PAUL
Apostle to the Gentiles

14

-7

2

22

24

D1344389

PAUL
APOSTLE TO THE GENTILES

Studies in Chronology

Gerd Lüdemann

SCM PRESS LTD

Translated by F. Stanley Jones from the German
Paulus, der Heidenapostel, vol. 1: *Studien zur Chronologie* (FRLANT 123), published 1980 by Vandenhoeck
& Ruprecht, Göttingen. This translation, supervised
and authorized by the author, constitutes a new
edition. See Postscript for details.

© Vandenhoeck & Ruprecht 1980
Translation © Fortress Press 1984

All Rights Reserved. No part of this publication may be
reproduced, stored in a retrieval system, or transmitted, in any form or by any means, electronic, mechani-
cal, photocopying, recording or otherwise, without the
prior permission of the publisher, SCM Press Ltd.

Unless otherwise noted, biblical quotations are from
the Revised Standard Version of the Bible, copyrighted
1946, 1952, © 1971, 1973 by the Division of Christian
Education of the National Council of the Churches of
Christ in the USA, and are used by permission.

Lüdemann, Gerd
    Paul, apostle to the Gentiles : studies in
    chronology.
    1. Paul, *the Apostle, Saint* ——Chronology
    I. Title   II. Paulus der Heidenapostel.1.
    Studien zur Chronologie.*English*
    225.9'24   BS2506

    ISBN 0-334-02246-0

334 02246 0

First published in Britain 1984 by
SCM Press Ltd
26–30 Tottenham Road, London N1 4BZ

Typeset in the United States of America
and printed in Great Britain at
The Camelot Press Ltd, Southampton

Undergraduate Lending Library

JOO9I / 6

CONTENTS

CONTENTS

CONTENTS

viii

CONTENTS

ix

CONTENTS

CONTENTS

CONTENTS

FOREWORD

The request of both author and publisher that I write the Foreword to the first edition in English of this very significant volume offers me a most welcome opportunity. I regard it as a great privilege to introduce to a new audience a biblical scholar of distinguished accomplishment and even more distinguished promise, whose published work hitherto has been almost entirely in German. The present book is the first volume in a proposed trilogy on *Paul, The Apostle to the Gentiles*, but it is a complete work in itself—a contribution of great importance to the study of Paul's life. This importance lies in the methodology the author adopts with regard to the use of sources and in the faithfulness and skill with which he applies it.

Traditionally, "lives" of Paul—and especially accounts of his apostolic career—have been based largely on the Book of Acts, which is the most ancient attempt to present a consecutive narrative of the earliest period of Christianity's development and expansion. The major portion of that narrative is concerned with Paul's evangelistic activity. Since Paul's own letters, illuminating as they are as to his character, religious experience, and thought, refer only occasionally—and usually only incidentally—to the circumstances and events of his career, it is natural that biographers of Paul have, for the greater part, given their attention to the Acts story, harmonizing with it, as well as they could, the pieces of biographical information which the letters provide. In recent decades, however, there has been a growing recognition that Acts has deficiencies as a dependable source for Paul and that if the autobiographical statements and hints in the letters are carefully studied, they come nearer to giving us a complete picture of the general course of Paul's life as an apostle than had been previously supposed.

The extraordinary significance of Gerd Luedemann's book lies in its being the first full-length, full-bodied, and fully documented study of Paul's apostolic career which is based solely on the letters. It is the author's aim to use material from Acts only when it supports what the letters either state or suggest. Although earlier writers on Paul's life have adopted the same method, none has attempted to cover Paul's career so comprehensively and in such detail.

The last section of the book is devoted to an illuminating exemplification, based on a comparison of the eschatological ideas expressed in 1 Thessalonians and 1 Corinthians respectively, of the important bearing of the chronology of Paul's career on his theology. This section gives us a hint of what is to be fully developed in the third part of this trilogy.

Gerd Luedemann, a German born in 1946, was on this side of the Atlantic from 1977 to 1982. After serving two years as Visiting Assistant Professor at McMaster University, he became Assistant Professor and later Associate Professor of New Testament at Vanderbilt University. In 1983 he was appointed Professor of New Testament and Director of the Institute of Early Christian Studies at Georg August University, Göttingen. He received his higher education chiefly at the same university, earning his Doctor of Theology degree in 1974. He spent 1974–75 at Duke University, doing graduate work under the supervision of W. D. Davies. He then returned to Göttingen for further study (Habilitation in New Testament Studies). During his student days at the German university, he had important tutoring and lecturing responsibilities. Besides a number of articles in German and English, his publications include *Investigations into Simonian Gnosis* (Göttingen: Vandenhoeck & Ruprecht, 1975), the original German edition of the present book (1980), *Paul, The Apostle to the Gentiles*, vol. 2: *Antipaulinism in Early Christianity* (Göttingen: Vandenhoeck & Ruprecht, 1983), and *Paul and Judaism* (Munich: Chr. Kaiser Verlag, 1983).

I have no doubt that this book will have a constructive and continuing influence on Pauline studies, and we can look forward eagerly to the succeeding volumes.

JOHN KNOX

ABBREVIATIONS

The abbreviations are generally the same as those in Siegfried Schwertner, *Internationales Abkürzungsverzeichnis für Theologie und Grenzgebiete* (New York and Berlin: Walter de Gruyter, 1974) and Gerhard Kittel, ed., *Theological Dictionary of the New Testament*, trans. and ed. G. W. Bromiley, 10 vols. (Grand Rapids: Wm. B. Eerdmans, 1964–76), 1:xvi–xl. The following list is provided for reference.

Unless otherwise indicated, the translations are taken from the Loeb Classical Library (Cambridge, Mass.: Harvard University Press; London: William Heinemann) and the Revised Standard Version of the Bible.

References to a modern author by name alone refer to that author's commentary on the passage under discussion.

AGG	*Abhandlungen der Gesellschaft der Wissenschaften zu Göttingen. Philologisch-historische Klasse*
AGJU	Arbeiten zur Geschichte des antiken Judentums und des Urchristentums
ALGHL	Arbeiten zur Literatur und Geschichte des hellenistischen Judentums
AnBib	Analecta biblica
AncB	The Anchor Bible (Garden City, N.Y.: Doubleday & Co.)
ANF	*Ante-Nicene Fathers* (Grand Rapids: Wm. B. Eerdmans)
Aristotle	
Eth. Nic.	Aristotle, *Ethica Nicomachea*, The Nicomachean Ethics
AThANT	Abhandlungen zur Theologie des Alten und Neuen Testaments
AThR	*Anglican Theological Review*
Barn.	*Epistula Barnabae*, Letter of Barnabas
Bauer, Lexicon	Walter Bauer, A *Greek-English Lexicon of the New Testament and Other Early Christian Literature*, 2d ed. (1979)

BBB	Bonner biblische Beiträge
BEvTh	Beiträge zur evangelischen Theologie
BFChTh	Beiträge zur Förderung christlicher Theologie
BGBE	Beiträge zur Geschichte der biblischen Exegese
BHTh	Beiträge zur historischen Theologie
BiBe	Biblische Beiträge
BiH	Biblische Handbibliothek
Bill.	Paul Billerbeck, *Kommentar zum Neuen Testament*
BJRL	*Bulletin of the John Rylands Library*
Bl.-Debr.	Friedrich Blass and Albert Debrunner, *A Greek Grammar of the New Testament and Other Early Christian Literature* (1961)
BNTC	Black's New Testament Commentaries = HNTC (London: A. & C. Black)
BR	*Biblical Research*
BSGRT	Bibliotheca scriptorum Graecorum et Romanorum Teubneriana (Leipzig: B. G. Teubner)
BU	Biblische Untersuchungen
BWANT	Beiträge zur Wissenschaft vom Alten und Neuen Testament
BZ	*Biblische Zeitschrift*
BZNW	Beihefte zur *Zeitschrift für die neutestamentliche Wissenschaft*
CB.NT	Coniectanea biblica, New Testament Series
CBQ	*Catholic Biblical Quarterly*
Cicero	
De Invent.	Cicero, *De inventione*, Treatise on Rhetorical Invention
De Orat.	Cicero, *De oratore*, Treatise on Oration
(Pseudo-) Cicero	(Pseudo-) Cicero, *Rhetorica ad Herennium*, Treatise on Rhetoric
CJTh	*Canadian Journal of Theology*
1 Clem.	*Epistula Clementis ad Corinthios I*, First Letter of Clement of Rome
Clement	
Ex. Theod.	Clement of Alexandria (Clemens Alexandrinus), *Excerpta ex Theodoto*, Excerpts from Theodotus
Strom.	Clement of Alexandria, *Stromata*, Miscellanies
CNT	Commentaire du Nouveau Testament (Neuchâtel: Delachaux et Niestlé)
ConNT	*Coniectanea neotestamentica*
CP	*Classical Philology*
CPJ	Corpus Papyrorum Judaicorum

CRI	Compendia Rerum Iudaicarum ad Novum Testamentum
CSEL	Corpus scriptorum ecclesiasticorum Latinorum (Vienna: C. Geroldi)
CSM	*Christian Science Monitor*
CTL	Crown Theological Library
CTM	*Concordia Theological Monthly*
CwH	Calwer Hefte zur Förderung biblischen Glaubens und christlichen Lebens
Dg.	*Epistula ad Diognetum*, Letter to Diognetus
Did.	*Didache*
Dio Cassius	Dio Cassius, *Historia Romana*, Roman History
Diodorus of Sicily	Diodorus Siculus, *Bibliotheca historica*, Library of History
EETH	Einführung in die evangelische Theologie
EHPhR	Études d'histoire et de philosophie religieuses
EHS.T	Europäische Hochschulschriften. Series 23: Theologie
EKK.V	Evangelisch-katholischer Kommentar zum Neuen Testament. Vorarbeiten
Eras.	*Erasmus*
ET	*Expository Times*
EtB	Études bibliques (Paris: J. Gabalda)
Eth. En.	*Ethiopic Enoch*
Euripides	
Med.	Euripides, *Medea*
EvTh	*Evangelische Theologie*
Exp.	*Expositor*
FEUC	Forschungen zur Entstehung des Urchristentums, des Neuen Testaments und der Kirche
FKDG	Forschungen zur Kirchen- und Dogmengeschichte
Fortunatianus	Fortunatianus, *Ars rhetorica*, Art of Rhetoric
FRLANT	Forschungen zur Religion und Literatur des Alten und Neuen Testaments
FzB	Forschung zur Bibel
GCS	Die griechischen christlichen Schriftsteller der ersten drei Jahrhunderte
GGA	*Göttingische gelehrte Anzeigen*
Gn.	*Gnomon*
Gn.r.	*Genesis rabba*, Midrash on Genesis
GNT	Grundrisse zum Neuen Testament
GTA	Göttinger theologische Arbeiten
GTB	Van Gorcum's theologische bibliotheek
HAW	Handbuch der Altertumswissenschaft

HC	Hand-Commentar zum Neuen Testament (Freiburg: J. C. B. Mohr [Paul Siebeck])
Hermeneia	Hermeneia—A Critical and Historical Commentary on the Bible (Philadelphia: Fortress Press)
Hesp.	*Hesperia*
HHS	Harvard Historical Studies
Hippolytus	
Ref.	Hippolytus of Rome, *Refutatio omnium haeresium*, Refutation of All Heresies
Hist.	*Historia*
HNT	Handbuch zum Neuen Testament (Tübingen: J. C. B. Mohr [Paul Siebeck])
HNTC	Harper's New Testament Commentaries = BNTC (New York: Harper & Row)
HThK	Herders theologischer Kommentar zum Neuen Testament (Freiburg: Herder)
HThR	*Harvard Theological Review*
HZ	*Historische Zeitschrift*
Iamblichus	
Vit. Pyth.	Iamblichus, *De vita Pythagorica*, Pythagorean Life
ICC	International Critical Commentary of the Holy Scriptures (Edinburgh: T. & T. Clark)
IDB	*Interpreter's Dictionary of the Bible*
*IDB*Sup	*Interpreter's Dictionary of the Bible*, Supplement
Ignatius	
Magn.	Ignatius of Antioch, *Epistula ad Magnesios*, Letter to the Magnesians
Phld.	Ignatius of Antioch, *Epistula ad Philadelphenses*, Letter to the Philadelphians
R.	Ignatius of Antioch, *Epistula ad Romanos*, Letter to the Romans
Interp.	*Interpretation*
Irenaeus	
Haer.	Irenaeus of Lyon, *Adversus haereses*, Against Heresies
JAAR	*Journal of the American Academy of Religion*
JBL	*Journal of Biblical Literature*
JBR	*Journal of Bible and Religion*
JKAW	*Jahresbericht über die Fortschritte der klassischen Altertumswissenschaft*
JNES	*Journal of Near Eastern Studies*
Josephus	
Ant.	Flavius Josephus, *Antiquitates*, Antiquities
Ap.	Flavius Josephus, *Contra Apionem*, Against Apion
Bell.	Flavius Josephus, *De bello Judaico*, Jewish War

JR	*Journal of Religion*
JSJ	*Journal of the Study of Judaism in the Persian, Hellenistic, and Roman Period*
JSNT	*Journal for the Study of the New Testament*
JThS	*Journal of Theological Studies*
Jud.	*Judaica*
Justin	
Apol.	Justin Martyr, *Apologia*, Apology
Kairos	*Kairos. Zeitschrift für Religionswissenschaft und Theologie*
KBANT	Kommentare und Beiträge zum Alten und Neuen Testament
KEK	Kritisch-exegetischer Kommentar über das Neue Testament (Göttingen: Vandenhoeck & Ruprecht)
KP	K. Ziegler and W. Sontheimer (eds.), *Der Kleine Pauly: Lexikon der Antike* (Stuttgart: Druckenmüller)
KuD	*Kerygma und Dogma*
LCL	Loeb Classical Library
LeDiv	Lectio divina
Lv.r.	*Leviticus rabba*, Midrash on Leviticus
MThSt	Marburger theologische Studien
NGG	*Nachrichten von der königlichen Gesellschaft der Wissenschaften zu Göttingen. Philologisch-historische Klasse*
NT	*Novum Testamentum*
NTA	Neutestamentliche Abhandlungen
NTD	Das Neue Testament Deutsch (Göttingen: Vandenhoeck & Ruprecht)
NT.S	*Novum Testamentum*, Supplement
NTS	*New Testament Studies*
Origen	
Cels.	Origen of Alexandria, *Contra Celsum*, Against Celsus
Orosius	Paulus Orosius, *Historiae adversum paganos*, Histories against the Pagans
Ovid	
Ars	Ovid, *Ars amatoria*, Art of Love
Pauly-W.	A. Pauly and G. Wissowa (eds.), *Realencyclopädie der classischen Altertumswissenschaft* (Stuttgart: Druckenmüller)
Philo	
Leg. Gaj.	Philo of Alexandria, *Legatio ad Gajum*, Embassy to Gaius
Pindar	
Olymp.	Pindar, *Olympia*

Plato
Ap.	*Apologia*, Apology
Ep.	*Epistulae*, Letters
Euthyd.	*Euthydemus*
Gorg.	*Gorgias*
Prot.	*Protagoras*
Resp.	*Respublica*, Republic
Soph.	*Sophista*, Sophist
Theaet.	*Theaetus*

Plutarch
Lib. Ed.	Plutarch, *De liberis educandis*
QD	Quaestiones disputatae
Quintilian	Quintilian, *Institutio oratoria*
RAC	T. Klauser (ed.), *Reallexikon für Antike und Christentum* (Stuttgart: Hiersemann)
RB	*Revue biblique*
REG	*Revue des études grecques*
RGG	K. Galling (ed.), *Religion in Geschichte und Gegenwart*, 3d ed. (Tübingen: J. C. B. Mohr [Paul Siebeck])
RHPhR	*Revue d'histoire et de philosophie religieuses*
RHR	*Revue de l'histoire des religions*
RMP	*Rheinisches Museum für Philologie*
RNT	Regensburger Neues Testament
RSR	*Recherches de science religieuse*
S. Bar.	*Syriac Apocalypse of Baruch*
SBL	Society of Biblical Literature
SBLMS	Society of Biblical Literature Monograph Series
SBS	Stuttgarter Bibelstudien
SBT	Studies in Biblical Theology
SC	Sources chrétiennes (Paris: Éditions du Cerf)
SCBO	Scriptorum Classicorum Bibliotheca Oxoniensis (Oxford: At the Clarendon Press)
SEA	*Svensk Exegetisk Årsbok*
SG	Sammlung Göschen
SHAW.PH	*Sitzungsberichte der Heidelberger Akademie der Wissenschaften. Philosophisch-historische Klasse*
Sib.	*Sibyllines*
SJ	Studia Judaica
SJLA	Studies in Judaism in Late Antiquity
SJTh	*Scottish Journal of Theology*
SNT	Schriften des Neuen Testaments
SNTSMS	Society for New Testament Studies Monograph Series

ABBREVIATIONS

SPAW.PH	*Sitzungsberichte der preussischen Akademie der Wissenschaften. Philosophisch-historische Klasse*
SQAW	Schriften und Quellen der Alten Welt
StANT	Studien zum Alten und Neuen Testament
StD	Studies and Documents
StEv	*Studia Evangelica*
StNT	Studien zum Neuen Testament
StTh	*Studia Theologica*
StUNT	Studien zur Umwelt des Neuen Testaments
Suetonius	Suetonius, *De vita Caesarum*, Lives of the Caesars
Caes. Claudius	Claudius
Caes. Tiberius	Tiberius
Tacitus	
Annals	Tacitus, *Annales*, Annals
TB	Theologische Bücherei
TDNT	G. Kittel and G. Friedrich (eds.), *Theological Dictionary of the New Testament*
TEH	Theologische Existenz heute
Theophrastus	
Char.	Theophrastus, *Characteres*, Characters
ThF	Theologische Forschung
ThHK	Theologischer Handkommentar zum Neuen Testament (Berlin: Evangelische Verlagsanstalt)
ThLZ	*Theologische Literaturzeitung*
ThR	*Theologische Rundschau*
ThT	*Theologisch tijdschrift*
ThW	Theologische Wissenschaft
ThZ	*Theologische Zeitschrift*
tr.	translator's own translation
TU	Texte und Untersuchungen zur Geschichte der altchristlichen Literatur
TynB	*Tyndale Bulletin*
TzF	Texte zur Forschung (Darmstadt: Wissenschaftliche Buchgesellschaft)
UB	Urban-Bücher
UTB	Uni-Taschenbücher
VF	*Verkündigung und Forschung*
VigChr	*Vigiliae Christianae*
vl.	*varia lectio*, alternative reading
WA	Luther, M., *Werke*. Weimarer Gesamtausgabe
WdF	Wege der Forschung
WMANT	Wissenschaftliche Monographien zum Alten und Neuen Testament

WuD	*Wort und Dienst*
WUNT	Wissenschaftliche Untersuchungen zum Neuen Testament
ZKG	*Zeitschrift für Kirchengeschichte*
ZNW	*Zeitschrift für die neutestamentliche Wissenschaft und die Kunde der älteren Kirche*
ZRGG	*Zeitschrift für Religions- und Geistesgeschichte*
ZSTh	*Zeitschrift für systematische Theologie*
ZThK	*Zeitschrift für Theologie und Kirche*
ZWTh	*Zeitschrift für wisssenschaftliche Theologie*

1

A CRITICAL SURVEY OF RESEARCH
INTO THE CHRONOLOGY
OF PAUL

1.1 INTRODUCTION

Notwithstanding substantial differences of opinion in certain areas, New Testament research generally proceeds from a few basic assumptions such as the (modified) two-source theory in synoptic exegesis and a relatively uniform chronology of Paul and of primitive Christianity up to 70 C.E.[1] (differences of two or three years matter little here). However, dogmas in historical scholarship always appear suspect to the spirit of scientific inquiry and methodical doubt. In what follows we shall present a critical survey of the results of previous research into the chronology of Paul. Thereafter we shall develop a new proposal for Pauline chronology that is conceived as a preliminary study for a new interpretation of Paul.

Both our critique of previous research and our positive construction have to a large extent been evoked by the work of two Americans, J. Knox[2] and D. W. Riddle,[3] whose ideas on Pauline chronology either have remained almost totally unknown[4] or have been described with considerable distortion.[5] In my judgment, the provocative results of redaction-historical investigation into Luke's two-volume work provide a basis for amplification and decisive improvement of the chronology of these two Americans. First, however, the conventional reconstruction of the chronology of Paul will be reviewed.

1.2 THE CONVENTIONAL RECONSTRUCTION
OF THE CHRONOLOGY
OF PAUL

To determine the contours of Pauline chronology, one usually proceeds as follows. The sole[6] absolute datum is found in the reference to the governor Gallio in Acts 18:12. In the light of an inscription found in Delphi, Gallio's tenure of office as proconsul may be reckoned as falling approximately in the year 51/52 C.E.[7] Assuming the historical accuracy of Acts' report of Paul's stay in Corinth at the time of Gallio (i.e., the accuracy of Acts' report of the trial before Gallio), one then conventionally charts out an absolute chronology for the time both before and after this fixed point.

Before we present the details involved in charting out this chronology, we should mention one more report in Acts 18 which, according to conventional scholarship, provides further confirmation of this absolute datum in Pauline chronology. Acts 18:2 recounts that on his arrival in Corinth, Paul met "a Jew named Aquila, a native of Pontus, lately come from Italy with his wife Priscilla, because Claudius had commanded all the Jews to leave Rome." Such a decree by Emperor Claudius is mentioned by Suetonius in his *Lives of the Caesars*: "Iudaeos impulsore Chresto assidue tumultuantes Roma expulit" ("Since the Jews constantly made disturbances at the instigation of Chrestus, he expelled them from Rome"; *Caes. Claudius* 25). While Suetonius does not specify a date for the expulsion, Orosius (*Historiae adversum paganos* 7.6.15)[8] states that it took place in Claudius's ninth year (49 C.E.).

This dating clearly fits in well with the absolute datum in the chronology of Paul mentioned above. Thus, according to the conventional interpretation, Aquila and Priscilla, together with other Jews (Jewish Christians), were expelled from Rome in 49 C.E. They proceeded to Corinth and there met Paul who, according to Acts, was in Corinth ca. 51/52 C.E.

After Paul's visit to Corinth described in Acts 18, Paul visited Ephesus. This visit is confirmed both by Paul's composition of 1 Corinthians in Ephesus (1 Cor. 16:8) and by Acts' report of a stay in Ephesus after Paul's departure from Corinth. This visit is not, however, the stopover mentioned in Acts 18:19–20. Rather, the conventional view is that after his initial missionary trip to Corinth, Paul traveled to Palestine by way of Ephesus (completion of the second missionary journey) and then returned to Ephesus on his third missionary journey. This second stay in Ephesus (Acts 19–20) is supposed to be identical with the one mentioned in 1 Cor. 16:8. After this, Paul is said to have passed through Macedonia (Acts 20:1) and to have again spent some time in Corinth, for Acts 20:2–3 could refer to no other place. Further, the occurrence of this visit may be deduced from the Corin-

2

thian correspondence (2 Cor. 12:14; 13:1) and, moreover, from the fact that Romans was probably composed in Corinth.

It is said that Paul next traveled to Jerusalem in order to deliver the collection (Rom. 15:25). According to the passage just mentioned, and in contrast to the point of time when 1 Cor. 16:8 was written, the collection had now been completed. Thus Acts' report of the trip to Jerusalem as following directly on the visit to Macedonia and the stay in Corinth (Acts 20:1–3) would again fit in well with the relative chronology established on the basis of Paul's letters. In Jerusalem, Paul was taken prisoner (Acts 21) and was then transferred to Rome (Acts 27–28). Though there are no indisputable references in Paul's own letters to verify these last two events (it is, however, possible that Philippians was composed during the imprisonment in Rome), the martyrdom of Paul in Rome is nevertheless seen as being absolutely confirmed by the witness of 1 Clem. 5:4–7 from the end of the first century C.E.[9] Since we have no absolute dates for Paul's imprisonment and transference to Rome (the change of the proconsulate from Felix to Festus [Acts 24:27] cannot be dated with certainty; see above, n. 6), and since we also have no relative chronological references comparable to the numeric references in Galatians 1–2, scholarly opinions differ most greatly concerning this last part of Paul's life. The importance of this divergence seems to be diminished, however, in the light of the generally acknowledged fixed point for the absolute chronology of Paul, the reference to Gallio.

For the period *before* 51/52 C.E., the combination of Acts 15–17 with 1 Thessalonians 3 and Galatians 1–2 supplies relative dates that may be accommodated into the absolute chronology based on the reference to Gallio. In 1 Thess. 2:2, Paul mentions his stay in Philippi, and in 3:1, his stay in Athens. During the intervening time, Paul was in Thessalonica, as the retrospect in 1 Thess. 1:2ff. shows. Later he wrote 1 Thessalonians in Corinth. The same stations implied by Paul for the journey (Philippi, Thessalonica, Athens, Corinth) are also found in the report in Acts 16–18. Hence one need not wonder at the general consensus that Paul's mission in Macedonia and Achaia occurred during the second missionary journey. Further, according to the statements of Acts, this second journey took place *after* the Jerusalem Conference. It is generally agreed that Acts 15 and the second visit to Jerusalem mentioned by Paul refer to the same event, especially since both Paul and Acts report that a difference of opinions resulted in the separation of Paul and Barnabas immediately *after* the conference (Acts 15:36–39 [Gal. 2:13 more indirectly]). Even though we have no indications of years or other numbers, the events before 51/52 C.E. may be arranged in the following order: Jerusalem Conference; separation from Barnabas in Antioch; journey to Philippi, Thessalonica, Athens, and Corinth. One may then supplement this list with the stations that have been determined for the period *after* 51/52 C.E.: Ephesus; journey to Palestine as the transition from the second missionary journey to the third; Ephesus; Macedonia; Corinth; Jerusalem; Rome.

According to the conventional view, the contours of the period before the Jerusalem Conference may be delineated on the basis of Paul's statements in Galatians 1–2. There Paul enumerates years, and thus greater precision is possible for this period than for the periods between the Jerusalem Conference, the stay in Corinth, and the third trip to Jerusalem. According to Paul's own statement, fourteen or, following the majority opinion, seventeen years elapsed between his conversion and his second visit to Jerusalem (for the Jerusalem Conference). Three years after God "was pleased to reveal his Son" to Paul, Paul went to Jerusalem to become acquainted with Cephas (*historēsai*) and remained there two weeks (Gal. 1:18). Fourteen years later, or eleven years later if one computes the fourteen years as beginning with the conversion, Paul traveled with Barnabas to Jerusalem (Gal. 2:1).

Gal. 1:21 is understood to specify the place of Paul's activity between his first and second trips to Jerusalem: Directly after Paul's report of his first visit to Jerusalem, he writes, "Then I went into the regions of Syria and Cilicia." Accordingly, Paul worked for fourteen or eleven years in these localities. It is further supposed that Paul was working under the auspices of the Antiochene congregation. This thesis concerning Paul's activities between his first and second visits to Jerusalem is considered probable also because Acts 13–14 depicts Paul and Barnabas (Paul's superior) working as missionaries commissioned by the Antiochene congregation and traveling together as delegates of this congregation to the conference in Jerusalem. Furthermore, this report agrees with Paul's statement in Gal. 2:1 that he went to Jerusalem with Barnabas.

If the period from the trial before Gallio to the Jerusalem Conference is estimated to be three years, the absolute date for Paul's second visit to Jerusalem would be 48/49 C.E. The date of the conversion would be 31 C.E. (or 34 C.E.).[10]

For theological reasons, one may be inclined to be wary of exaggerating the importance of determining the "right" chronology of Paul. Nevertheless, it can be shown that the conventional chronology involves an important preliminary decision for the theological interpretation of Paul's letters, and that the chronological question is thus of supreme interest even for theologians. According to the standard chronology of Paul, all the genuine letters (to set Philippians to one side for the moment) originate from the time of the second or third missionary journeys. Thus the intervals between the letters would be fairly short, while the period between the conversion and the first letter (around nineteen years) would be about four times as long as that between the first and last letters. We should then have before us the letters of a man who had already completed a long period of missionary activity. As concerns the interpretation of the letters, this dating implies (a) that there remains hardly any room for the recently renewed[11] thesis of theological development in Paul's thought and (b) that to a still greater extent than has been usual up to now one may employ the letters to interpret one another, or to rephrase this last implication: For the interpretation of the extant letters, even the historian can use the theological principle "Scriptura ipsius interpres" ("Scripture is its own interpreter").[12] So much for the theological implications of the chronology of Paul!

1.3 VARIOUS CRITICAL OBJECTIONS

The chronology of Paul just reviewed is distinguished by the way in which it utilizes the information of Acts whenever it agrees with Paul's own statements while it ignores information in Acts that contradicts Paul's letters. The most recent proponent of this method, P. Vielhauer, writes: "One cannot be totally skeptical of Acts. Critical use of the book and considered combination of its information with that of the letters allows one to gain a general idea of the chronological framework of Paul's activity."[13] The most famous example of the results of this critical method is the rejection of the historicity of Acts 9:26ff., a passage that recounts that shortly after his conversion Paul traveled to Jerusalem. Here Acts' report has been properly countered by reference to Paul's emphatic statement in Galatians 1 that after the incident near Damascus he did *not* travel to Jerusalem. The most important example of combination of Paul's own statements with those of Acts is the chronological specification of Paul's stay in Corinth based on Acts' reference to Gallio (see above).

In the following section we shall list diverse critical objections to the chronology of Paul presented in section 1.2.

1.3.1 Was Paul a Delegate of Antioch and a Junior Partner of Barnabas before the Jerusalem Conference?

The thesis that Paul was a delegate of Antioch and a junior partner of Barnabas[14] before the Jerusalem Conference is propounded with the greatest assurance today.[15] Nevertheless, this thesis has serious weaknesses that become evident when it is evaluated in the light of Paul's own statements.

First, in Gal. 2:1–2 Paul emphasizes that he went to Jerusalem (to the conference) with Barnabas because of a *revelation*. It is not logical to infer Paul's subordination to Barnabas from this statement. (On the other hand, it must be admitted that Paul is writing apologetically, which might have led him to accentuate his independence and to emphasize his own will.) Second, Paul evidently associates his visit to Jerusalem with the intention of presenting to those in Jerusalem the gospel that *he* proclaims among the Gentiles (2:2). This statement, however, allows the inference that Paul was operating an *independent* mission at the time. Third, Paul took with him the Gentile Christian Titus who, as is well known, is never mentioned in Acts. This action witnesses to considerable self-consciousness on Paul's part.[16] Also, this symbolic action, which emphasizes the inclusion of Gentiles in the eschatological people of God, and the fact that we know Titus only from Paul's European mission[17] similarly render it plausible that Paul had operated a mission independent of Antioch even before the Jerusalem Conference.[18]

1.3.2 On the Date of the Expulsion of the Jews from Rome

The dating of the expulsion of the Jews from Rome in 49 C.E. rests on the report of Augustine's student Orosius, who attributes this information to Josephus ("Iosephus refert," "Josephus reports"). However, in the works of Josephus, which have been preserved in their entirety,[19] no such dating is found, even though in several passages Josephus deals at length with the administrative period of Claudius. Even if we must assume with Harnack[20] that Orosius took the date as well as the reference to "Josephus" from tradition (Harnack speculates that Julius Africanus was the originator), the witness to this dating is too late to warrant uncritical adoption. This dating merits even less credence since Suetonius does not date the expulsion and since Dio Cassius 60.6.6 mentions an imperial decree from the beginning of Claudius's administrative period (41 C.E.) which was issued in connection with Jewish riots. The measure mentioned by Dio Cassius must be identical with that mentioned by Suetonius, for Dio Cassius appears to refer (indirectly) to the tradition preserved by Suetonius. Is it then methodologically permissible to prefer the dating of Orosius to that of Cassius?

1.3.3 The Indeterminate Nature of the Chronological Concatenation of Episodes in Acts

The episodes reported in Acts are joined to one another by vague indications of time, for example, 12:1: "about that time"; 19:23: "about that time"; 6:1: "now in these days" (see, similarly, 11:27). If one further compares the span of time treated by Acts with the chronological information provided by Paul, it may be observed that the report in Acts 9:5–26 (the conversion of Paul until the first stay in Jerusalem) covers a period of at least two to three years and that Acts 11:26— 15:1ff. (Paul in Syria until the second stay in Jerusalem) covers at least thirteen to fourteen years, whereas the remaining fourteen chapters of Acts report on a period that spans at most six years.[21]

"For the historian the importance of this observation is clear: we are dealing with selected episodes, not with a continuous history."[22] If one considers this style of selective presentation along with the indeterminate nature of the chronological information mentioned above, it is clear that one must be skeptical with regard to the chronological information of the entire book. It could well be that Luke omitted some of the main events in the chronology of Paul and that he mistakenly connected unrelated episodes by means of his vague chronological references.[23]

The expression "many days" also permits no conclusions regarding specification of periods of time in Acts or regarding Luke's knowledge of such. Haacker[24] decidedly maintains a different opinion regarding this expression. Acts 9:23 recounts that after many days had passed, the Jews wanted to murder Paul in Damascus. Paul is then let down over the city wall in a basket and proceeds to Jerusalem, where he attempts to join the disciples. Haacker combines the specification "many days" with Paul's own report that he proceeded to Jerusalem for the first time after three years. He follows Schlier in dating Paul's stay in Arabia as lasting a year, and he thus arrives at the conclusion that Paul was in Damascus for about one and a half years.

Contra Haacker, we must say that Haacker presumes what should first have been proven, namely, Luke's knowledge of the length of Paul's stay in Damascus. Since Luke is either uninformed or badly informed about the particulars of the stay (according to Paul's own report [2 Cor. 11:32–33], he was persecuted not by the Jews but by the governor of King Aretas) and of the preceding period in Arabia, his chronological knowledge is probably not very good. Finally, "many days" is a common Lukan indication of time and by no means always designates a period of eighteen months. Haacker equates the reference to eighteen months (18:11) with the "many days" in 18:18 in the following sentence: "Though *hēmerai hikanai* in Acts 9:23 can represent one and one-half years, the information in Acts 18:18 does not provide any clues about when within the eighteen months of his activity in Corinth Paul stood before Gallio's tribunal" (p. 254). This argument already breaks down in light of the fact that in the phrase "after this Paul stayed many days longer" the "many days" are intended as a period distinct from the eighteen months and as representing an additional period of stay (i.e., after Paul had stayed in Corinth for eighteen months, he remained there for many more days and then departed).

Does Haacker also want to say that Peter's stay in Joppa (9:43) and the delay during the voyage (27:7) lasted eighteen months?

On the other hand, a few passages in the part of Acts dealing with Paul do provide explicit information regarding the chronological periods (see above, n. 21). These may be evaluated only after Paul's chronology has been reconstructed solely on the basis of the letters. Nevertheless, when taken together with the indeterminate chronological information mentioned above, they are evidence of Luke's historical interest.

That Luke's historical interest is one for world history is apparent above all from the references to events of universal history in the Lukan volumes. In the following section, we shall analyze the historical reliability of these references.

1.3.4 Contradictions between Luke's Chronological Information and Data from World History

As previously stated, research into Pauline chronology finds its only essential datum of absolute chronology in the reference to Gallio in Acts 18. It may be possible to counter the objections that have been raised until now against the conventional chronology of Paul by modifying this chronology (i.e., one can acknowledge the objections but still generally abide by the conventional view). In the following we shall launch a full-scale attack on the conventional chronology by means of fundamental criticism of the propriety of accepting any absolute datum of world history from Luke (without confirmation from Paul). We shall demonstrate that Luke's chronological references to world history are often incorrect[25] and thereby deny the methodological right of developing a chronology of Paul on the basis of the reference to Gallio.[26] To do this, we shall examine the relevant passages in the order of their appearance in the Lukan writings.

Luke 2:1ff.: Luke dates the birth of Jesus during the reign of Herod the Great and at the time of the census of Quirinius. Now, (a) the census of Quirinius occurred a decade after Herod's death, and (b) Luke has an incorrect conception of the census: Contra Luke, the census was limited to Judaea and Syria. For both (a) and (b), see Josephus, *Ant.* 17.355 and 18.1ff. The attempts of Zahn and others to identify a census by Quirinius which differs from that mentioned by Josephus and to connect this one with Luke 2:1ff. are apologetic.[27]

Luke 3:1: In older research it was sometimes supposed that Luke perpetrated a gross historical blunder in his reference to Lysanias as the tetrarch of Abilene (this is the view of Holtzmann and Hilgenfeld). Older research thought that Lysanias reigned from 40 to 36 B.C.E. and was put to death by Antonius. This suspicion has been damped, though in my opinion not completely muffled, by the discovery that there was evidently another, later Lysanias (who died between 28 and 37 C.E.).[28]

Luke 3:2: On Annas and Caiaphas, see below on Acts 4:6.

Luke 3:19–20: Luke's formulation follows Mark 6:17. However, in contrast to Mark, Luke identifies "the tetrarch" and corrects by omitting "Philip." This example demonstrates that Luke did not proceed without criticism and investigation, for Philip married Salome, the daughter of Herodias (Josephus, *Ant.* 18.137). Herodias was thus the mother-in-law of Philip and not his wife, contra Mark 6:17–18.

Further, Luke generalizes when he allows the admonition of John the Baptist to cover also "all the evil things" that Herod the tetrarch had done. Characteristics of Lukan redaction are already evident here. Though we shall later thematically explicate the relevance of these characteristics for the evaluation of Luke's chronological information, we should note here that Lukan redaction is completely conspicuous when Luke does not employ the tradition preserved in Mark regarding the end of John's life. For Luke, this event merits only brief notice (here Luke follows Mark 6:16). "The exit of John has no particular importance."[29]

Josephus gives a completely different reason for the imprisonment of John by Herod the tetrarch. Only with great difficulty can this reason be harmonized with that provided by Mark and Luke.[30] For Josephus the reason is not John's moral condemnation of Herod but rather Herod's fear that political rioting might be incited by John's proclamation. *Ant.* 18:118 reads: "Herod decided that it would be much better to strike first and be rid of him before his work led to an uprising, than to wait for an upheaval, get involved in a difficult situation and see his mistake."

Our conclusion regarding Luke 3:19–20 may now be summarized. Luke correctly alters details in his source. He does not, however, critically investigate the received tradition, for example, by comparing it with other sources.

Luke 13:1: The slaughter of the Galileans by Pilate has no parallel in Josephus. To state that Luke's report is historically probable simply because the Galileans had a penchant for insurrection (cf. Acts 5:37) and because Pilate was cruel is hardly a convincing case. More important for this question is the observation that Josephus (*Ant.* 18.85ff.) reports that Pilate instigated a blood bath among the Samaritans at Mount Gerizim, though this event should be dated after Easter 35 C.E. If Luke has this blood bath in mind, as seems probable, then Luke has jumbled names and places.[31]

Acts 4:6: "Annas the high priest and Caiaphas." One should probably also interpret Luke 3:2 as referring only to Annas as the high priest, for "the same hand is setting the titles in both passages" (Schürmann, 151). Luke incorrectly thinks that Annas (6–15 C.E.), and not Caiaphas (high priest from 17/19 to 37 C.E.), was the ruling high priest. Luke thereby again proves himself to be badly informed. The counterargument raised by Jeremias, Schürmann, and others,[32] that it was customary for a former high priest to retain the title even after his term of office, *cannot* explain why Luke would withhold the title from Caiaphas when he actually held the office of high priest at the time.[33]

Acts 5:36ff.: In this passage, (the Lukan) Gamaliel hardly sets the two revolutionaries, Theudas and Judas, in proper chronological order. According to Josephus (*Ant.* 20.97ff.), Theudas entered public life at the time of the procurator Fadus (ca. 44 C.E.). According to Acts 5:36, this occurred before Gamaliel's speech and even before the census (6 B.C.E.). The text says that Judas the Galilean appeared during the days of the census, *after* Theudas. There has been an attempt to exonerate Luke from this mistake by postulating the existence of another Theudas who was not known to Josephus (note the parallel to the argument regarding Luke 2:1ff.). However, (a) the name Theudas is extremely rare, (b) the reference to Theudas in Acts 5 is meaningful only

10

if Theudas, like Judas, initiated an important movement, and (c) if this were the case it is unlikely that Josephus would have overlooked this Theudas.[34] On the other hand, Luke does properly date Judas's revolt by connecting it with the census (cf. Josephus, *Ant.* 18.3ff.), even though he has an incorrect conception of the census and dates it incorrectly (see above).

Acts 11:28: The idea of a worldwide famine in the days of Claudius contradicts the information available to us from secular historians as well as the immediate context of Acts 11. Since the Antiochene congregation assisted the brothers in Judaea, it was evidently not affected by the famine. Sources witness to regional famines during the period in question,[35] but the notion of a worldwide famine is a Lukan fiction. "The discrepancy that such a famine would also have affected Antioch went unnoticed by Luke."[36]

Whether Luke derived the notion of a *worldwide* famine from the tradition about Agabus,[37] or, as appears more probable, universalized the prophecy of a local famine by adding "over all the world," it is certain that Acts 11:28 is historically incorrect. If the former is the case, we have another example of uncritical adoption of information regarding world history. If the latter is the case, we have an incorrect transformation of a local tradition into something universal.[38] This would be roughly parallel to Luke's extension of the census that was limited to Judaea and Syria to the entire Roman empire (see Luke 2:1: "all the world").

Acts 18:2: The statement that *all*[39] the Jews were expelled from Rome contradicts secular history, since such an expulsion would have been impossible owing to the large number of Jews in Rome, as Dio Cassius correctly notes (see below, pp. 164–65). The report in Acts 18:2 may be a typical Lukan generalization, as were the reports on the census and the famine in the days of Claudius.

Let these examples be enough to admonish scholars seeking to construct a critical chronology of Paul not to adopt chronological and historical information from Luke's two volumes[40] that is not confirmed in Paul's letters. Before we proceed to construct our chronology of Paul, further arguments against the conventional view must be collected.

1.3.5 The Redactional Nature of Luke's Chronological References

In the preceding section, we examined Luke's references to world history by comparing them with the available secular historical sources.

11

Characteristics of Lukan redaction were already evident there (see on Luke 3:19 and Acts 11:28). In the following, we shall focus on this latter question and collect the material in both volumes that shows how information about places, dates, and persons derives from Luke's redaction.

1.3.5.1 HEROD AND THE PASSION STORY

Luke 13:31ff.: Here we find a biographical apothegm peculiar to Luke. Though it "is perhaps in some way related to the similarly obscure story in Mark 6:14–16 par., one would rather expect to find it situated in the time *before* a journey toward Jerusalem was explicitly begun" (Klostermann, 147). The report that it was Herod's intention to kill Jesus cannot be verified from non-Christian sources. One begins to suspect redaction when one recognizes that the figure of Herod served Luke to explicate a thesis. This is evident from the next passage.

Luke 23:6ff.: The depiction of Jesus before Herod I is probably dependent on Ps. 2:1–2, as Dibelius has shown.[41] Either early Christian theology or Luke himself assumed, in light of this Old Testament passage, that there was a friendly relationship between Herod and Pilate (see esp. Acts 4:27, where scriptural proof for their joint action *against* the anointed one is found in Psalm 2). After what has been said, it should be clear that the portrayal of Herod in Luke's writings may not be employed at all for the question of the *historia Jesu*. Rather, it should be investigated in terms of Luke's redactional intention. Then, light is also shed on Luke 13:31ff. According to Luke's understanding of Herod's intention to kill Jesus, Jesus' statement in v. 33b, "For it cannot be that a prophet should perish away from Jerusalem," has the following meaning. Only after the end of the period that was free from Satan, which in Luke extends from 4:13 to 22:3,[42] is the adversary able to overpower Jesus. Herod, among others such as Judas, is depicted as an instrument of the adversary. Further, Herod is apparently a climactic figure insofar as he serves as the foil for the saving event and for the period of salvation that becomes manifest in Jesus. Herod lays hands on Christ's forerunner and witness (in Luke 3:19–20) and then in Luke 13:31ff. pursues Christ himself until the prophecy of Ps. 2:1–2 is fulfilled in Luke 23:6–12.

In sum, the *Lukan passion story* can raise no claims to be a historical and factual representation. Since Conzelmann has demonstrated, in a fair rebuttal of Streeter, that the theory of a proto-Luke is superfluous, and since the assumption of a peculiar Lukan source[43] for the passion story is unnecessary, the changes, transpositions, and additions undertaken on the Markan passion story should mostly be ascribed to Luke's redaction.[44] Luke is responsible for styling the passion of Jesus as a martyrdom and for presenting Jesus as a martyr.[45]

It is clear that this reinterpretation of Mark should be explained solely on the basis of literary and redaction criticism. In any event, this finding discredits Luke the "objective" historian, though not Luke the theologian.

1.3.5.2 THE JOURNEY(S) OF JESUS AND PAUL AS A STYLISTIC DEVICE FOR LUKE'S PRESENTATION OF THE PROPAGATION OF THE GOSPEL FROM JERUSALEM TO ROME

We shall proceed under the assumption that the travel narrative in the Gospel of Luke (9:51—19:27) derives from Lukan redaction.[46] This initial assumption, which is shared by the majority of investigators, gives us reason to ask whether the presentation of Paul's activity in the form of a journey may be understood as part of Lukan redaction.[47]

We shall approach this question by comparing the travels of Paul as depicted in Acts with the information supplied by the letters. This comparison will demonstrate the difficulties involved in harmonizing the two sources.

It is conventional[48] to differentiate the following journeys:

1. *The first missionary journey* (Acts 13–14) with Barnabas through Cyprus and Pisidian Antioch and back to home base, that is, Antioch on the Orontes.

2. The *second missionary journey* (Acts 15:40—18:22), which is undertaken by the main character, Paul. Its major stations are Philippi, Thessalonica, Athens, Corinth, Ephesus, and Palestine (the starting point is again Antioch; the final destination is unclear since a visit to Jerusalem seems to be reflected in 18:22; on this problem, which can only be solved on the basis of literary observations, see below, p. 141).

3. The *third missionary journey* through Galatia, Phrygia, Ephesus, Macedonia, Miletus, and Jerusalem (Acts 18:23—21:16).

4. The *journey to Rome* (Acts 27:1—28:16).

The report in Acts 11:27ff. concerning the support for those in Jerusalem from the congregation in Antioch also formally belongs here. It recounts a *journey* of Barnabas and Saul to Jerusalem. Nevertheless, convincing arguments have been brought against the historicity of this journey. The depiction

13

should "be understood as a Lukan composition created by combining various traditional elements."[49] Alongside the travel narrative in the Gospel of Luke, it is a further witness to Luke's manner of presenting history.

The same method that gave rise to inquiry into the historicity of Paul's second trip to Jerusalem as portrayed in Acts 11:27ff., that is, a comparison of the statements in Acts with those in Paul's letters, will now be used to evaluate the four journeys of Paul that are recounted in Acts.

Neither the stops recorded for the *first missionary journey* nor Barnabas as a fellow traveler on such a journey are mentioned in the letters. Of course, these could be merely fortuitous omissions. On the other hand, these discrepancies should warn investigators against blind adoption of Luke's information, all the more since the information can be explained on the basis of Lukan redaction (more on this shortly). The reports about the period preceding this journey (Acts 9:30: Paul in Tarsus/Cilicia; 11:26: Paul in Syrian Antioch) do not contradict Paul's own statements in Gal. 1:21, since during Paul's lifetime Syria and Cilicia *campestris* formed *one* Roman province.[50]

The correspondence of the stops mentioned in Acts 16ff. for the *second missionary journey* with those that may be inferred from 1 Thessalonians, even with regard to the order of the stations, is astonishing. The letters and Acts witness the following order: Philippi, Thessalonica, Athens, and Corinth. Further comparison of details in 1 Thessalonians and Acts 17–18 reveals the following differences. Acts 17:14 reports that Silas and Timothy remain behind in Beroea. The command for them to rejoin Paul as soon as possible is to be relayed to Silas and Timothy by the members of the congregation who accompany Paul to Athens (v. 15). Acts 18:5 then relates that Paul's command is carried out: Silas and Timothy come from Macedonia to Corinth. Evidence *contrary to this report* is that (a) in 1 Thessalonians 3, Paul mentions only Timothy and not Silas and (b) Paul sends Timothy from Athens to Thessalonica (v. 2), that is, he does not leave him behind in Beroea. Only the place where Paul and Timothy rejoin one another, Corinth, is the same in Acts and 1 Thessalonians.

The stops of the *third missionary journey*, too, seem to correspond with events in the life of the historical Paul, even with regard to the order of the stations (Ephesus, Philippi, Thessalonica, and Corinth can be inferred). The case is thus similar to that of the second missionary journey. A different question, however, is whether the chronological placement of this journey is correct. The possibility that Paul visited

Jerusalem between his stay there for the conference and the journey there to deliver the collection seems to be *excluded*.[51] For this reason, the present form and chronological location of this journey in Acts is hardly acceptable.

The *journey to Rome* cannot be verified through Paul's letters. It is generally assumed, and rightly so, that Paul died in Rome, probably as a martyr (*1 Clem*. 5:5–6). Thus Paul either undertook a trip to Rome or was brought there (as a prisoner). One must distinguish this historical judgment from the question of whether Luke stylized the trip to Rome as a *journey*. This question should probably be answered in the affirmative, since Luke composed the voyage and the shipwreck in chap. 27 according to a schema also used in ancient parallels.[52]

In sum, our comparison of the Lukan depiction of Paul's missionary journeys and his trip to Rome with the changes in locality that can be inferred from the letters (and from other reliable traditions) brings us to the following noteworthy observation: With the exception of the journey through southern Galatia and Cyprus, most of the stations in Acts, and even their order, are confirmed by the letters. The journeys of Paul under discussion here thus *differ* in character from the so-called second journey to Jerusalem reported in Acts 11:27ff. The traditions that have been incorporated into these reports may well derive from something other than just isolated bits of information. On the other hand, the letters give rise to doubts about Luke's chronological placement of the third missionary journey. One general observation is that Luke styled at least some parts of the trip to Rome as a journey. This observation justifies our question of whether stylistic intentions played a role in Luke's depictions of Paul's journeys, regardless of the reliability of the traditions he used.

We shall now *positively* demonstrate that Luke employed the journey as a stylistic device.[53] Luke conceives of the continuity of salvation history as a course (*dromos*) or way (*hodos*). See the (Lukan) speech of Paul in Pisidian Antioch: "And as John was finishing his course [*dromos*] . . ." (Acts 13:25). The proclamation of John occurred before Jesus' entrance into the world (*eisodos*, 13:24). Acts understands Christian existence in general as a *hodos* (9:2; 19:9, 23; 22:4; 24:14, 22). In the summary of Paul's missionary activity in his farewell speech at Miletus (Acts 20:18ff.), Paul describes the termination of his activity as the completion of his course (*dromos*, 20:24).[54]

Luke's overarching theological reason for understanding and presenting the activity of Paul (the apostles, Jesus, and John the Baptist) as a course arises from his conception of salvation history. The history of salvation presents the path of the gospel from Jerusalem (Luke 24:47) all the way to Rome (cf. Acts 1:8 and the end of Acts). The worldwide missionary activity (i.e., throughout the Roman empire; see Luke 2:1) and the person of Paul form the focus of the presentation. Everything else—the beginning in Galilee, the crisis in Jerusalem involving the death and resurrection of Jesus, the church in Jerusalem, and the experimental mission of the Hellenists (in Luke's perspective)—leads toward this one goal. The Jerusalem Conference is located in the middle of Acts as the "pivotal point" (Conzelmann). It separates "the primitive period of the church from the present"[55] and forms the presupposition for Paul's independent mission that begins after his separation from Barnabas (Acts 15:39–40).[56] When the Gentile Christians accept the Apostolic Decree,[57] the Pauline era is meshed with, and legitimized by, the holy past as the era of the church. The first missionary journey serves a preparatory and copulative function. On the one hand, Luke uses this journey to illustrate "the problem that will be the concern of the Apostolic Council, which immediately follows in Acts 15. It is as if the fact and success of the proclamation of the gospel to the Gentiles in Antioch in Acts 11:20f. were projected onto the map and emphasized by means of this 'geographical hyperbole.'"[58] On the other hand, the journey is consciously stylized by Luke to present Paul in the place of Barnabas as the great missionary to the Gentiles (see Acts 13:13, 16, 43, 45, 50; 14:20; and the well-known transformation of Saul to Paul in 13:9). In the second part of Acts, Paul alone steps to the center of the stage.[59] The depiction of the course of the Pauline mission all the way to Rome[60] thus rests on theological motives, and its chronological placement *after* the Jerusalem Conference serves to demonstrate the continuity of the Lukan church with the primitive church in the history of salvation. The reasons for this placement are *not* primarily chronological:

> Luke makes no separation between chronological and soteriological significance. On the contrary, to him the historical sequence as such is of *fundamental* importance. Yet he is not a modern, "secular" historian, he is a man of faith. In other words, when he has discovered the redemptive significance of an event, he can go on *to deduce from it the "correct"* *chronology*, which means, among other things, that he can begin to modify Mark. . . . *The correctness of the chronology cannot be demonstrated "historically."*[61]

If these results thus indicate that we should understand the journeys of Paul in the framework of Luke's theology of salvation history, it should further be emphasized that what has just been said about the relationship of salvation history and chronology also raises a fundamental objection to the employment of the secular historical data in Luke's two volumes for a critical chronology of Paul. When Luke writes in his prologue that he intends "to write an orderly account for you," the order he is speaking of "does not necessarily mean chronological order."[62] This statement of intention should be understood as the basic principle also underlying the composition of Acts.[63] The prologue indicates the geographical itinerary of the events in Luke and Acts. "The way of Jesus begins in Nazareth. . . . The worldwide mission starts in the holy city [Jerusalem] and finally reaches its goal in Rome, the capital of the world."[64]

1.3.5.3 A PECULIAR FEATURE IN LUKE'S USE OF LOCAL TRADITIONS

There is a peculiar, seldom observed,[65] and to my knowledge never-evaluated feature in the way Luke groups together local traditions in Acts. Although Paul may visit a given locality two or three times, the various information about his visits is always summarily presented together in a single passage. This is the case for Corinth in 18:1ff., even though Paul also stays there for three months during his third missionary journey (20:2–3); for Thessalonica in 17:1ff., which, as Luke reports, Paul also visits later (20:2); and for Philippi in 16:11ff., which Paul later visits two more times (20:2, 3–6).

The episodes involving Lystra also belong in this category, for only Acts 14:8–20 reports traditions, whereas Acts 14:21 merely mentions briefly that Paul passed through Lystra, and Acts 16:1–3 is redactional (see below, pp. 153–54). Nor is Ephesus an exception. Acts 19 presents several traditions about Paul's activity in this city, while 18:19ff. should be viewed as a Lukan composition that uses tradition only to serve as preparation for the presentation of the stay in Ephesus in chaps. 19–20 (see pp. 144ff.).

It is unlikely that Luke should have large amounts of material for some stations of the second missionary journey and little or none for other stations, while precisely the inverse should be the case for the third missionary journey. Hence one is led to suppose that the reasons for Luke's arrangement of local traditions are not chronological in nature.[66] If it is at all possible to determine the original chronological place of the incidents reported in Luke's summaries of local traditions, this may be done only in the light of Paul's letters. For the chronology we intend to develop below, these observations mean the following. Even if we think that Luke's report of Paul's trial before Gallio reflects historical traditions, we still do not know during which of Paul's visits with the Corinthian congregation this trial occurred.

1.3.5.4 CHRONOLOGICAL AND WORLD-HISTORICAL DATA AS AN APOLOGETICAL STYLISTIC DEVICE

We shall first point out the passages that most clearly create the impression that Luke was writing with one eye on the Roman state and that he wanted to illustrate the politically inoffensive nature of Christianity.[67]

The *passion story* (see already Luke 13:31ff.) portrays Jesus dying as a martyr and thereby wards off every possible political interpretation of this event in the sense of Jewish (political) messianism.[68] When the Roman Pilate cross-examines Jesus, he is unable to find anything that warrants condemnation (see also Acts 3:13) and, as is well known, is completely cleared of guilt for Jesus' death.

The first Gentile convert to Christianity is a Roman centurion (Acts 10). Further, the way that Roman officials treat Christians who have been denounced by Jews is exemplary (cf. what was already said regarding Pilate and, further, the portrayals of Gallio, Felix, and Festus). Indeed, the main character in Acts, Paul, is himself a Roman citizen.

These tendencies in Luke's two volumes, which should clearly be classified as apologetic, shed light on other tendencies that have less often been designated "apologetic."

John the Baptist's sermon on the *responsibilities of people of various ranks*, a Lukan compendium, ends with prescriptions for soldiers. Though the soldiers are not at all concerned about the baptism of John, the ethical advice in Luke 3:14, "Rob no one by violence or by false accusation, and be content with your wages," indicates that they should be loyal to the state.

Since Luke's *census* has failed to pass the test of historical verification (see above, p. 9), we can surprisingly identify an apologetic element in this report: Even Jesus' parents demonstrate their loyalty to the Roman state when they undertake the difficult journey (moreover, Mary is pregnant) from Nazareth to Bethlehem (note that Matthew differs here).[69]

1.3.5.5 CHRONOLOGICAL DATA AS AN EXPRESSION OF THE URBANITY OF CHRISTIANITY

Closely related to the apologetic aspect in Luke's two volumes is Luke's conspicuous attempt to present Christianity as urbane, that is, as meet-

18

ing all the demands of Hellenistic culture.[70] Not only does the portrayal of "primitive Christian communism" in Acts demonstrate that the Christians have turned Greek ideals into reality (cf. Acts 2:44–45 and 4:32 with Iamblichus, Vit. Pyth. 30.168: *koina gar pasi panta* ["For all things are common to all," tr.]),[71] but the *clausula Petri* in Acts 5:29 (see already 4:19) also shows that Christians are followers of Socrates. Socrates similarly said to his judges, "I shall obey the god rather than you" (Plato, Ap. 29 D). Paul the apostle received a Hellenistic education, just as the triplet in Acts 22:3[72] and Paul's artistic speech at the Areopagus in Acts 17 illustrate.

As regards the *social* aspect of Christianity, Acts predominantly has upper-class people interested in Christianity, for example, the Ethiopian treasurer (8:26ff.), the proconsul Sergius Paulus (13:6ff.), and Dionysius of Athens (17:34). Further, Paul always has an upper-class audience. See merely 25:23ff., where Luke presents the king Agrippa, his sister Bernice, their court, the governor Festus, the tribunes, and the prominent men of the city of Caesarea as Paul's audience.

The claim for Christianity's renown that is apparent here is complemented by an understanding of Christianity in terms of *world history*. Christian history is an integrated part of universal history (Luke 2:1ff.; 3:1ff.; also Acts 11:28). Even the opponents of Christianity must necessarily acknowledge its expansion throughout the world (Acts 17:6; 24:5). Acts 26:26 illustrates well this universal claim of Christianity when Paul says to Festus, "This was not done in the corner."

From what was said in section 1.3.4 and from what has just been said, the nonhistoricity of all the chronological or world-historical references in Luke's two volumes certainly does not *eo ipso* follow. The redactional tendencies that have been identified do, however, forbid any chronology of Paul deserving of the name "critical" to use even one of these references without support from the primary source, the letters of Paul.

1.3.6 Paul as a Historian?

While previous research has been concerned with testing or occasionally correcting Acts' information on Paul through the use of Paul's statements in the genuine letters, the preceding sections have criticized this method for not being radical[73] enough. This section argues that even the previous use of Paul's letters was not critical enough. A careful examination of the decisive passage, Galatians 1–2, will make this clear.

(a) In Galatians, Paul is writing not as a neutral historian[74] but rather in response to accusations. He is defending himself. Before the data supplied by Paul in retrospect is transposed without further ado onto the historical drawing board (as has become conventional in recent investigations), the genre of Galatians as a whole and, above all, of Galatians 1–2 in particular must be determined.

(b) Nearly everyone maintains that Gal. 1:15ff. indicates that Paul worked for fourteen (eleven) years in Syria and Cilicia. Paul, however, says only, "[After my first visit to Jerusalem,] I went [aorist] into the regions of Syria and Cilicia." After mentioning the publicity that his proclamation of the gospel received (Gal. 1:23), Paul evidently bypasses the period between his stay in Syria and Cilicia and his second visit to Jerusalem. The statement about where Paul went after his visit with Cephas does not permit us to say anything about where Paul stayed during the fourteen years.

(c) What is the reference point of Paul's chronological statements? We mentioned above (p. 4) that research is currently debating whether the "fourteen years" in Gal. 2:1 should be counted from the time of the conversion or from the time of the first visit to Jerusalem. If one reads the text carefully, both suggestions could be wrong. Each time Paul uses the word *epeita* (Gal. 1:18, 21; 2:1), he connects what follows with what immediately preceded. Thus it seems that we should count the fourteen years from the time he completed his trip to Syria and Cilicia. This insight similarly applies to the question of Paul's reference to "three years" (Gal. 1:18). Here research is unanimous in the opinion that the apostle is speaking of three years since his conversion. In any event, it is more probable that Paul reckons the three years from the time of his return to Damascus (for further substantiation of these theses, see below, pp. 61–64).

(d) It is generally considered self-evident that the controversy in Antioch, which Paul recounts in Gal. 2:11ff., should be located chronologically after the Jerusalem Conference. The fact that Paul does not commence his report with the word *epeita*, however, speaks against this view. Rather than introducing this event as he had introduced the incidents in the previous chronologically ordered account, he begins with *hote*. Further, the account of Paul's speech to Peter leads directly into the body of the letter. This indicates that Paul was concerned to place this speech at precisely this point in the letter. The position of the speech has material importance as the conclusion of the historical report. This observation raises the question of whether the location of Gal. 2:11ff. reflects material rather than chronological priorities. We shall have to raise the question of whether the literary genre of Galatians 1–2 knew of such a transposition in the chronological order for the purpose of emphasizing a certain point.

1.4 THE TASK AND THE APPROPRIATE METHOD

Now that the conventional mode of establishing a critical chronology of Paul has been subjected to a decisive critique, we turn to the matter of determining the proper procedures and material priorities that should underlie and guide a new chronology.

1.4.1 The Absolute Priority of Paul's Own Witness for a Chronology of Paul

Ever since P. Vielhauer demonstrated in his article "On the 'Paulinism' of Acts"[75] that the content of Paul's speeches in Acts derives from Lukan theology, research has generally refrained from using any of Paul's speeches in Acts for the presentation of Paul's theology. Vielhauer's thesis, which at that time sounded revolutionary to many an ear,[76] was based on a comparison of Paul's letters with the speeches attributed to Paul in Acts. As is well known, Vielhauer's article was followed by the productive redaction-historical phase in synoptic studies. This new method was first tested on Luke's two volumes, where Vielhauer's refutation of the supposed Paulinism of Luke led to Conzelmann's determination of Luke's redactional intentions. It was then that Luke was first taken seriously or, one might even say, discovered as a theologian, though the relevance of this discovery was perceived in several different ways.[77] Vielhauer's starting point for his refutation of the "Paulinism" of Luke, a comparison of the letters with Acts, thus lay readily at hand as the starting point for our investigation of the chronology of Paul.[78] After we had determined the incompatibility of Paul's statements with the chronological framework of Acts (refutation), we then proceeded to the positive construction, that is, to the determination of Luke's redactional intention in his chronological references. Now if the historical reliability of Luke's chronological framework deserves just as negative a verdict as the reliability of his presentation of Paul's theology, then a reconstruction of the chronology of Paul, and not just the presentation of Paul's theology, must employ the letters as the primary source.[79] This parallel in method may

21

be extended one more step. Just as a sketch of Paul's theology must consider the original context of the letters and the genres employed in the letters,[80] so too must a reconstruction of Paul's chronology. Before one can transpose Paul's biographical statements onto a historical chart, one must deal with the question of the genre of the passage and with the related question of the situation that gave rise to these statements. As was seen in section 1.3.6, Paul by no means presents an absolutely continuous and unambiguous report. A *first section* in this study will thus provide an exegesis of Galatians 1–2, with particular attention to the form of Paul's statements. The goal will be to determine the relative chronology of the period between the conversion and the Jerusalem Conference. Closely connected with this task, an analysis of the agreements of the conference, insofar as they are mentioned in Galatians, will be undertaken. The agreements possibly provide important chronological information regarding the time before and after the conference.

Next, the topographical and (again, relative) chronological references of all the genuine letters will be employed to reconstruct the order of events in Paul's life. This reconstruction will also involve the question of the place and time of the composition of these same letters (any attempt to break out of this circle by, for example, using Acts would be a step backward). In determining the order of the letters, we shall *deliberately* abstain from using *internal* criteria (e.g., developments in Paul's thought) in preference for an *external* criterion that allows the specification of a particular order of the letters and their chronological relations to one another. We find this external criterion in the agreement that was indubitably made at the Jerusalem Conference and that obliged Paul (and Barnabas) to undertake a collection for the congregation in Jerusalem. Since, as is well known, Paul's efforts to organize the collection after the conference are reflected in most of his letters, it is possible to determine the chronological order of the letters[81] on the basis of the stage in the organization of the collection that each of the letters reflects.[82] When, for example, Rom. 15:25 mentions the immediately impending journey to Jerusalem in order to deliver the collection, it is evident that Paul wrote this later than 1 Cor. 16:1ff., where Paul explains how the collection should be gathered in Corinth. One may therefore conclude that Romans was written *after* 1 Corinthians. The presupposition of such a procedure is, of course, that the collection mentioned in the letters is the same collection agreed on at the Jerusalem Conference and that in Gal. 2:10b ("which very thing I was eager to do") is not referring to a collection that Paul had already delivered. The validity of this premise must first be demonstrated in the section on Galatians 1–2. Finally, one more task for the analysis of Galatians 1–2, which is closely related to the following step in the investigation, should also be mentioned here. It is well known that 1 Thessalonians[83] and Philippians do not mention the collection. Does this indicate that these two letters were not composed during the time of the collection? The analysis of Galatians 1–2 will show us whether we should keep the possibility open that Paul might have been in an area where he could have written 1 Thessalonians and Philippians even before the time of the conference. In the event of positive indications of this possibility, the question should be raised whether—apart from Galatians 1–2—other statements by the apostle contain hints of an early mission in Europe.

Since our overarching goal in this section will be the construction of a (relative) chronology based solely on Paul's letters, for reasons of method we shall consider Acts only afterward.

1.4.2 The Acts of the Apostles and Its Traditions

1.4.2.1 Integration of the Traditions of Acts Dealing with the Chronology of Paul into the Chronological Framework Attained Solely on the Basis of the Letters and the Means for Identifying and Isolating These Traditions

The substantiated thesis that Luke cannot have been a companion of Paul[84] provoked scholarly research to ask about the historical value that may be placed on Acts' witness to Paul's life as a whole. The principles listed above in section 1.4.1 exacerbate the problem even more, for they employ the collection as an external criterion for determining the order of the letters, whereas the impartial reader of Acts could never imagine the importance the collection had for Paul. This last observation is one more reason not to view Luke as a companion of Paul and not to trust his historical information. Nevertheless, a study of the collection provides a strong argument in favor of the value of the *traditions* Luke reworked. In his speech before Felix (Acts 24:10ff.), Paul mentions in passing the reason for his trip to Jerusalem: "Now after some years I came to bring to my nation alms and offerings" (24:17), that is, "to refute the charge of *stasis* and to demonstrate Paul's solidarity with his people."[85] While no one not knowing the letters of Paul would understand the historical importance of this sentence (a further warning against uncritical adoption of Luke's historical references), it is unmistakable, on the other hand, that the tradition reworked by Luke contained a correct bit of information about the purpose of Paul's last visit to Jerusalem (a weighty argument *for* the value of the traditions contained in Acts).

This minute observation also demonstrates that Acts may not be left to one side when one is concerned with the construction of a critical chronology of Paul. Rather, on the basis of the chronology that has been attained exclusively from the letters, one must dedicate a special section to determine the traditional value of Acts (that is, the value of the traditions contained therein) and, accordingly, order this material into the previously attained *vita* of Paul.

In this stage of the investigation, the following questions should be differentiated: Which traditions or passages clearly derive from Luke? Where does Luke formulate statements based on tradition, and how does he interpret the tradition? Can (and how can) tradition and redaction be cleanly distinguished in Acts?

In the preliminary comparison of Acts with Paul's letters (above, pp. 14ff.), some results were already achieved. For example, we saw that the stations mentioned in Acts' second and third journeys are closely paralleled by the routes recognizable from the letters and that they, in contrast to the so-called second trip of Paul to Jerusalem (Acts 11: 27ff.), may derive from a cohesive body of traditions. This traditional material must be carefully compared with the chronological data in Paul's own statements. In this process, what we observed above about Luke-Acts must be taken into consideration, and Luke's proclivities must not be allowed to distort our view. The chronological arrangement of the traditions about the journeys of Paul in Acts is of a *dogmatic* nature and should not be confused with critical chronology. (As was seen above, the Pauline mission *had* to be after the Jerusalem Conference and would not have been *allowed* before it.) Further, mention should be made of a methodological difficulty in separating tradition and redaction in Acts. It has been correctly observed that Luke composes more freely in Acts than he does in his gospel.[86] If this judgment is correct, the consequences for identifying and isolating sources in Acts are sobering. Imagine, for example, that we did not possess the Gospel of Mark. If this were the case, it would be impossible to reconstruct Mark on the basis of Luke. If Luke composes even more freely in Acts, the difficulty, if not impossibility, of identifying

24

and isolating the sources in Acts is apparent. *That* Luke used sources is, of course, certain. One may observe in the pericope on Simon in Acts 8, for example, how a tradition concerning the Hellenists originally reported Philip's mission in Samaria[87] and how Luke corrected this tradition by having the mission sanctioned by Jerusalem, for the Holy Spirit is granted only on the arrival of Peter and John from Jerusalem. This modification is enough to satisfy the demands of the Lukan program for Samaria, too, to be missionized by the apostles from Jerusalem (Acts 1:8).

The way Luke here reworked a source about the Hellenists is paralleled by his use of the second story about Philip (Acts 8:26ff., which probably derives from the same source as Acts 8:5ff.). This story of the conversion of the Ethiopian, which was "evidently recounted in the circles of the Hellenists as the first conversion of a Gentile,"[88] is employed by Luke as a prelude to the competing story of the conversion of Cornelius. These examples, among others (e.g., 5:1ff.; 6:8ff.; 7:54ff.; see Conzelmann, ad loc.), demonstrate that one must reckon with the use of written sources in the composition of Acts. It is another question, which in my opinion should be answered in the negative, whether reconstruction of these sources is possible. That a convincing restoration of these sources has not yet been published and that the old proposals about a Jerusalem source and an Antiochene source have not been able to establish themselves result from the difficult nature of the task[89] and further should *not* lead to the conclusion that an understanding of the meaning of the text at the level of redaction presupposes a precise delineation of the source.[90] "It was a matter of pride for the ancient author to transform his sources in such a way that the texts that he used remained barely recognizable and that the mark of his own individual style, in contrast, came all the more to the fore."[91]

While these observations are a clear caveat against rashly reconstructing the sources of Acts, we must still deal with the often-repeated thesis that an eyewitness report underlies the second part of Acts (the problem of the "we"-reports and of the itinerary). The importance of this question is apparent, for if this thesis were correct, we should possess the report of a companion of Paul.[92]

1.4.2.2 On the Question of an Itinerary of Paul's Journeys

The first issue arises from the "we"-reports in Acts 16:10–17 (journey from Troas to Philippi), 20:5–15 (from Philippi to Miletus), 21:1–18 (from Miletus to Jerusalem), and 27:1—28:16 (from Caesarea to

Rome [in addition to these passages, there is the secondary "we" in the Western text of 11:28]). Is a companion of Paul speaking in these passages, and may these parts in the first-person plural be attributed to a source? The "we" alone is not a sufficient criterion, for (a) it appears abruptly, (b) it does not stand in tension with the context but rather fits in well,[93] and (c) it could derive from the author of Acts, who would be feigning a temporary presence.[94] Dibelius clearly recognized these difficulties and refrained from using the "much discussed" "we" as the foundation stone for the hypothesis of a travel report.[95] Nevertheless, he does *accept* the question about a written travel report used in Acts that was posed by the sort of research that viewed the "we" as a criterion for source criticism.

Research has taken too little notice of this point. It should also be recalled that, according to Dibelius, Luke the physician (Col. 4:14; Philemon 24) was both the author of Acts and a companion of Paul. In my view, it is still meaningful, especially under this presupposition and after refraining from the reconstruction of the travel report on the basis of the "we"-passages, to draw into consideration the possibility that there was a continuous itinerary. Particularly if the author of Acts accompanied Paul along the stations mentioned in the itinerary, it is both conceivable and reasonable that he would have recorded the events for himself in an itinerary and that he could have used this later.

If, on the contrary, one follows Vielhauer in denying that the author of Acts was a companion of Paul, further questions arise regarding how such a relatively comprehensive itinerary was transmitted and how Luke[96] got his hands on it.

For the sake of fair discussion, it should be emphasized that, in his reconstruction of the itinerary, Dibelius left the question of the authorship of Acts totally to one side.[97] An affirmative answer to the question whether Luke was a companion of Paul would nevertheless provide weighty supplementary support for the thesis of an itinerary, even more, in my opinion, than its last defender, P. Vielhauer,[98] realizes.

Dibelius bases his reconstruction of the travel report, which he calls an itinerary, on the following observations on Paul's journeys in Acts:[99]

1. The stations are listed in marked regularity. "Had the writer worked without such a source and used only local traditions of the communities, he would probably have considered certain stations more fully, but excluded others" (pp. 5–6).
2. The author incorporates such irrelevant reports as Acts 21:16, which mentions the early disciple Mnason. "The sentence in

20:13, 14 which is completely unimportant for both the story of the mission and for the biography of Paul belongs here also: 'But going ahead to the ship, we set sail for Assos, intending to take Paul aboard there; for so he had arranged, intending himself to go by land. And when he met us at Assos, we took him on board and came to Mitylene'" (p. 197).

3. Doublets have sometimes arisen where an isolated tradition has been inserted into the itinerary. "The Lystra-story is told in 14:8–18 although, according to the itinerary, the stay of the missionaries in Lystra, and also in Derbe, the next station, has previously been reported (14:6–7)" (p. 6). Dibelius finds yet another insertion into the itinerary at 13:14, where the speech in vv. 15–42 interrupts the itinerary, which is picked up again in v. 43. Further, "the context of the Areopagus speech also suggests that through the introduction of the speech the proper sequence has been interrupted" (p. 6).

In our assessment of Dibelius's thesis, we need to ask (a) whether the thesis properly evaluates the text of Acts and (b) whether the reports of the itinerary that Dibelius reconstructs from Acts 13:4—14:28 and 15:35—21:16 correspond to the data on the journeys in Paul's letters. This last question is especially important, because the itinerary is supposed to derive from a companion of Paul.

We shall begin with (b). First, the contradiction between 1 Thessalonians and Acts 17–18, which was noted above (p. 14), must be attributed to the itinerary. Second, the agitated to and fro movement of trips between Ephesus and Corinth, which may be reconstructed from the Corinthian correspondence (see pp. 93–96), is not reflected at all in the itinerary. Third, indications of the first missionary journey are not found in Paul's letters.

With regard to (a), we may note that the supposed tension between Acts 14:6–7 and 14:8, which is maintained by Dibelius and is taken as the basic reason for employment of source criticism, is contrived rather than real. Verses 6–7 may be understood as a "redactional preview" (Conzelmann, ad loc.) in the sense that they describe the general missionary field while vv. 8ff. offer particulars. When Vielhauer criticizes Conzelmann for leaving it to the reader to imagine what he means by this statement,[100] Vielhauer is not presenting a material argument. Further, Vielhauer should have asked why Luke did not present the story directly after mentioning Lystra but rather continued to follow the "itinerary" up to "Derbe and the surrounding country." With his thesis that an itinerary note is involved here, Vielhauer has to assume awkwardness on the part of Luke. The derivation of the material mentioned under 2 from written sources is correct, of course. It is another question, however, whether this material should be connected with the thesis of a comprehensive itinerary. The concessions that Vielhauer makes to Conzelmann in the light of the texts give rise to the question whether the usual form of the itinerary thesis has lost its usefulness. Vielhauer writes:

> One will of course need to modify Dibelius's hypothesis to accommodate for the fact either that more than one document was used or that the author of Acts possessed the itinerary in a fragmentary, rather than complete, form. Decisions as to precisely what belonged to the itinerary may vary in the details; Dibelius himself sometimes corrected his delineation. One will also have to reckon with more thorough redaction by the author. One must refrain from the attempt to reconstruct the precise wording of the source, for while the author bases his work on this source, he literally quotes it only in certain passages; one must be content with discovering remnants of the source.[101]

It is not clear why Vielhauer, who assumes that *several* itineraries were used,[102] criticizes Conzelmann's circumspect view that the author of Acts employed specialized sources (including lists of stations). At least, the difference between Vielhauer and Conzelmann on this point does not appear to me to be irreconcilable. On the other hand, other, basic differences between the two proponents do exist. Vielhauer reckons with the existence of fragments from itineraries that derive from *companions of Paul*. In Conzelmann's work, one receives the impression that, according to his opinion, the *author of Acts* himself determined what many of Paul's stops were by using a map.[103] Further, Vielhauer apparently still seriously reckons with the possibility of reconstructing the fragments of the itineraries solely on the basis of Acts. He considers these fragments to be of great value for determining the chronology of Paul, for they "permit the establishment of the order of certain journeys and thus enable one to determine the chronological order and approximate date of Paul's letters."[104] This possibility seems to be greatly diminished, however, by the concession that several itineraries were used. Vielhauer's view also seems to be ruled out (unless support for it is found in the letters) because, as Conzelmann properly noted, Luke derives the "proper" chronology from the importance that an event has for the history of salvation. That is to say, Luke could well have inserted a fragment from an itinerary at an incorrect spot, chronologically considered.

One final consideration for the problem of whether particular episodes belonged to the itinerary is that the Lukan manner of dealing
with local traditions (see above, pp. 17–18) excludes the possibility
that this problem can be solved solely on the basis of Acts.

Our discussion of Dibelius's thesis of an itinerary and its modification by Vielhauer leads to the conclusion that without previous consideration being given to Paul's own statements, it is (contra Dibelius and
Vielhauer) hopeless that one will arrive at useful results. Contra
Conzelmann, it must be emphasized that the old thesis of an itinerary
has its moment of truth in that Acts has reworked some traditions that
were of a continuous nature. This was the impression we received in
our comparison of the stations in Acts with those found in Paul's letters
(see above, p. 15). In Chapter 3 we shall see whether this impression
may be established with certainty.

NOTES

1. See M. Hengel, "Christologie und neutestamentliche Chronologie," in
Neues Testament und Geschichte: "In view of other divergences in German
research, the present relative consensus on Pauline chronology—and that simultaneously means New Testatment chronology up to A.D. 70—is amazing" (p. 44 n. 5).

2. J. Knox, *Chapters in a Life of Paul*; idem, "'Fourteen Years Later': A
Note on the Pauline Chronology"; idem, "The Pauline Chronology."

3. D. Riddle, *Paul: Man of Conflict*. Riddle writes in the preface (p. 9) that
Knox's article "'Fourteen Years Later'" provided the impetus for his own
book. There is thus no reason for W. G. Kümmel, *Introduction to the New
Testament*, 252–54, to have mentioned Riddle before Knox. Kümmel probably did this on the unmentioned assumption that Knox, inspired by his
teacher Riddle, made his statement before Riddle could actually write his
monograph.

A sympathetic introduction to the methods of Knox and Riddle is given by
J. C. Hurd, "Pauline Chronology and Pauline Theology," in *Christian History and Interpretation*. See also Hurd, "The Sequence of Paul's Letters";
idem, s.v. "Chronology, Pauline," *IDB* Sup: 166–67. Also methodologically
important is C. Buck, "The Collection for the Saints." Buck's work has suffered almost total neglect from research, probably because he propounded the
untenable thesis that "the collection took place before the Jerusalem council
and not after it" (p. 27). See also J. C. Hurd, *The Origin of 1 Corinthians*,
3–42; and, above all, H. L. Ramsey's diss. (supervised by J. Knox), "The
Place of Galatians in the Career of Paul." Ramsey offers a good presentation
of Knox's working procedure (pp. 126–36). Attention should be given to

Ramsey's work in future discussions of Pauline chronology, even though neither his main thesis, that Gal. was written during the imprisonment in Caesarea (pp. 305ff.), nor his late date for the conversion of Paul (37 C.E., pp. 151ff.) is probable. Further, the title of the dissertation says too little about its content. Ramsey actually presents a complete chronology of Paul. On the reception of Knox's position, see also A. J. Mattill, Jr., "Luke as a Historian in Criticism since 1840" (Ph.D. diss., Vanderbilt University, 1959), 453–55.

4. Even in North America, Knox's procedure is often rejected without a real knowledge of his thesis. See E. E. Ellis, *Paul and His Recent Interpreters*, who in an otherwise informative book describes (p. 17) Knox's thesis imprecisely and does not even mention Knox's equation of Acts 18:22 with the visit for the Jerusalem Conference (see Knox, *Chapters in a Life*, 68f.). D. R. A. Hare, *The Theme of Jewish Persecution of Christians in the Gospel According to St. Matthew*, accurately describes the treatment Knox's chronology has received: "While few subsequent Pauline biographies show the same primary regard for the Pauline data, . . . the main arguments of John Knox stand unrefuted. These arguments have often been ignored, but they have not been answered!" (p. 62 n. 2). Knox's chronology is not even mentioned by W. F. Orr and J. A. Walther, *1 Corinthians* ("Introduction with a Study of the Life of Paul," 1–131).

5. Knox's chronology, if mentioned at all, is usually dismissed with the remark that his identification of the ecstatic experience described in 2 Cor. 12 with the conversion is incorrect. This is done, e.g., by Béda Rigaux, *Paulus und seine Briefe*, BiH 2 (Munich: Kösel-Verlag, 1964), 122, and even by E. Haenchen, *The Acts of the Apostles*, 67 (see 544f. n. 6). A. Suhl, *Paulus und seine Briefe*, by contrast, properly noted that Knox no longer maintained this thesis in his *Chapters in a Life of Paul*. Suhl (p. 89) misrepresents Knox, however, when he says that Knox's proposal in the two articles mentioned above (n. 2) is based on the equation of the ecstatic experience in 2 Cor. 12 with the conversion. Knox, *Chapters in a Life*, 78 n. 3, writes to the contrary that his "scheme has never depended upon the interpretation of this passage" (viz., 2 Cor. 12).

In the following, we assume that the ecstatic experience in 2 Cor. 12 does not have anything to do with Paul's conversion. The same observation that caused Knox to make this identification, the chronological reference "fourteen years ago," actually speaks against it: (a) Knox had to reckon the fourteen years in Gal. 2:1 from the conversion, something that is unlikely (see below, pp. 61–62), and (b) it would be necessary to assume that 2 Cor. 12 was written the same year the Jerusalem Conference took place, a possibility that should be ruled out because 1 Cor. 16:1ff. (1) was written before 2 Cor. 12 and (2) presupposes that the organization of the collection had been under way for at least a year (see below, pp. 82–83). P. Hartmann, "Das Verhältnis des Galaterbriefs zum zweiten Korintherbrief," who prior to Knox tried to evaluate the reference to fourteen years in Gal. 2:1 and 2 Cor. 12 for chronological purposes, consequently dates 1 Cor. *before* the conference. Recently C. Buck and G. Taylor, *Saint Paul*, 104, 222, have again presented the thesis that the ecstatic experience in 2 Cor. 12 should be identified with the conversion.

6. According to the majority of investigators, we do not have any other datum of absolute chronology, for the change of governors from Felix to Festus (Acts 24:27) cannot be dated precisely (see H. Conzelmann, *Die Apostelgeschichte*, and the literature cited there). For the present, we shall refrain from explicating this passage, for it deals with a period in Paul's life not covered by the letters.

7. Thanks to A. Plassart (see below, pp. 185–86 n. 57), we know of nine fragments (no longer only four [seven] as at the time of Deissmann; see below, p. 163) from the letter of Claudius that enable us to determine the date of the proconsulate of Gallio. Kümmel, *Introduction*, 253 n. 2, speaks of "recent discoveries" instead of Plassart's determination that *existing, known* fragments belonged to the Gallio-inscription.

8. According to B. Altaner and A. Stuiber, *Patrology*, 280, the work was composed at Augustine's request in the year 417/418.

9. The Roman imprisonment of Paul is witnessed even earlier by Hebrews. See W. Wrede, *Das literarische Rätsel des Hebräerbriefs*, 62–63.

10. According to this mode of reckoning, Paul's stay in Arabia began shortly after the year 31 (34). If Paul is referring to this period in 2 Cor. 11:32–33, then Paul's visit with Cephas in Jerusalem occurred, at the latest, in the year 41, for Aretas ruled only until 40, and the date of this visit should be reckoned as "three years after" (Gal. 1:18; equivalent to two years, see p. 118 n. 54) Paul's return to Damascus (see p. 63). On the relationship of Acts 9:23ff. to 2 Cor. 11:32–33, see C. Burchard, *Der dreizehnte Zeuge*, 150ff., and the literature cited there. R. Jewett, *A Chronology of Paul's Life*, 30–33, believes he can demonstrate that "Paul's escape occurred sometime within the two year span until the death of Aretas in A.D. 39. This is a datum whose historical solidity is capable of anchoring a chronology" (p. 33). Jewett neither disproved the view that some followers of Aretas were (just) watching the city gates at Damascus nor proved that Aretas had power over Damascus (and further that this was the case during the two years before Aretas's death). "The only information 2 Cor. 11:32–33 provides is that Paul must have fled from Damascus before the death of Aretas" (Suhl, *Paulus*, 315). See Burchard, *Zeuge*, 158f. n. 100, and the literature cited there.

11. See, most recently, J. Becker, *Auferstehung der Toten im Urchristentum*. In German research it is easily forgotten that the notion of a development in Paul's thought has long been of great importance in English and American (and also French) research. This comment is applicable to J. Baumgarten, *Paulus und die Apokalyptik*, 236–38, who deals with this ques-

tion in two pages and discusses German literature exclusively. See merely C. H. Dodd, "The Mind of Paul: Change and Development," *BJRL* 18 (1934): 69–110 (= *New Testament Studies* [New York: Charles Scribner's Sons, 1954], 83–128). For criticism of this attempt, see John Lowe, "An Examination of Attempts to Detect Developments in St. Paul's Theology," *JThS* 42 (1941): 129–42. See, most recently, the work of Buck and Taylor, *Saint Paul*. For criticism of this book, see V. P. Furnish, "Development in Paul's Thought"; and J. W. Drane, "Theological Diversity in the Letters of St. Paul." See also W. D. Davies, *The Gospel and the Land*, 208ff., and the survey in Hurd, *Origin*, 8ff. On the question of development in Paul's theological thought, see also the important report by Werner Georg Kümmel, "Das Problem der Entwicklung in der Theologie des Paulus," *NTS* 18 (1971/72): 457–58.

12. See Martin Luther, WA 7.97.23: "[Scriptura sacra] sui ipsius interpres." On this principle, see Karl Holl, *Gesammelte Aufsätze zur Kirchengeschichte*, vol. 1: *Luther*, 7th ed. (Tübingen: J. C. B. Mohr [Paul Siebeck], 1948), 558ff.

13. P. Vielhauer, *Geschichte der urchristlichen Literatur*, 71–72.

14. The expression "junior partner of Barnabas" derives from Ernst Käsemann, *Commentary on Romans*, ed. and trans. G. Bromiley (Grand Rapids: Wm. B. Eerdmans, 1980), 4.

15. On the other hand, see Wolf-Henning Ollrog, *Paulus und seine Mitarbeiter: Untersuchungen zu Theorie und Praxis der paulinischen Mission*, WMANT 50 (Neukirchen-Vluyn: Neukirchener Verlag, 1979), 17–18. Ollrog argues, on partially dubious grounds, that Paul had become the leader of the Antiochene congregation before the conference.

16. I consider it improbable that someone such as Paul, whose letters reflect such a developed self-consciousness, could have spent around twenty years working for a mission that was not his own. I think that Paul's missionary strategy changed little throughout the years. Rather, he understood himself very early to be the apostle to the Gentiles (Rom. 11:13). Too much must be given up to maintain the picture of a Paul who was domesticated during the first twenty years, unless one resigns oneself to the explanation that "Paul (and the Hellenists) stayed within this small area [Syria and Cilicia] because at that time the parousia was expected immediately; there was no time for a worldwide mission" (M. Hengel, "Die Ursprünge der christlichen Mission," 21 n. 25). A man who intends to "transverse" the world all the way to Spain (on this expression, see A. von Harnack, *The Mission and Expansion of Christianity*, 1: 73–74) would not remain in a small area for such a long time. This appears all the more to be the case since the expectation of the imminent parousia is documented precisely in a letter, 1 Thess., which was composed outside the "small" area of Syria and Cilicia. It is incorrect to say that "in the years after the 'council,' according to his own understanding Paul became *the*

missionary to the Gentiles (1 Cor. 15:10; Rom. 11:13)" (M. Hengel, *Acts and the History of Earliest Christianity*, 119). According to Paul's own understanding, he became *the* apostle to the Gentiles at his conversion. Paul's understanding of his mission has been discussed most recently by Wolfgang Wiefel, "Die missionarische Eigenart des Paulus und das Problem des frühchristlichen Synkretismus," *Kairos* 17 (1975): 218–31. These problems will be discussed extensively in the third part of this trilogy.

17. Riddle, *Man of Conflict*, 97, states: "Barnabas accompanied him. Titus was included also—which proves without possible doubt that Paul went from the West, and that his work there was already far advanced. For it was in his western work that he brought this able assistant into the movement." See below, p. 193 n. 106.

18. On the thesis that Gal. 2:11ff. proves that Paul was still active in the Antiochene mission after the conference, see below, pp. 75–77.

19. See B. Schaller, "Iosephos," in *KP* 2: cols. 1440–1444, esp. col. 1441.

20. A. von Harnack, "Chronologische Berechnung des 'Tags von Damaskus,'" 674–75.

21. See the discussion by A. von Harnack, "Die Zeitangaben in der Apostelgeschichte des Lukas." For criticism of this view, see below, pp. 177–79 and p. 194 n. 113).

22. K. Lake, "The Chronology of Acts," in *The Beginnings of Christianity*, 5: 474.

23. Hurd, *Origin*, 23, correctly notes: "The intervals of time specified in Acts do not add up to fourteen years throughout the entire book!" I cannot refrain from remarking that Hurd's book has not received sufficient attention in the German-speaking lands. This judgment also applies to the commentaries published after Hurd's book. Regardless of whether one agrees with Hurd's reconstruction of the correspondence between Paul and the Corinthians, his book is an invaluable aid for exegesis of 1 Cor. See, nevertheless, W. G. Kümmel's review of *The Origin of I Corinthians* by J. C. Hurd in *ThLZ* 91 (1966): cols. 505–8. The article that Kümmel considers to have raised "problematic" issues (ibid., col. 508) for Hurd's theses, T. H. Campbell, "Paul's 'Missionary Journeys' as Reflected in His Letters," is critically discussed by Hurd in "Chronology," 228ff.

24. K. Haacker, "Die Gallio-Episode und die paulinische Chronologie." Suhl, *Paulus*, 121, also correctly notes that *hēmerai hikanai* is a "typically Lukan temporal reference" that has no chronological value.

25. It would be a modern misunderstanding to characterize Luke as a fraud because of this fact.

26. On the question of whether the reference to Gallio belonged to an itinerary and thus supplies a reliable datum, see below, pp. 18–19 and pp. 25–29.

27. The discussion of the census up to approximately the year 1971 has

been evaluated in the new English edition of E. Schürer, *The History of the Jewish People in the Age of Jesus Christ*, 1:399ff. See also S. Safrai in *The Jewish People in the First Century*, 1:372–74. The relevant source material is presented with clarity by E. Klostermann, *Das Lukasevangelium*, 32–34. See also J. Finegan, *Handbook of Biblical Chronology*, 236.

28. See Schürer, *History*, 1:567ff.; and E. Meyer, *Ursprung und Anfänge des Christentums*, 1:47–49. Whether John the Baptist entered public life in the fifteenth year of Tiberius (28 C.E.) cannot be verified through other sources. Doubts about the reliability of this report arise from consideration of (a) the history of redaction and (b) the history of traditions. On (a): The synchronism in Luke 3:1 is motivated by "the attempt . . . to draw attention to the universal importance of the Christ-event" (H. Schürmann, *Das Lukasevangelium*, 1:151). On (b): "There could have been, at most, a tradition that dealt with the year in which John was imprisoned or executed, but there would not have been a tradition about his appearance as a prophet, which was not occasioned by any particular event" (E. Schwartz, *Charakterköpfe aus der antiken Literatur*, 100).

29. H. Conzelmann, *The Theology of St. Luke*, 26.

30. Contra Schürer, *History*, 1:346. Of course, even Josephus's report calls for a redaction-historical explanation, especially since the content of John's proclamation, as depicted by Josephus, "seems to be adapted to Graeco-Roman taste" (ibid.). The solid historical kernel of the report in Josephus is Herod's measure to place John in prison because he was afraid of political implications. The admonition not to misuse marriage is more congruous with the moralistic perspective of Christian tradition. On the martyrdom of John, see further Joachim Gnilka, "Das Martyrium Johannes' des Täufers (Mk 6,17–29)," in *Orientierung an Jesus: Zur Theologie der Synoptiker. Für Josef Schmid*, ed. P. Hoffmann, N. Brox, and W. Pesch (Freiburg: Herder, 1973), 78–92, and the literature cited there.

31. For this problem, see Schürer, *History*, 1:385ff.; uncritical: Josef Blinzler, "Die Niedermetzelung von Galiläern durch Pilatus," *NT* 2 (1958): 24–49; contra Blinzler, and rightly, P. Winter, *On the Trial of Jesus*, 74ff. nn. 8–10, and the literature cited there.

32. J. Jeremias, *Jerusalem in the Time of Jesus*, 157–58.

33. Is the statement by Schürmann that Caiaphas came into office by a procedure that was "actually contrary to the law" (Schürmann, *Lukasevangelium*, 1:151) supposed to be a response to this problem? Did Luke know that? A consideration from the history of traditions also speaks against the reliability of the combination in Luke: The oldest Gospel (Mark) does not even mention the name of the high priest who was in office at the time of Jesus. Later the high priest is identified as Annas (substratum of the Gospel of John; see 18:12, 19). Then he is correctly identified as Caiaphas (John 11:49; 18:13–14; Matt. 26:3). Luke combines the two names.

34. The possibility that there is an error in Josephus, as maintained by F.

Dexinger, "Ein 'Messianisches Szenarium' als Gemeingut des Judentums in nachherodianischer Zeit?" (261 n. 61), is unlikely. More likely is that Luke had read Josephus, where Judas is mentioned in a paragraph that follows *Ant.* 20.97, namely, 20.102. The incorrect order in Acts 5 would thus have arisen from a hasty reading of this text in Josephus. In Josephus, however, only the *sons of Judas* are mentioned, and furthermore, Josephus's reports on Theudas and on the crucifixion of the sons of Judas are not connected by a smooth transition. Thus one should follow M. Dibelius, "The Speeches in Acts and Ancient Historiography," in *Studies in the Acts of the Apostles*, 138–85, 186–87, in rejecting this proposal. The reason that F. F. Bruce, *The Acts of the Apostles*, 2d ed., 1951 (reprint, Grand Rapids: Wm. B. Eerdmans, 1973), gives in support of the historicity of a second Theudas is also insufficient. Bruce cites Origen, *Cels.* 1.57, where it is said, "Among the Jews there was one Theudas before the birth of Jesus." He differentiates this Theudas from the one mentioned by Josephus (*Acts*, 147). This argument is faulty, since in this passage Origen is using Acts, as is apparent from his reference to Simon the magician in 1.57 (cf. Acts 8) and also from the reference to Judas (Acts 5). Acts is responsible for the order "Theudas—Judas." Origen concludes that Theudas was active in the pre-Christian era on the basis of Acts 5:37, where it is said that Judas arose in the days of the census, i.e., at the time of the birth of Jesus but *after* the days of Theudas. On this problem, see further Schürer, *History*, 1:456–57, and the literature cited there.

35. See Conzelmann, *Apostelgeschichte*, on Acts 11:28; and Suhl, *Paulus*, 62.

36. Conzelmann, *Apostelgeschichte*, 76.

37. G. Strecker, "Die sogenannte zweite Jerusalemreise des Paulus (Act 11,27–30)," 73 n. 40.

38. Word statistics point in this direction. *Oikoumenē* is one of Luke's favorite words: Luke 2:1; 4:5; 21:26; Acts 17:6, 31; 19:27; 24:5 (elsewhere in the New Testament only in Matt. 24:14 and Rom. 10:18). The construction *holos ho* is also Lukan: Luke 4:14; 7:17; 8:39, 43 (vl.), and frequently; fifteen times in Acts.

It should also be taken into consideration that the announcement of a worldwide famine would correspond well with apocalyptic, early Christian prophecy (this comment is made in reference to E. Plümacher, *Lukas als hellenistischer Schriftsteller*, 24).

39. R. O. Hoerber, "The Decree of Claudius in Acts 18:2," investigates the use of *pas* in Luke's two volumes and concludes that it is used in a "hyperbolic" way in our passage (the case is different, e.g., in Acts 13:44). If this is correct, the historical value of Luke's information is hardly enhanced.

40. Strong doubts about the reliability of Luke as a historian also arise in light of his ignorance of the geography of Palestine, the main setting for his history of the church (see Conzelmann, *Theology of Luke*, 60ff.).

41. M. Dibelius, *From Tradition to Gospel*, 199; see also the literature

cited there. See also Karlheinz Müller, "Jesus vor Herodes: Eine redaktionsgeschichtliche Untersuchung zu Lk 23,6–12," in *Zur Geschichte des Urchristentums*, ed. G. Dautzenberg, H. Merklein, and K. Müller (Freiburg: Herder, 1979), 111–41; and Erwin Buck, "The Function of the Pericope 'Jesus before Herod' in the Passion Narrative of Luke," in *Wort in der Zeit: Festgabe für Karl Heinrich Rengstorf zum 70. Geburtstag*, ed. W. Haubeck and M. Bachmann (Leiden: E. J. Brill, 1980), 165–78. This observation renders void the considerations of Jewett on the chronological value of Luke 23:12 (*Chronology*, 28). A one-sided historicizing approach is also taken by H. W. Hoehner, "Why Did Pilate Hand Jesus over to Antipas?" in *The Trial of Jesus*, 84–90.

42. On this, see R. Bultmann, *The History of the Synoptic Tradition*, 365; and, further, Conzelmann, *Theology of Luke*, 152. A different view is presented by S. Brown, *Apostasy and Perseverance in the Theology of Luke*, 6ff.

43. See F. Rehkopf, *Die lukanische Sonderquelle*. For criticism of this thesis, see Hans Conzelmann, review of *Die lukanische Sonderquelle: Ihr Umfang und Sprachgebrauch* by Friedrich Rehkopf, *Gn.* 32 (1960): 470–71.

44. This has been shown for the pericope on Gethsemane (Luke 22:40–46) by E. Linnemann, *Studien zur Passionsgeschichte*, 11–40. On Luke 23:6ff., see what was said above in the text. Most recently, V. Taylor, in a posthumously published work, has spoken out in favor of a special Lukan source for the passion story. See Vincent Taylor, *The Passion Narrative of St. Luke*. For criticism of this book, see Georg Strecker, review of *The Passion Narrative of St. Luke* by Vincent Taylor, *ThLZ* 101 (1976): cols. 33–35.

45. Detailed proof of this statement is found in Dibelius, *Tradition*, 199ff.; and H.-W. Surkau, *Martyrien in jüdischer und frühchristlicher Zeit*, 90–100.

46. See G. Sellin, "Komposition, Quellen und Funktion des lukanischen Reiseberichtes (Lk. IX 51—XIX 28)."

47. J. Knox could pungently write, "If you had stopped Paul on the streets of Ephesus and said to him, 'Paul, which of your missionary journeys are you on now?' he would have looked at you blankly without the remotest idea of what was in your mind" (*Chapters in a Life*, 41–42). Apparently of a completely different opinion is Nils Alstrup Dahl, "Paul: A Sketch," in *Studies in Paul* (Minneapolis: Augsburg Publishing House, 1977), 5. Knox's critique of the method of subdividing Paul's mission into three missionary journeys by no means implies that the apostle proceeded without a plan. On the contrary, Paul's "over-all conception of his apostolic mission would not have been of a series of missionary journeys between Jerusalem and various points in Asia Minor and Greece, but rather of one great journey beginning and ending at Jerusalem, but encompassing the whole Mediterranean world in its scope" (John Knox, "Romans 15:14–33 and Paul's Conception of His Apostolic Mission," *JBL* 83 [1964]: 1–11, esp. 11).

48. It is doubtful whether the conventional differentiation of the second

and third missionary journeys is in accord with Luke's own ideas. If Luke did have such a division in mind, he would have distinguished the two journeys more clearly (thus, correctly, Suhl, *Paulus*, 80–81). This observation does not affect what was said above about Luke's use of journeys as a stylistic device. Rather, after the model journey in Acts 13–14, which starts and ends in Antioch, "the apostle's activity after the conference [seems to form] one single great journey, which reaches its end with the arrest in Jerusalem in Acts 21:17ff." (Suhl, *Paulus*, 81). Or would it not be more appropriate to say, "Which reaches its end with the arrival in Rome"?

49. Strecker, "Jerusalemreise," 75.

50. See D. Magie, *Roman Rule in Asia Minor to the End of the Third Century after Christ*, vol. 2, *Notes*: 1419f. n. 68, 1439f. n. 27; Hengel, "Ursprünge," 18 with n. 15. See also the map in W. M. Ramsay's *Pauline and Other Studies in Early Christian History*, following p. 48.

51. See C. Weizsäcker, *The Apostolic Age of the Christian Church*, 2:11; Davies, *Gospel*, 277; and Conzelmann, *Apostelgeschichte*, 117. That Paul visited Jerusalem only three times after his conversion is in my opinion certain. The possibility of a further journey to Jerusalem between the visit to become acquainted with Cephas and the visit for the conference is, contrary to Acts, ruled out by Gal. For internal and geographical (distance) reasons, it is unlikely that there was a visit after the conference and before the trip to Jerusalem to deliver the collection. The tradition that glimmers through in Acts 21:18ff. does not know anything about an intermediary visit to Jerusalem (vv. 18–19 refer back to 15:4, 12; see Conzelmann, *Apostelgeschichte*, 117, 131). One may consider it a fortunate coincidence that Paul's letters enable such certainty regarding the visits to Jerusalem and thus provide us with a sure cornerstone for the chronology of Paul. On the other hand, J. J. Gunther, *Paul: Messenger and Exile*, again reckons with five visits by Paul to Jerusalem. This position involves an indefensible equation of primary and secondary sources.

52. See M. Dibelius, "The Acts of the Apostles in the Setting of the History of Early Christian Literature," in *Studies in the Acts of the Apostles*; Conzelmann, *Apostelgeschichte*, 156–57, and the literature cited there; and V. K. Robbins, "The We-Passages in Acts and Ancient Sea-Voyages."

53. For the following, see W. C. Robinson, "The Theological Context for Interpreting Luke's Travel Narrative" (see also idem, *Der Weg des Herrn*, 39ff.); F. V. Filson, "The Journey Motif in Luke-Acts," in *Apostolic History and the Gospel*. See also F. Hauck and S. Schulz, "Poreuomai," *TDNT* 6: 566–79, esp. 574–75.

54. See Robinson, "Theological Context," 26.

55. Hans Conzelmann, "Luke's Place in the Development of Early Christianity," in *Studies in Luke-Acts*, ed. L. Keck and J. Martyn (Nashville: Abingdon Press, 1966), 306. See also Haenchen, *Acts*, 461–62.

56. Paul's independent mission is actually motivated not by the Jerusalem

Conference but by his separation from Barnabas (reference from Prof. Luz). Nevertheless, Paul's worldwide mission would have been an impossibility in Luke's view without the Jerusalem Conference, even in spite of Paul's separation from Barnabas, for otherwise the Lukan church would be without past (understood in terms of salvation history). To this extent, the conference provides the internal justification for the Pauline mission and thus for freedom from the law in Gentile Christianity (contra Jervell, see below, n. 57).

57. This assertion should be understood in terms of salvation history and not as a historical assertion, as if the Lukan church still observed the minimal demands of the law (this comment is made in reference to J. Jervell, "The Law in Luke-Acts," 33 [= *Luke and the People of God*, 133–51]). In Luke's time, the problem of mixed congregations was no longer current, and the Lukan James does not understand the decree as law (Acts 15:19–20; see Haenchen, *Acts*, 459). Unfortunately I cannot accept Jervell's programmatic thesis that Luke wrote in a Jewish Christian milieu. See also Burchard, *Zeuge*, 167 n. 23, and the animated protest of Hans Conzelmann, "Literaturbericht zu den Synoptischen Evangelien (Fortsetzung)," *ThR*, n.s. 43 (1978): 44–45. See further W. Eltester, "Israel im lukanischen Werk und die Nazarethperikope," in *Jesus in Nazareth*, esp. 122ff.; and S. G. Wilson, *The Gentiles and the Gentile Mission in Luke-Acts*, 219–38. On the other hand, see also the important contribution by N. A. Dahl, "The Purpose of Luke-Acts," in *Jesus in the Memory of the Early Church*, esp. 94ff.

58. Suhl, *Paulus*, 80.

59. That the first missionary journey is consciously being related to the second part of Acts is also shown by the dispute over John Mark (13:13; 15:37ff.). "Luke related the incident [in Acts 13:13] only because later it is to separate Barnabas and Paul" (Haenchen, *Acts*, 415).

60. The precedence topography has over chronology in Luke's two volumes is emphasized and demonstrated well by R. W. Funk, "The Enigma of the Famine Visit."

61. Conzelmann, *Theology of St. Luke*, 33 (emphasis added). These observations, which were made primarily on the Gospel of Luke, are probably equally valid (even from Conzelmann's perspective) for Acts.

62. Funk, "Enigma," 133.

63. On *kathexēs*, see, most recently, F. Mussner, "*Kathexēs* im Lukasprolog," in *Jesus und Paulus*, and the literature cited there; and Gerhard Schneider, "Zur Bedeutung von *kathexēs* im lukanischen Doppelwerk," ZNW 68 (1977): 128–31.

64. E. Lohse, "Lukas als Theologe der Heilsgeschichte," in *Die Einheit des Neuen Testaments*, 145–64, esp. 149–50.

65. See Buck and Taylor, *Saint Paul*, 193; Hurd, *Origin*, 29.

66. See, however, the observations already made by G. Schille, "Die Fragwürdigkeit eines Itinerars der Paulusreisen," cols. 170ff.

67. See Conzelmann, *Theology of St. Luke*, 137ff., on Luke's apologetic tendencies. It should be recalled with J. Knox, *Marcion and the New Testament*, 132 n. 26, that the apologetic tendencies in Luke's two volumes were already analyzed by F. C. Baur: "The apologetic character of Luke-Acts, especially the Acts section, was first conspicuously emphasized by F. C. Baur, from whom we undoubtedly have more to learn than, in our reaction from his more extreme positions, we have been willing to recognize" (ibid.).

68. See Conzelmann, *Theology of St. Luke*, 139: "The concept of the Davidic Lordship is replaced by the simple title of King, the non-political sense of which is preserved (xix, 38)." E. Brandenburger, *Frieden im Neuen Testament*, 35 n. 38, is more cautious in his judgment.

69. See H. R. Moehring, "The Census in Luke as an Apologetic Device," in *Studies in New Testament and Early Christian Literature*, 144–60.

70. See Plümacher, *Lukas*.

71. Further Hellenistic parallels may be found in ibid., 17.

72. That the triad *gegennēmenos—anatethrammenos—pepaideumenos* corresponds to a set (Hellenistic) biographical schema was lucidly shown by Willem C. van Unnik, *Tarsus or Jerusalem* (London: Epworth Press, 1962) (= *Sparsa Collecta*, NT.S 29 [Leiden: E. J. Brill, 1973], 1:259–320). Nevertheless, to conclude that Paul was raised in Jerusalem (so van Unnik) or that he was educated under Gamaliel I in the Holy City (so J. Jeremias, *Der Schlüssel zur Theologie des Apostels Paulus*, 9–10, 14, who expressly emphasizes van Unnik's proof) too rashly neglects the *redactional* tendency of the formula demonstrated above. On Acts 22:3, see also Burchard, *Zeuge*, 31ff., and the literature cited there.

73. The philologian E. Schwartz believed not only that Acts does not provide solutions to the enigmas of the letters regarding Paul's journeys but also that it very often further complicates these enigmas (Schwartz, *Charakterköpfe*, 118–19).

74. See W. Wrede, *Paul*, 67: "The Acts of the Apostles has certainly distorted things a little; but also Paul's report, which is that of an eyewitness, leaves something to be wished; it contains obscurities, was written too in a passionate moment, and pursues the definite aim of establishing his independence of the apostles in Jerusalem." It should not be forgotten, however, that Paul had to provide absolutely correct information at *one* point in order to retain credibility, namely, when stating the number of visits to Jerusalem (cf. Gal. 1:20). Thus it is an exaggeration when J. T. Sanders writes that because of the character of Gal. 1–2 as a retrospect "suspicion should have arisen regarding the historicity of the chronology" ("Paul's 'Autobiographical' Statements in Galatians 1–2," 337). See, correctly, G. Eichholz, *Die Theologie des Paulus im Umriss*, 17–18; Ramsey, "Place of Galatians," 169–70.

75. P. Vielhauer, "On the 'Paulinism' of Acts."

76. Vielhauer's recognition that the picture of Paul in Acts bears Lukan

contours was in itself not new. See H. J. Cadbury's *The Making of Luke-Acts*; Riddle, *Man of Conflict*, 185ff.; Knox, *Chapters in a Life*; Burton Scott Easton, *The Purpose of Acts* (London: SPCK, 1936) (= *Early Christianity*, ed. Frederick C. Grant [New York: Seabury Press, 1954], 31–118, esp. 57ff.). In general, one may notice how much Vielhauer's epoch-making article (seen in retrospect) is obliged to the analyses of Overbeck. On this point, see Johann-Christoph Emmelius, *Tendenzkritik und Formengeschichte: Der Beitrag Franz Overbecks zur Auslegung der Apostelgeschichte im 19. Jahrhundert*, FKDG 27 (Göttingen: Vandenhoeck & Ruprecht, 1975), 16.

77. Thus O. Cullmann is able to accept Conzelmann's results and use them for his own theology of salvation history, while Vielhauer, Conzelmann, and Käsemann, to name just a few, stand in the tradition of dialectical theology and use the results to criticize the "early catholicism" of Luke. On this issue, see U. Wilckens, "Interpreting Luke-Acts in a Period of Existentialist Theology."

78. We compared, further, the chronological information of Luke with the extant profane historical data and, in light of the frequent contradictions, were led to skepticism with respect to Luke's information. The statement in the text above is intended to indicate clearly that my own approach to the reconstruction of Pauline chronology is an *extension* of Vielhauer's approach, for what is right for the study of Pauline theology is also applicable to the study of Pauline chronology. In his method of combining the chronological data of Acts with that of Paul's letters, a method here subjected to thorough criticism, Vielhauer proved himself guilty, in my opinion, of inconsequently carrying out his original plan (on the thesis of an itinerary, see below, pp. 25–29). The contradictions between the letters and Acts, such as in the case of the so-called second journey of Paul to Jerusalem (Acts 11:27ff.), Paul's stay in Arabia, Paul's proclamation in Jerusalem (Acts 9:28–29), and so forth, could be neglected because Vielhauer and most other critical investigators since Vielhauer refrain from harmonizing attempts in these cases. These cases are mentioned here in passing in order to emphasize what has been said in the text. See also n. 79, below.

79. The approach of G. Ogg, *The Chronology of the Life of Paul*, reverts to a position less critical than that presented under section 1.2 and will therefore not be considered extensively here. For example, Ogg relativizes the difference between Acts 9 and Gal. 1 in the following manner: "It seems best to conclude that the writer of Acts had not heard of the Arabian visit" (p. 15). The review of the works of J. Knox by G. Ogg, "A New Chronology of Saint Paul's Life," also deals in effect with the letters of Paul and Acts as sources of equal value and thus represents a retrogression.

80. This need has not been adequately recognized in the exegesis of Paul. In light of the fruitfulness of this method for synoptic exegesis, the need should be apparent, especially since H. D. Betz, *Der Apostel Paulus und die*

sokratische Tradition, has shown the type of results such an inquiry can produce. Dibelius, "Zur Formgeschichte des Neuen Testaments (ausserhalb der Evangelien)," spoke about the genres present in the letters in an article that has remained little known.

81. In his commendable book *Der Standort des Galaterbriefes*, U. Borse designates this method "the method of measurement" and differentiates from this a method of equal value (because it employs *external* criteria), the method of accommodation. As is apparent from its name, this method seeks to fit the letters into various historical situations and, for example, concludes on the basis of the absence of a reference to a prospective visit in Gal. and the set plan to travel to Jerusalem in Rom. that Gal. was written close to the time of the composition of Rom. Gal. is thus accommodated to the situation of Rom. (so Borse, *Standort*, 27, following C. E. Faw, "The Anomaly of Galatians"). The method of accommodation is, however (contra Borse), probably inferior to the method of measurement, for (a) (to use the example given above) Paul's travel plans could have changed (see 2 Cor. 1 for an example of this) and (b) a situation is usually susceptible to several interpretations, a description of it usually involves inferences, and where the situation is presented in clear terms, such as in a travel plan, it could change quickly because of special circumstances. In contrast to this, reference to the collection is a surprising constant in most of the letters, and its connection with the Jerusalem Conference is not based on inference.

82. A similar procedure is employed by J. Knox in his works on chronology (cf. also C. H. Buck, "Collection") and also by P. S. Minear, "The Jerusalem Fund and Pauline Chronology."

83. Contrary to Walter Schmithals (review of *Die Geschichte der Kollekte des Paulus für Jerusalem* by Dieter Georgi, *ThLZ* 92 [1967]: 668–72), I think that Georgi properly did not use 1 Thess. 2:3–12 as a text relevant to the collection. This text is not a response to accusations, and even if it were it does not refer to the collection at all. 1 Thess. 2:3ff. should probably be understood as part of the apostle's "standard apologetics" (thus O. Kuss, *Paulus*, 88 n. 5).

84. For the reasoning behind this thesis, see Kümmel, *Introduction*, 178ff., and the literature cited there.

85. Conzelmann, *Apostelgeschichte*, ad loc.

86. M. Dibelius, "The First Christian Historian," 124.

87. On the analysis of Acts 8:5ff., see G. Luedemann, *Untersuchungen zur simonianischen Gnosis*, 39ff.

88. Conzelmann, *Apostelgeschichte*, 63; P. Vielhauer agrees in his review of Conzelmann's *Die Apostelgeschichte*, 18.

89. When C. Burchard remarks that research into Acts has neglected the question of pre-Lukan traditions (*Zeuge*, 17), he seems to have underestimated the difficulties involved in this question. His own attempt to isolate re-

lated traditions in Acts is hardly satisfactory. For example, the thesis that Saul belongs to the tradition about Stephen and that Acts 7:58 (Saul as the one who guards the garments) is not a Lukan insertion that serves as a transition to the following material ("One can defend . . . the view that Paul was already mentioned before Luke . . . as the one who watched the garments," p. 30) is not convincing, despite its approval by M. Hengel, "Zwischen Jesus und Paulus," 172 n. 80. Burchard's query of how, on the assumption that Acts 7:58 is a Lukan insertion, one should explain the contrast with the later story of the raging Paul (*Zeuge*, 28) should be met with a counterquestion: How did such a minor detail as the fact that the garments were laid at the feet of a young man named Saul merit documentation? Burchard appears to have faced this question when he explains the harmless characterization of Paul in the martyrdom of Stephen by saying that the Hellenists wanted to protect their own man (p. 30 n. 23). This is already a hypothesis of a second degree. Burchard's own question, mentioned above, may be answered as follows: There is a dramatic climax when Paul appears as the guard of the garments in 7:58, consents to the murder of Stephen in 8:1, and finally becomes an active persecutor in 8:3.

E. Grässer ("Acta-Forschung seit 1960," 23) similarly considers it "certain" that Luke is responsible for connecting Paul with the martyrdom of Stephen.

90. Thus Burchard: "What he intended and created can first be clarified, and in any event first established as certain, when there is clarity about which material he used to write his book and which of the leading ideas were there before him" (*Zeuge*, 17).

91. Hengel, "Jesus," 156.

92. A report on Dibelius's thesis of an itinerary is found in Schille, "Fragwürdigkeit," cols. 165–69.

93. See the convincing demonstration by A. von Harnack in *New Testament Studies I: Luke the Physician*, 26–27. See also Harnack, *New Testament Studies II: The Date of the Acts and of the Synoptic Gospels*, 1–29. For Harnack, this meant that the whole of Acts (not just the we-passages) is of great historical value.

94. See M. Dibelius, "The Acts of the Apostles as an Historical Source," 102–8, 104–5: "The frequently used 'we', which, under the influence of modern historical ideas, used at one time to be taken as the earliest element of the whole account of the journey, was, perhaps, only introduced by Luke into his version in order to make it clear that he himself took part in Paul's journeys."

95. See M. Dibelius, "Acts in the Setting," 196ff. After comparing Hellenistic, Jewish, and Christian texts, Dibelius comes to this conclusion: "Thus the finding of this survey is that the occurrence of 'I' or 'we' may equally well indicate either an old source or a new literary work" (p. 204).

96. In our work we are using "Luke" as the name of the author of the Third Gospel and Acts.

97. M. Dibelius, "Style Criticism of the Book of Acts," 1–25.

98. Vielhauer, review of Conzelmann's *Apostelgeschichte*; idem, *Geschichte*, 388–93.

99. The page numbers refer to Dibelius, "Style Criticism" and "Acts in the Setting."

100. Vielhauer, review of Conzelmann's *Apostelgeschichte*, 10.

101. Ibid., 11.

102. See now Grässer's approval of the itinerary thesis in his "Acta-Forschung," 188ff. All that is necessary to say regarding the book by W. Ward Gasque, *A History of the Criticism of the Acts of the Apostles*, BGBE 17 (Tübingen: J. C. B. Mohr [Paul Siebeck], 1975), was said by Charles H. Talbert in his review in *JBL* 95 (1976): 494–96; see further Hans Conzelmann, in *Eras.* 28 (1976): cols. 65–68, and the summarizing opinion of Grässer, "Acta-Forschung," 68: Gasque's book is "a retrogression insofar as owing to its apologetical aim all previous investigators are judged on the basis of whether they affirm the historical reliability of Acts. *This* method . . . really involves 'oversimplification' . . . because the numerous literary critical and theological problems do not even come into view."

For the question of the historicity of the traditions contained in Acts, the judgment of Dibelius is still fully applicable: The question "can be resolved only after the style-criticism has been carried out; any premature solution of the problems will do more than endanger the integrity of the style-critical method; it will obscure our understanding of the stories themselves. Intrinsically these stories are far removed from the problems of historiography, and it is only when we begin to look away from the questions which have been raised in connection with them that we learn to listen to what the story-tellers have to say to us" ("Style Criticism," 25).

103. Conzelmann, *Apostelgeschichte*, 6: "The question thus arises whether . . . the author formed a whole for the routes from individual pieces of information. That he added unimportant intervening stations can be explained on a purely literary basis." As Vielhauer, review of *Die Apostelgeschichte*, 11, correctly notes, Conzelmann assumes, on the other hand, that Luke had sources for Paul's routes in Acts 18:18ff. (and elsewhere) that were more than just individual pieces of information.

104. Vielhauer, review of Conzelmann's *Apostelgeschichte*, 12.

2

THE RECONSTRUCTION
OF A CHRONOLOGY OF PAUL
SOLELY FROM THE WITNESS OF
THE EPISTLES

2.1 AN EXEGESIS OF GAL. 1:6—2:14
AS THE CENTRAL PILLAR FOR
A CHRONOLOGY OF PAUL

Among the reliable results of recent Pauline exegesis is the realization that Paul was a controversial figure not only after his death but also during his lifetime. Though precise specification of the opponents and of their theology has often become entangled in rather abstruse arguments, there is no avoiding the fact that at least in Galatians and 2 Corinthians Paul stands in a constant struggle with antagonists. When we deal with the question of the position of Paul and the position of his opponents, we are involved in a circular process of understanding. For example, the assertions in an epistolary section, or those statements that we hold to be Paul's own, lead us to a particular picture of the opponents he is fighting. This in turn brings us to a more vivid perception of the import of the statements directed against the adversaries. As regards method, one should normally proceed in exegesis from the question of the surface meaning of the text, for any specification of the opponents' position remains to a great extent hypothetical. On the other hand, it is clear that knowledge of the adversaries' position is invaluable for determining Paul's intention. For this reason, I view it as methodologically permissible to start with an examination of the opponents' position in the exegesis of the letters in which the opponents' statements may be virtually gleaned from the text without resort to hypotheses. This will be the procedure followed below, where we shall start by gathering together the main characteristics of the opponents' position on as broad a basis as possible.

2.1.1 The Opponents' Position

In specifying the opponents' position in Galatians, research has arrived at an amazingly broad consensus: (a) the opponents preach a gospel that differs from Paul's (Gal. 1:7); (b) the opponents have introduced legal observances that are described more precisely in Gal. 4:10: observation of days, months, and years;[1] (c) the opponents are promoting circumcision for the Galatians (Gal. 6:12); (d) the opponents have attacked Paul's apostleship (Gal. 1:1, 12).

As we said, these four points have been recognized by the majority of investigators as an appropriate characterization of the opponents. However, various possible and contradictory explanations of the opponents remain. I believe, nevertheless, that I will be allowed here to spare the reader a discussion of the thesis of Gentile Christian origin of the opponents (Munck, M. Barth) or of their gnostic provenance (Schmithals). Both proposals are, in my judgment, on the wrong track.[2]

Paul's opponents in Galatia[3] should rather be seen as Palestinian Jewish-Christians who were offended by the Pauline proclamation of the gospel without the law. For them, the true gospel, which included observation of the law, could be taught probably only in Jerusalem or by a mission dependent on Jerusalem. In their opinion, Paul had diverged from this true gospel in an inadmissible way, even though he had received his gospel from those in Jerusalem. That is to say, the Galatian opponents were apparently spreading a very particular version not only of the Jerusalem Conference but also of Paul's relations with the apostles in Jerusalem before the conference. This should be deduced, in my opinion, from Paul's repeated negations in Galatians 1–2: "Nor did I go up to Jerusalem [after my conversion]," 1:17; "I saw none of the other apostles. . . . (In what I am writing to you, before God, I do not lie!)," 1:19–20; and "Those, I say, who were of repute added nothing to me," 2:6, end.

It nevertheless seems questionable whether the Galatian opponents could have stigmatized Paul solely on the basis of disregard for Jerusalem or for tradition. It is doubtful whether reference to the differing opinion of those in Jerusalem would have had an effect on the Gentile Christian congregations in Galatia.[4] The attempted introduction of legal observances in Galatia could succeed, however, if the opponents maintained that Paul's proclamation was dependent on Jerusalem.[5] Such proof would give them the right to modify the Pauline gospel in a few points by adding Jewish norms. That is to say, they polemicized against the Pauline gospel (and the apostleship of Paul) by pointing out Paul's dependence on Jerusalem and thus his subordinate position.

Paul's defense is contained in the letter to the Galatians.[6]

45

2.1.2 Form-critical Section

2.1.2.1 ON THE FORM-CRITICAL ANALYSIS OF PAUL'S LETTERS

Form-critical investigation of the letters in the New Testament is still in its rudimentary stages. It is true that especially since the fundamental work by A. Seeberg,[7] research has reached a consensus that the letters contain such forms as hymns, catalogs of virtues and vices, tables of conduct, and prayer formulas and that these forms may be isolated by employing certain criteria.[8] Nevertheless, analysis of the form "letter" has hardly proceeded beyond the work of A. Deissmann.[9] This situation may be explained partly by the fact that at the beginning of this century such influential scholars as P. Wendland,[10] E. Norden,[11] and F. Overbeck[12] staunchly refused to view Paul's letters as real literature[13] and to recognize in them elements of ancient rhetoric.[14] Whatever the biases that underlay this refusal and the related dichotomy set up between Paul and Hellenism,[15] the discussion has again—with this field still wide open for research—come to life, particularly because of contributions from American scholarship. Here we may only mention in passing the desideratum of a form-critical investigation of Paul's letters, for it is generally recognized that knowledge about the form of a letter can say something about its occasion[16] and simultaneously place the content in proper perspective. Has any progress been made in the form-critical analysis of the letter to the Galatians?

We stated above that work on a critical chronology of Paul must begin with Galatians 1–2 as its most important witness, and further that this epistolary section is far from being a complete chronology. This encourages us to test the developing form-critical analysis of Paul's letters on Galatians, especially since Galatians has a feature much more peculiar than the biographical retrospect already mentioned: It does not contain a thanksgiving. We shall proceed by starting with the recent article of H. D. Betz.[17] The main focus of our form-critical experiment will of course be the "biographical section," Galatians 1–2. Its form and meaning, however, cannot correctly be determined without analyzing the form of the entire letter.

2.1.2.2 GALATIANS AS AN "APOLOGETIC LETTER"

Betz's classification of Galatians as an apologetic letter is based on a thorough analysis of the entire letter.[18] He concludes that the structure of Galatians corresponds exactly with the structure of the apologetic speech in ancient rhetoric, the constitution and aim of which are described in the handbooks of ancient rhetoric.[19] Apart from the proem occasioned by the epistolary situation, Betz identifies the following structure of Galatians:

1:6–11   *exordium* (introduction)
1:12—2:14   *narratio* (narration)
2:15–21   *propositio* (indication of the point of the proof)
3:1—4:31   *probatio* (statement of proof)
5:1—6:10   *paraenesis* (admonition)
6:11–18   *peroratio* (conclusion)

The last section, the *peroratio*, is clearly marked by epistolary characteristics: Gal. 6:11–18 was *written* by Paul himself. This feature seems to complicate the comparison of this part of the *letter* with the concluding part of an apologetic *speech*. Nevertheless, Betz is able to offer striking parallels from the *peroratio* of ancient rhetoric precisely for the structure and content of this section. Betz's explanation of the *letter* to the Galatians on the basis of a form of *speech* in ancient rhetoric, which strikes one at first sight as somewhat far-fetched, thus actually receives support from a comparison of Gal. 6:11–18 with the structure of a *peroratio*.[20] Before we check this part of Betz's thesis, the *peroratio* should be defined:

> The general purpose of the *peroratio* is twofold: it serves as a last chance to remind the judge or the audience of the case, and it tries to make a strong emotional impression upon them. The three conventional parts of the *peroratio* carry out this task: the *enumeratio* or *recapitulatio* (*anakephalaiōsis*) sharpens and sums up the main points of the case, the *indignatio* arouses anger and hostility against the opponent, and the *conquestio* stimulates pity.[21]

Verification:

Gal. 6:12–13: This poignant polemic against the opponents is a clear expression of the *indignatio*.

Gal. 6:14 summarizes Paul's position just as he had presented it in the letter (*recapitulatio*).

Gal. 6:16: The conditional wish for peace implies a curse on anyone who does not stand in accord with the Pauline canon. This conditional wish for peace forms the positive complement to the conditional curse in the *exordium* and thereby connects the end of the letter with the beginning.[22]

Gal. 6:17: The reference to the marks of Christ corresponds to the *conquestio*. According to Quintilian, among the ways that were eminently used by Cicero to win the approval of the judges were references to numerous persecutions and to scars from wounds received in battle (Quintilian, 6.1.21).

This spot check[23] of Betz's classification of Gal. 6:11–18 shows that (preliminary) adoption of the view that a literary form underlies the structure of Galatians is justified. Betz's analysis of the form[24] of Galatians will thus be adopted in the following analysis of the chapters that are so important for a chronology of Paul, Galatians 1–2. Our adoption of Betz's analysis will not occur, however, without checking his conclusions for each passage (as was done above for Gal. 6:11–18). In the event that our tests verify his analysis, it will be both possible and permissible to draw important conclusions for the interpretation of the letter from the fact that Paul employs a specific rhetorical form.

2.1.2.3 FORM-CRITICAL ANALYSIS OF GAL. 1:6—2:14: *Exordium* and *Narratio*

2.1.2.3.1 Gal. 1:6–9: First Part of the Exordium: Principium

Galatians is the only letter of Paul's that does not contain a thanksgiving. While this negative finding has properly been explained up to now as occasioned by the situation in Galatia and by the reports that reached Paul from there, the question should be raised whether this feature corresponds with something positive, namely, the structuring of Galatians in accord with the form of an apologetic speech.

Paul sees that his relationship with the congregations has been disturbed, and he no longer considers it even possible to include a thanksgiving. Instead, he begins his apology immediately after the prescript, which itself was *consciously* composed to indicate the subsequent theme of direct derivation of his apostleship from Christ.[25] There was general consensus among the teachers of rhetoric about the proper commencement of the apologetic speech, the *exordium*, of which there were two types, *insinuatio* and *principium*. The *insinuatio* should be employed when the audience has an antagonistic attitude toward the speaker: "Insinuatio est oratio quadam dissimulatione et circumitione obscure subiens auditoris animum" ("Insinuation is an address which by dissimulation and indirection unobtrusively steals into the mind of the auditor"; Cicero, *De Invent.* 1.15.20; cf. Lausberg, secs. 280–81). One employs the *principium* when there is a good possibility of arousing the esteem of the audience: "Principium est oratio perspicue et protinus perficiens auditorem benivolum aut docilem aut attentum" ("An introduction is an address which directly and in plain language makes the auditor well-disposed, receptive and attentive"; Cicero, *De Invent.* 1.15.20). We shall first examine whether there is a *principium* in Gal. 1:6ff.

There were four rules about how one should arouse the esteem of the audience in the *principium*: one must speak *ab nostra, ab adversariorum, ab iudicum* [= *auditorum*] *persona, a causa* [= *re ipsa*] ("from our own persons, from the person of the opponents, from the persons of the jury, from the case itself"; Cicero, *De Invent.* 1.16.22). These rules are applicable to our section. In Gal. 1:7 Paul speaks of those who trouble the Galatians (*persona adversariorum*). It is clear, too, that the *persona iudicum* (*auditorum*) (as the object of the opponents' turbulence) also appears in our text. Further, the *persona oratoris* (*nostra persona*) is present in v. 8, and so is the matter of concern (*causa*), the gospel that is being threatened in Galatia: Any attack on the gospel that Paul preached to the Galatians is also an attack on the apostleship of Paul himself, and vice versa.[26] For this reason, the theme, the *res ipsa*, in our text is also the main concern in 1:11ff., which deals with the derivation of Paul's apostleship directly from Christ and thus also with the one gospel that is being threatened among the Galatians by the opponents.

By pronouncing a *curse* on everyone who preaches contrary to "his" gospel, Paul employs a stylistic means in the *exordium* (and also in the *peroratio*) that was reserved for extreme cases, the threat.

The idea of being able to curse someone else[27] (cf. 1 Cor. 5:3ff.; 16:22) was known to the apostle from the primitive Christian environment, probably from the sphere of the "sentences of holy law."[28]

In correspondence with an example from Quintilian (4.1.21), where the speaker threatens the judge, Paul pronounces a conditional ban on any of his readers who stands at variance with his gospel. He does this, of course, in order to confront his congregations with the *decision* they have to make, for he apparently has not yet given up hope for them. Taken together with the points noted above, this observation gives us the right to designate Gal. 1:6ff. as a *principium*.

Our positive proof that 1:6–9 is a *principium* leads to the negative conclusion that 1:6–9 is not an *insinuatio*.

Now the second "let him be accursed" in v. 9 forms a marked conclusion, and the opening question in v. 10, "Am I now seeking to persuade men?" is apparently a new starting point. The question that needs to be asked is how far—judged form-critically—the *principium* extends. Does v. 10 belong to it? Further, while it is clear that Paul is presenting a sort of historical retrospect at the latest in v. 13, how does v. 10 relate to this section? Does the concluding statement in v. 9, "let him be accursed," indicate that v. 10 is closely connected to vv. 13ff.? Or, does v. 10 have a point of its own, and does it possibly reflect further accusations by Paul's opponents? In order to clarify these questions, it seems advisable, within the framework of a form-critical analysis of Gal. 1:10, to start with a detailed exegesis of this verse.

2.1.2.3.2 Gal. 1:10: Second Part of the Exordium: Insinuatio

2.1.2.3.2.1 Exegesis of Gal. 1:10

Exegetes of the letter to the Galatians have ever again raised the question of whether v. 10 should be connected with the preceding or with the following. A statement that is almost identical with Gal. 1:11 and that introduces a new section is found in 1 Cor. 15:1. Compare "Now I would remind you, brethren, in what terms I preached to you the gospel" (1 Cor. 15:1) with "For I would have you know, brethren, that the gospel which was preached by me . . ." (Gal. 1:11).[29] One further reason for setting the start of the new unit first at Gal. 1:11 is the thesis that v. 10 employs general rhetorical *topoi*, while the claims of the opponents are reflected first in v. 11. This thesis will be verified in the following.

Our starting point is the observation that "seeking the favor of men" should be interpreted by the "pleasing men," which directly follows, and that here the phrase cannot have a qualified positive meaning (see below, n. 33), as it does in 2 Cor. 5:11. The verb *peithein* in this passage should be translated "persuade."[30] This, however, does not exclude the possibility that v. 10 derives from the opponents, for the accusation "He persuades men and seeks to please them" is readily conceivable as coming from the lips of an opponent, especially if the two charges are understood in the sense of an ironical "both this and that."[31] Such an interpretation runs into difficulty, however, in explaining the phrase "or God?" and must revert, for example, to the interpretation of this phrase as containing something "like a zeugma" (Oepke, 53–54; Mussner, 63). "The words . . . are a side comment, and the continuation of the sentence is found in the second question"

(Oepke). If one understands, as the syntax and wording indicate, "to persuade God" as a complete question alongside "to persuade men," then (a) these words should be translated in a manner analogous to the first question ("do I even persuade God?"), and (b) the first half of the verse does *not* make sense on the assumption that it represents accusations by the opponents. No one would have claimed that Paul persuades men *and* God.[32]

While it is therefore probable that accusations by the opponents do not stand behind Gal. 1:10, this result, which was obtained through faulting previous interpretation, will be positively confirmed by the following proof that v. 10 may be readily understood in the light of ancient rhetorical traditions.

The phrase "to persuade men" embodies the definition and goal of rhetoric. Compare Plato, *Gorg.* 452 E:

> [Gorgias says: It is the greatest good] to persuade with speeches either judges in the law courts or statesmen in the council-chamber or the commons in the Assembly. . . . And I tell you that by virtue of this power you will have the doctor as your slave, . . . your money-getter will turn out to be making money not for himself, but for another—in fact for you, who are able to speak and persuade the multitude. (Cf. 458 E, 462 C, 453 A, 454 E; *Prot.* 352 E; *Theaet.* 201 A; see Lausberg, sec. 257)

Accordingly, philosophical writers ever since the time of Plato have maintained an extremely negative judgment of the art of persuasion (*hē pithagorikē technē*) (see also Plato, *Soph.* 222 C) and have equated it with deception and witchcraft (see also Plato, *Euthyd.* 289 D—290 A). This negative evaluation of the *peithein* of humans is shared by Paul[33] and the Christian tradition.[34]

The other phrase, "persuading God," is a polemical description of the activity of religious charlatans, as is apparent from Plato, *Resp.* 364 C. Here Plato compares the sophists with soothsayers who, with the help of magical enticements and curses, persuade/cajole the gods to serve them (*tous theous . . . peithontes . . . hypēretein*).[35] Oepke (pp. 53–54) and, following him, Suhl do not pay enough attention to the context when they translate *peithein* here as "make oneself well-disposed."[36]

The third characterization of Paul's activity which is rejected by him, "pleasing men," also has a rich (negative) tradition in ancient ethics and rhetoric.[37] The one who pleases men is a well-known character in ethics: Aristotle, *Eth. Nic.* 2.7.13; 4.6.1; 9.10.6; Plutarch, *Lib. Ed.* 4 D, 6 B; Theophrastus, *Char.* 5.[38]

Rhetoric traditionally connects *areskein* with *peithein*. To persuade others in a way that pleases them is the goal and method of rhetoric. Plato, *Gorg*. 462 C: Socrates is asked, "Then you take rhetoric to be something fine—an ability to gratify people?" (*charizesthai hoion te einai anthrōpois*). Socrates answers in contrast: "[It is] a certain habitude . . . of production of gratification and pleasure" (*empeiria . . . charitos kai hēdonēs apergasias*, 462 D–E).[39] The art of speaking is also involved in political demagogy (see Plato, *Ep*. 4.321 B; Diodorus of Sicily 13.53.3; 17.115).

This survey has shown that all three of the activities rejected by Paul in Gal. 1:10 (persuading men, persuading God, and pleasing men) were well known and predominantly negatively valued *topoi* in ancient philosophy. It was revealing that already at the time of Plato "persuading men" and "pleasing men" were connected traditionally and that the *topos* "persuading the gods" was also known as a negative description of the activities of soothsayers and charlatans.

Thus, when Paul asks in Gal. 1:10a, "Am I seeking to persuade men or God?" he is not rejecting accusations[40] of the opponents, as is generally assumed. He is rather on the offensive in an ironical way. Paul takes up common charges against sophists and charlatans and, insofar as he rejects them for himself, holds them up as a mirror for his opponents. Verse 10b goes one step further. From the same tradition as "persuading men" and "persuading God," the negatively characterized activity "pleasing men" is declared to be incompatible with being a servant of Christ. Rejection of this sort of activity follows from positive affiliation with Christ. The opponents (thus seems to be the unspoken consequence even for Paul), who are not servants of Christ, are absorbed in pleasing men.[41]

2.1.2.3.2.2 Explication of the Form-critical Problem of Gal. 1:10

Above we left open the question of how v. 10 should be judged form-critically. Having undertaken a detailed exegesis of the verse, we may now return to this question. It should be clear that our verse merits form-critical classification, for it is preceded by a unit that closes with the emphatic "let him be accursed" and is followed by an introduction to a new section, "for I would have you know." It is also clear that v. 10 cannot be understood as a second *principium*. Here anything but the audience, the opponents, Paul, and the issue at hand is addressed in a direct manner, and the situation no longer seems to be that Paul is able to draw the audience to his side at any moment. It looks rather as if one should follow Betz in classifying v. 10 as the *insinuatio* type of *exordium*. The characteristics and tasks of this type were as follows: "Dissimulatione et circumitione obscure subiens auditoris animum" ("by dissimulation and indirection unobtrusively steals into the mind of the auditor"; Cicero, *De Invent.* 1.15.20). This is also the structure of v. 10. Paul does *not* deal with the claims of the opponents, and thus the reader acquainted with these (pertaining to Paul's relationship to Jerusalem) is not at first able to understand the meaning of v. 10. But then Paul's words subtly lead the reader to a correspondingly negative view of the opponents.

We may thus say that Gal. 1:6–9 corresponds to the *principium* type of *exordium* in ancient rhetoric, while Gal. 1:10 corresponds to the *insinuatio* type. "This mixture of the *principium* and the *insinuatio* may be peculiar, but it conforms precisely to the situation with which Paul sees himself confronted."[42] On the one hand, Paul is still able to hope that he will be able to draw the audience, which still belongs to his congregations, to his side. On the other hand, the Galatians have almost fallen to the opponents.

2.1.2.3.3 Form Criticism of Gal. 1:11–12: Transition from Exordium *to* Narratio

"For I would have you know" leads into a new section (vv. 13ff.), the content of which may be described as follows: The direct derivation of the Pauline gospel from Christ as is also demonstrated by the historical sketch of Paul's relations with the apostles in Jerusalem. This means that vv. 11–12 prepare for the following and, in a certain sense, serve a titular function for vv. 13ff. When Paul says that he received the gospel through a revelation of Jesus Christ, he not only says something about the nature of the gospel but also implicitly refers to a historical place and time at which the revelation of Christ occurred. There is more said about this event in the following verses (vv. 15–16). Paul then explicates the "not from man," referring back to v. 12. He explains how it was that he did not receive the gospel *from men*: After the revelation he did not go to Jerusalem (v. 17), where alone, according to the opinion of the opponents in Galatia, the true gospel could be taught, and between the first and second visits to Jerusalem at least fourteen years passed (2:1). Our remarks thus form a second observation that confirms the preparatory and transitional character of vv. 11–12 and the explicative character of vv. 13ff. Finally, there is a third connection between vv. 11–12 and the following. The statement that

Paul's gospel is not "according to man" (v. 11) is explicated in vv. 13ff. through the contrast established between the periods in Paul's life before and after he became a Christian. The leap from the rash and violent persecutor of the church to the proclaimer of the gospel cannot be the result of a religious development—otherwise the gospel would really be "according to man"—but may be explained only on the basis of a revelation of Jesus Christ. Thus the gospel is "not according to man." (The contrast of "then" and "now" is found a second time in v. 23.)

If it is clear from the interrelationship demonstrated above that vv. 11–12 are transitional in character, then light is shed for the form-critical classification of our verses. According to the handbooks of rhetoric, a smooth transition should be made from the *exordium* to the *narratio* (see Lausberg, sec. 288, and, e.g., Quintilian, 4.1.79: "Ut non abrupte cadere in narrationem, ita non obscure transcendere est optimum" ("Although we should not be too abrupt in passing to our statement of facts, it is best to do nothing to conceal our transition"). Since vv. 11–12 not only lead into vv. 13ff., as we have seen above, but also relate to 1:6–9 insofar as both sections discuss the character of the Pauline gospel (1:6–9 emphasize the *one* gospel), these verses may be classified, in accord with the structure of the apologetic speech in ancient rhetoric, as the transition from the *exordium* to the *narratio*.

2.1.2.3.4 Form-critical Investigation of Gal. 1:13—2:14: Narratio

According to the handbooks of ancient rhetoric, the *exordium* is followed by the *narratio* (*diēgēsis*). Before we survey its main rules, a statement by Quintilian should be taken as a warning against rashly defining the structure of the *narratio* too rigidly. Quintilian writes that the rules for defense are variable within certain limits: "Neque enim est una lex defensionis certumque praescriptum" ("For there is no single law or fixed rule governing the method of defense"; 4.2.84).

Having mentioned this introductory rule of caution, we may now list the main characteristics of the *narratio*. The *purpose* of the *narratio* is to unravel and clarify the issues involved in the controversy between the speaker and his opponents. One might describe these issues as the antecedent history of the case at hand. "Narratio est . . . oratio docens auditorem, quid in controversia sit" ("The *statement of facts* is . . . a speech instructing the audience as to the nature of the case in dispute"; Quintilian, 4.2.31). This model might also lie behind Gal. 1:13ff. Since Paul's opponents have maintained that the Pauline gospel is dependent on Jerusalem and, closely related to this claim, have cast doubts on his apostleship, Paul begins his rectification of these slanders by presenting a sketch of his relations with the apostles in Jerusalem (1:13ff.). He presents the controversial antecedent history of the present case, where the issue is the propriety of the Pauline apostleship and, closely related to this, the propriety of proclaiming to Gentile Christians the gospel that did not include works of the law.

The handbooks of ancient rhetoric prescribe that the *narratio* should have the following *characteristics*. Almost all rhetoricians agree that the *narratio* must possess three qualities: brevity, clarity, and credibility ("Oportet igitur eam tres habere res: ut brevis, ut aperta, ut probabilis sit"; "It ought to possess three qualities: it should be brief, clear, and plausible"; Cicero, *De Invent.* 1.20.28; see Lausberg, secs. 294–334). Brevity is achieved by leaving out everything not relevant to the point of concern. Clarity and credibility are achieved by presenting a report based on facts, persons, times, places, and causes (see Quintilian, 4.2.36: "Distincta rebus, personis, temporibus, locis, causis"; "a distinct account of facts, persons, times, places, and causes"). Nevertheless, the *narratio* does not offer a complete, objective report but rather is conceived from the (involved) standpoint of the speaker and is intended to convince the judge. This does not mean that the reported facts are false. It does mean, however, that particulars which could weaken the position of the speaker could be left to one side (the *narratio* must nevertheless remain credible; see above). For expediency the *narratio* uses phrases such as "you recall" (*meministi*) or "perhaps it is unnecessary to recall/to spend time mentioning that" (*fortasse supervacuum fuerit hic commorari*) to link up with something the hearer already knows about the antecedent history of the case (see Quintilian, 4.2.22). It leads only to the point where the actual controversy begins (see Fortunatianus, 2.20 [Halm 113:12–14]: "Quid in narratione novissimo loco observabimus? ut ibi narrationem finiamus, ubi est initium quaestionis, et ut subtiliter ad eam descensum faciamus, ne quaestiones abrupte incohemus." "What shall we observe as regards the last part of the narration? We should be careful to end the narration at the point at which the case at hand begins and to make a smooth approach to it, lest we address the matters at hand abruptly," tr.). This characteristic also implies that the transition from the end of the *narratio* to the *propositio* should be smooth and gradual (see Lausberg, 188).

This last point brings us to the question of whether in view of the

55

most prominent characteristics of the *narratio* just listed Gal. 1:13—2:14 should be designated a *narratio*. The following points support such a designation.

1. We noted already that Paul's speech to Peter in Antioch leads directly into the speech of the apostle to the Galatian congregations. At the end of the *narratio* stands the controversial point of concern in Galatia: Should Gentile Christians accept the law, and should the opponents be allowed to force the Galatians to live as Jews (*pōs ta ethnē anagkazeis ioudaizein*)?

2. Gal. 1:13, the beginning of Paul's report, uses *ēkousate* to link up with something the Galatians know about a particular of the antecedent history of the case.

3. Paul does not expound on many particulars of his own life and activity. The best explanation of this is that, in accord with the style of the *narratio*, Paul leaves everything out of the report that does not relate directly to the case at hand.[43]

4. In Gal. 1:13ff. Paul presents a report that revolves around facts, persons, times, places, and reasons:

He reports on his two visits to Jerusalem and on what transpired there (*facts*: 1:18: he became acquainted with Cephas and saw none of the other apostles, with the exception of James; 2:1ff.: nothing was added).

He lists the *persons* involved in each event: Cephas (1:18; 2:8–9, 11, 14), James (1:19; 2:9 [12]), Barnabas (2:1, 13), Titus (2:1, 3), the false brethren (2:4), John (2:9), certain ones from James (2:12).

He reports about the locations of the events (*places*): Arabia (1:17), Damascus (1:17), Jerusalem (1:18; 2:1ff.), Syria (1:21), Cilicia (1:21), Judaea (1:22), Antioch (2:1ff.).

He supplies *reasons*: The first visit to Jerusalem enabled him to become acquainted with Cephas (1:18). The second time, he traveled to Jerusalem because of a revelation (2:2).

Finally, Paul also structures his report through *chronological* references. *Epeita* thrice introduces an immediately subsequent event (1:18; 1:21; 2:1). In two of these cases, a reference in numbers of years is also supplied (1:18; 2:1). The length of his first stay in Jerusalem is specified as two weeks.

The last chronological reference reveals a related interest. The statement "fourteen days" is supposed to indicate that the first visit to Jerusalem was a short one and thereby to protect Paul further from the charge that he is dependent on Jerusalem. This should similarly be said of the two other explicit

56

chronological references (three and fourteen years): Their purpose is to separate the apostle both temporally and materially from the apostles in Jerusalem and thus to underline his independence once more.

This brings us to the end of our verification and to positive results. Gal. 1:13ff. was structured in accord with one part of the apologetic speech in ancient rhetoric, the *narratio*. This result, itself derived from the text, may be used as one of the bases for our subsequent exegesis of the same text (circle).

Before we analyze Gal. 1:13ff. further, however, another form-critical question must be addressed, namely, the question left open above whether the *narratio* of ancient rhetoric only knew and recommended a presentation of events in their chronological order. As concerns the reconstruction of the chronology of Paul, the answer to this question will provide important information for dating the event reported in Gal. 2:11ff.

2.1.2.3.4.1 On the Question of the Maintenance of Chronological Order in the Narratio: Gal. 2:11–14

We must remember that according to the handbooks of ancient rhetoric the *narratio* was required to be credible. At the same time, however, the aim of the *narratio* was to convince the judge. In view of this last point, it is understandable that the *narratio* of events could be arranged not only in *ordo naturalis* (*more Homerico*) but also in *ordo artificiorum*. That is, if it was required by *utilitas*, the chronological order of events could be abandoned. See Quintilian, 4.2.83: "Namque ne eis quidem accedo, qui semper eo putant ordine, quo quid actum sit, esse narrandum, sed eo malo narrare, quo expedit" ("Neither do I agree with those who assert that the order of our *statement of facts* should always follow the actual order of events, but have a preference for adopting the order which I consider most suitable"). There is not just *one* law for defense and not just *one* rule: "Pro re, pro tempore intuenda quae prosint, atque ut erit vulnus, ita vel curandum protinus" ("We must consider what is most advantageous in the circumstances and nature of the case, and treat the wound as its nature dictates"; 4.2.84). It is interesting that Quintilian is thinking not of a thoroughgoing rearrangement of the events but of the rearrangement of one or a few events. This is clear from the remarks that follow on the quotation given above from 4.2.83: "(Sed eo malo narrare, quo ex-

pedit). Quod fieri plurimis figuris licet. Nam et aliquando nobis excidisse simulamus, cum quid utiliore loco reducimus, et interim nos
reddituros reliquum ordinem testamur, quia sic futura sit causa lucior:
interim re exposita subiungimus causas, quae antecesserunt" ("[but
have a preference for adopting the order which I consider most suitable.] For this purpose, we can employ a variety of figures. Sometimes, when we bring up a point in a place better suited to our
purpose, we may pretend that it had escaped our notice; occasionally,
too, we may inform the judge that we shall adhere to the natural order
for the remainder of our statement, since by so doing we shall make
our case clearer, while at times after stating a fact, we may append the
causes which preceded it"). That is, according to Quintilian, it is possible to take an event out of the chronological order ("aliquando nobis
[aliquid] excidisse simulamus") so that it might be presented at the end
as the *causa*, after everything else has been reported in *ordo naturalis*
(*re exposita*).

To be sure, Quintilian does not wish to generalize this rule. The
ordo naturalis should normally be preferred to the *ordo artificiorum*:
"Neque ideo tamen non saepius facere oportebit, ut rerum ordinem
sequamur" ("On the other hand this is no reason for not following the
order of events as a general rule"; 4.2.87). Further, as we have already
seen, rearrangement is limited to particular events within *one narratio*.
Apparently other rhetoricians,[44] though not all,[45] were of a differing
opinion when they prescribed that the *ordo naturalis* should always be
given preference ("Ne *eis* quidem accedo, qui *semper* eo putant ordine,
quo quid actum sit, esse narrandum" ["Neither do I agree with those
who assert that the order of our *statement of facts* should always follow
the actual order of events"; Quintilian, 4.2.83]).

In sum, our remarks have shown that there is a form-critical possibility that Paul could have abandoned the chronological order of the
narratio in his presentation of the controversy in Antioch. The question remains to be asked whether there are indications in the content
that Gal. 2:11ff. really does reflect a chronological rearrangement (out
of interest for the issue at hand), that the event should be chronologically located before the Jerusalem Conference, and that this event may
have been *the* occasion for the conference. These possibilities, which
will be dealt with further below, could at least find support in form
criticism when one remembers Quintilian's statement quoted above.
This said that one part (or a few parts) could be taken out of the *ordo
naturalis* of the *narratio* and—*re exposita*—be presented at the end as
the *causa(e)*. Whether one may prove that this possibility is the case in

the narration of the conference and the event in Antioch will be seen in the following sections of our examination. In any case, the passage from Quintilian that was just mentioned would provide good confirmation of such a conclusion.

With the form-critical part of the exegesis of Gal. 1:6—2:14 now complete, we turn, following our theme, to explicate the specific problems in Galatians 1–2 with which a critical chronology of Paul must deal.

2.1.3 Explication of the Specific Problems in Galatians 1–2 for a Critical Chronology of Paul

It has been shown that the letter to the Galatians, as well as Gal. 1:6—2:14, may be understood in the light of ancient rhetorical traditions. The following is concerned with applying the knowledge gained in the form-critical section to our work on a chronology of Paul. The following groups of problems must be addressed.

1. Does the statement in Gal. 1:21, that (after the first visit to Jerusalem) Paul went into the regions of Syria and Cilicia, indicate anything about where Paul spent the period between the first and second visits to Jerusalem?

2. Beginning with which date are the years in Gal. 1:18 and 2:1 enumerated?

3. What was the issue of concern at the Jerusalem Conference? The answer to this question will provide answers to the next two questions.

4. How was the conference related to the controversial incident at Antioch?

5. What was the purpose of the collection, which is the external criterion for our reconstruction of the chronology of Paul?

We shall investigate these groups of problems in the order in which they were just listed.

2.1.3.1 GAL. 1:21: "THEN I WENT INTO THE REGIONS OF SYRIA AND CILICIA"

Verse 21 describes one of Paul's changes in location again with the simple verb "I went" (see v. 17: "I went up," "I went away"; v. 18: "I went up"). Nothing more specific is said. How he went there is not said. From the following verses, vv. 22–23 (the churches in Judaea heard: The one who once persecuted us is now preaching the faith he once tried to destroy),[46] we are able (more or less against Paul's inten-

59

tion in this section) to conclude that Paul worked as a missionary in the area of Syria and Cilicia. Although Paul did not write vv. 22–23 for biographical reasons,[47] vv. 22–23 nevertheless contain, as did vv. 16–17, the schema of "then" and "now."[48] This schema serves to demonstrate the special quality of the Pauline gospel, that it is not according to men (the special nature of the gospel is demonstrated in the person and commission of the apostle). The statement "they only heard it said," together with "I was still not known by sight," provides a further argument for Paul's distance from Jerusalem. If he is unknown by sight to the churches of Judaea, and if (for this reason) they are able only to *hear* something about him, then a real proximity of Paul (both spatially and thus also materially) can never have really been the case.

Back to v. 21: The form-critical laws prescribe that the *narratio* section of the apologetic speech should mention only persons, places, and events that are directly related to the case at hand. The opponents claimed that Paul's gospel was dependent on Jerusalem. Paul limits his reports about the journeys he had undertaken to those relevant to this controversy. Apart from the journeys *away from* Jerusalem or *toward* Jerusalem (in each of these cases an indication of the year is given), Paul does not mention any[49] changes in locality.[50] The description of the conflict in Antioch is a special case (see below, pp. 75ff.), but even this report contains characters from Jerusalem.

If one admits that all the references to times, places, and persons in Galatians 1–2 stand in direct connection with "Jerusalem," one may then ask hypothetically about the place that a report about any (hypothetical) missionary activity in Macedonia before the conference would have taken in the *narratio*. The report about the reaction of the Judaean Christians to Paul's proclamation of the gospel finds its proper place only after v. 21, for the news "He who once persecuted us is now preaching the faith . . . " is a quotation in which the speakers are the Christians from the area of Syria and Cilicia. If the report of a journey to Macedonia would thus not have a logical place after v. 21, its placement after v. 24 (where it would fit chronologically) would be even less logical. This would have involved giving a biographical detail weight of its own, something that would break the form-critical law of *brevitas* and also the rule evident in Gal. 1:13ff., to leave out everything not directly related to Jerusalem. The opinion sometimes expressed—that if Paul had had a mission in Macedonia he would never have failed to mention that in his argument in Galatians 1, for it especially would have emphasized his independence from "Jerusalem"—fails to give sufficient consideration to the structure of Paul's argument as shown above and to the form-critical issue. Further, greater spatial distance from Jerusalem by no means implies Paul's independence from Jerusalem. Such independence, however, would become more probable in the eyes of the opponents and the congregations if Paul had not been to Jerusalem for fourteen years. *This* was the argument that did not escape Paul!

Form-critical studies are not the only ones, however, that have arrived at the conclusion that Paul's reference to "Syria and Cilicia" does not (intend to) specify the entire sphere of the apostle's activity during the time between the first and second visits to Jerusalem. "Gal. 1:21 cannot be taken to mean that for the fourteen years he worked *only* in Syria and Cilicia. The statement merely indicates the point from which his work at that time began."[51] Paul is concerned primarily to prove that he was *not*[52] in Jerusalem, and thus he is not concerned to the same degree to give a comprehensive description of the localities or the nature of his activity.[53]

As the result of this section, it may be said that Gal. 1:21 does not indicate anything about where Paul stayed during the time between his first and second visits to Jerusalem. It is certain only that after a two-week stay in Jerusalem he went into the regions of Syria and Cilicia, and that he returned to Jerusalem only after fourteen years. But from which point in time should these fourteen years be counted? This question will be addressed in the next section.

2.1.3.2 ON THE REFERENCE POINT OF THE ENUMERATIONS OF YEARS IN GAL. 1:18; 2:1

Research stands in unanimous agreement regarding the reference point of the enumeration of years in Gal. 1:18: When Paul says, "Then after three years I went up," he is enumerating these three years from the time of the conversion that was described in v. 15.[54] As regards the interpretation of the chronological statement in Gal. 2:1, research vacillates *exclusively* between the following two alternatives: to enumerate the fourteen years either from the time of the conversion or from the time of the first visit to Jerusalem. The most recent advocate of the first alternative known to me is A. Suhl.[55] He properly emphasizes that Paul's concern "in this context is to prove his independence from Jerusalem" (p. 47). The "objective of the argument [makes] it likely that when Paul had two numbers to choose from [sic] for the dating in Gal. 2:1, he necessarily chose the larger. This was the number that enumerated from the date of the conversion and not from the first visit to Jerusalem" (ibid.). Suhl also thinks that there is *linguistic* support for his thesis that the fourteen years should be reckoned from the time of the conversion: "The triple *epeita* in 1:18, 21; 2:1 is chronologically specified only by the statements *meta tria etē, epemeina pros auton hēmeras dekapente* in 1:18 and *dia dekatessarōn etōn* in 2:1. In 1:18, Paul employs *meta* to refer to the immediately preceding chronological statement in v. 15. When 2:1 has *dia*, in contrast, this makes it likely that Paul has in mind the entire period since the conversion, during which his relationship to Jerusalem had not changed" (ibid.).

With regard to the linguistic observations, Suhl's thesis is based, on the one hand, on the fact that Paul uses *dia* instead of *meta* in 2:1. The function of *dia* here, however, is to emphasize more strongly than is possible with *meta* the span and length of time during which Paul had not been in Jerusalem.[56] There is no material difference between the use of the two prepositions. For this reason, Suhl cannot support his thesis on the basis of the change of prepositions. On the other hand, Suhl maintains that the triple *epeita* is chronologically specified only by the explicit temporal references. The *epeita* in 1:18, however, is not connected with the temporal reference "two weeks." Paul mentions the brevity of his stay in Jerusalem in order to emphasize his independence from Jerusalem. The chronological specification of *epeita* does not need to be explicated by another temporal reference. As an adverb, *epeita* already contains temporal meaning in that it joins up with the preceding and introduces the following (this temporal sense is also apparent in 1 Cor. 15:5ff. and elsewhere).[57]

This rebuttal of Suhl's linguistic contentions also invalidates his first argument, that when Paul had the choice of two numbers he naturally chose the larger. This argument rests on an invalid differentiation of *dia* and *meta*. Further, how did it happen that Paul had the "choice" of two numbers?

Suhl's exegesis also seems to rest on the assumption shared by most other investigators that we can extract exact chronological information from this passage "because of the chronological precision that is intended here."[58] If this were the case, would not Paul have expressed himself in clearer terms? And was it even necessary for Paul to be chronologically exact in every detail in order to achieve his main objective, proof of his independence from Jerusalem? The chronological reference "fourteen years," along with Paul's statement that after two weeks' stay in Jerusalem he departed for Syria and Cilicia, is rather intended as an independent argument emphasizing Paul's distance from Jerusalem (see above, p. 56). The chronological point of reference here depends on the referent of the particle *epeita* (more on this shortly).

The other, probably predominant group of investigators reckons the "fourteen years" from the time of the first visit to Jerusalem, insofar as the matter is not just left unresolved. Lightfoot, Schlier, and Bonnard[59] write that the statement in 2:1 "I went up again" shows that the "fourteen years" should be reckoned from the time of the first visit. While this propc al is grammatically possible, one must nevertheless ask whether the numeric reference in 2:1 should not rather be understood as standing in reference to the event with which *epeita* links up. This interpretation would then be parallel to the accepted interpretation of 1:18, where *epeita* is also followed by a numeric reference. This suggestion may serve as a springboard for a new proposal concerning how one should reckon the enumerations of years in Galatians 1–2. While research has vacillated between counting the "fourteen years" either from the time of conversion or from the time of the first visit to Jerusalem, there is a third possibility that, in my opinion, should be preferred over the other two. We shall examine this possibility in the following.

Paul uses the particle *epeita* three times in Gal. 1:18—2:1. With the exception of 1 Cor. 12:28, Paul always uses this particle in a temporal sense (cf. 1 Cor. 15:5, 6, 7, 23, 46; 1 Thess. 4:17). *Epeita* links up with what immediately precedes and introduces what follows. If one understands Gal. 1:18 on the basis of this usage, then the *epeita* links up with the return to Damascus, and the "three years" should be enumerated from this same return to Damascus.[60] From the perspective of this proposal, Paul says *nothing* about how long he stayed in Arabia.

The generally accepted interpretation of *epeita* in v. 21 indicates that our interpretation is on the right track. No one would ever take *epeita* here in reference to the conversion mentioned in v. 15. Rather, *epeita* clearly stands in reference to the completed first visit to Jerusalem.

Gal. 2:1 should be interpreted in an analogous manner: *epeita* separates the new trip to Jerusalem from what preceded. This indicates that one should probably follow J. Weiss in reckoning the fourteen years mentioned after the *epeita* as starting from the immediately preceding event.[61] However, contra Weiss, what immediately precedes is not the first trip to Jerusalem but rather the journey to the province of Syria and Cilicia.[62]

On the basis of what has been said, we may construct the chart shown in Figure 1.

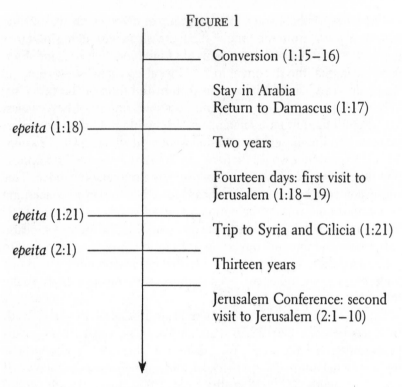

FIGURE 1

Conversion (1:15–16)

Stay in Arabia
Return to Damascus (1:17)

epeita (1:18)

Two years

Fourteen days: first visit to
Jerusalem (1:18–19)

epeita (1:21)

Trip to Syria and Cilicia (1:21)

epeita (2:1)

Thirteen years

Jerusalem Conference: second
visit to Jerusalem (2:1–10)

2.1.3.3. The Content and Occasion of the Jerusalem Conference

When we approach the question of the content and occasion of the Jerusalem Conference, there is good reason to start with an examination of Paul's own report of the agreement made with the apostles in Jerusalem. If we are able to discern old tradition here, then we may use this information as a secure starting point for dealing with the question of the occasion of the conference. If, however, our attempt fails, we must alter our approach to the question in order to accord with the findings in the text.

2.1.3.3.1 Redaction and Tradition in Gal. 2:7–8

To reconstruct the agreement at the conference, or a part of this agreement, we must proceed from the following observation: In Gal. 2:7, 8, Paul diverges from his usual way of referring to the disciple Simon as Cephas (see, in the immediate context, 2:9, 11, and previously, 1:18) to designate him rather as Peter.

This deviation from the rule calls for an explanation. We shall use it as a springboard for the assumption that in these verses Paul is reproducing the agreement as it was drawn up in Jerusalem. The text reads: "I had been entrusted with the gospel to the uncircumcised, just as Peter had been entrusted with the gospel to the circumcised (for he who worked through Peter for the mission to the circumcised worked through me also for the Gentiles)." Now, it is inconceivable that the first-person singular should be used in a written agreement. Thus, presuming for the moment the correctness of the assumption made above, we should reconstruct the agreement by replacing *pepisteumai* with *Paulos pepisteutai* and, similarly, "me" with "Paul."

We shall now analyze these two verses in detail, starting with v. 7.

Pepisteumai with the accusative is also found elsewhere in Paul's writings (cf. 1 Thess. 2:4: "to be entrusted with the gospel"; 1 Cor. 9:17: "I am entrusted with a commission"; Rom. 3:2: "entrusted with the oracles of God"). The expression is also used, however, in post-Pauline tradition (1 Tim. 1:11; Titus 1:3) and elsewhere in early Christian writings (Ignatius, *Magn.* 6:1; *Phld.* 9:1; *Dg.* 7:1) and in Hellenistic Jewish writings (Josephus, *Bell.* 1.667). These findings do not necessarily mean we are dealing with Pauline redaction,[63] and it is methodologically justified to object to such a rash conclusion, because when one approaches Galatians 2 with "questions regarding the origin of the terminology, it [must] be taken into consideration that Paul certainly had no less influence on the formulation of the agreement than in the negotiations that led to the agreement."[64] On the other hand, these findings on *pepisteumai* do not in themselves provide unequivocal support for the traditional character of v. 7.

"The gospel to the uncircumcised/to the circumcised": A glance at the concordance reveals that neither of these two concepts has a parallel in the Pauline writings. While this finding may be indicative of pre-Pauline origin,[65] the following two arguments have been made against this conclusion. First, "apart from a few exceptions, 'uncircumcised—circumcised' is found as an antithetical pair of concepts only in the Pauline writings and in those writings influenced by Paul."[66] "There are, to my knowledge, no non-Christian witnesses of the abstract *hē peritomē* meaning the Jews. Only seldom does *hē akrobystia* mean the Gentiles."[67]

Second, the attempt to translate the two expressions back into Aramaic/Hebrew indicates that the Jerusalem congregation must have employed *ha-bᵉsōrah* in an absolute manner. Such a use cannot, however, be verified for this congregation.[68]

In response to these objections, we may say that, as concerns method, the second argument impermissibly excludes the possibility that Paul (and Barnabas) could have had any part in formulating the result of the conference and neglects *a priori* the possibility that the compromise could have been expressed in monstrous formulations.

As concerns the first argument, the word *peritomē* with the meaning "Jew" is witnessed in the New Testament other than just in the Pauline writings, as Acts 10:45 and 11:2 (cf. Eph. 2:11; Col. 3:11; 4:11; Titus 1:10) show. The same applies for *akrobystia* with the meaning "Gentile"; cf. Acts 11:3. Thus the linguistic evidence in favor of Pauline origin of this antithetical pair of concepts is not necessarily convincing. Wilckens's remark that the antithetical pair "circumcision—uncircumcision" is found with few exceptions only in Paul's writings should be countered with the remark that the passages in Paul's letters that employ the pair in the ethnological sense of "Jew—Gentile" as in Gal. 2:7–8, namely, 1 Cor. 7:19; Gal. 5:6; 6:15; Rom. 3:30; 4:9 (Rom. 2:25ff. presents a figurative use!), all reflect traditions whose *Sitz im Leben* was baptism.

As regards Gal. 6:15, "For neither circumcision counts for anything, nor uncircumcision, but a new creation," the above conclusion is probable, since "new creation" is set in opposition to the antithetical pair. The erstwhile partition and separation of humankind into Jews and Gentiles have lost their validity in the light of the Christ-event. See 2 Cor. 5:17: If someone is *in Christ*, then that person is a *new* creation. "Being-in-Christ" effects the new creation. Thus, the new creation is christologically grounded. We may therefore use such statements as Gal. 6:15, which relativize the importance of membership in groups of people and nations, as parallels for our passage, which can be employed in the detailed exegesis (e.g., regarding the question of *Sitz im Leben*).

One parallel is found in 1 Cor. 12:13: "We were all baptized into one body—Jews or Greeks, slaves or free." Here the relativization of the various groups follows from belonging to Christ, which was established at baptism. There is a further parallel in Gal. 3:26–28: "For in Christ Jesus you are all sons of God, through faith. For as many of you as were baptized into Christ have put on Christ. There is neither Jew nor Greek, there is neither slave nor free, there is neither male nor female; for you are all one in Christ Jesus." In contrast to the preceding passage, this passage contains the pair "male—female," which Paul probably did not accidentally leave out of 1 Corinthians (most likely because of the enthusiastic misunderstanding of transcendence of the factual that also found expression in emancipatory tendencies and that called forth a response such as 1 Cor. 14:33ff.).[69]

These two passages, whose structure is identical with Gal. 6:15, render it plausible that baptism was also the *Sitz im Leben* of Gal. 6:15. The following observation on Gal. 3:26–28 shows that the same conclusion is necessary for the second text in question, Gal. 5:6: "For in Christ Jesus neither circumcision nor uncircumcision is of any avail, but faith working through love." In Gal. 3:26–28, Paul expands the tradition that he had received by adding *dia pisteōs*.[70] He is thus able to employ this tradition in his theology of justification. Accordingly, *pistis* for Paul is directly related to embodiment "in Christ," which occurs at baptism. For this reason, *pistis* in Gal. 5:6 can be understood as abolition of the former antithesis between Jews and Gentiles. While the antithesis "*pistis*—circumcision/uncircumcision" indubitably derives from Paul, this is not the case for the antithesis "*peritomē*—akrobystia," which is also reflected in Gal. 5:6 and which derives from a baptismal *Sitz im Leben*. In 1 Cor. 7:19, "For neither circumcision counts for anything nor uncircumcision, but keeping the commandments of God," the (previously applicable) antithesis "circumcision—uncircumcision" is contrasted with observation of the commands of God. We may note that in the preceding passage it is *pistis*, which becomes effective through *agapē*, that is contrasted with this antithetical pair. This observation gives us the right to connect *agapē* and the observance of the commands of God closely with *pistis* in Paul's thought. *Agapē* and observance of God's commands are the human response to the grace granted at baptism. Thus not only *pistis* but also observance of the commands of God are constituents of the new being, and they fundamentally relativize the state in which the Christian finds herself or himself (1 Cor. 7:20). To this extent, the antithesis in 1 Cor. 7:19, "Jew/Gentile—observance of the commands of God" (Gal. 5:6: faith active in love), which, just as the antithesis in Gal. 5:6, was created by Paul, reflects the baptismal situation and is a variation of the (new) antithesis of "Jew/Gentile—new creation/in Christ" that was affirmed at baptism.

Since Rom. 4:9ff. merely repeats the antithetical pair already found in Rom. 3:30 and has no peculiar significance of its own, only Rom. 3:30 remains to be investigated: ". . . since God is one; and he will justify the circumcised on the ground of their faith and the uncircumcised through their faith." "The style of v. 30 seems somewhat ceremonial and seems to reflect a confession" (Michel).[71] The relative *hos*, the parallel structure, and Paul's formulaic use of the *heis theos* predication elsewhere (1 Cor. 8:6) lead to the conclusion that our passage is based on a formula corrected by Paul through the addition of *ek pisteōs* and *dia pisteōs* as well as through replacement of the present or aorist by the future (whether logical or not). The underlying formula stated that God justifies Jews and Gentiles in baptism. This formula is based on a present eschatology, just as are the previously analyzed formulas.

This demonstration of the relationship of the antithesis "*akrobystia—peritomē*" in the history of traditions to present-oriented, enthusiastic baptismal traditions[72] shows that Wilckens's claim that this antithesis derives from Paul is not convincing Further, the argument in favor of the traditional character of the expressions "gospel of circumcision" and "gospel of uncircumcision" finds even more support in the fact that the division of the gospel into these two types strictly contradicts Paul's normal word usage.[73]

It is thus probable that v. 7 is part of a tradition. Nevertheless, these observations do not yet positively confirm that Paul is here quoting the protocol drawn up at the conference. Some things actually speak against this: (1) the first-person singular, which as it stands certainly could not have been in the protocol;[74] (2) *pisteuthēnai* with the accusative is also good Pauline usage; and (3) the order "Paul—Peter" could not, as it stands, have been in a protocol. We thus arrive at the following conclusion regarding v. 7: It contains tradition, even if this tradition is not a protocol from Jerusalem.

Verse 8 reads as follows: "For he who worked through Peter for the mission to the circumcised worked through me also for the Gentiles."

Energein: According to Wilckens,[75] this word and its derivatives are typically Pauline words. This is a somewhat exaggerated statement, for *energein* is found, for example, also in Mark 6:14 and *Barn.* 2:1. The construction with *dativus commodi* is found only here in the New Testament.

Petros: On this, see above, p. 64.

Apostolē is found in non-Pauline writings in Acts 1:25 (alongside *diakonia*) and in the Pauline writings in 1 Cor. 9:2 and Rom. 1:5.

Ethnē is good Pauline usage (see the concordance), though in the rest of the New Testament and in Judaism it was also a *terminus technicus* for non-Jews.

Conclusion regarding v. 8: The derivation of v. 8 as a part of a protocol is no more convincing than the supposition of thoroughgoing Pauline redaction.

These findings force us to abandon our preliminary hypothetical assumption that in Gal. 2:7–8 Paul is quoting the agreement drawn up at the conference. We must search for other possible explanations of the above observations on the text of Gal. 2:7–8.

We may note that up to now Gal. 2:7–8 has been discussed with the following alternatives in view: Does the text derive from a protocol, or does it present a Pauline paraphrase of the agreement that can no longer be recovered? Both these alternatives do, however, share *one* assumption, namely, that Gal. 2:7–8 is directly related to the conference. In my opinion, this shared assumption has been imposed on the text and is responsible for having raised a question which involves alternatives that lead to an impasse: Is the text part of the protocol or merely a Pauline formulation? It seems to me that this shared assumption is false and that it has kept researchers from finding a satisfactory explanation of the text. In the following we shall attempt to demonstrate that the tradition contained in Gal. 2:7–8 actually goes back to the period prior to the Jerusalem Conference. (This demonstration will also simultaneously show that v. 9 is referring to an agreement made at the conference.)

2.1.3.3.2   Gal. 2:7–8 as Part of a Personal Tradition[76] about Paul before the Conference

Even after redaction and tradition in Gal. 2:7–8 have been separated, the exegetical possibilities for understanding this passage have not been exhausted. One absolutely decisive argument against the thesis that vv. 7–8 derive from the agreement drawn up at the Jerusalem Conference has unfortunately not received sufficient attention.[77] Verse 9 says that the pillars, James, Cephas, and John, gave Paul and Barnabas the right hand of fellowship and that the pillars went to the Jews while Paul and Barnabas went to the Gentiles. The situation reflected in this verse evidently differs from that reflected in vv. 7–8. In v. 9, (1) nothing more is said of the juxtaposition "Peter—Paul"; (2) Paul again uses the name "Cephas"; (3) Paul and Barnabas are mentioned together; and (4) James stands at the head of the list.[78] This comparison of vv. 7–8 with v. 9 demonstrates the tension between the two statements and leads to the conclusion that vv. 7–8 cannot derive from the agreements drawn up at the Jerusalem Conference.

We saw above, however, that vv. 7–8 do reflect tradition, even though they contain elements of Pauline vocabulary. Now we want to ask whether this tradition may be relegated to a specific chronological period. The opening words of v. 7 provide one clue in this regard: They *saw* "that I had been entrusted with the gospel to the uncircumcised, just as Peter had been entrusted with the gospel to the circumcised." The wording shows that the tradition contained in this verse was already presupposed at the conference and thus that this tradition should be relegated to the period *before* the conference. The information in the tradition about Paul's mission to the Gentiles (the gospel of the uncircumcised) has a parallel in Gal. 2:2: Paul goes to Jerusalem in order to present the gospel he proclaims among the Gentiles. Paul's mission to the Gentiles was both assumed (*idontes*) and recognized at the conference (v. 7), and in the same breath Paul mentions Peter as the one who operated the mission to the Jews that corresponded to Paul's mission to the Gentiles. The three pillars give Paul (and Barnabas) the right hand of fellowship precisely because Paul had been entrusted with the gospel among the Gentiles even up to the time of the conference (perfect: *pepisteumai*).

Verses 7–8 not only say something about the present state of Paul's being entrusted with the mission to the Gentiles. Rather, v. 8 is a parenthetical remark in the aorist that has the same content as v. 7. The aorist indicates that Paul and Peter were entrusted with their respective missions at a particular time before the conference, probably long in the past. Further, the particle *gar* in the sentence "for he who worked . . ." allows us to conclude that Paul can assume that the Galatians know of this tradition about his person, just as he can for the tradition in 1:13. Paul includes the parenthetical statement in order to remind the Galatians of this tradition. We may cautiously conclude that the historical root of this piece of personal tradition about Paul, which was current among the *Greek-speaking* Pauline congregations (this view alone explains the Greek form of the name *Petros*), was Paul's first visit to Jerusalem to become acquainted with Cephas. Even at that time, Peter and Paul may have made an agreement that is directly related to the personal tradition about Paul reflected in Gal. 2:7 and that was current among Paul's congregations. It should be clear that the parity of Peter and Paul expressed in this tradition is not historical in nature but should rather be attributed to the followers of Paul or to Paul himself.

It should not be doubted that personal contact during the first visit to Jerusalem could have been accompanied by a type of regulatory agreement such as the one above. W. D. Davies once picked up on a statement by C. H. Dodd and remarked humorously, "Certainly Paul and Peter did not spend their time 'talking about the weather.'"[79]

The above considerations give rise to a clear argument for Paul's marked apostolic consciousness of mission before the conference, something that does not harmonize with the thesis that Paul was the junior partner of Barnabas (Barnabas does not appear at all in the old tradition in Gal. 2:7). Further, if Paul parenthetically plays on a personal tradition from the period *before* the conference which was also known to the Galatian congregations, this is an indication that the Galatian congregations were founded before the conference. It is indeed improbable that traditions about Paul from the period before the conference would still be circulated after the conference, especially since the tradition of "Paul—Peter" was modified by the expansion of the list to "Paul/Barnabas—James/Cephas/John."[80]

A further argument for the founding of the Galatian congregations before the conference can be found in Gal. 2:5. Paul does not yield to the false brethren in order that "the truth of the gospel might be preserved for you." The "in order that" (hina) has been understood as introducing an ideal goal (Lietzmann, 11; Bonnard, 144). A simpler interpretation is that the Galatian congregations already existed before the conference, even if this interpretation is "not absolutely necessary" on the basis of the hina.[81] On to proteron in Gal. 4:13, see pp. 90–92.

By contrasting the personal tradition with the agreement of the conference, we have already touched on the next problem; the question of the occasion and result of the conference. This question should be dealt with on the basis of the regulation established at the conference and contained in Gal. 2:9.

2.1.3.3.3 The Occasion and the Result of the Jerusalem Conference Explained on the Basis of the Tradition in Gal. 2:9 That Derives from the Conference

We may assume as certain that Paul operated a mission to the Gentiles before the conference and that he did not require his new Christians to be circumcised. This situation is clearly documented in the fact that Paul took the Gentile Christian Titus with him to Jerusalem and in the emphatic statement that Titus was not forced to be circumcised at the conference (something which presupposes that Paul did not have the Gentile Christians in his congregations circumcised).

The conference affirmed the propriety of Paul's mission to the Gentiles free of the law, just as is particularly clearly expressed in the statement "Those, I say, who were of repute added nothing to me" (v. 6). Nevertheless, the freedom of the Gentile Christians from the law was not undisputed at the conference, for Paul himself reports that he did not yield to the false brethren in order that the truth of the gospel (freedom from the law) remain for the Galatian congregations that already existed at the time (vv. 4–5).

It may be remarked in passing that some investigators[82] adopt the reading of D*, Ir[lat], Tert, Ambst, Pelag at Gal. 2:5, *hois pros hōran eixamen*, and believe that Paul did allow Titus to be circumcised in Jerusalem. According to this view, Paul's agitation over this concession gave rise to the confused structure of the sentence. It may be said against this view that if this were correct, Paul's *narratio* would have provided the Galatians with a splendid example of his dependence on Jerusalem.[83]

Why does Paul use the compound verb *prosanatithēmi*,[84] and why does he place *emoi* in such an emphatic position at the beginning of the sentence? Do not these phenomena reflect a tradition about the agreement at the conference which knew of some addition to the Pauline gospel and which Paul is denying in the statement cited above? D. Georgi recommended:

> One should translate (in order to give due weight to the *pros*-) . . . , "To me those of repute added *nothing additional*," and one should understand this as a play on the so-called Apostolic Decree (Acts 15:24–29). What Paul intends to say here is that there is a special injunction that supplements what was once dealt with and agreed on in Jerusalem, but this arose later and without my approval.[85]

I think that at this point Paul is actually thinking of a regulation similar to the Apostolic Decree, but I believe that this regulation stands in a *direct* relationship with the Jerusalem Conference. It is possible to support this thesis solely on the basis of the injunction contained in Gal. 2:9.

In the agreement preserved in Gal. 2:9, the worldwide mission is divided into two parts, the mission to the Jews and the mission to the Gentiles. This is not a geographical division of the areas for the mission in the sense that those from Jerusalem would be responsible for Palestine while Paul and Barnabas would be responsible for the mission in the rest of the world.[86] The division is rather made from an ethnographical[87] perspective.[88] It cannot be objected that, according to this thesis, Paul would have lost the possibility of approaching the Gentiles who were best prepared for Christianity, the fearers of God,[89] for these were not fully Jews and were reckoned according to Pauline and Jewish understanding to the *ethnē*.[90] Serious attention should be given to the fact that in his preserved letters Paul nowhere speaks of a *mission* by himself to the Jews.[91]

Conzelmann and Lindemann have correctly observed that the usual uncomplicated communal life of Jewish and Gentile Christians in the same congregation before the conference was turned into a problem by the agreement of the conference reflected in Gal. 2:9.[92] Before the Jerusalem Conference, communal life of Jewish and Gentile Christians without further ado was possible and usual in the congregations established by the Hellenists.[93]

The theological stance reflected in the uncomplicated communal life and in the table fellowship of these congregations—it was probably primarily ecclesiologically conceived as the concrete realization of the eschatological unity of Jews and Gentiles as the new people of God— presupposes a position critical of the law (even though we know nothing about the degree of reflection on this matter). "The practical problem of the mission and the theological problem were intertwined, and were even identical."[94]

If one compares such a situation with the division intended by the conference, the agreement "we to the Gentiles, you to the Jews" clearly appears to be a restriction and revocation of the realization of the unity of the people of God. "Yes, one may almost assume that this communal life became a problem only because of the decision made in Jerusalem: While Jews and Gentiles up to then had apparently been members of the same congregation without complications, now the Jewish Christians could be obliged to strict observance of the law."[95] Behind all this was the demand for the separation of Jewish and Gentile Christians who belonged to the same congregation. Because "the problem of the open communal life of Jews and Gentiles in a Christian congregation was precisely *not* solved by the decision of the conference concerning the division of the areas for mission and concerning the mission to the Gentiles free of the law,"[96] it is often assumed that the Apostolic Decree mentioned in Acts 15:24ff. arose in a mixed congregation after the conference. The purpose of the Apostolic Decree would have been to fill the gap left by the decision of the conference or to resolve the problem this decision created.[97] In my view, however, it is inconceivable that the conference could have bypassed such a fundamental problem of the mixed congregations, especially since the conflict over the law that led to the Jerusalem Conference may have occurred precisely in mixed congregations which up to that time had known an uncomplicated communal life of Jewish and Gentile Christians. Also, as the decision of the conference is preserved by Paul (Gal. 2:9), it reads as if it is an undoing of church relationships as they existed in mixed congregations before the conference. If one does not want to attribute complete remoteness from reality to the representatives of the mixed congregations, or to their representative, Barnabas, then for the *internal* reasons mentioned above one is forced to assume that the Jerusalem Conference drew up a document similar to the Apostolic Decree as a legal injunction for mixed congregations. Only such a regulation enabled the maintenance of the unity of the congregation after the rise of the conflict over the law and the division of the areas for missionary activity.

Thus, when Paul says that nothing additional was added to him, he is referring to the decree that henceforth was valid in the mixed congregations and that was apparently enjoined on Barnabas as the representative of the Antiochene congregation, though not on Paul himself for his congregations, since his congregations as well as the Galatian congregations consisted (primarily) of Gentile Christians.

Despite this injunction for the *mixed* congregation in Antioch,[98] the stipulation "we to the Gentiles—they to the Jews" still makes good sense, for the mission to the Gentiles was the prerogative of the Pauline and Antiochene mission. That is, so to speak, the valid form of the decision of the conference for the Pauline congregations. For the congregation in Antioch this stipulation will have been accompanied by an additional clause that was similar to the Apostolic Decree and that regulated the communal life of Jewish and Gentile Christians.

If Luke is dependent on Antiochene traditions in Acts 15, one need not wonder that the Apostolic Decree appears as the main part of the agreement in Acts, for it was this regulation that primarily affected the mixed Antiochene congregation. Similarly, when Paul fails to mention explicitly the Apostolic Decree in Galatians 2, one need not wonder, for he is speaking from the perspective of his missionary work where probably no additional stipulation was applicable.

In light of what has been said, it is improbable that, for example, primarily the demand for the circumcision of the Gentile Christians was the direct occasion for the conference.[99] This demand more probably *arose out of* the problem of further communal life between Jews and Gentiles in the mixed congregations. Once the communal life had been turned into a problem, the possibility of solving the conflict by having Gentile Christians completely adopt the law also arose.[100] That some Jewish Christians had considered solving the problem in this manner is apparent from the demand for the circumcision of Titus that was raised at the conference (cf. Acts 15:1, 6, 24). The implicit presupposition for such a demand was, however, first of all the complication of the previously uncomplicated communal life of Gentile and Jewish Christians in the same congregation that will have brought about the conference.

74

Aside from providing a new[101] view of the Jerusalem Conference, this section has led us to the conclusion, which is not unimportant for the chronology, that it is possible to find indications of a Pauline mission that occurred before the conference and was independent of Antioch even in the tradition in Gal. 2:9 that derives from the agreement at the conference. Only in the Pauline mission was nothing added to the "gospel of the uncircumcised," precisely because the Pauline congregations (such as the Galatian congregations) consisted mainly of Gentile Christians and up to the time of the conference had not experienced the problem that had arisen in the mixed congregations. (It is another question, which will not be dealt with here, whether Paul would have sanctioned something similar to the Apostolic Decree for his congregations even if this problem had arisen there.)

2.1.3.3.4 The Incident in Antioch: Gal. 2:11ff.

In the following we shall present the reasons that speak for dating the incident in Antioch *before* the Jerusalem Conference (the form-critical possibility was already demonstrated above).

1. The demands of the opponents in Antioch[102] and the demands of the ones who occasioned the conference are similar. The opponents at the conference demand the withdrawal of Jewish Christians from Gentile Christians, as may be indirectly concluded on the basis of the regulation "we to the Gentiles—you to the Jews." The opponents in Antioch demand the same thing, and when they do this, Barnabas, Cephas, and the other Jews withdraw.

2. The phenomenon of *uncomplicated* communal life in a mixed congregation, as is found in Gal. 2:11ff., is probably conceivable only before the conference.

3. From point 2 it follows that questioning of the table fellowship of Jewish and Gentile Christians, as in Gal. 2:11ff., would, it seems, no longer be possible in mixed congregations after the conference (for this fellowship would have been regulated by a clause similar to the Apostolic Decree; see the conclusion above).

One may ask why Paul did not maintain the chronological order in the *narratio*. To the extent that this can be explained in the following, the thesis of locating the incident in Antioch chronologically before the conference will be simultaneously confirmed. The reason for placing the report about the incident in Antioch after the report about the conference was that this would serve to demonstrate the independence of the Pauline gospel and *apostleship*, something very important for the present situation in Galatia. Only in Antioch did Paul prove himself to be of equal rank with one "pillar" of Jerusalem. Paul even accused him as guilty (*kategnōsmenos*).

Basically, what Paul says after Gal. 2:11ff. seems to involve a violation of the compromise established at Jerusalem. In the following sections of the letter, the law, which the Jerusalem agreement had maintained to be applicable for the Jewish Christians, is criticized in a fundamental manner.[103]

At the Jerusalem Conference the right of the mission to the Gentiles free from the law was confirmed. Paul emphasizes this several times in order to incriminate his Galatian opponents with breach of contract for intruding into Gentile Christian congregations. Thus in this point Paul finds support in the agreement made in Jerusalem. On the other hand, there was one controversial point in the present conflict where Paul could *not* call on the events and the agreement of the conference, namely, the question of recognition of his apostleship.[104] The tradition in Gal. 2:9 that derives from the conference speaks only of Barnabas and Paul's mission to the Gentiles, something that in no way implies recognition of the title "apostle." Further, the personal tradition about Paul in v. 8 contains a statement about the *apostolē* of Peter to the Jews but no express statement about Paul's *apostolē* to the Gentiles. Sometimes it is assumed that Paul is employing here an abbreviated manner of speaking (Lietzmann, 13; cf. vv. 7b and 9) and that he assumes the recognition of his own rank as an apostle (equal to those in Jerusalem) at the conference. Paul, however, would not have passed over any tradition connected with the conference that documented recognition of his apostleship from the side of Jerusalem.[105] Furthermore, v. 8 is not part of the agreements drawn up at the conference, for we were able above (p. 70) to show that the kernel of v. 8 is a personal tradition current in the Pauline congregations before the time of the conference. It was also said that the equality of Peter and Paul[106] expressed in this tradition cannot be historical (e.g., reflecting an agreement between Peter and Paul in which Peter admits that Paul is of equal rank). The idea of this equality derives from later interpretation either by Paul or by his congregations. The actual question is whether the personal tradition contained a pronouncement about the *apostolē* of Peter *and* Paul or did not contain this predication at all. (The third possibility, that the statement was current as it is quoted by Paul, drops out, for if this were the case—to leave the first-person singular to one side—one would expect greater correspondence in the wording of the statements about Peter and Paul.)

It seems likely to me that Paul introduced the word *apostolē* into the tradition in order to connect *indirectly* his own claim to this rank with the Jerusalem Conference (see also v. 9a and n. 104).

Result: Because Paul saw that the agreements (and the things not agreed on) at the conference could not offer him final support in the Galatian controversies, the apostle presented the conference and the incident at Antioch *ordine artificiorum* rather than maintaining the chronological order.

The view that the *hote de* in 2:11 continues the narrative (Oepke, 87–88) is just an antiquated exegetical convention that is unable to explain why *epeita* is not used. On *hote de*, however, see 1:15.

If these three points and these observations on the placement of the report about the incident in Antioch after the report about the conference have demonstrated it to be probable that the incident in Antioch occurred before[107] the conference,[108] we may now in closing suggest that precisely the incident in Antioch was the direct occasion for Paul, Barnabas, Peter, and "those from James" to travel to Jerusalem. Though the fragmentary character of the sources perhaps prohibits absolute judgment of this possibility, reasons of content and form criticism (see above, p. 75, first point) give this suggestion considerable probability.[109]

2.1.3.3.5 The Collection[110] for the Poor

In Gal. 2:10, Paul mentions one (single: *monon*) qualification of the agreement about the division of areas for the mission described in v. 9: "Only they would have us remember the poor, which very thing I was eager to do." In the agreement, both partners from the side of the Gentile Christians committed themselves to remember the poor.[111] This is apparent from the first-person plural in v. 10a, though v. 10b mentions only Paul's zeal in fulfilling this obligation (*espoudasa*). One further difference between v. 10a and v. 10b that should be noticed in the exegesis is that v. 10a employs the present subjunctive while v. 10b uses the first aorist.

On *mnēmoneuōmen*: The present tense of the verb expresses a continuing action. For the interpretation of v. 10a, this means "either that the course of action referred to is one which having already been begun is to be continued, or that there is distinctly in mind a practice (not a single instance) of it in the future."[112] The first possibility for understanding the present subjunctive has often been used by research to maintain that Paul and Barnabas delivered a collection before the conference, for Acts 11:27ff. mentions such a transaction. This view collapses in the light of Paul's own statement that he had not visited Jerusalem between the time of his visit with Cephas and the trip to Jerusalem for the conference.

Other investigators[113] expressly acknowledge Paul's statement[114] but connect the trip of Paul and Barnabas to Jerusalem for the conference with a collection. They understand the present subjunctive *mnēmoneuōmen* as a request for continuation of this relief work (it is supposed that in Acts 11:27ff. Luke mistakenly doubled the journey of Paul and Barnabas to the conference).

Against this view stands, first, the fact that Paul says nothing in Gal. 2:1 about such a purpose for the journey. He says that the journey was undertaken because of a revelation and in order to present to those in Jerusalem the gospel that he preaches among the Gentiles. Second, when Paul describes his zeal for the collection in v. 10b, he characterizes it as something that corresponds to the agreement established in Jerusalem and that was subsequent to the agreement.[115] Further, on the basis of Paul's report about the observance of the agreement and without Acts 11:27ff., no one would conclude that Paul had already delivered a collection. The aorist *espoudasa* actually excludes the possibility that Paul's action (in fulfillment of the agreement at Jerusalem) stands in any connection whatsoever with a relief action for the poor that had occurred (continuously) either at the time of the conference or before it. "A reference to an effort on behalf of the poor at that very time [the time of the conference] in progress is impossible in view of the meaning and tense of *espoudasa.* . . . This would have required an imperfect tense" (Burton, 100). However, this is what is assumed by the proponents of the opinion that *mnēmoneuōmen* indicates a relief action had already occurred. They would like to translate "Only that we should *continue* to remember the poor."[116]

The outcome of our considerations on *mnēmoneuōmen* is that at the conference in Jerusalem it was agreed that in the future the Gentile Christian congregations would continuously provide support for the poor in Jerusalem.

One recent detailed investigation of the present subjunctive *mnēmoneuōmen* provides us with the opportunity to explain in the next couple of paragraphs the meaning and importance of the term "poor" and thus make a contribution to the broader clarification of the "collection." For D. Georgi, the tense of the verb *mnēmoneuein*, which indicates that the assistance was of a continuing nature, means that the expression must not be understood as indicating primarily "economic assistance for the congregation in Jerusalem." The expression rather "has in mind constant remembrance by the Gentile Christians of the situation, importance, and accomplishments of the Christians in Jerusalem, thus primarily an inner attitude but also the outward expression of this attitude in recognition, thankfulness, and petition and then also economic assistance."[117] In my opinion, Georgi arrives at this interpretation only because he understands *ptōchoi* as a well-known title of the Christians in Jerusalem. "The absolute use of the term in Gal. 2:10 and the fact that it does not need an explanation speak for this being a well-known title of the Christians in Jerusalem" (p. 23). To this statement one may raise the question of how Paul would have had to express himself if he wanted *ptōchoi* to be understood in a sociological sense. How else other than the way he does in Gal. 2:10?[118] Further, Georgi has yet to prove that *ptōchoi* was a designation of honor in the early period of Christianity.[119] Gal. 2:10 is not a witness for this meaning, since a literal understanding is more natural and since in Rom. 15:26, "to make some contribution for the poor among the saints in Jerusalem," where Paul speaks of the same collection (see below), the *ptōchoi* are clearly understood, as Georgi also admits (p. 23 n. 51), as a (sociological) group in the congregation which as a whole receives the eschatological prediction *hagioi* (see Rom. 1:7; 1 Cor. 1:2; 2 Cor. 1:1).[120]

While maintaining that *mnēmoneuōmen* means continuous remembrance (constant and repeated assistance), we have thus shown that, contra Georgi, the *ptōchoi* in the agreement at the conference were a sociological[121] group and correspondingly that the assistance should be understood as economic support.[122]

The immediate occasion for this request of the Gentile Christian churches remains uncertain. The sabbatical year in 47/48 C.E., which led to a famine in Palestine, deserves consideration (see Josephus, *Ant.* 20.101; Tacitus, *Annals* 12.43; Orosius, 7.6.17). Also possible is that the request was part of the general care for those of a low social status. The tense of the verb *mnēmoneuōmen* speaks for this view, as does the observation that Paul would have delivered the collection only after any immediate need had faded away (otherwise he must have been in Jerusalem for a second time during the same year, against which speaks the evidence of the letters[123]).[124]

After this detailed exposition of Gal. 2:10, we may now return to the actual problem relevant for our reconstruction and ask whether there is proof for our assumption that the collection mentioned in Gal. 2:10 is the same as the one mentioned in the letters to the Corinthians and the Romans. One condition for the correctness of this assumption is that the reference in Gal. 2:10 is not looking back on a collection that had already been delivered. This is clear from the following. It was said above that the regulation established at the conference envisioned continuing assistance by the Gentile Christian congregations for those of lower social status in the Jerusalem congregation. According to his own statement, Paul strove (*espoudasa*) to fulfill this request. This points (a), because of the *tense* of the verb, to an effort that is already in progress toward the fulfillment of the wish but (b), because of the *expression* "to strive," not to its completion. The collection is evidently still fully in progress. While this last sentence can be supported further only by an analysis of the statements about the collection in all the letters,[125] one may not doubt that, as at the time of Galatians so too at the time of the letters to the Corinthians and the Romans, Paul is striving for the completion and delivery of the collection. This provides us with a solid basis for the use of the comparative method in the following, for the analysis of Gal. 2:10 has confirmed that all the references to the collection in Paul's letters (a) point back to the regulation established at Jerusalem and (b) should be related to one and the same campaign.

A secondary result arising from the last section (2.1.3.3.5) for the chronological question is that Gal. 2:10 is most easily understood as indicating that Paul took up the obligation of the collection for his own congregations while Barnabas did so for the Antiochene congregation. This gives us another point in support of an independent Pauline mission before the conference. Compare the considerations that led to the same conclusion in the analyses of Gal. 2:5 (p. 71), Gal. 2:7–8 (pp. 69–71), and Gal. 2:9 (pp. 71–75).

2.2 THE COLLECTION AS AN EXTERNAL CRITERION FOR THE DETERMINATION OF A CHRONOLOGICAL FRAMEWORK

It was already remarked above (p. 22) that at the time of the composition of Romans, Paul is looking back on the completion of the collection in Macedonia and Achaia, while in 1 Cor. 16:1ff. he is still speaking about the manner in which the money should be gathered. One should start with this evidence of progress in the process of the collection. Not only should one chronologically order the letters of Paul in relationship to one another according to their position in the progress of the collection (1 Corinthians was clearly written *before* Romans), but one should also ask whether the references to the collection permit a preliminary sketch of the period before 1 Cor. 16:1ff. and the period between 1 Cor. 16:1ff. and Rom. 15:26. The leading question in this inquiry is what stage of development the collection has reached in the separate congregations.

2.2.1 The Commencement of the Collection in Corinth: 1 Cor. 16:1ff.[126]

2.2.1.1 ON THE ANTECEDENT HISTORY OF 1 COR. 16:1FF.

In 1 Cor. 16:1ff., Paul explicates the manner in which the collection should be gathered, just as he had done for the churches in Galatia ("as I directed the churches in Galatia, so you also are to do"). Paul here compares not the "that" of the collection in Corinth and Galatia, but rather the "how."[127] The collection itself was initiated sometime in the past. For the *Corinthian* congregation that is also evident from the beginning of v. 1, "Now concerning the contribution for the saints." The *peri de* and the article before *logeia* make it evident that Paul is speaking about something with which the readers are already familiar. The question is whether the *peri de* refers back to a question raised by the Corinthians and, if that is the case, how the congregation received the first instructions regarding the collection.

It is certain that *peri de*s in 1 Cor. 7:1, 25; 8:1; and 12:1 refer back to questions raised by the Corinthians in a letter.[128] In 7:1 a letter of the Corinthians to Paul is expressly mentioned. The other passages (with the exception of 12:1) are found in the same section, and 12:1 deals with the situation in Corinth, something that makes it likely that this passage too was a response to a question in a letter.

All this makes it likely that 1 Cor. 16:1 (and accordingly also 16:12) should be understood, in analogy to the other sections of the letter introduced with *peri*, as a response to a letter by the Corinthians.[129]

Nevertheless, one cannot obtain complete certainty in this question, for Paul also introduces new sections with *peri* in 1 Thess. 4:9, 13; 5:1, where it is not as simple (as, e.g., in 1 Cor. 7:1) to conclude that there was a letter of the Thessalonians to Paul, since these questions could also have been raised orally.[130]

But even if one refers to 1 Thessalonians and decides that it is more probable that the question about the collection was raised orally[131] rather than through a letter, it is still clear that the congregation was familiar with the collection before the composition of 1 Corinthians. If we ask about the time and means of the introduction of the collection in Corinth, there are the following possibilities:

1. The Corinthians received news from the Galatians that a collection was being taken up in the Pauline congregations in Galatia. They adopted for themselves Paul's instructions that had initiated the collection in Galatia (Barrett, 385).[132]

2. Paul was in Corinth and arranged for the collection when he was there.[133]

3. Paul had Timothy, Titus, or other assistants convey instructions for the collection to Corinth.

4. Paul wrote about the collection that should be begun also in Corinth in the "previous letter" (1 Cor. 5:9).

On possibility one: In 1 Cor. 16:1ff. a comparison is drawn, as was shown above, with regard to the manner for gathering the money in Galatia and in Corinth and not with regard to the fact that a collection was being undertaken in both places. With the words "as I directed the churches in Galatia," Paul is not taking up a question of the Corinthians such as "Should we gather together a collection as the Galatians are doing?" He is rather arranging a means for the collection, just as he had done for the Galatians. If one wants to admit this observation and nevertheless maintain the essentials of the thesis described under possibility one, the question raised by the Corinthians must be assumed to have been "Should we gather the collection together in the same way the Galatians are gathering it?" Since such a question presupposes knowledge of the way the collection was being gathered in Galatia, one cannot explain why Paul deems it necessary to repeat in 1 Corinthians 16 the details of the manner of collection, which were already known to the Corinthians. For this reason, possibility one must be ruled out.[134]

The same applies for possibility two. Paul had not been in Corinth for a long time (1 Cor. 4:18). Between his founding visit and the writing of 1 Corinthians, Paul wrote the "previous letter." Since Paul is answering a question of the Corinthians about the collection in 1 Corinthians and, throughout the letter, responding to questions prompted by his previous letter and posed orally and through the letter of the Corinthians, it is in any event more likely that Paul initiated the collection in the previous letter rather than at the founding visit, which, moreover, occurred long in the past.[135] The rejection of possibility two adds strength to possibility four, but possibility three is not excluded, for the apostle could have sent instructions to his congregation by a means other than the previous letter.

In any event, Stephanas deserves serious consideration as a possible transmitter of Paul's instructions for the initiation of the collection (and of the Corinthians' question). Paul knows that the household of Stephanas had been particularly concerned with the collection (1 Cor. 16:15). This view would also explain why the collection is treated at the end of the letter, for Stephanas arrived in Ephesus only at the end of the composition of 1 Corinthians.[136] It is, however, at least as possible that Stephanas had been a strong advocate of the collection that had been instituted by the previous letter.

Whether the collection in Corinth was initiated by the previous letter[137] or orally by one of Paul's acquaintances, it seems certain in either case that Paul's instructions had been issued not long ago. "The nature of the Corinthians' questions concerning the collection for the saints implies that they had been informed of this project only shortly before."[138]

These observations provide us with the following order of events:

1. Introduction of the collection by the previous letter or by an acquaintance.

2. (Not much later) The Corinthians' question (by means of a letter or through a messenger) regarding the manner in which the collection should be gathered together.

3. Composition of 1 Cor. 16:1ff.

In the exegesis of 1 Cor. 16:1, we encountered Paul's reference to his instructions about the manner for gathering the collection in Galatia. In the following it will be asked how our reconstructed order of events of the collection in Corinth relates to the progress of the collection in Galatia, which is presupposed in 1 Cor. 16:1ff. As we deal with this question, we shall draw on what was said above about Gal. 2:10.

2.2.1.2 THE CAMPAIGN FOR THE COLLECTION IN 1 COR. 16:1FF. AND ITS ANTECEDENT HISTORY IN RELATIONSHIP TO THE DRIVE FOR THE COLLECTION IN GALATIA

The results of our exegesis of Gal. 2:10 were: (1) Paul speaks here of his zeal for the collection as if this zeal were known to the Galatians (notice further the other things mentioned in Galatians 1–2 that were known to the Galatians: persecution by Paul [1:13]; "Peter to the Jews, I to the Gentiles" [2:8]); (2) the collection has not yet been completed.

Can one exegetically extend these results in the light of the information in 1 Cor. 16:1ff. that Paul had instructed the Galatians about the manner for gathering the collection? Before we attempt to answer this question, we must first deal with D. Georgi's theses, which would deny the propriety of this question. Georgi writes:

> The instructions for the collection in Galatia mentioned in 1 Cor. 16 must have been delivered after the composition of the letter to the Galatians, for they are not mentioned in that letter. Judged according to 1 Cor. 16:1, the request for the Corinthians' participation in the collection followed directly after corresponding instructions to the Galatians.[139]

It is correct that Galatians does not say anything about the organization of the collection. The collection is nevertheless mentioned in Gal. 2:10b, and Paul's zeal, as stated above, is presumed to be something known to the Galatians. In view of the letter to the Galatians, the collection appears to have been fully under way until the opponents arrived. Georgi, however, denies both the organization of the collection and Paul's zeal in carrying out the collection at the time of the composition of Galatians.

Concerning the *organization* of the collection, Georgi writes, "There is no mention . . . of an organization of the collection, not even when he talks about the collection in his report about Jerusalem. If the collection had already begun in Galatia, one would expect there at least an 'as you know'" (pp. 32–33). This is a *petitio principii*. If the collection in Galatia was in full operation up to a short time before the letter, the reference to Paul's zeal is enough (it is a different matter with the "you have heard of my former life . . ." [1:13]; here Paul refers to a personal tradition), and everyone would understand Paul's reference. Also, in the face of overwhelming opposition, Paul had concerns other than the organization of the collection. The collection is not dealt with in Galatians because of the existing situation.

In denial of Paul's *zeal* for carrying out the collection at the time of Galatians, Georgi writes that when Paul says "which very thing I was eager to do," he means "clearly his zealous efforts for the completion of the second part of the agreement *after* the conference. Here he speaks of his zeal, however, as something of the past" (p. 30). According to this view, the collection was begun by Paul with zeal directly after the conference. Then it was broken off because of the incident in Antioch[140] but later renewed in Paul's independent mission after Paul had

84

won back the Galatians.[141] The first witness of this renewal is considered to be 1 Cor. 16:1.

The following four observations speak against this view.

1. Georgi's assumption that Paul was able to win back the Galatians through his letter is problematical. If Paul was unsuccessful— something that is more probable in light of the content and genre of the letter—then Galatians would have been written *after* 1 Corinthians. Otherwise the reference to the Galatians in the section about the collection (1 Cor. 16:1) would not be understandable, for one may conclude on the basis of this reference that the relationship between the Galatian congregations and Paul is intact. That is to say, in the event that Galatians was written before 1 Corinthians and that Paul lost the congregations, one could hardly understand how Paul could instruct the Corinthians to gather the collection together just as the Galatians were doing.

2. Galatians is noticeably similar to Romans. This observation, which makes it probable that Galatians was written shortly before Romans, may be defused only partially by reference, for example, to specific similarities between 1 Corinthians and Romans (1 Cor. 1:20 / Rom. 1:22; 1 Cor. 3:20 / Rom. 1:21; 1 Corinthians 12–14 / Rom. 12:3ff.; 1 Corinthians 8–10 / Rom. 14:1—15:6),[142] for the parallelism between the sections of the letters dealing with justification (Galatians 3/Romans 4; cf. also Gal. 4:1–6 with Rom. 8:2–16) not only relates the letters to one another but also separates them from all Paul's other letters[143] (with the exception of Phil. 3:2ff.).[144]

3. There are similarities in style and language between Galatians and 2 Corinthians 10–13, just as Borse has recently shown in detail.[145]

The most important common features are the following. *Language and structure*: Gal. 1:6–9 / 2 Cor. 11:4–5; *several specifics* (Damascus, oath, fourteen years): Gal. 1:17—2:2 / 2 Cor. 11:11—12:4; *terms*: *pseudadelphoi*: Gal. 2:4 / 2 Cor. 11:26; *katadouloun*: Gal. 2:4 / 2 Cor. 11:20; *katesthiein*: Gal. 5:15 / 2 Cor. 11:20; *aggelos*: Gal. 1:8; 4:14 / 2 Cor. 11:14; 12:7; *catalogs of vices*: Gal. 5:20 / 2 Cor. 12:20. In evaluating this last parallel for the temporal proximity of Galatians and 2 Corinthians, one should note the following point not mentioned by Borse. Borse sees that the two passages mentioned contain four vices in the same order within a longer list. But it should also be noted that three further vices in 2 Cor. 12:21, *akatharsia*, *porneia*, and *aselgeia*, which are somewhat set apart from the catalog in 2 Cor. 12:20, stand at the head of the list in Gal. 5:20, though here the order varies: *porneia, aka-*

tharsia, aselgeia.[146] The constant recurrence of standard vices in New Testament catalogs of vices does not undermine this argument, for the argument here does not deny this fact but rather proceeds solely from the *singular* agreement in the order of the vices (together with the other points mentioned above) to argue that Galatians and 2 Corinthians belong chronologically close together.

According to Borse, these findings "make sense only if the statements of the one letter were still alive in the thoughts of the apostle as he dictated the other, so that he was able to repeat these statements in the later writing in a varied but nevertheless surprisingly similar manner."[147]

4. In the passage already mentioned above, Rom. 15:26, Paul reports to the Romans that "Macedonia and Achaia have been pleased [*ēudokēsan*] to make some contribution for the poor among the saints at Jerusalem." If the collection in Galatia is supposed to have been undertaken in connection with the collection in Achaia (Corinth), why does Paul fail to mention Galatia here? Or had the collection from Galatia already been delivered? If this were the case, it is surprising that the Galatian collection is not mentioned even in 2 Corinthians 8–9, a section dealing with the collection which was composed before Rom. 15:26.[148] For this reason it seems highly probable that Paul was not able to report that the Galatians had decided to support the poor among the saints in Jerusalem because the collection in Galatia had been overthrown.[149]

If this *argumentum e silentio* (namely, that the collection was overthrown in Galatia) is accepted as justified in view of the absence of a reference to the collection from Galatia in Rom. 15:26 (and 2 Corinthians 8–9), then those who defend the chronological priority of Galatians over 1 Corinthians must explain how Paul is able to refer in 1 Cor. 16:1 to the (overthrown) organization of the collection in Galatia.[150]

It is most probable that Asia (Ephesus) did not organize a collection[151] because the apostle could not (any longer?) gain a foothold there. Paul's intimations regarding his persecutions in this locality (1 Cor. 15:32; 2 Cor. 1:8) should also be noted.

Thus, contra Georgi,[152] everything speaks in favor of the view that Galatians was written after 1 Corinthians.

The question raised at the beginning about the relationship of 1

Cor. 16:1ff. to Gal. 2:10[153] and about the antecedent history of the collection in Galatia should therefore be answered as follows. Gal. 2:10 and 1 Cor. 16:1ff. look back on an initiative for the collection in Galatia that had proceeded beyond the initial stage. It is presupposed by 1 Cor. 16:1ff. that detailed instructions about the manner of gathering the collection had already been given (there is evidently agreement about the "that" of the collection!). Paul's zeal for the collection, which is reflected in Gal. 2:10, is similarly understandable only if the collection in Galatia had already made some progress, and this fits well with 1 Cor. 16:1.[154] After this time we do not hear anything more about the collection in Galatia. Because it is not mentioned in Rom. 15:26 and 2 Corinthians 8–9, we are able to conclude with a degree of probability approaching certainty that the collection was overthrown in connection with the adversaries' opposition to Paul. Details about the time when the collection was instituted may be deduced only after an analysis of the progress of the collection in Corinth and on the basis of a comprehensive proposal for Pauline chronology developed on the basis of the letters (see below, pp. 107–8).

2.2.2 The Continuation of the Collection in Corinth: 2 Corinthians 8–9

The collection in Corinth has clearly progressed since the time of 1 Cor. 16:1ff. Paul is sending Titus (as a courier with 2 Corinthians?; see below, pp. 97–98) to Corinth so that he might complete the organization of the collection (2 Cor. 8:6). Paul exhorts the Corinthians "now to complete the deed so that your readiness in desiring it may be matched by your completing it out of what you have" (2 Cor. 8:11, tr.). The Corinthians "began to desire this a year ago" (8:10, tr.). "The *thelein* refers to the Corinthian inquiry presupposed in 1 Cor. 16:1–4, where Paul speaks of *hē logeia* as something with which the Corinthians are acquainted."[155] For this reason Paul was able to boast to the Macedonians of the Corinthians' willingness to raise the collection (9:2).

At the time of the composition of 2 Corinthians 8–9, Paul is in Macedonia. This is evident from 9:4, where he announces that he will arrive with some Macedonian brethren and where he asks the Corinthians to have completed the collection by the time of their arrival, "lest if some Macedonians come with me and find that you are not ready, we be humiliated—to say nothing of you—for being so confident" (9:4).

87

The division of 2 Corinthians 8 and 9 undertaken by D. Georgi following H. Windisch, and the characterization of these chapters as "The Letter of Recommendation for Titus and His Companions" (chap. 8) and "The General Letter for the Congregations of Achaia" (chap. 9), in no way does justice to the text. Is the view that chap. 9 encourages the completion of the collection while chap. 8 encourages that the collection be taken up again (Windisch, ad loc.; Georgi, *Geschichte der Kollekte*, 57) really an argument that could justify the division? The sending of Titus to Corinth to organize the completion of the collection (8:6) fits in well with the request for the collection to be completed when Paul arrives with the Macedonian brethren. One could almost construct an internal connection: Paul sends Titus to Corinth so that when he arrives with the Macedonian brethren the collection will have been completed.[156]

Beyond the reference to the advanced stage of the collection, the relative indication of the year ("what a year ago you began," 8:10), and the indication of Paul's location at the time of the composition of 2 Corinthians 8–9, these two chapters contain one further important piece of information relating to the history of the collection: Macedonia also sponsored a collection (2 Cor. 8:1–6a). Since Paul boasts to the Corinthians of the example set by the Macedonians, the beginning of the collection in Macedonia occurred probably not later than it did in Corinth. Paul evidently sought to correspond with the second part of the Jerusalem agreement through the organization of a collection also in the Macedonian congregations (Philippi, Thessalonica).

We may now summarize section 2.2 by a list of the events in their order.

1. Paul's initiation of the collection in Galatia, Achaia, and Macedonia
2. More detailed specification of the manner for gathering the collection (directly witnessed for Corinth and Galatia)
3. Breakdown of the collection in Galatia, continuation in Macedonia and Achaia
4. Completion[157] of the collection in Macedonia and Achaia (Rom. 15:26)

It should now be asked whether this list, which already indicates a specific order of events, may be expanded and made more specific through the use of topographical and chronological data, which was already surfacing above. In the following section, we shall review the texts just dealt with and examine them for chronological and topographical data.

2.3 TOPOGRAPHICAL AND CHRONOLOGICAL INFORMATION IN THE PASSAGES DEALING WITH THE COLLECTION IN PAUL'S LETTERS

2.3.1 1 Cor. 16:1ff.

In the immediate context of 1 Cor. 16:1ff., we find a statement that contains both topographical and chronological information. Paul writes in v. 8, "But I will stay in Ephesus until Pentecost." Pentecost here is the Jewish festival, for it is questionable whether a Christian Pentecost already existed at that time.[158] Lietzmann considers it best not to combine this passage with 1 Cor. 5:7b ("for Christ, our paschal lamb, has been sacrificed") in order to date 1 Corinthians as falling between Passover and Pentecost, for *etuthē* could "only be said of the one time at Golgotha and not of the ceremony of remembrance."[159] Nevertheless, 1 Cor. 5:7 assumes that the Corinthians are acquainted with Jewish Passover rites.[160]

As a whole, Lietzmann is not convincing in arguing that the nonexistence of a Christian Passover at the time of the composition of 1 Corinthians renders the terminology of the Passover in 1 Corinthians (combined with 1 Cor. 16:8) irrelevant for dating the letter. The presence of the recurrent Passover motif in 1 Corinthians (see the next note) is satisfactorily explained by the view that Paul "was at the time of writing engaged in preparations for, or in celebration of, the Passover."[161]

Other investigators conclude from 1 Cor. 16:8 that Paul was planning to spend the coming winter in Ephesus. In support of this view, Conzelmann (p. 296) evidently calls on 1 Cor. 16:9, where Paul supplies the following reason for remaining in Ephesus: "For a wide door for effective work has opened to me, and there are many adversaries." Against this view speaks (a) that Paul does not mention a plan to stay through a winter (on the contrary, see v. 6) and (b) that Paul is explaining why he is coming at Pentecost, which indicates that his arrival has been delayed, and in 1 Cor. 4:19 he announces that he will come soon. For Paul, the presence of "many" adversaries is a reason to persevere. Thus one may not read out of 1 Cor. 16:8 a plan to stay through the winter. Nevertheless, the following considerations regarding when and where the collection was initiated speak for a stay in Ephesus that was not too short and thus for Paul having spent a winter there. As the place from which the collection was initiated, only Ephesus really comes into consideration. The agitated travels between Corinth and Ephesus indirectly indicate that the collection was initiated from Ephesus, be it that Paul had mentioned the collection in the previous letter or that he had informed the Corinthians of the collection through a courier. How else than through the previous letter or through that messenger did the Corinthians learn of the place where Paul was staying and write a letter in return or send him their questions orally? (The assumption that Paul had changed his locality and had nevertheless received the Corinthian letter is more complicated.) A further reason in favor of a longer stay in Ephesus is found in 1 Cor. 15:32, if this brief statement ("What do I gain if, humanly speaking, I fought with beasts at Ephesus?") refers to a past imprisonment in Ephesus. In contrast to 2 Cor. 1:8, Paul here assumes that there is a certain distance between this event and his present situation.

As the result of this section, it may be said that 1 Cor. 16:8 was written in the spring in Ephesus and that Paul had spent at least one winter in this city. Paul's previous letter and the initiation of the collection thus derive from the preceding year.

2.3.2 Topographical and Chronological Data for Galatians?

In 1 Cor. 16:1, Paul mentions his description of the manner for gathering the collection in Galatia. Paul's description could have been included in a letter now lost, could have been transmitted orally by a personal acquaintance, or could have been given during a personal visit by the apostle. In contrast to the order of events in Corinth, it is possible that the initiation of the collection and the description of the manner for the collection occurred at the same time in Galatia. In the following it is requisite to examine, first, the only chronological reference in Galatians in order to use this as a basis for reconstructing Paul's visits to Galatia and for determining the time of the initiation of the collection.

Gal. 4:13: "You know it was because of a bodily ailment that I preached the gospel to you at first [to proteron]." In this sentence Paul refers to the founding proclamation in Galatia (see 1:8). The interpretation of to proteron is controversial. The interpretation of this phrase decides whether Paul's founding visit was his first and last stay in Galatia and thus whether the apostle had visited the congregations a second time. Should to proteron be translated "earlier" or "the first time"? The last possibility would necessarily presuppose that Paul had visited Galatia a second time. The first possibility would not necessarily include a second visit and could mean that Paul is referring to his first and only visit. When dealing with this question, we must refrain from the usual side references to Acts. Lexical considerations should be made first. "*Proteros* has surrendered the meaning 'the first of two' to *prōtos* and means only 'earlier'" (Bl.-Debr., sec. 62). This statement can hardly be maintained in its apodictic form,[162] all the more since there is no doubt that even *prōtos* should not always be translated as "the first of two." Consider *ta prōta erga*, which means "the previous works" in Rev. 2:5 (tr.; cf. 1 Tim. 5:12).[163]

Lexically, neither of the two views may be confirmed (see *proteros* in Bauer, *Lexicon*, 721–22). If a substantiated decision is possible at all, the criteria for the decision must be found in the context in Galatians itself.

Kümmel thinks that the expression *to proteron* here could not mean "the only previous time," for "in that case the introduction of this expression into Gal. 4:13 would be completely superfluous. 4:13 on the basis of the more usual meaning presupposes rather two visits of Paul to Galatia."[164] Borse objects to this explanation by saying that "the addition is sufficiently understandable if Paul intends to remind the Galatians emphatically of his visit, which lay some time in the past, meaning something like: 'but you remember how it was then as I preached the gospel to you in the weakness of the flesh.' In this case, however, one must assume that a relatively long period of time had elapsed between Paul's stay with the Galatians and the composition of Galatians."[165]

Neither opinion is satisfactory. Contra Kümmel, *to proteron* is sufficiently understandable as serving to contrast the situation then, when the Galatians did everything for Paul, with the present situation in which, according to Paul, they were on the verge of betraying him in an ignominious manner. On the basis of this same observation, it should be said, contra Borse, that a considerable period of time must not necessarily have elapsed between the founding visit and the present (only the contrast is important) and that the possibility of a second visit should not be excluded.[166] A glance at Phil. 4:15 and 2 Cor. 1:19 reveals how Paul can bypass all the secondary visits to refer to his first stays in Philippi and Corinth.

We conclude that even when *to proteron* is seen in the context of Galatians, the expression gives no indication of the number of Paul's visits to Galatia.[167] Even the time[168] of the mission—before or after the Jerusalem Conference—eludes specification on the basis of this text. That the mission in Galatia occurred *before* the conference was a result of our examination of Galatians 1–2 and may thus be assumed here.

One further bit of information important for chronology is found in the first half of Gal. 4:13. Paul preached the gospel to the Galatians "because of a bodily ailment." The founding of the Galatian congregations arose from the circumstance that Paul was forced to stay in Galatia because of sickness.[169] During this stopover, Paul undertook a mission. He was probably merely passing through to some other destination, or else he had come to Galatia for some unknown reason.

These considerations on Gal. 4:13 yield the following result regarding topographical and chronological data for the letter to the Galatians and the collection:

(The Galatian congregations were founded before the Jerusalem Conference.) The initiation of the collection and—what probably occurred at the same time in Galatia—specification of the manner for organizing the collection took place during a second visit by Paul or, less probably, through a lost letter or through oral instructions by a courier.

In the last two cases, Paul will have sent the message from Ephesus, where he had been staying already in the year prior to the composition of 1 Corinthians. If Paul initiated the collection and gave directions for its organization during a second visit, this will have occurred in the year prior to the composition of 1 Corinthians. Paul will have come to Ephesus by land and have passed through Galatia. That Paul could provide directions for the organization of the collection at the same time that he initiated the collection there, while in Corinth instructions regarding the manner for gathering the collection were imparted only at a second stage (after the "that" had been explained in the previous letter or by a messenger), is explainable on the basis that Paul was able to provide instructions for both during his personal visit to Galatia. Since Paul was not present at the time in Corinth, and since he had not been there for a considerable period of time, he had to be more careful with the Corinthians (and employ tact).

The chronological proximity of Galatians to Romans and 2 Corinthians was already demonstrated above on the basis of comparisons of style and language. More specific information about the time and place of the composition of the letter to the Galatians will be obtained after the following analysis of the chronological and topographical data of 2 Corinthians.

2.3.3 The Topographical and Chronological Data Presupposed in 2 Corinthians 8–9

We may proceed on the basis of the observation made above that at the time of the composition of 2 Corinthians 8–9 Paul is in Macedonia and is looking back on the initiation of the collection in Corinth in the preceding year. In the following, we must deal with (1) the route of the journey from Ephesus to Macedonia, (2) the organization of the collection in Macedonia, and (3) the meaning of the expression "a year ago."

2.3.3.1 THE ROUTE OF PAUL'S JOURNEY FROM EPHESUS TO CORINTH

When Paul states in 1 Cor. 16:8 that he intends to stay in Ephesus until Pentecost, he has already mentioned his plan to come to Corinth via Macedonia (v. 5) so that he might spend the winter in Corinth (v. 6). This winter can only be the winter of the same year (i.e., the winter following the Pentecost spoken of in v. 8), for otherwise Paul would have mentioned the long intervening period. (He speaks of "staying the winter" as if its meaning is evident and of his coming as lying not too far in the future.)[170] He is striving to have the collection completed at the time of his arrival:

(On the first day of every week, each of you should put something in the moneybag, as he may prosper,) "so that contributions need not be made when I come. And when I arrive, I will send those whom you accredit by letter to carry your gift to Jerusalem. If it seems advisable that I should go also, they will accompany me" (1 Cor. 16:2–4).

Prior to this time, Paul had sent Timothy to Corinth (4:17). The request for the Corinthians to receive Timothy well when he arrives (16:10–11) assumes that the letter will reach Corinth before Timothy, who had already set out. The only explanation for this state of affairs is that Timothy had taken the route by land (via Macedonia) while the letter was sent by sea.

In 2 Corinthians, Paul again writes about his travel plans:

2 Cor. 1:15–16: "I wanted to come to you first, so that you might have a double pleasure; I wanted to visit you on my way to Macedonia, and to come back to you from Macedonia and have you send me on my way to Judea."

A comparison with the plans in 1 Corinthians 16 shows that (a) the possibility that Paul would travel to Jerusalem to deliver the collection, which was left open in 1 Corinthians 16, has now become a definite intention; (b) the route planned for the trip to Corinth (again from Ephesus) had been changed; and (c) a double visit to Corinth had been envisioned. Paul wanted to travel directly to Corinth from Ephesus (instead of taking the route by land as reflected in 1 Corinthians 16), then to go to Macedonia, and then to come back to Corinth *again* in order to set out for Jerusalem from there.

In the immediate context of 2 Cor. 1:15–16, Paul has to defend himself against the charge of thoughtlessness (v. 17: *elaphria*) with regard to this decision, and a little later he writes, "But I call God to witness against me—it was to spare you that I refrained from coming to Corinth" (*pheidomenos hymōn ouketi ēlthon eis Korinthon*, v. 23).

What had caused Paul to refrain from a further visit to Corinth? Should the "further visit" be taken in reference to a second or a third visit? Information relevant to this question is provided by 2 Cor. 2:1: "For I made up my mind not to make another painful visit" (*to mē palin en lupē pros hymas elthein*). Evidently there had been a painful visit after the founding visit.[171] It was during this visit that Paul had been offended, and this visit was the occasion for the so-called letter of tears (cf. 2 Cor. 2:3–9; 7:8–12). The first part of the plan in 2 Cor. 1:15 ("I wanted to come to you first, so that you might have a double pleasure") was evidently carried out.[172] The apostle was offended during this visit and for this reason does not want to appear again before his congregation under similar circumstances.

In 2 Corinthians 1–2, Paul defends (a) the changed and already partially completed travel plans (instead of Ephesus—Macedonia—Corinth, now Ephesus—Corinth—Macedonia—Corinth) and (b) the fact that he has not come a further time (i.e., a third time) to Corinth. From this defense we may conclude: (a) The travel plans that had been changed from those in 1 Corinthians 16 and that had been partially carried out were the occasion of the Corinthians' accusation that Paul was vacillating ("With Paul the Yes and the No amount to the same"; see 1:17). (b) When Paul's intention to visit the Corinthians a third time—an intention Paul probably expressed during his second visit—did not materialize, there was a new occasion for the same accusation as above.[173] Paul counters this accusation with the response that he did not want to make another painful visit.

From what has been said, we obtain the following order of events:

The composition of 1 Corinthians in Ephesus
The journey from Ephesus to Corinth
The precipitate return
The composition of the letter of tears in Ephesus

After this, things turn out to Paul's advantage, and he begins preparation to come to Corinth for a third time (2 Cor. 12:14; 13:1).

How did it come to such a turn of events? After the return from the
second visit to Corinth and the composition of the letters of tears, Paul
went to Troas (2 Cor. 2:12) after having escaped a deadly dangerous situation in Asia (2 Cor. 1:8).[174] He then traveled to Macedonia, where
after some time he met Titus, whom he had failed to find in Troas (2
Cor. 7:6–7). Titus told Paul of the Corinthians' positive reaction to
the letter of tears. This reaction was the presupposition for the intended third visit and for the request for the Corinthians to complete
the collection, which no doubt had suffered during the quarrel between the apostle and the congregation. Paul is able to send Titus to
Corinth for a second time[175] because Titus and the unnamed brethren proved themselves to be free of greed during their first visit, which
was connected with the organization of the collection (2 Cor. 12:17–
18; cf. 8:6).

With regard to the question of the time of Titus's first journey to
Corinth, one may assume that Titus was the one who conveyed the
letter of tears. That his trip to Corinth was part of a detailed plan by
Paul is evidenced by the precise agreement about the time and place
for his return, which is clear from the fact that Paul was waiting for his
companion in Troas. Since in 2 Cor. 7:5ff. Paul speaks of Titus's return, of his hearty reception in Corinth, and of the resolution of the
situation that led to the letter of tears, one cannot but conclude that
Titus had taken the letter of tears to Corinth and that he was now able
to report to Paul in Macedonia of the change of feelings to Paul's advantage in Corinth.

If sufficient reasons for this initial assumption have thus been supplied, it is similarly certain that Titus's first visit to Corinth was also
connected with the collection (see above). The time of Titus's first
journey should be reckoned as, at the latest, during the summer of the
year in which 1 Corinthians was written.

These considerations yield the following order of events for Paul's
journey from Ephesus to Macedonia and for the organization of the
collection:

95

The sending of Timothy by land to Corinth
The composition of 1 Corinthians in Ephesus
The journey from Ephesus to Corinth (Paul's intervening visit)
The precipitate return
The letter of tears from Ephesus / The sending of Titus to convey the letter of tears, the suppression of the opponents, and the organization of the collection that had been drawn into danger
The deadly danger in Asia
The journey from Ephesus to Troas
The journey from Troas to Macedonia
The return of Titus from Corinth to Paul in Macedonia.

2.3.3.2 THE ORGANIZATION OF THE COLLECTION IN MACEDONIA

Since the two preserved letters to the Macedonian congregations, Philippians and 1 Thessalonians, do not contain any references to the collection, we must work from the other letters if we want to deal in the following with the organization of the collection in Macedonia. Paul's other letters report on the collection in Macedonia in two passages. In Rom. 15:26, Paul writes that Macedonia and Achaia had decided to help the poor among the saints in Jerusalem and that he is on the verge of taking their collection to Jerusalem (vv. 31–32). He is thus looking in retrospect at the completion of a collection of money in Macedonia. In 2 Cor. 9:4, Paul mentions a Macedonian legation that will accompany him to Corinth with the collection that had been gathered in the Macedonian congregations.

The statement in 2 Cor. 9:4, "lest if some Macedonians come with me and find that you are not ready, we be humiliated—to say nothing of you—for being so confident," is meaningful only if Paul expects that the Macedonians will come with their completed collection. Otherwise, they would themselves be humiliated, not just the Corinthians.

Paul is even able to report that the Macedonians participated in the collection of their own free will, without being urged (2 Cor. 8:3–4). While this sentence may not be pressed to mean that the collection there was not initiated by Paul or that there were absolutely no problems there,[176] it nevertheless indicates that the collection in Macedonia was by far not as problematical as it was in Corinth (note the order in Rom. 15:26: Macedonia, Achaia). Macedonia is like a calm between the renegade congregations in Galatia, Corinth (which had almost betrayed him), and Ephesus, where he could no longer set foot.[177] When we connect this general impression of the Macedonian congregations with the completion of the collection expected in 2 Cor. 9:4 and reported in Rom. 15:26, the probability increases for the *argumentum e silentio* that the collection in Macedonia occurred without complication.

The time and manner of Paul's initiation of the collection in Macedonia are evident from 1 Cor. 4:17 and 16:10, which presuppose that Timothy was sent to Corinth by land, that is, through Macedonia. This provides a further argument for the above thesis that the collection in Macedonia was less problematical than it was in Achaia. Paul was so certain of the Macedonian congregations that he sent Timothy on to the real center of problems, Corinth, rather than having him return to Ephesus to report on his reception in Macedonia.

It should be assumed that Timothy was sent to organize the collection during the spring of the year in which 1 Corinthians was written (this would mean, however, that a surprisingly short stay in Macedonia was planned) or, more likely, that he was sent in the summer or the fall of the preceding year and stayed the winter in Macedonia.

2.3.3.3 THE MEANING OF THE PHRASE "A YEAR AGO" (*apo perysi*, 2 COR. 8:10)

In 2 Cor. 8:10–11, Paul writes, "It is best for you now to complete what a year ago [*apo perysi*] you began not only to do but to desire, so that your readiness in desiring it may be matched by your completing it." The desire of the Corinthians had manifested itself in some action such as their inquiry regarding the organization of the collection. After the vacillations that resulted from the waxing influence of the opponents in Corinth and the related threat to overthrow the collection were subdued precisely through the success of Titus's mission, Paul encouraged the Corinthians finally to convert their readiness in principle for the collection into action. Since the time of the initiation of the collection in Corinth and the present situation, the year had changed.

It is difficult to determine which calendar Paul is using for his computation in this passage, the Roman calendar (where the year begins on January 1) or the Jewish-Oriental calendar (where the year begins in the fall). More important than the solution to this question is the observation that between the time of the initiation of the collection in Corinth and the time of the composition of 2 Corinthians 8–9 a winter had passed.[178] This is clear from the numerous and various events that had occurred after the composition of 1 Corinthians, as a glance at the list on p. 96 will show. It is probable that Paul remained in Ephesus during the winter following the composition of 1 Corinthians 16. From here he will have traveled to Troas in the spring, and he probably met Titus in Macedonia in the summer of the same year. The composition of 2 Corinthians, which followed this event, will then have occurred in late summer of the same year. This means that the expression "since last year" refers to the Corinthian letter or oral report in the spring of the previous year, when the Corinthians declared their intention to gather a collection. The two situations would perhaps be separated by a period of around sixteen months.

If one maintains the unity of 2 Corinthians for lack of a better solution, then one should postulate the same time for the composition of Galatians as for the composition of the last part of 2 Corinthians, chaps. 10–13, that is, late summer. The bad news from Galatia will have reached Paul not long after the arrival of Titus from Corinth.

From what has been said, it is clear that Titus spent the preceding winter in Corinth and that he will also spend the coming winter there in order to bring the collection to completion.

Paul remained in Macedonia for this winter and journeyed with the Macedonian brethren and their collection to Corinth in the spring/ summer. Here, during his third stay in this city, he would finally make completion of the Corinthian collection certain. Paul is evidently looking back on this in Rom. 15:26 (see above); that is, Paul wrote Romans in the following winter in Corinth[179] and traveled from there to Jerusalem in the spring. By this visit to Corinth, Paul fulfilled his original plan to stay the winter in Corinth (1 Cor. 16:6), though there had been some delays and changes. The possibility mentioned there in v. 4, that Paul himself would transport the collection to Jerusalem, had in the meantime become a definite intention (2 Cor. 1:16),[180] which the apostle maintained up to the time directly before his departure (Rom. 15:25).

The arrangement of Timothy's trips into the chronological framework presents no difficulties. Before 1 Corinthians was sent, Timothy had taken the route by land to Corinth, and Paul was expecting his return to Ephesus (1 Cor. 16:11). He then appears as a co-sender of 2 Corinthians and thus was evidently with Paul in Macedonia. He will have reported to Paul the inadequate effect of 1 Corinthians as well as the failure of his own mission. This will have formed the direct occasion for the apostle's unplanned intervening visit. Accordingly, it is clear that Timothy then stayed with Paul in Ephesus through the winter and that he thereafter accompanied Paul to Macedonia via Troas.

2.4 PRELIMINARY RESULT

In the following, we shall summarize the results of an initial step of the investigation, where the collection, as reflected in its various stages in Paul's letters, was used to establish a chronological framework (i.e., the "before" and the "after"), and the results of a second step, where the topographical and chronological data connected with the collection in Paul's letters were analyzed to help refine and fill out the framework. To provide an overview we shall employ a chart (what is less certain is placed in parentheses):

Fall	The sending of Timothy to Corinth via Macedonia; the previous letter to Corinth with instructions for the collection (or this latter through a messenger)
First winter	Paul in Ephesus, Timothy in Macedonia
Spring	Letter of the Corinthians with a question about the collection (or this by oral questioning)
Before Pentecost (around Easter)	1 Corinthians
Summer	After bad news from Corinth by Timothy, Paul's intervening visit to Corinth, precipitate return to Ephesus; the letter of tears and the sending of Titus to Corinth
Second winter	Paul in Ephesus (in deadly danger: 2 Cor. 1:8)
Spring	Paul's journey with Timothy to Troas, further journey to Macedonia
Summer	The arrival of Titus in Macedonia from Corinth; bad news from Galatia; the composition of 2 Corinthians 1–9, 2 Corinthians 10–13/Galatians; the sending of Titus (with 2 Corinthians) to Corinth to organize the completion of the collection
Third winter	Paul in Macedonia: completion of the collection there
Spring/summer	The journey to Corinth; Paul's third stay in Corinth; completion of the collection there
Fourth winter	Paul in Corinth: Romans

Two things had to be left out of this chart: the events before Paul's arrival in Ephesus and the events after his third stay in Corinth. The latter should be fairly clear. Paul probably effected his plans in Romans 15 and traveled to Jerusalem to deliver the collection in the spring. Research usually has a ready answer for the former issue. It states that Paul traveled to Ephesus after his founding visit in Corinth and after having previously founded congregations in Philippi and Thessalonica; soon after this, on the third missionary journey, Paul returned again to Ephesus and wrote 1 Corinthians.

It was shown above that this thesis must not seek support by combining Paul's own statements with those of Acts (see pp. 14ff.). Since this does not exclude the possibility that the letters reflect the chronological proximity of the apostle's activities in Greece to the stay in Ephesus, the following will examine the passages relevant to this possibility.

2.5 ON THE QUESTION OF A FOUNDING VISIT BY PAUL TO GREECE IN THE PROXIMITY OF THE STAY IN EPHESUS REFLECTED IN 1 COR. 16:1FF.

2.5.1 The Question of the Relevant Sources. On Method

So far we have reconstructed Paul's chronology by using the collection as an external criterion to obtain a chronological framework. We were able to arrange events in Paul's life on the basis of their relationship to the collection. The result was a relatively exact chronology of a period of three to four years in Paul's life that were devoted to organization of the collection. If we ask about the time of the founding of the Pauline congregations in Greece, the answer depends on the decision of whether Paul had been in Corinth long before the stay in Ephesus (1 Cor. 16:1ff.). If the stays in Corinth and Ephesus lie in temporal proximity, then it may be concluded, with a degree of probability that approaches certainty, that the European mission occurred during Paul's mission after the Jerusalem Conference, especially since Paul had been in Corinth only once before 1 Cor. 16:1ff. was written. According to this view, Paul departed from Corinth after this founding visit and took the ship to the place where he wrote 1 Corinthians, namely, Ephesus.[181] For this reason it should first be asked in the following what the letters that reflect Paul's organization of the collection (only 1 and 2 Corinthians are relevant) say about the founding of the Corinthian congregation and whether they contain indications of the temporal relationship of this founding visit to Paul's stay in Ephesus. If one assumes along with the conventional chronology that the founding of the Corinthian congregation stands in temporal proximity to the stay in Ephesus reflected in 1 Cor. 16:1ff., then it should be supposed that Paul would have said something in his letters about this relative proximity.

The letters that contain extensive remarks about the founding of the congregations in Greece and that were not employed up to now for reasons of method, 1 Thessalonians and Philippians, are also excluded for the time being from this stage of the investigation, for the concern here is with determining the interval of time between the organization of the collection and the founding visit. This question permits the use of only those letters that reflect *both* the collection *and* the founding visit. This is not the case for 1 Thessalonians and Philippians. Only if it should become clear that the two events lie temporally rather distant from another do we receive the right to employ the letters that speak about the founding visit without mentioning the collection and to ask whether, in light of these letters, a time other than that after the Jerusalem Conference should be assumed for the founding of the congregations in Corinth and Macedonia.

2.5.2 The Absence of Documentation in the Pauline Letters for the Temporal Proximity of the Founding Visit to the Stay in Ephesus

In several passages in the Corinthian correspondence, Paul speaks of the founding of the congregation. Paul planted, Apollos watered (1 Cor. 3:6). As a skilled master builder, Paul laid the foundation (1 Cor. 3:10). (Up to now) Paul could feed the Corinthians only milk (1 Cor. 3:2). The apostle came to the Corinthians in fear and trembling, but the proclamation occurred not with persuasive ploys but with the demonstration of the Spirit and of power (1 Cor. 2:4). As a father, he begat the Corinthians through the gospel (1 Cor. 4:15). The gospel was proclaimed by Paul, Silvanus, and Timothy (2 Cor. 1:19). Unfortunately, none of these passages supplies an answer to the question whether the congregation was founded a short time or a long time before the stay in Ephesus mentioned in 1 Corinthians 16.

Other observations make it likely that Paul had been absent from Corinth for a fairly long period after his founding visit. Paul had sent Timothy (1 Cor. 4:17). This action, the announcement of a sudden arrival (4:19), the reasons supplied for the extended stay in Ephesus until Pentecost (16:8), and the following observations render it probable that Paul had not been in Corinth for a long period of time: (1) Between the time of the founding visit and 1 Corinthians, Paul's previous letter and the Corinthian letter had been composed and had changed hands. (2) Apollos had evidently stayed in Corinth long after Paul had completed his first visit (1 Cor. 3:6). In the meantime, he had already made his way back to Ephesus and had been with Paul (1 Cor. 16:12). (3) The new, problematical situations, of which Paul learns by an oral report or that he is able to infer on the basis of the Corinthian letter, are conceivable only as having arisen after a relatively long absence of Paul. (4) In 1 Cor. 11:30, Paul assumes that "many"[182] have fallen asleep (*koimōntai hikanoi*) because of the abuse of the Lord's Supper that had arisen since his departure.

While these observations make it clear that a long time passed between the founding of the Corinthian congregation and the composition of 1 Corinthians, it remains to be demonstrated in a *positive* way that the founding visit occurred *before* the Jerusalem Conference. This thesis already appears somewhat more probable in the light of the following consideration.

We saw above that the collection was *not* instituted during Paul's first stay in Corinth. One possible argument against employing this finding for chronological questions, namely, that Paul did not mention the collection during the first visit for tactical reasons (being indulgent with the young congregation), does not hold water because the institution of the collection a little later could not help but produce the same effects and, owing to the apostle's absence, would have had less chance of success.

Any reference to 1 Thessalonians to show that Paul did not mention the collection during the founding of that congregation either is ruled out for reasons of method. It would first have to be demonstrated—solely on the basis of Paul's letters—that 1 Thessalonians was composed after the Jerusalem Conference.

The more likely preliminary assumption thus seems to be that Paul could bridge the subject of the collection for the poor only through a letter or a messenger, because at the time of the founding visit there was no reason to initiate the collection. That is, at the time of the founding visit the second part of the agreement at the conference in Jerusalem, which prescribed that the Gentile Christian communities should remember the poor, did not yet exist.

It has been shown above that Paul's stay in Ephesus at the time of the composition of 1 Corinthians 16 and the founding visit in Corinth should be viewed as being separated by a fairly long period of time. That there is no evidence that the collection was a topic during the founding visit in Corinth also speaks for dating the mission in Corinth before the Jerusalem Conference. For these reasons, we now have the right to ask in the following if the information on the founding visits in those letters that do not mention the collection provides indications of the date of Paul's European mission.

2.6 THE TIME AND THE CIRCUMSTANCES
OF PAUL'S MISSION
IN EUROPE

Phil. 4:10ff. enables us to gain an insight into the circumstances and the time of Paul's mission in Europe. In Phil. 4:10–11, Paul thanks the Philippians for a gift of money that the Philippian congregation sent him through Epaphroditus (v. 18): "I rejoice in the Lord greatly that now at length you have revived your concern for me" (v. 10). This support should be differentiated from the gifts Paul calls to mind retrospectively in vv. 15–16: "And you Philippians yourselves know that in the beginning of the gospel, when I left Macedonia, no church entered into partnership with me in giving and receiving except you only; for even in Thessalonica you sent me help a couple[183] of times" (tr.).

Verse 15 is usually read in light of 2 Cor. 11:8–9 (Paul does not accept money from the Corinthians; see already 1 Cor. 9:12, 15): "I robbed other churches by accepting support from them in order to serve you. And when I was with you and was in want, I did not burden any one, for my needs were supplied by the brethren who came from Macedonia." Since Paul is looking forward to a third visit to Corinth at the time of the composition of 2 Cor. 11:8–9 (2 Cor. 12:14; 13:1), and since the second stay was probably a short one, the support could have been brought to him only during the founding visit.

Is it permissible to combine Phil. 4:15 with 2 Cor. 11:8–9?[184] This combination is confronted with the following difficulties: (1) Phil. 4:15 speaks of support from Philippi, not from Macedonia. (2) Phil. 4:15–16 does not mention aid that was sent to Paul in Corinth, but only a couple of times in which it was sent to Thessalonica. On (2): This observation does not exclude the possibility that a gift was also brought to Corinth. Because Philippi was the only congregation from which Paul accepted money (in Thessalonica, as in Corinth, Paul held it to be important to be a burden to no one [see 1 Thess. 2:9], even though he had a right to accept money: cf. 1 Thess. 2:7 with 1 Cor. 9:6), this possibility is actually probable. Further, Phil. 4:16 sounds (*"even* in Thessalonica you sent me help a couple of times" [tr.]) as if the Philippian support in Thessalonica was just one example among others. On (1): Paul often employs the name of a province for larger cities in the province. In view of what was just said about 1 Thess. 2:9, Thessalonica is excluded as a possible origin for the aid mentioned in 2 Cor. 11:8–9. Since we know of Paul's special relationship with Philippi, the Philippian congregation is a possible origin. Paul's use of the plural ("I robbed other *churches*") is not an argument against this possibility. One must be aware here that Paul wants to emphasize the contrast: I robbed other congregations in order to be able to preach the gospel to *one* congregation, you.

In the light of all this, it is permissible to conclude that the Philippians assisted Paul during his (first) mission in Europe not only in Thessalonica but also in Corinth.[185]

A further circumstance of the Pauline mission in Greece may be determined from the reflections of 1 Thessalonians on the founding of the Thessalonian congregation. In 2:2, Paul mentions maltreatment and sufferings in Philippi. This short statement gives us a vivid picture of how Paul was not immune to attacks from governmental officials and from the Jews (?) despite his close relationship with the Philippian congregation. The list in 2 Cor. 11:23ff. reflects reality.

These indications of the circumstances of Paul's initial mission in Greece do not, of course, say anything about the date of the mission. The following will address this question. The key to a solution seems to be the exegesis of the statement mentioned above, Phil. 4:15: "In the beginning of the gospel, when I left Macedonia. . . ." Here Paul specifies the time of the first assistance by the Philippians. It occurred "in the beginning of the gospel." Research has two basic ways of understanding the phrase "in the beginning of the gospel" (a few other suggestions will be discussed in the footnotes).

(a) The majority of exegetes think that Paul formulates here from the standpoint of the Philippians: After I preached the gospel to you the first time (you sent gifts for me to Thessalonica).[186]

Dibelius, for example, translates "At the time of the beginning of the mission, when I started out from Macedonia, no congregation other than yourselves alone entered with me into a relationship of mutual exchange. . . ; you also assisted me in Thessalonica . . . ," and he explicates "in the beginning . . ." with the following words: "From the standpoint of the readers, 'when I made a beginning among you'; Paul adds in explanations: 'as I started out from Macedonia (i.e., from Philippi . . .).' Thus 4:15 probably refers to the mission in Philippi, 4:16 to that in Thessalonica."[187]

This thesis is not likely, because Paul connects "in the beginning of the gospel" not primarily with a mission in Philippi (even though this is certainly presupposed in 4:15) but rather with his *own* setting out from Macedonia ("when I left Macedonia").[188]

(b) For this reason others think that Paul formulates here from his own perspective and view this statement as reflecting the apostle's opinion that the mission on European soil was the real beginning of the gospel / proclamation of the gospel for Paul. The previous phase of the mission as an Antiochene delegate should not be considered proclamation of the gospel in the real sense of the words.[189]

Gnilka connects this thesis with the hypothesis that Paul's decision for a Macedonian mission was "determinative for his own activity from the beginning" (p. 177). Lohmeyer connects it with the following consideration: "When . . . Paul nowhere previously appears as the leader of a mission but rather as one commissioned alongside Barnabas, when a vision in a dream is supplied as the special reason for the passage to Macedonia, a consciousness of the historical importance of the passage to European soil is disclosed. . . . Everything that was achieved before this 'beginning of the gospel' simultaneously ceased . . . to exist" (p. 185).

Despite correct insights contained in the theses of Gnilka and Lohmeyer (see below), they are beset with untenable elements. Lohmeyer's statements suffer from an impermissible harmonization of Acts and Paul's letters. Gnilka should be asked how it happened that Paul worked in another locality for more than fourteen years when his actual goal was Europe.

Nevertheless, both investigators have correctly determined the point of reference for "the beginning of the gospel." They understand it as referring to Paul's setting out from Macedonia. "When I left Macedonia" would then relate to the Pauline mission that started out from Macedonia and that included the proclamation of the gospel in Achaia. In this period of the mission, called the "beginning of the gospel," the Philippians were the only ones who supported Paul financially. This is evident, even apart from Phil. 4:15, from the fact that Paul did not accept money from the congregations he founded in this same period (1 Thess. 2:9; 1 Cor. 4:12; 9:15). Paul probably would not have received any money anyway.

The expression "gospel" should be understood in our passage not as an absolute entity[190] but rather as a *nomen actionis*, and it should be translated as "proclamation of the gospel" (see Bauer, *Lexicon*, 318 [1.b]). The word "beginning" does not yet have the technical sense it assumed two generations later in the Lukan and Johannine writings. There it indicates the very beginning of the church.[191] Here it should be understood as a relative term indicating the *early* period generally. This means that in Phil. 4:15 the word should in no circumstances be pressed to mean "the very beginning."

Since Paul formulates primarily from his own perspective in Phil. 4:15 and not from the perspective of the Philippians,[192] *en archē tou euaggeliou* is best translated as "in the beginning of my proclamation of the gospel," for Paul views his mission in Greece which set out from Macedonia as the initial period of his evangelistic activity.[193] Since it is certain that Paul was active as a missionary before the conference, that he operated a Gentile mission independent of Antioch (Titus), and that he could hardly have designated a mission that began thirteen to seventeen years after his conversion as the beginning of his missionary activity, it should be concluded that Paul was in Greece before the Jerusalem Conference. This will have occurred within the thirteen years before the Jerusalem Conference that are briefly mentioned in Gal. 2:1 but not further explicated.

In view of Paul's relative understanding of *archē*, it is quite possible that Paul could have reckoned his provably prior activity in Arabia (uncertain), Damascus, Syria/Cilicia, and South Galatia (probable) to the initial period (i.e., the early phase) of his proclamation of the gospel. Since Christian congregations probably existed in these localities at a very early date, and since Paul does not want to preach "where Christ has already been named, lest I build on another man's foundation" (Rom. 15:20), it is understandable that Paul left Palestine/Syria soon after his conversion and came to Greece.[194] Here he was really able to lay a foundation (1 Cor. 3:10). He could allow others to build or plant on this. For example, he could allow Apollos to water (1 Cor. 3:6).

If Paul's mission that started out from Macedonia (and included Philippi) should thus be understood in general as an early stage of his evangelistic activity, then it is highly probable that 1 Thessalonians derives from that first phase of the European mission. While the absence of a reference to the collection in 1 Thessalonians already led us above to assume that this letter was not composed within the period in which Paul wanted to satisfy the second part of the Jerusalem agreement, the date suggested above becomes even more certain for the following reasons: (a) Phil. 4:15–16 presumes that a mission in Thessalonica was connected with the initial period of proclamation (v. 16), and (b) Paul looks in retrospect at the founding of the congregation in 1 Thessalonians. See merely 1:9–10, a summary of Paul's missionary sermon in Thessalonica, and 2:1, where Paul speaks about the acceptance he encountered in the Macedonian city.

As already mentioned above, the references in Philippians to the support that the Philippian congregation provided for Paul in Thessalonica (4:16) fit in well with the statements in 1 Thessalonians about Paul working day and night in Thessalonica (as in Corinth) and about him—so we may conclude—not receiving any financial aid from that congregation.

The first letter to the Thessalonians provides us with much information about the route Paul took during his founding mission in Greece. The apostle travels from Philippi to Athens,[195] sends Timothy from here to Thessalonica, and meets this assistant again at the place where 1 Thessalonians was composed, probably in Corinth. One will not go wrong in assuming that the Corinthian congregation had just been founded about the time 1 Thessalonians was composed.[196]

This positive proof that the founding visit to Corinth did not occur during the period in which the collection was being organized, but rather before the Jerusalem Conference, is a further argument against the thesis that Paul founded the Corinthian congregation shortly before his stay in Ephesus (at the time of the composition of 1 Corinthians). We can thus make the following suggestion about the route of Paul's journey to Ephesus.

2.7 PAUL'S ROUTE PRIOR TO HIS STAY IN EPHESUS AS PRESUPPOSED IN 1 COR. 16:1FF.

At the conference in Jerusalem, Paul and Barnabas promised to remember the poor. We know from Paul that he had striven to fulfill this second part of the agreement. Nothing indicates that we should either take away from or add to Paul's express assertion by assuming that his zeal had been suspended for a while. If one takes the literal meaning of *espoudasa* seriously, one can arrive only at the assumption that Paul soon got under way to his congregations in order to organize the collection, that is, to the Galatian congregations,[197] the founding of which arose from Paul's being sick, and to the Corinthian, Philippian, and Thessalonian congregations. On the way to these latter congregations and after his second visit to Galatia, he stayed the winter in Ephesus. Since "a door had opened" for him in Ephesus, he undertook the preparations for the collection in Corinth and Macedonia by sending out letters and messengers from Ephesus. On the basis of the existing references in the letters, we presented above a chronological sketch of this period, which spans three to four years. In the following, we shall add the data obtained in section 2.5–7 on Paul's activity before and directly after the Jerusalem Conference and also the data derived from Galatians 1–2. The following table can serve as a summary of a chronology reconstructed solely on the basis of Paul's letters.

2.8 SUMMARY

	Paul's conversion in/near Damascus
x years	Stay in Arabia
	Return to Damascus
2 years	(Probably in Damascus)
14 days	First visit to Jerusalem
y weeks	Journey to Syria and Cilicia
13 years	Mission with Barnabas there and in South Galatia. Founding visit to Greece: Philippi, Thessalonica, Corinth; founding of the Galatian congregations owing to sickness Incident in Antioch
z months	Second visit to Jerusalem: Jerusalem Conference; then the journey to organize the collection in the Pauline congregations
Summer	Paul in Galatia
Fall	Paul in Ephesus: mission; sending of Timothy to Macedonia and Corinth; previous letter to Corinth with instructions pertaining to the collection (or this latter through a messenger)
First winter	Paul in Ephesus, Timothy in Macedonia
Spring	Letter of the Corinthians with question about the collection (or this by oral inquiry)
Before Pentecost (around Easter)	1 Corinthians
Summer	After bad news from Corinth by Timothy, Paul's intervening visit to Corinth, precipitate return to Ephesus; letter of tears and sending of Titus to Corinth

108

Second winter	Paul in Ephesus (in deadly danger: 2 Cor. 1:8)
Spring	Paul's journey with Timothy to Troas, further journey to Macedonia
Summer	Arrival of Titus in Macedonia from Corinth; bad news from Galatia; the composition of 2 Corinthians 1–9, 2 Corinthians 10–13 / Galatians; the sending of Titus (with 2 Corinthians) to Corinth to organize the completion of the collection
Third winter	Paul in Macedonia; completion of the collection there
Spring/summer	Journey to Corinth; Paul's third stay in Corinth; completion of the collection there
Fourth winter	Paul in Corinth: Romans
Spring	Journey to Jerusalem in order to deliver the collection

2.9 OPEN AND HALF-OPEN QUESTIONS

The following problems have remained unsolved in various degrees.

(a) The question of the time of the founding of the Galatian congregations (nevertheless, even on the sole basis of the letters of Paul, the North Galatian hypothesis is more probable; see above, p. 138 n. 197 on Gal. 3:1). While it is certain that the Galatian congregations were founded *before* the Jerusalem Conference, there is absolutely no way of deciding whether this took place before or after the mission in Greece.

(b) The question of the chronological location of the incident in Antioch could be answered with a great degree of certainty when it was said that it occurred *before* the Jerusalem Conference. Nevertheless, its occurrence directly before the conference must remain a hypothesis.

(c) This last hypothesis would, however, provide an illuminative explanation of the occasion of the conference. In view of the fragmentary nature of our sources, caution should be exercised here. That the conflict which led to the conference arose in mixed congregations does appear very plausible.

(d) One further open problem pertains to Paul's relationship to the Antiochene congregation and to Barnabas. Even though we had to reject the inference that Paul and Barnabas's joint trip to Jerusalem should be explained by assuming that they were jointly active in the Antiochene mission, there remains the question of why both went up to Jerusalem and of which role Paul played in the conflict that arose in the mixed congregations and that led to the conference. If our hypothesis that the incident in Antioch gave rise to the conflict proves incorrect, then we may ask whether Paul went to Jerusalem to present the apostles in Jerusalem with the gospel he was preaching to the Gentiles primarily for theological reasons, that is, because of the importance he attached to Jerusalem. This action by the apostle, which would have arisen ultimately from his ecclesiology—his conviction about the unity of the church of Jews *and* Gentiles—would then have assumed, in connection with the Judaistic demands and Paul's taking Titus along, an eminently polemical function when the right of the Gentile church to exist (free from the law) and thus Paul's proclamation to the Gentiles were drawn into question by the demand for Titus to be circumcised.

If there were *both* a Pauline mission *and* an Antiochene mission prior to the conference, as was shown above to be probable, then no difficulties are involved in the supposition that Paul traveled to Jerusalem together with the representative of the Antiochene mission, in which he himself had worked for a short time. The mission to the Gentiles was a concern of both parties.

In conclusion we should recall once more the gaps in the chronology and biography of Paul that we still have and that cannot be filled out by use of Acts. In view of these gaps, our own inability to locate the exact chronological place of the founding visit to Galatia and of the incident in Antioch, as well as the difficulty in determining Paul's relationship to the Antiochene mission and to Barnabas, does not seem overly important. These problems are of even less importance since Paul himself presents the mission in Greece as the initial period of his proclamation as a whole and since this statement provides us with a good basis for the thesis that the European mission occurred not long after the first visit to Jerusalem.

NOTES

1. See P. Vielhauer, "Gesetzesdienst und Stoicheiadienst im Galaterbrief," in *Rechtfertigung*.

2. Markus Barth, "The Kerygma of Galatians," *Interp.* 21 (1967): 131–46. On J. Munck, *Paul and the Salvation of Mankind*, see the reviews by Rudolf Bultmann, "Ein Neues Paulus-Verständnis?" *ThLZ* 84 (1959): cols. 481–86; W. D. Davies, "A New View of Paul—J. Munck: 'Paulus und die Heilsgeschichte,'" *NTS* 2 (1955/56): 60–72 (= *Christian Origins and Judaism*, 179–98); Morton Smith, "Pauline Problems," *HThR* 50 (1957): 107–31.

For predecessors of Munck's thesis that the Galatian opponents were Judaizing Gentile Christians, see the list in John Gale Hawkins, "The Opponents of Paul in Galatia" (Ph.D. diss., Yale University, 1971), 21f. n. 1. In the first chapter, Hawkins presents an instructive history of research into the question of Paul's opponents in Galatia (pp. 5–85).

On W. Schmithals, "The Heretics in Galatia," in *Paul and the Gnostics*, 13–64, see the balanced criticism by R. M. Wilson, "Gnostics—in Galatia?" and the literature indicated there.

For the reconstruction of the opponents in the letters of Paul, see the extensive remarks in the second part of this trilogy, Gerd Luedemann, *Paulus, der Heidenapostel*, vol. 2: *Antipaulinismus im frühen Christentum*, FRLANT 130 (Göttingen: Vandenhoeck & Ruprecht, 1983), 103–61.

3. H. D. Betz (*Galatians*, 5–9 and throughout) arrives at the same result regarding Paul's opponents as does the present work. A very welcome aspect of Betz's commentary is that it finally raises again the question of the relationship of the Galatian opposition to so-called heretical Jewish Christianity (see the frequent quotations in the commentary from the *Pseudo-Clementines*) and consciously links up with the research of the Tübingen school.

4. So, correctly, A. Suhl, *Paulus und seine Briefe*, 21.

5. Contra Suhl, who excludes this possibility in words that I cannot understand: "Such an accusation would not be understandable from people who themselves are connected with Jerusalem" (*Paulus*, 21–22). In my opinion, it is clear that "in the larger context of Gal. 1f., Paul always has in view the accusation of dependency on *Jerusalem* decisions" (G. Klein, "Die Verleugnung des Petrus," in *Rekonstruktion and Interpretation*, 83 n. 205). See what follows in the text.

6. For the more detailed reasoning of what is presented here thetically, see the following and Luedemann, *Paulus*, vol. 2: *Antipaulinismus*, 144–52. On the position of the opponents, see the summary in F. Mussner, *Der Galaterbrief*, 11–32.

7. A. Seeberg, *Der Katechismus der Urchristenheit*. On the one hand, Seeberg's thesis of the existence of a comprehensive creedal formula between the years 30 and 35 C.E. was dismissed long ago. On the other hand, this thesis was a productive mistake insofar as the search for traces of this formula in the New Testament directed attention to the individual formulas. On this book, see K. Weiss, *Urchristentum und Geschichte in der neutestamentlichen Theologie seit der Jahrhundertwende*, BFChTh 40.4 (Gütersloh: C. Bertelsmann, 1939), 19–29.

8. See E. Stauffer, *New Testament Theology*, 338–39 (Appendix 3: Twelve Criteria of Creedal Formulae in the New Testament).

9. G. A. Deissmann, *Bible Studies* and *Light from the Ancient East*. See now Erhardt Güttgemanns, *Offene Fragen zur Formgeschichte des Evangeliums*, BEvTh 54, 2d ed. (Munich: Chr. Kaiser, 1971), 110ff.; and K. Berger, "Apostelbrief und apostolische Rede/Zum Formular frühchristlicher Briefe." In the U.S., P. Schubert's pioneering work *Form and Function of the Pauline Thanksgivings* and his important article "Form and Function of

the Pauline Letters" were followed by several important studies of Pauline and ancient letters by R. W. Funk and his students. A report on research may be found in W. G. Doty, *Letters in Primitive Christianity*. See also the survey and the references to literature in H.-M. Schenke and K. M. Fischer, *Einleitung in die Schriften des Neuen Testaments*, vol. 1 of 2 vols.: *Die Briefe des Paulus und Schriften des Paulinismus*, 26–35.

10. P. Wendland, *Die hellenistisch-römische Kultur in ihren Beziehungen zu Judentum und Christentum*, 342ff.

11. E. Norden, *Die antike Kunstprosa vom VI. Jahrhundert v. Chr. bis in die Zeit der Renaissance*, 2:492–510 and the supplement on pp. 3–4.

12. F. Overbeck, "Über die Anfänge der patristischen Literatur" (= *Über die Anfänge der Patristischen Literatur*; on the letters of Paul, see pp. 19–20).

13. See also E. Schwartz, *Charakterköpfe aus der antiken Literatur*: "Because the letters are not literary polemical writings but rather products of the moment . . . , they do not reveal their driving force, the pulse of the language, in a uniform way. Nevertheless, Galatians and Second Corinthians show with shocking clarity that Paul's defense of his personal missionary call, independent of all the men of repute in the primitive congregation . . . , turned Paul into the creator of a new body of literature. This occurred contrary to his will. He was not thinking of the succeeding generations as he wrote his epistles" (p. 121). "A figure of world history is not the apostle to the Gentiles but rather the author Paul" (p. 122). It is only a small step from this judgment to an evaluation of the form of these writings.

14. See the illuminative remarks of Johannes Weiss: "The word 'rhetoric' already awakes horror in every upstanding man who maintains something of the saying 'pectus facit theologum'" (*Die Aufgaben der Neutestamentlichen Wissenschaft in der Gegenwart* [Göttingen: Vandenhoeck & Ruprecht, 1908], 16). "Against the majority of expositors, one must object that they are willfully denying themselves an essential part of the process of understanding insofar as they consider it beneath their dignity to deal with the rhetorical form of their texts" (ibid., 19).

15. Nevertheless, it should be remarked that the protest described above came mostly from philologians (Overbeck is a special case), while theologians such as G. Heinrici (see his commentaries on the letters to the Corinthians) viewed Paul more strongly from the perspective of the Greeks. See G. Heinrici, "Zum Hellenismus des Paulus," in *Der zweite Brief an die Korinther*, 436–58. This is an important appendix directed against E. Norden's approach (see above, n. 11).

16. Essentially, every letter (and every document) of the New Testament requires the development of an arsenal of methods that corresponds to its particular nature. In this regard, see Ernst von Dobschütz, *Vom Auslegen des Neuen Testaments* (Göttingen: Vandenhoeck & Ruprecht, 1927), 16, 25.

17. H. D. Betz, "The Literary Composition and Function of Paul's Letter to the Galatians." See also H. D. Betz, "In Defense of the Spirit: Paul's Letter to the Galatians as a Document of Early Christian Apologetics," in *Aspects of Religious Propaganda in Judaism and Early Christianity*; and Betz, *Galatians*, 14–15.

18. According to Betz, perhaps only J. B. Lightfoot subdivided Galatians according to the categories of ancient rhetoric. Other examples of such a procedure might be found in the older (precritical) commentaries, for Quintilian's work on rhetoric was used in the schools and his *termini technici* may have been used in exegesis. Quintilian was valued already by Luther. See U. Nembach, *Predigt des Evangeliums*, 130ff. After "Poggio rediscovered the Institutio oratoria . . . in 1415 in St. Gallen, . . . [Quintilian] came to be viewed as the leading pedagogical figure of his time" (Hermann Weimer and Heinz Weimer, *Geschichte der Pädagogik*, SG 145/145a, 17th ed. [Berlin: Walter de Gruyter, 1967], 39). See now Betz, *Galatians*, 14 n. 97.

19. The most important handbooks of rhetoric are Quintilian's *Institutes of Eloquence*, Cicero's *Treatise on Rhetorical Invention*, and Pseudo-Cicero's *Treatise on Oration*. These are dependent on older Greek textbooks on rhetoric that are mostly no longer extant. An indispensable aid is H. Lausberg, *Handbuch der literarischen Rhetorik*. See, further, J. Cousin, *Études sur Quintilien*, vol. 1 of 2 vols.: *Contribution à la recherche des sources de l'institution oratoire*; J. Martin, *Antike Rhetorik*, and the literature indicated there; and G. Kennedy, *The Art of Rhetoric in the Roman World 300 B.C.—A.D. 300*, and the literature indicated there.

20. Betz is probably right: "The form of the letter is [only] necessary, because the defendant himself is prevented from appearing in person before the jury. Therefore, the letter must serve to represent its author. Serving as a substitute, the letter carries the defense speech to the jury" ("Literary Composition," 377). Gal. 4:18–20 shows that Paul considers it a disadvantage that he is not present.

21. Ibid., 357.

22. See Betz, *Galatians*, 50: "The entire 'body' of the letter is bracketed in by this conditional curse and blessing."

23. Betz's analysis cannot be checked here in every detail. The following is thus, to a certain extent, experimental. If Betz's analysis should prove wrong or in need of correction at certain points, this would by no means cause the collapse of the present chronology. At the crucial points, the same results can be and have been reached on the basis of other analyses. See below, pp. 125–26 n. 108.

24. In the report on the 1974 Society of New Testament Studies conference in Sigtuna, where Betz presented excerpts of his article, Karl Kertelge wrote: "In spite of much recognition [of Betz's presentation], questions remained: To what extent was Paul's working method 'literary,' or are there rather only ele-

ments of such a form that arise naturally from the material intention?" (*BZ*, n.s. 19 [1975]:157). In terms of the history of literature, the dichotomy "literary—natural" is misguided.

25. On this, see Wendland, *Kultur*, 347: "Not only is the title 'apostle' emphasized, but there is also an energetic protest raised against the manner in which some of the Galatians derive this title from human origin or from human mediation. He emphasizes that he is writing on the basis of the understanding of *all* the Christians who are with him in order to exclude from the outset the possibility of another view of the gospel. Then follows the cool *tais ekklēsiais tēs Galatias* without any of the usual additions. This is indicative of the relationship of the sender to the addressees. Then the greeting is supplemented in a special way through the statement that Christ gave himself up in order to deliver us from the present evil age. One senses that bad times have arrived in Galatia. After this oppressive tone in the prescript, where one can already hear the thunder roaring, lightning follows: the double anathema against anyone who preaches another gospel."

26. See K. Kertelge, "Das Apostelamt des Paulus, sein Ursprung und seine Bedeutung"; and idem, "Apokalypsis Jesou Christou (Gal 1,12)," in *Neues Testament und Kirche*, 267; P. von der Osten-Sacken, "Die Apologie des paulinischen Apostolats in 1Kor 15,1–11."

27. Gal. is, so to speak, "sealed" with a curse that applies to any Christian who deviates from the *one* gospel of Paul. Hence, Betz characterizes Gal. as a *magical letter*. See Betz, "Literary Composition," 379; and Betz, "Defense," 112–13.

28. E. Käsemann, "Sentences of Holy Law in the New Testament," in *New Testament Questions of Today* (on Gal. 1:9, see p. 70).

29. With regard to Gal. 1:11, notice should be taken of the variant reading offered by P⁴⁶, ℵ *, A, and the majority text, *gnōrizō de*. Which reading is the *lectio difficilior* is uncertain.

30. Bauer, *Lexicon*, s.v. "Peithō," does not decide between "win over" and "persuade" for our passage. On the proposal to translate *peithein* in a positive sense and *areskein* in a negative sense, see below, n. 32.

31. The expression "ironical both this and that" indicates, on the one hand, that "persuade" and "please" stand in tension with each other (and both should actually not have been usable by the same group as accusations against Paul), for in persuasion the speaker changes the hearers while in pleasing the speaker accommodates himself to the hearers. On the other hand, a negative view of Paul would have held his art of persuasion to be something employed only when he could please the hearers with it. Persuasion and pleasing would thus be presented as the essence of swindling.

32. The attempt has been made to extract a positive meaning from *peithein ton theon*. The meaning of v. 10 would then be something like "I, Paul, refuse to persuade men but rather make God well-disposed." However, no one

yet has been able to explain what making God well-disposed would have involved in Paul's understanding. Further, it is awkward to attribute to *peithein* first a negative sense and then a positive sense when the word itself is not repeated.

R. Bultmann's proposal of the inverse explanation would yield the following paraphrase: "I, Paul, want to win over people and refuse to convince God and to please people" ("Peithō," *TDNT* 6:10–11). He must wrestle with the same problems as does the previous proposal (double meaning of *peithein*). There is also another problem: Bultmann's presupposition, that *peithein tous anthrōpous* characterizes legitimate apostolic proclamation, is indefensible. It cannot find support in the controversial passage 2 Cor. 5:11 (see n. 33, below).

33. 2 Cor. 5:11 is not a clear witness for a positive use of *peithein*, for this verb is immediately relativized in the following clause, *theō de pephanerōmetha*.

34. Cf. Ignatius, *R.* 3:3: "Christianity is a matter not of persuasion but of greatness" (tr.). See also *Treatise on Resurrection*, Nag Hammadi Codex 1.46.4–7, in *The Nag Hammadi Library in English*, ed. James M. Robinson (New York: Harper & Row, 1977), 51.

35. See, further, Plato, *Resp.* 390 E: "Gifts move the gods." This saying was understood in a negative sense at the latest by Plato, as the context shows: "It is certain that we cannot allow our men to be acceptors of bribes or greedy for gain. By no means. Then they must not chant: Gifts move the gods and gifts persuade dread kings." For this saying, see also Euripides, *Med.* 964: "Gifts sway the gods"; Pindar, *Olymp.* 2.144; from Latin-speaking areas: Ovid, *Ars* 3.653: "Munera, crede mihi, capiunt hominesque deosque" ("Gifts, believe me, win over both humans and gods," tr.). See A. Otto, *Die Sprichwörter und sprichwörtlichen Redensarten bei den Römern*, 233.

Also in Josephus, *Ant.* 4.123, the attempt to *peithein ton theon* by Balak and Balaam (Num. 23:13) in order to bind Israel with a curse should be understood in a negative sense, and the verb should be translated as "to cajole." *Ant.* 8.255–56 might, in contrast, present a neutral use of *peithein*.

On the whole issue of the relationship of charlatans and philosophers, see W. Burkert, "GOĒS: Zum griechischen 'Schamanismus'"; and H. D. Betz, *Der Apostel Paulus und die sokratische Tradition*, 33–34, the literature cited there, and 132ff.

36. Suhl, *Paulus*, 22.

37. *Anthrōpois areskein* should undeniably be negatively understood not only in this passage but also in 1 Thess. 2:4. The verb *areskein* is used by Paul in a positive sense (1 Cor. 10:33; Rom. 15:2) as well as in a negative sense (1 Cor. 7:33f.).

38. On this, see the commentary by P. Steinmetz, *Theophrast: Charaktere II*, Das Wort der Antike 7.2 (Munich: Max Hueber, 1962), 73ff.

39. For our treatment of *areskein*, the references by J. J. Wettstein in *HĒ KAINĒ DIATHĒKĒ: Novum Testamentum Graecum*, ad loc., were gratefully employed and were supplemented with other references.

40. According to Suhl (*Paulus*, 36), for example, vv. 13ff. are supposed to rebut the accusation behind v. 10 that Paul had strayed from the Jerusalem gospel in an impermissible way in order to please people.

41. Betz's exegesis of Gal. 1:10 (*Galatians*, 54ff.) agrees with the above exegesis and provides further justification for it. The only differences are that Betz understands *eti* in a temporal sense (p. 56) and that he leaves open the possibility that Paul had been accused of being a "man pleaser."

I differ from Betz in thinking that Paul employs the rhetorical questions in Gal. 1:10 to attack his opponents indirectly (cf. Gal. 5:11; 6:12). In light of the above presentation, the much-discussed *eti* should be understood not in a temporal way but in a cumulative sense, emphasizing that the opponents are presently pleasing men. The statement should be paraphrased as follows: "If I were, *on top of it all*, trying to please men as my opponents are doing. . . ."

42. Betz, "Literary Composition," 360.

43. The other possible conclusion on the basis of these findings, namely, that Paul left out events because they would have weakened his case, cannot be maintained exegetically because of other considerations that will be taken into account below. This possibility has been mentioned for the sake of completeness.

44. See, e.g., Isocrates, frag. 6 (Benseler and Blass, eds., p. 275); *Rhetorica ad Herennium* 1.9.15; Cicero, *De Orat.* 2.80.329.

45. Betz, "Literary Composition," 366–67, creates such an impression when he writes, "Quintilian disagrees with the general rule that the order of events in the *narratio* should always follow the actual order of events" (see idem, *Galatians*, 61). The passage in Quintilian, however, reads "ne eis quidem accedo. . . ." On the basis of this passage, it may not be concluded that those rhetoricians whom Quintilian does not follow represent the "general rule." See J. Cousin, "Théorie de la Narration," in his *Études*, 229–44. Dionysius of Halicarnassus, *De Isaeo* 15.615, also speaks in favor of using the *ordo artificiorum* in the *narratio*.

46. Contra C. Burchard, *Der dreizehnte Zeuge*, 50 n. 37, I do not think that *hēmas* in Gal. 1:23 should be taken as in reference to Judaean Christians and that it thus witnesses to persecution by Paul in Jerusalem, as Burchard would like to think. Our view is shared by K. Löning, *Die Saulustradition in der Apostelgeschichte*, 52. See also G. Strecker, "Befreiung und Rechtfertigung," in *Rechtfertigung*, 428f. n. 10.

47. In passing, we should remark that Paul apparently never of his own will speaks about himself; he does this when he is forced to by accusations from his opponents (see esp. 2 Cor. 11–12). Phil. 1 is a noteworthy exception. It is a different question whether traditions about his person were current fairly soon

in the Pauline congregations (see our proof of such in Gal. 1–2, below, pp. 69ff.).

48. On this schema, see P. Tachau, *"Einst" und "Jetzt" im Neuen Testament.*

49. In this passage, Paul understands "Syria and Cilicia" as one entity, as is shown by the common word governing both these genitives. See, correctly, J. B. Lightfoot, *The Epistles of St. Paul*, vol. 2, pt. 3: *St. Paul's Epistle to the Galatians*, 85: "The words *ta klimata* seem to show that 'Syria and Cilicia' are here mentioned under one general expression, and not as two distinct districts." The repetition of the article before *Kilikias* (notice, however, the vl.) does not necessarily contradict this. See also G. B. Winer, *A Treatise on the Grammar of New Testament Greek*, 159–63, esp. 159–60; Friedrich Blass and Albert Debrunner, *Grammatik des neutestamentlichen Griechisch*, rev. F. Rehkopf, 14th ed. (Göttingen: Vandenhoeck & Ruprecht, 1976), sec. 276.2, p. 226. Paul "does not at all want to indicate here the route he traveled" (F. Sieffert, *Der Brief an die Galater*, 72). This linguistic observation is supported by the historical fact that, at the time of Paul, Syria and Cilicia (*campestris*) were one Roman province (see above, p. 14 with n. 50). On this, see also E. M. B. Green, "Syria and Cilicia—A Note," *ET* 71 (1959/60): 52–53. The western part of Cilicia was counted as part of the province Galatia. See A. H. M. Jones, *The Cities of the Eastern Roman Provinces*, rev. Michael Avi-Yonah, 2d ed. (Oxford: Clarendon Press, 1971), 213, 439. The above explanation assumes that Paul also employs names of Roman provinces in matters of geography. In the light of 1 Cor. 16:19, 2 Cor. 1:8, and other passages (Gal. 1:2 differs), there should be no doubt about this point. The problem is nevertheless in need of further clarification. On this, see the important remarks by Marie Joseph Lagrange, *Saint Paul: Épître aux Galates*, 2d ed., EtB (Paris: J. Gabalda, 1950), xxii–xxiii. I am convinced neither by the assumption of W. M. Ramsay, *Pauline and Other Studies in Early Christian History*, that Paul always uses the names of the provinces nor by the assumption of Suhl (*Paulus*, e.g., 28 n. 3) that Paul exclusively uses the names of regions.

50. Even the stations "Arabia—Damascus" do not contradict the above, for the statement "and again I returned to Damascus" implicitly contains the negation "even this time I did not go to Jerusalem."

51. J. Weiss, *Earliest Christianity* (1970 ed.), 1:204. Weiss, however, excludes Greece as a possibility for the mission after the first visit to Jerusalem (ibid.), though he gives no reasons for doing that. See further, J. Knox, *Chapters in a Life of Paul*; H. L. Ramsey, "The Place of Galatians in the Career of Paul," 171–72; and Betz, *Galatians*, 84: "Paul does not reveal how long he stayed in Syria and Cilicia."

52. See M. Dibelius and W. G. Kümmel, *Paul* (Philadelphia: Westminster Press, 1953), p. 59, on Gal. 1:21: "In that very general indication, all the

emphasis is on negation; he was not in Jerusalem." Dibelius and Kümmel then use the information of Acts 13–14 to determine Paul's routes between the first and second visits to Jerusalem.

53. Munck, *Paul*, 101 n. 1, distorts the situation when he says that Paul's statements have the nature of an alibi. An alibi seeks to present positive proof of a stay in particular places. Paul's emphasis is: I was not in Jerusalem. Also incorrect is D. R. Catchpole, "Paul, James, and the Apostolic Decree," who thinks that Paul intended to say "where he was when he was not" in Jerusalem (p. 438). See Weiss, *Christianity*, who appropriately remarks that Gal. 1:21 has "merely the negative purpose of showing that he had removed himself far from the 'sphere of influence' of the original Apostles" (1:203). In contrast to this, see H. Kasting, *Die Anfänge der urchristlichen Mission*, who as many before him and after him defends the thesis that Gal. 1:21 shows that Paul stayed in Syria and Cilicia for thirteen years. He writes, "According to his own witness in Gal. 1, he [Paul] did not undertake any extensive journeys up to the time of the Apostolic Council" (p. 106). Aside from the fact that Kasting operates with the Lukan schema of the three missionary journeys (pp. 106–7), it should be objected that Kasting employs an *argumentum e silentio*. Paul does not say where he spent these thirteen years. Further, one can argue inversely that if the Galatian congregations were founded before the conference and after the mission in Cilicia, Paul did not need to indicate further locations of his activities, for these would have been known tc his congregations. On this, see also Ramsey, "Place of Galatians," 174. Admittedly, it is as impossible to draw this conclusion on the sole basis of Gal. 1:21 as it is to draw Kasting's widely disseminated conclusion that Paul worked for thirteen years in Syria and Cilicia. There are, however, other reasons that speak for the existence of the Galatian congregations before the conference.

54. Since the ancient mode of reckoning included years that had been only partially involved, one may strictly count only $x + 1 + y$ years (applied to the statement "after fourteen years": $x + 12 + y$ years). In the recurrent references to three and fourteen years in the following, this distinction will go unmentioned. Account will be taken of it in the summary, where we shall reckon with two and thirteen years. See below, p. 172 with n. 103.

55. Suhl, *Paulus*. The page numbers are supplied in the text.

56. Was *dia* occasioned by the fourteen years (instead of three years)?

57. The same view is taken by R. Jewett, *A Chronology of Paul's Life*, 52–53.

58. H. Lietzmann, *An die Galater*, 8.

59. Lightfoot, *Galatians*, 102; H. Schlier, *Der Brief an die Galater*, 64–65; P. Bonnard, *L'Épître de Saint Paul aux Galates*, 35–36.

60. See Ramsey, "Place of Galatians," 165, who then rejects this proposal without reason. On the possibility of the above thesis, see also W. F. Orr and J. A. Walther, *1 Corinthians*, 7; and Betz, *Galatians*, 76 n. 191.

61. Weiss, *Christianity*, 1:203 n. 1: "In view of the 'then after' (*epeita*) of Gal. 2:1, so pointedly contrasted with what precedes, it seems more natural to count the years from the last mentioned event."

62. Betz, *Galatians*, 83, also considers Gal. 1:21 to be the referent of the *epeita* in Gal. 2:1. He continues, "This connexion, to be sure, increases the difficulty of using the 14 years for an establishment of a Pauline chronology" (pp. 83–84).

63. This view is taken by U. Wilckens, "Der Ursprung der Überlieferung der Erscheinungen des Auferstandenen," in *Dogma und Denkstrukturen*, 72 n. 41.

64. G. Klein, "Galater 2,6–9 und die Geschichte der Jerusalemer Urgemeinde," *Rekonstruktion und Interpretation*, 118–19.

65. E. Dinkler, "Der Brief an die Galater: Zum Kommentar von H. Schlier," *Signum Crucis*, 282.

66. Wilckens, "Ursprung," 73 n. 41.

67. P. Stuhlmacher, *Das paulinische Evangelium I: Vorgeschichte*, 95.

68. Ibid., 96.

69. In agreement with G. Strecker, *Handlungsorientierter Glaube*, 21, I think that 1 Cor. 14:33b–35 (36) is perhaps an original part of 1 Cor.

70. See the proof by H. D. Betz, "Spirit, Freedom, and Law," 148.

71. O. Michel, *Der Brief an die Römer*, ad loc.

72. On the formulas analyzed in the text, see also M. Bouttier, "Complexio Oppositorum"; D. Lührmann, "Wo man nicht mehr Sklave oder Freier ist," 60ff.; and R. Gayer, *Die Stellung des Sklaven in den paulinischen Gemeinden und bei Paulus*.

73. See Stuhlmacher, *Evangelium*, 96: "For Paul there is . . . only one gospel, the one revealed and commissioned to him by God" (Stuhlmacher has this in spaced print).

74. For this reason, Wilckens is in a sense right when he objects, "The formulation of Gal. 2:7f. [is] . . . thoroughly marked by the (irremovable) first-person singular (of Paul!)" ("Ursprung," 72 n. 41).

75. Ibid.

76. A result of the following analysis is that one must take into consideration, more than has been done previously, the existence of personal tradition(s) about the leading figures of early Christianity even in the earliest period. With respect to this matter, I am able to agree totally with the programmatic theses of Jacob Jervell, "The Problem of Traditions in Acts," in *Luke and the People of God*, 19–39, and would like to draw attention to these theses. However, our finding above does not mean that it is possible to delineate exactly the traditions in Acts. Jervell (ibid., 36) evidently considers this to be possible (contra Dibelius). On this article by Jervell, see also Burchard, *Zeuge*, 20.

Above, I have used the term "personal tradition" in a descriptive manner. It would be desirable to develop a form-critical definition of this term, with consideration also being given to non-Christian personal traditions.

77. See, however, G. Strecker, "Das Evangelium Jesu Christi," in *Jesus Christus in Historie und Theologie*, 503–548, esp. 526–27, and the literature cited there. Recently, H.-M. Schenke, "Das Weiterwirken des Paulus und die Pflege seines Erbes durch die Paulus-Schule," has attempted to remove the tension between vv. 7–8 and v. 9 by dismissing vv. 7–8 as a gloss (p. 517). See also Schenke and Fischer, *Einleitung*, 79–80. For criticism of this thesis, which was already promoted by Barnikol, see Strecker, "Evangelium," 526–27 n. 102.

78. I think that Klein ("Galater 2,6–9") is basically right when he says that on the basis of this order and its tension with v. 7 one should conclude that a change of power had taken place in the primitive congregation or that "vv. 7f. and v. 9 reflect the state of authority in Jerusalem at different times" (Klein, "Verleugnung," 81). In my opinion, however, the change of power had already occurred before the conference and was an accomplished fact at the conference (this view is also held by O. Cullmann, *Peter: Disciple, Apostle, Martyr*, 42–43). Klein's interpretation, which sees the change of power as having occurred between the conference and the composition of Galatians, is confronted with the difficulty that the change would have had to have taken place within a relatively short period (ca. two years). Further, Klein's interpretation of *ēsan* is not convincing. According to Klein ("Galater 2,6–9," 112–113), "*dokountes* . . . [should] be taken in reference to the present ('those who are of repute today'), and the clearly constructed imperfect sense of the parenthesis with *ēsan* stands in reference to the state of affairs at the time of the conference." Against this: (1) *ēsan* derives from *attractio temporis* and can be translated in the present (see E. Schwyzer, *Griechische Grammatik*, vol. 2 of 3: *Syntax und syntaktische Stilistik*, 279). The imperfect was occasioned by the report, which deals with something in the past (see Mussner, *Galaterbrief*, 115–16). (2) *pote* may not be translated as "once" (see Bl.-Debr., 14th ed., sec. 303.2, p. 251) and is thus not able to support Klein's expressly imperfect understanding of *ēsan*, namely, that it refers to the power structure at the time of the conference. For criticism of this thesis by Klein, see also W. Schmithals, *Paul and James*, 83 n. 13; Kasting, *Anfänge*, 78 n. 78.

79. W. D. Davies, *The Setting of the Sermon on the Mount*, 454.

80. The view that Gal. 2:7b–8 reflects *Paul's* attempt to provide a new interpretation of the agreement formulated at the conference (v. 9) (thus E. Haenchen, "Petrus-Probleme," in *Gott und Mensch*, 1:55–67, esp. 62) breaks down because Paul elsewhere never employs the name *Petros*. Further, it would be a curious anachronism if Paul were to have introduced this new interpretation as the *reason* for the agreement with the pillars (see v. 7: "When they saw that I had been entrusted with the gospel to the uncircumcised, just

as Peter had been entrusted with the gospel to the circumcised . . . , [v. 9] they . . . gave to me . . . the right hand of fellowship"). On vv. 7–8, see above, pp. 64ff.

81. W. Bousset, "Der Brief an die Galater," 37. Correctly, Ramsey, "Place of Galatians," 173.

82. So again J. Gunther, *Paul: Messenger and Exile*, 51–52.

83. On the problem, see B. W. Bacon, "The Reading *hois oude* in Gal. 2:5"; and C. K. Barrett, "Titus," in *Neotestamentica et Semitica*, 1–14.

84. On this verb, see E. W. Burton, *A Critical and Exegetical Commentary on the Epistle to the Galatians*, 89–91.

85. D. Georgi, *Die Geschichte der Kollekte des Paulus für Jerusalem*, 19–20. So also A. Strobel, "Das Aposteldekret in Galatien," 184–85. Strobel thinks that the Galatian disturbances arose because of the decree (against this: the issue in Galatia was circumcision!), and he speculates that Paul later revised his initial rejection of the decree (ibid., p. 189).

86. Stuhlmacher, *Evangelium*, 99, is correct here and gives examples of the incorrect interpretation described above.

87. This view is shared by W. Schmithals (*Paul*, 45), Cullmann (*Peter*, 45–46), and Betz, *Galatians*, 100. Stuhlmacher, *Evangelium*, rejects this interpretation and says rather that "the world that was to be missionized [was divided] from eschatological perspectives into missionary spheres" (p. 99). Are the implications of this view really any different?

88. C. Andresen phrases well when he speaks of "purposeful subdivision of the missionary field" (*Geschichte des Christentums*, vol. 1: *Von den Anfängen bis zur Hochscholastik*, 1).

89. On God-fearers, see Kasting, *Anfänge*, 22ff.; and F. Siegert, "Gottesfürchtige und Sympathisanten."

90. See K. G. Kuhn and H. Stegemann, "Proselyten," *Pauly-W.*, supp. 9: cols. 1248–83, esp. col. 1282:27ff. Critical research stands in a consensus that Paul's stereotyped initial visits to the Jews in the reports of Acts reflect a Lukan schema and, at least in this exclusive manner, have nothing in common with Paul's missionary method.

91. Neither 1 Cor. 9:20 nor 2 Cor. 11:24 reflects a mission among the Jews. Wayne A. Meeks (*The First Urban Christians: The Social World of the Apostle Paul* [New Haven and London: Yale University Press, 1983], p. 26) curiously regards these passages as evidence of such a mission.

92. H. Conzelmann and A. Lindemann, *Arbeitsbuch zum Neuen Testament*, 413. Similarly, Betz appropriately says, "The agreement also meant the sacrifice of the unity of the church" (*Galatians*, 82; cf. 100–101).

93. See M. Dibelius, *From Tradition to Gospel*, 30: "In consequence of the fact that proselytes and 'God-fearers' had been received into these Churches, the boundary between Gentiles and Jews was not unsurmountable." See also Conzelmann and Lindemann, *Arbeitsbuch*, 413.

94. H. Conzelmann, A *History of Primitive Christianity*, 183.

95. Conzelmann and Lindemann, *Arbeitsbuch*, 413.

96. Ibid.

97. See E. Hirsch, "Petrus und Paulus," 65. Similarly, F. Hahn, *Mission in the New Testament*, 72–73. See, further, the representatives of this view mentioned by E. Haenchen, *The Acts of the Apostles*, 468, and, most recently, Catchpole, "Apostolic Decree," 442. Haenchen (*Acts*, 468–69) warns against too quickly combining the decree in Acts 15:24ff. with the scene reported in Gal. 2:11ff. It should also be noted that the four prescriptions of the decree do not deal exclusively with table fellowship between Jews and Gentiles. With regard to such table fellowship, one would expect there to be regulations governing pork and libatory wine. Luke will, however, have gotten the decree, together with the addressees (Antioch, Syria, Cilicia), from a source and not from Gentile Christianity of his time (contra ibid., 470). Gentile Christianity of his time was no longer faced with the problem of mixed congregations (H. Conzelmann, *Die Apostelgeschichte*, 93) and the decree was no longer in effect.

We cannot enter into the discussion of the relationship of Acts 15 and Gal. 2 (see the commentaries). Our concern was to reconstruct the events of the conference on the sole basis of the primary source. I think that I have shown, nevertheless, that for *internal* reasons the conference must have produced an agreement for the mixed congregations that was similar to the Apostolic Decree and that regulated the common life of Gentile and Jewish Christians. In light of this insight, Acts 15 needs to be reanalyzed. Despite the reservations expressed above, the decree in Acts 15 will have been related in the history of traditions to the decree formulated at the conference. It may be remarked in passing that no prescriptions regarding food were necessary in Jerusalem, for nothing that was forbidden ever came to the table there.

98. A decisive assumption of the above reconstruction is that the Antiochene congregation was a mixed congregation. I consider this assumption to be completely certain, since Gal. 2:13 presupposes that resident Antiochene Jewish Christians were eating with the Gentile Christians before the arrival of the people from James. This is also correctly seen by W. A. Meeks, "Jews and Christians in Antioch in the First Four Centuries," in *SBL Seminar Papers*, 40. See, in the same volume, the contribution by Robert L. Wilken, "The Jews of Antioch," 67–74. A different view is evidently taken by Betz, *Galatians*, 104, 110 n. 473.

99. Gal. 2:4 could point in this direction. See Jost Eckert, *Die urchristliche Verkündigung im Streit zwischen Paulus und seinen Gegnern nach dem Galaterbrief*, BU 6 (Regensburg: F. Pustet, 1971), 185–86. Paul could, however, have selected this wording here in light of the demand of the Galatian opponents for circumcision. The view that the conflict arose in mixed congregations is supported by the general consideration that just as the Jews were not

concerned about the morals of the Gentiles, so the Jewish Christians were not concerned about transgressions of the law by Gentile Christians. See also Albert Schwegler, *Das nachapostolische Zeitalter in den Hauptmomenten seiner Entwicklung*, 2 vols. (1846; reprint, Graz: Akademische Druck- und Verlagsanstalt, 1977), 1:120–21.

"But what brought the situation to a sharp point was this, that the Gentile mission was not homogeneous: everywhere there were believing Jews by the side of the converted pagans. The two parts formed but one community" (W. Wrede, *Paul* [London: P. Green, 1907], 65). See the description of the Antiochene congregation by C. Weizsäcker, *The Apostolic Age of the Christian Church*, 1:189: "No sort of Jewish observance was imposed on the Gentiles. The Jews, similarly, neither held by the legal ordinances about food, nor troubled themselves about the numerous defilements to which this intercourse exposed them."

100. See Suhl, *Paulus*, 71: "The only possibility that remained for the Gentile Christians was to submit to circumcision in order to be able to participate again in the table fellowship that had formerly been practiced with the Jewish Christians." In contrast to this view, G. Dix (*Jew and Greek*, 2nd ed. [Westminster: Dacre Press, 1955], 44) thinks that the intention of the separation of Jewish and Gentile Christians (at the Lord's Supper) was to prevent the circumcision of the latter group. "S. Peter and S. Barnabas and 'the other Jews' are trying to maintain the 'freedom of the Gospel' while avoiding its dangerous practical consequences for the Jewish-Christian Church" (ibid.).

Catchpole, "Apostolic Decree," thinks that the occasion of the incident in Antioch was the delivery of the Apostolic Decree of Acts by the people from James (Gal. 2:12). The following may be said against this view. On the one hand, Catchpole proceeds in a one-sided, historicizing manner (see also above, n. 97) that arises from his inadequate methodology for employing Acts in relationship to Paul's letters. On the other hand, it is difficult to understand why the Apostolic Decree of the people from James should lead to the *immediate* withdrawal of the one group when the decree was supposed to preserve the unity of the congregation (Catchpole, "Apostolic Decree," 441). Further, the addressees of the decree in Acts are Gentile Christians, whereas the people from James evidently address Jewish Christians. Catchpole's thesis is not entirely new. In addition to the investigators that Catchpole (ibid., 442 n. 3) names, mention should be made of Harnack's student A. C. McGiffert, *A History of Christianity in the Apostolic Age*, 216.

101. The attempt has sometimes been made, even by critical investigators, to relate the Apostolic Decree to the conference. See Schlier, *An die Galater*, 2d ed. (1951), 42 n. 4. The above proposal nevertheless deserves to be characterized as "new" because we developed it solely on the basis of Galatians, without keeping an eye on Acts.

102. Contrary to Suhl, *Paulus*, 72, and frequently elsewhere (also contrary

to Dix [*Jew*, 43]; Schmithals [*Paul*, 66ff.], and others), *hoi ek peritomēs* are in any event not unbelieving Jews. See, correctly, E. Earle Ellis, "'Those of the Circumcision' and the Early Christian Mission," in *StEv* 4, ed. F. L. Cross, 390–99 (= *Prophecy and Hermeneutic in Early Christianity*, WUNT 18 [Tübingen: J. C. B. Mohr (Paul Siebeck), 1978], 116–28). They are Jewish Christians from Jerusalem (just as *hoi loipoi Ioudaioi* in Gal. 2:13 are Antiochene Jewish Christians), and they are probably identical with the people from James. See Mussner, *Galaterbrief*, 141, and the literature cited there.

Suhl's explanation of the incident in Antioch through political factors is, at least, one-sided. Nothing in the text of Gal. 2:11ff. indicates that the incident was occasioned by "delegates from the Jerusalem congregation who, by reference to the possibility that the Jews could endanger the church, enforced the demand for circumcision in a mixed congregation of Jewish and Gentile Christians that was free from the law" (Suhl, *Paulus*, 18). Suhl's dating of the incident "before the delivery of the collection for the sabbath year 47/48" (ibid., 73) is speculative. Equally speculative is his next thesis that the incident in Antioch should "be evaluated, in terms of content, as the attempt . . . to establish conditions even in Antioch that would allow the acceptance of this second [*sic*] collection without endangering the congregation in Jerusalem" (ibid., 73–74). The subsequent history of Jewish Christianity also makes it clear that the demand for observance of the law was founded in an autonomous theological position that cannot be one-sidedly explained through political factors. Contra Suhl, it seems that the incident in Antioch must be related to waxing Jewish Christian tendencies in the primitive Jerusalem congregation. These tendencies were on the rise, especially because James the brother of the Lord had assumed the leading role (see the second part of this trilogy, G. Luedemann, *Paulus, der Heidenapostel*, vol. 2: *Antipaulinismus im frühen Christentum*, FRLANT 130 [Göttingen: Vanderhoeck & Ruprecht, 1983] on this). They are thus evident (according to the reconstruction presented here) *before* the conference. The understanding of *diōkein* as "persecute" (with the use of physical force), which Suhl proposes in this context and in his exegesis of Gal. 6:12 (ibid., 13ff.), should be rejected. On this, see the balanced discussion by D. R. A. Hare, *The Theme of Jewish Persecution of the Christians in the Gospel According to St. Matthew*, 60ff.

103. This will be discussed extensively in the third part of this trilogy. For the time being, see A. von Harnack, *New Testament Studies II: The Date of the Acts and of the Synoptic Gospels*, 40–66, esp. 56–57, 76–77.

104. On the apostolate in early Christianity, see the summary presentation by F. Hahn, "Der Apostolat im Urchristentum," 54–77, and the literature cited there. The question of whether Paul's apostolate was a subject of debate in Jerusalem usually does not receive sufficient attention from exegetes. Generally, reference to Gal. 2:9a ("when they perceived the grace that was given

to me") is used to support an affirmative answer to this question (moreover, it is believed that Paul's apostolate was recognized in Jerusalem), for Paul elsewhere connects *charis* with *apostolē* (see Mussner, *Galaterbrief*, 118). Verse 9a, however, was formulated by Paul, and in general one should differentiate Paul's intepretation from what actually occurred in Jerusalem. It was evidently this indecisive stance on Paul's apostolate that first made possible opposition to Paul in Galatia and Corinth. In both cases Paul has to defend his apostolate (see 1 Cor. 9:1; 15:8ff.). "Through a powerful act of usurpation Paul placed himself on the same level with the legitimate primitive congregation. No one after him ventured such a move, and the spirit very soon takes the place of the resurrected one" (Eduard Schwartz, "Zur Chronologie des Paulus," in *NGG* [1907]: 262–99 [= *Gesammelte Schriften*, 5 vols. (Berlin: Walter De Gruyter, 1938–63), 5:124–69, esp. 141]).

Betz, *Galatians*, 98–99, also thinks that Paul's apostolate was not discussed at the conference and therefore calls the conference the "Jerusalem conference." I cannot believe that Paul "did not call himself 'apostle'" at the time of the second visit to Jerusalem (Betz, *Galatians*, 99 n. 395; cf. 82; see above, pp. 32–33 n. 16).

105. See R. A. Lipsius, *Briefe an die Galater, Römer, Philipper*, HC 2.2 (Freiburg: J. C. B. Mohr [Paul Siebeck], 1891), 22.

106. Peter is mentioned first in v. 8 because of the chiastic construction. On chiasmus in Paul's writings, see J. Jeremias, "Chiasmus in den Paulusbriefen."

107. H. D. Betz objects (in a letter of 14 October 1977): "In the commentary I emphasized the oral character ('rule of thumb') of 2:9. The 'rule of thumb' regulates missionary activity, not communal life in the mixed congregations, which is a different problem. I should strictly differentiate these two." The two, of course, are not the same. I do, however, ask myself whether an agreement that dealt with the mission and that arose because of Judaistic objections could bypass the problem of mixed congregations. Precisely these congregations formed the area of danger for the Jewish Christians. The usual exegesis assumes an act of stupidity by those involved in the agreement: The incident in Antioch was, so to speak, provoked by the results of the conference.

108. This thesis has occasionally been presented in research. It has been defended by Zahn, Munck, and most recently, Henricus-Maria Féret, *Pierre et Paul à Antioche et à Jérusalem* (Paris: Éditions du Cerf, 1955). See also the remarkably careful considerations on the chronological placement of the incident in Antioch by J. Hainz, *Ekklesia*, BU 9 (Regensburg: F. Pustet, 1972), who remarks on Gal. 2:11ff., "An unhistorical composition would thus be thoroughly possible" (p. 121). With regard to the book by Féret, see J. Dupont, "Pierre et Paul à Antioche et à Jérusalem," (= *Études sur les actes des Apôtres*; on p. 187 Dupont mentions other earlier representa-

tives of the view that Gal. 2:11ff. refers to the period before the conference). Discussion with Dupont cannot be pursued here, for our primary concern is to obtain a chronology solely on the basis of the letters.

109. A. Lindemann, *Paulus im ältesten Christentum*, recently spoke out against our placement of the incident in Antioch before the Jerusalem Conference. His reasons are unintelligible to me. According to Lindemann (ibid., 167 n. 133), "The scene presented in Acts 15:1f. . . . [was] the occasion for this conference," even though Luke is supposed to have composed this scene on the basis of Gal. 2:11ff. (ibid., 167–68 with n. 134). If Acts 15:1ff. is redactional, then it provides no basis for an argument against the proposal presented here. A position on the relationship of Gal. 2:11ff. and Acts 15:1ff., which is similar to Lindemann's position, is taken by M. S. Enslin, "Once Again, Luke and Paul," 263. I should like to emphasize here that I arrived at the above results without keeping an eye on Acts and that I consider it improbable (contra Lindemann, *Paulus*, 167–68) that Luke knew Gal. 2, much less used it. In contrast to Lindemann's apparent assumption (and, in an extreme form, Enslin, "Once Again"), it should be emphasized that Luke had access to valuable traditional material that reached him from sources other than Paul's letters (e.g., traditions about Paul's final stay in Jerusalem; this remark should be taken in reference to Lindemann [*Paulus*, 169–70], who would like to derive Acts 21:21 from Luke's knowledge of Gal. 5:6; 6:15; 1 Cor. 7:19).

110. Keith F. Nickle's *The Collection: A Study in Paul's Strategy* (London: SCM Press, 1966) appeared after Georgi's book on the collection. For our study, it presents nothing of importance. Important comments on the theological meaning of the collection are found in W. D. Davies, *The Gospel and the Land*, 195ff.; and N. A. Dahl, "Paul and Possessions," in *Studies in Paul*, 31–32, 37.

111. The *hina* does not stand in clear reference to anything in the text and is not, for example, the continuation of the preceding *dexias edōkan*. Such a view would again make the collection the *conditio sine qua non* of the Gentile mission free of the law. Following the meaning of the text, one should supplement something like *parakalein* before the *hina*.

112. Burton, *Galatians*, 99. See also idem, *Syntax of the Moods and Tenses in New Testament Greek*, 96. Burton himself believes, "The former as the more common implication of a present tense in the dependent moods is somewhat more probable" (*Galatians*, 99).

113. J. Jeremias, "Sabbathjahr und neutestamentliche Chronologie"; A. Oepke, *Der Brief des Paulus an die Galater*, 83.

114. "A second visit to Jerusalem before Acts 15 can by no means be harmonized with Gal. 1" (Jeremias, "Sabbathjahr," 236).

115. Sieffert, *An die Galater*, 123, speaks of "the *kai*, which characterizes the *espoudasa* as something that stands in accord with the agreement, thus, as

something that follows upon the agreement." P. S. Minear, "The Jerusalem Fund and Pauline Chronology," correctly remarks, "If the reference were simply to a continuance of almsgiving one wonders why the matter should have been included in the agenda of the council" (p. 391).

116. Recently, Suhl has again connected—against the grammar and against Paul's own witness—the second trip to Jerusalem with the purpose of delivering a collection ("Paul had no reason to place special emphasis on this motive of his journey since it was already known" [*Paulus*, 63]). The impossibility of such a view, in terms of both grammar and content, has already been demonstrated in the context of an analysis of Gal. 2:10 by Hans Windisch, "Literatuurberichten: Neues Testament I. Zur Chronologie des Paulus," *ThT* 53 (1919): 167–75, esp. 171–72.

117. Georgi, *Geschichte der Kollekte*, 29.

118. With the same justification as Georgi uses for Gal. 2:10, one could maintain that "poor" is used in a titular sense also in Luke 6:20.

119. In any event, the designation of the later Ebionite Jewish Christians (*ebjōnim = ptōchoi*) probably does not stand in any genetic relationship with the early primitive congregation. See George Strecker, "On the Problem of Jewish Christianity," app. 1 to W. Bauer, *Orthodoxy and Heresy in Earliest Christianity*, 272–73 (in correction of what had been said following H. Lietzmann in G. Strecker, "Ebioniten," *RAC* 4: cols. 487–500, esp. 487). This of course does not mean that the (heretical) Ebionites witnessed in the second century are a phenomenon of the postapostolic period, as the heresiologists maintain, and that there is no historical continuity between them and the Jerusalem congregation. For this problem, see Luedemann, *Paulus*, vol. 2: *Antipaulinismus*.

120. This is also the view of Georgi, *Geschichte der Kollekte*, 81–82.

121. Contra Georgi's thesis, see also W. Schmithals in his review of Georgi's *Geschichte der Kollekte*, in *ThLZ* 92 (1967): col. 671; H. Löwe, "Christus und die Christen," 27. Löwe (pp. 21ff. ["Die ekklesiologische Bedeutung der Kollekte"]) shows that a primarily sociological understanding of "the poor" does not exclude the ecclesiological meaning of the collection for Paul. A recent work dealing with this matter is K. Berger, "Almosen für Israel." Berger attempts to render it probable (see esp. pp. 195ff.) that the collection was instituted in Jerusalem and collected in the Pauline congregations in order that "they would be able to assume the traditional status of the group 'the fearers of God'" (p. 200). Berger seems to know too much about the meaning those in Jerusalem attached to the collection (the same applies to Stuhlmacher, *Evangelium*, 100ff.). Berger's exposition does, however, deserve a serious evaluation, which cannot be undertaken here.

122. No one should deny that Jewish piety with respect to poverty exercised an influence on early Christianity. See James 1:9ff.; 2:5ff.; 5:1ff., and M. Dibelius, *James*, 39–45.

123. H. Conzelmann's statement that the collection was a "one-time" gift (*History*, 87) is capable of creating misunderstanding. He comes to this one-sided conclusion in light of the observation that the collection "from this point on . . . runs like a red thread through the life of Paul" (p. 86). The tense of *mnēmoneuōmen* speaks against this. The one collection by Paul is part of the continuous assistance to which the Antiochene congregation had also obligated itself.

124. For reasons of method, I consider dubious the manner in which Suhl employs the sabbatical year as a fixed point for the chronology of Paul. See, e.g., the judgment he makes on p. 327: Paul had "planned the collection from the beginning in consultation with those in Antioch for the time of need during the sabbatical year 54/55." Suhl erroneously assumes that there was *always* a famine during the sabbatical years and that the collection can be explained through reference to concrete needs in Jerusalem. See, correctly, Berger, "Almosen," 196, and what is said above in the text. That the so-called consultation with those in Antioch finds no support in the letters will be shown below (pp. 142–44). B. Z. Wacholder, "Sabbatical Year," in *IDBSup.*: 762–63 (see also the literature cited there), recently expressed the view that the sabbatical year took place in 55/56 (instead of in 54/55).

125. On Georgi's thesis that the collection had been discontinued and that Paul is speaking of "his zeal as past zeal" (*Geschichte der Kollekte*, 30), see below, pp. 84–86.

126. I shall not discuss the hypotheses for division of the letter, and I shall assume the integrity of 1 Cor. (with H. Conzelmann, *1 Corinthians*, 2–3).

The method employed in this chapter renders it superfluous to take a position on the literary-critical problem of 2 Cor., for the chronological and topographical data on the collection in 2 Cor. permit construction of a clear order of events independent of literary-critical decisions. It is a weakness in Suhl's method that he first presents a particular hypothesis for the division of 2 Cor. and then reconstructs the order of events on the basis of this (see Suhl, *Paulus*, 224ff.).

127. One possible objection to the thesis presented above, that *diatassō* cannot describe the manner of the organization of the collection, may be countered with reference to the use of *diatassō* in 1 Cor. 11:34. Here the verb is used in the context of *specific* directions for regulation of the communal life of the congregation. This usage can thus be evaluated as a parallel to our passage.

128. See J. C. Hurd, *The Origin of 1 Corinthians*, 65–74.

129. J. Weiss, *Der erste Korintherbrief*, 381: "perhaps"; Conzelmann, *1 Corinthians*, ad loc.: "cannot with certainty be inferred"; affirmative answer: C. K. Barrett, *First Corinthians*, 385; W. Schrage, "Zur Frontstellung der paulinischen Ehebewertung in 1Kor 7,1–7," 214–15; Hurd, *Origin*, 73–74 (see the literature cited there).

130. This comment is made in reference to Chalmer E. Faw, "On the Writing of First Thessalonians," *JBL* 71 (1952): 217–25. On this problem, see the survey in Hurd, *Origin*, 64 nn. 1, 2.

131. Stephanas could have transmitted the question of the Corinthians (see below, p. 83).

132. See the same opinion in C. K. Barrett, "Titus," in *Neotestamentica et Semitica*, 7.

133. See D. J. Selby, *Toward the Understanding of St. Paul*, 224–25: Paul "had apparently started the collection while still in Corinth." For criticism, see also Hurd, *Origin*, 233 n. 3.

134. Does 1 Cor. 16:1 presuppose that the Galatian congregations were founded before the Corinthian congregation so that Paul could tell the Corinthians about them during the founding visit? We should really like to know more about the relationship of 1 Cor. to Gal. and of the congregations to one another.

135. See below, pp. 101–3.

136. Conzelmann, *1 Corinthians*, 298 n. 9.

137. See the material in Hurd, *Origin*, 233 n. 3.

138. Ibid., 233.

139. Georgi, *Geschichte der Kollekte*, 37 n. 119. (In the following, references to pages in this book will be made in the main text.) In passing, two corrections to the quoted statement may be added. These corrections do not in themselves refute Georgi's thesis, but they do serve the purpose of precision. (1) In 1 Cor. 16 there is nothing about the institution of the collection among the Galatians; rather, it refers, first, to regulation of the form for the collection. (2) In 1 Cor. 16:1 there is no request for the Corinthians to participate in the collection; rather, it presupposes their participation.

140. "The incident in Antioch disrupted the relationship of trust that had been established anew in Jerusalem" (Georgi, *Geschichte der Kollekte*, 33).

141. For criticism of Georgi's thesis of an interruption of the collection, see Davies, *Gospel*, 214ff.

142. See U. Borse, "Die geschichtliche und theologische Einordnung des Römerbriefes"; G. Bornkamm, "The Letter to the Romans as Paul's Last Will and Testament," in *The Romans Debate*.

143. See U. Wilckens, "Was heisst bei Paulus: 'Aus Werken des Gesetzes wird kein Mensch gerecht'?" (= *Rechtfertigung als Freiheit*; see pp. 84–85).

144. See F. Hahn, "Das Gesetzesverständnis im Römer- und Galaterbrief," 59.

145. U. Borse, *Der Standort des Galaterbriefes*, 84ff. These similarities also pertain to 2 Cor. 1–9.

146. A synoptic table is found in A. Vögtle, *Die Tugend- und Lasterkataloge im Neuen Testament*, 13.

147. Borse, *Standort*, 87.

148. P. Vielhauer, *Geschichte der urchristlichen Literatur*, 111, thinks that the silence about the Galatian collection in 2 Cor. 8–9 provides no justification for chronological conclusions. He does not, however, mention the surprising silence regarding the Galatian collection also in Rom. 15:26. (See, however, ibid., 125.)

I further consider it impermissible in terms of method to follow Ramsey, "Place of Galatians," 265–66, in concluding on the basis of Acts 20:4 (Gaius of Derbe as a member of Paul's entourage headed toward Jerusalem) that the Galatian congregations delivered a collection: Derbe is located in South Galatia, this information is only found in Acts, and precisely in Acts 20:4 there are no names from congregations that we know with certainty to have participated in the collection and sent along escorts (Corinth, Philippi). On Acts 20:4, see also Wolf-Henning Ollrog, *Paulus und seine Mitarbeiter*, WMANT 50 (Neukirchen-Vluyn: Neukirchener Verlag, 1979), 52ff.

149. Cf. A. Pincherle, "Paul à Ephèse," in *Congrès d'Histoire du Christianisme*, 2:51–69, esp. 64.

150. If one maintains the chronological order Gal.—1 Cor., there is the theoretical possibility that Paul wrote 1 Cor. without having yet experienced the result of the Galatian conflict. However, 1 Cor. 16 does not contain even a trace of a conflict, while Gal. already presupposes that the collection is in abeyance.

151. How do Schenke and Fischer, *Einleitung*, 45, know that a collection was gathered in Ephesus?

152. The dating of Gal. after 1 Cor. 16 is correctly upheld, in criticism of Georgi's theses, also by Suhl, *Paulus*, 217–23. H. Hübner, *Das Gesetz bei Paulus*, 151, rejects Suhl's thesis without having countered Suhl's main argument (1 Cor. 16:1). Instead, he limits himself—in a manner weak in terms of method—to listing internal criteria in order to render probable the order Gal.—1 Cor. (ibid., 150–51).

153. Nils Alstrup Dahl, "Paul's Letter to the Galatians, Epistolary Genre, Content, and Structure" (a 1973 unpublished work kindly made available to me by the author and obtainable directly from the Yale Divinity School Library; see Jacob Jervell and Wayne A. Meeks, eds., *God's Christ and His People: Studies in Honour of Nils Alstrup Dahl* [Oslo: Universitetsforlaget, 1977], 16), arrives at the same result as regards the relationship of 1 Cor. 16:1 and Gal. 2:10 (pp. 72ff.). He also thinks that reference to the collection is being made in Gal. 6:6–10 (similarly, L. W. Hurtado, "The Book of Galatians and the Jerusalem Collection," *JSNT* 5 [1979]: 46–62).

154. Nevertheless, one probably cannot determine exegetically that the collection in Galatia had already been completed. This statement is made in reference to U. Wilckens, "Über Abfassungszweck und Aufbau des Römerbriefs," in *Rechtfertigung als Freiheit*, 136.

I am also unable to follow Ramsey, "Place of Galatians," 305ff. and elsewhere, in the view that Gal. was written during the imprisonment in Caesarea. The view that Gal. is an imprisonment letter has also been considered by John Knox; see Knox, "Galatians," in *IDB* 2:342–43.

155. H. Lietzmann, *An die Korinther I.II*, 135.

156. On the literary unity of 2 Cor. 8–9 (and of 2 Cor. 1–9), see Dahl, "Possessions," 38–39.

157. Suhl thinks, in contrast, that Rom. 15:26 does not reflect the *completion* of the collection "but only that it [the collection] appears established with certainty. Paul also speaks of the collection by the Corinthians as a settled issue in 2 Cor. 8:10f.; 9:2" (*Paulus*, 266). Suhl also thinks that 2 Cor. 9 was written at the same time as Romans or later (ibid., 282). In contrast to this, it must be noted that Rom. 15:26 clearly reflects an advance in the Pauline collection, even if one accepts Suhl's observation quoted above. When the collection in Corinth is established with certainty (Rom. 15:26), this represents a stage advanced beyond the decision to undertake a collection. In 2 Cor. 9, Paul is trying to establish the collection in Corinth with certainty, even though a decision for the collection had already been made. The chronological order 2 Cor. 9—Rom. 15:26 thus seems to be protected against Suhl's objection.

158. E. Lohse, "Pentēkostē," *TDNT* 6:44–53, considers it uncertain "whether a Christian Pentecost was already being celebrated in Ephesus or Corinth" (6:50).

159. Lietzmann, *Korinther I.II*, 24 (so also, in dependence on this formulation, Conzelmann, *1 Corinthians*, 99 n. 49).

160. It is a controversial matter whether there was already a Christian Passover at the time of the composition of 1 Cor. In affirmation, Lohse, "Pentēkostē," 49 n. 35, with reference to J. Jeremias, "Pascha," *TDNT* 5:896–904, esp. 901–2, who in turn refers to the results of his student B. Lohse (*Das Passafest der Quartadezimaner*; on 1 Cor. 5, see pp. 101ff.). (For criticism of B. Lohse's thesis that Melito was a Quartodeciman, see W. Huber, *Passa und Ostern*, 31–45.) On this controversial point, see Hurd, *Origin*, 139 n. 3, and the literature cited there. Hurd's own solution: "Whether or not the Corinthians were themselves celebrating a Christian Passover, the theme of 1 Cor. 5:6–8 may well have been suggested to Paul by the season" (ibid., 139).

161. Barrett, *1 Corinthians*, 130. One should deal separately with the question of whether Paul systematically introduces Passover concepts into his theology. This question should be answered in the negative (with Conzelmann, *1 Corinthians*, 99). A different question, which in my opinion should be answered in the affirmative, is whether the noticeably recurrent Passover terminology in 1 Cor. (1 Cor. 5:7; 10:1ff.; 11:23ff.; 15:23) may be evaluated so as to conclude that 1 Cor. was written around the time of the Passover. See also W. D. Davies, *Paul and Rabbinic Judaism*, 250; and Suhl, *Paulus*, 215–16.

162. Note the passages that D. Tabachovitz, in the supplement to Bl.-Debr., 13th ed., p. 12, collected for *proteros* meaning *prōtos*.

163 See W. Michaelis, "Prōtos," *TDNT* 6:865–868, esp. 866.

164. W. G. Kümmel, *Introduction to the New Testament*, 302. A similar view is presented by Suhl, *Paulus*, 137.

165. Borse, *Standort*, 49.

166. Ibid., 48.

167. Suhl, *Paulus*, 137, would like to find a reference to a second visit in Gal. 5:7 (*etrechete kalōs*). This is not evident from the wording of the passage.

168. I also do not think that Gal. 1:6 (expression of astonishment at how *quickly* the Galatians have fallen away) may be employed for chronological purposes, for example, to conclude that the congregations were founded not long before. "Quickly" refers to the suddenness of the desertion.

169. See Bl.-Debr., 13th ed., sec. 233, p. 143: "The widespread understanding as 'while sick, while weak,' which the Vulgate's *per* (not *propter*) *infirmitatem* makes likely, would require *di' astheneias*" (contra Oepke, *An die Galater*, 142). Mussner, *Galaterbrief*, ad loc., correctly notes, "The sickness certainly made the conditions for the mission unfavorable, but it was . . . the actual occasion for the mission among the Galatians." This is denied—vainly—by E. Güttgemanns, *Der leidende Apostel und sein Herr*, 173–77 (see also the literature cited there). See, correctly against this denial, Schenke and Fischer, *Einleitung*, 78; and Suhl, *Paulus*, 114 (differently on p. 136?). On the basis of Gal. 4:13, Ramsey, "Place of Galatians," 241 and frequently, goes so far as to present the thesis that the Galatians were already Christians when Paul stayed with them for the first time.

170. This is also stated by C. H. Buck, "The Collection for the Saints," 3.

171. Despite the denial of this visit by N. Hyldahl, "Die Frage nach der literarischen Einheit des Zweiten Korintherbriefes." Hyldahl does not find any accomplished second visit reflected in 2 Cor. Contra this, *palin* is most readily taken with *en lupē*, and this phrase is most easily understood as containing a reference to a second visit of an unfortunate nature. Further, the statement in 2 Cor. 13:1, "This is the third time I am coming to you," clearly indicates that Paul was going to Corinth for the third time and that he had already been there twice (first, founding visit; second, intermediary visit). Two more passages, 1:15–16 and 12:14, which are not completely clear in themselves, should be interpreted in light of this statement. Hyldahl attempts to escape this conclusion by translating 2 Cor. 13:1 as follows: "I am coming to you this third time (in contrast to the previous times when I was ready to come but did not)" (ibid., 303). The following points speak against this view: (a) one cannot demonstrate that there were two planned trips to Corinth that fell through, and (b) the clear wording of 2 Cor. 13:1 (with Lietzmann, *Korinther I.II*, 160). An interpretation similar to Hyldahl's is presented by S. Dockx, "Chronologie paulinienne de l'année de la grande collecte." In other respects, Hyldahl's article is a noteworthy attempt to understand 2 Cor. as a unity.

172. With Lietzmann, *Korinther I.II*, 102–3. "It is linguistically possible to interpret the *deutera charis* as a reference to the stay on the return journey from Macedonia that was planned but not carried out (Schmiedel, Windisch)" (ibid., 103). This, however, would have no consequences for the above reconstruction.

173. Another accusation may have been that Paul traveled to Ephesus (rather than to Macedonia) after his second visit to Corinth.

174. The account sounds as if the reported event had occurred recently. The event should probably be dated after the letter of tears. In contrast to this, Suhl thinks it improbable that the "affliction in Asia mentioned in II 1:8 refers to an event in the most recent past" (*Paulus*, 257 n. 5). According to Suhl, "the imprisonment at the beginning of the stay in Ephesus, which alone fits this description, . . . is intended" (ibid.). Contra this view: The introductory words in 2 Cor. 1:8, "For we do not want you to be ignorant" (on this formula, see also below, pp. 214–15), show that the Corinthians had previously known nothing about this affliction. This event must thus be differentiated from the occasion referred to in 1 Cor. 15:32 (contra ibid., 140, who maintains the identity of the two). The deadly danger in Asia therefore occurred after 1 Cor. and before 2 Cor. (1:8). Thus, Suhl's conjectures about an imprisonment of Paul at the beginning of his stay in Ephesus (ibid., 144–202), during which Philippians A (Phil. 1:1—3:1a; 4:10–23) is supposed to have been written, are superfluous.

According to Suhl, Paul's opponents are Jews "who have denounced Paul before officials because of his proclamation of Christ and who are now trying to discredit him on the basis of 'proclamation of Christ' [see Phil. 1:15]" (ibid., 171). In my opinion, this possibility too is excluded by Phil. 1:18, where Paul refers to the facticity of the proclamation of Christ.

175. It is unnecessary to assume (as Vielhauer, *Geschichte*, has done most recently) that Titus visited Corinth *three* times before Paul's third visit. According to Vielhauer, Titus was in Corinth "first to deal with the collection (8:6; 12:17ff.) and later to win back the congregation" (*Geschichte*, 145). The announced visit for the purpose of completing the collection is supposed to be the third. Against this view: It does not require much imagination to assume that the rise of the opponents in Corinth also endangered the collection (cf. the example of Galatia and n. 180). A better solution is to connect Titus's first visit to deliver the letter of tears and to confute the opponents with the purpose of continuing the collection. Then the announced visit is the second one.

According to C. K. Barrett, *A Commentary on the Second Epistle to the Corinthians*, 325 (see already H. Windisch, *Der zweite Korintherbrief*, 405), in 2 Cor. 12:17–18 Paul is looking back on a visit by Titus to Corinth that still lies in the future in 2 Cor. 8–9. Barrett assumes this to be the case because of the similarity of expression in 2 Cor. 12:18, "I urged Titus to go, and sent the brother with him," and 2 Cor. 8:18, "With him we are sending the brother" (in reference to the second trip). "But in this case Paul would have had to have spoken of two brothers whom he had sent along. One of them (8:18) had actually been asked by Paul and appointed by the congregations with all due ceremony to supervise the monies. His witness would, however, have been decisive here and could not have been passed over in silence. Thus, in our passage the first trip of Titus is in view" (Lietzmann, *Korinther I.II,* 159).

176. Later Paul is able to declare to the Roman readership that Achaia had decided to raise the collection (Rom. 15:26) without mention of the previous difficulties.

177. The early history of Christianity in Ephesus needs to be analyzed thoroughly, though this cannot be undertaken here. It is a concern of Luke to demonstrate the priority of the Pauline proclamation in this city and to domesticate Apollo's Christianity (see Ernst Käsemann, *Essays on New Testament Themes,* SBT 41 [Naperville: Alec R. Allenson, 1964], 136–48, whose exegesis I follow). Luke also seems to know that opposition to Paul had the upper hand in Ephesus. See Acts 20:17ff. The analysis should also take into consideration the question of the addressees of Eph., 1 Tim. 1:3ff., Rev. 2:1–7, and Ignatius, *Epistle to the Ephesians* and the problem of the group of traditions of John connected with Ephesus.

178. Theoretically, the expression "a year ago" can cover a period of one to twenty-three months.

179. With reasons that are in my opinion insufficient, Suhl denies that Romans was composed in Corinth (*Paulus,* 265).

180. The reason for this change should be sought in the increasing endangerment of the collection by the opponents, who according to our analysis had already stopped the collection in Galatia.

181. This is evidently assumed by Conzelmann and Lindemann, *Arbeitsbuch,* 197. A similar position is probably also assumed by D. Lührmann, "Sklave," 59 n. 20, when Lührmann views Acts 18:18ff. as a Lukan construct (so also Weizsäcker, *Apostolic Age,* 2:1). According to the conventional chronology, Paul first undertook the trip Ephesus—Caesarea—Jerusalem—Antioch and then wrote 1 Cor. from Ephesus during the third missionary journey. Even in this case, however, the time between the stay in Ephesus and the founding visit is not great. On the average, it is reckoned as three to four years.

182. *Hikanoi* should clearly be translated as "many" or "numerous" (Weiss, *Korintherbrief,* 291). The translation by Conzelmann (*1 Corinthians,* 193) and Hurd (*Origin,* 230 n. 1) as "some" is too weak.

183. On this translation, see the extensive remarks by Suhl, *Paulus,* 103ff.

184. On the assumption that Phil. is spurious, F. C. Baur could nevertheless write, "The explanation of this is, in our opinion, that the author had the passage 2 Cor. xi. 9 before him, and drew from it a conclusion which it does

(not warrant, failing to allow due weight to the other passage" (*Paul*, 2:57).

185. In passing, we should mention Suhl's thesis "that Paul originally wanted to go from Thessalonica to Rome, but this plan was crossed and Paul went out of his way toward the south in order to go to Corinth" (*Paulus*, 96). Suhl further states that this view "renders Rom. 15:19 readily understandable: Paul left Thessalonica in order to go to Rome and attained to Illyricum" (ibid., 94). Against this view: (a) The expression "as far round as Illyricum" (Rom. 15:19) need not be understood in an inclusive sense (the same applies to the conjectures by Vielhauer, *Geschichte*, 80). (b) The primary sources offer no indications of this attempt by Paul to reach Rome. This also applies to "the information of 1 Thess. 2:18 . . . , according to which Paul had attempted several times to visit the congregation in Thessalonica once more before he sent Timothy there from Athens" (Suhl, *Paulus*, 94–95). In my opinion, Suhl's considerations (ibid.) regarding the routes in Greece fail to render his theses worthy of discussion. Why should there not have been occasion for a statement such as 1 Thess. 2:18 during the trip from Thessalonica to Athens?

186. This is the view of the majority. See, most recently, Josef Ernst, *Die Briefe an die Philipper, an Philemon, an die Kolosser, an die Epheser*, RNT (Regensburg: F. Pustet, 1974), ad loc.; G. Friedrich, "Der Brief an die Philipper," NTD 8 (Göttingen: Vandenhoeck & Ruprecht, 1976), 125–75, ad loc.; also Strecker, "Evangelium," 530–31.

The following assumes the integrity of Phil. (on this, see Kümmel, *Introduction*, 332–35). Of course, a decision on this question is only of subordinate importance for our topic, for in any event it is certain that Phil. 4:10ff. does not derive from the period of the founding visits since Paul differentiates this period, in which he received support from Philippi, from his situation at the time of the composition of the letter. (On the hypotheses for dividing the letter, see also Suhl, *Paulus*, 149ff.)

187. M. Dibelius, *An die Thessalonicher I.II, An die Philipper*, 2d ed., ad loc. In the third edition of his commentary (1937), Dibelius offers another translation of *en archē tou euaggeliou*. Instead of "at the time of the beginning of the mission," it reads "(then) when the mission began." In the exegetical remarks, Dibelius comments on Lohmeyer's exegesis, which had been published in the meantime: "*en archē tou euaggeliou* could strike one as peculiar because Paul had already been active as a missionary. Lohmeyer thinks that Paul's independent mission probably first began in Philippi. More simple is the supposition that in Philippi one spoke of that time as the 'beginning of the proclamation of salvation'" (p. 96). What does "that time" mean here? Dibelius was misled by Lohmeyer's punctual understanding of *archē* (see n. 189), which located the beginning of the Pauline mission exclusively in the mission at Philippi. In contrast to this view, it should be emphasized that while a mission in Philippi is implied in Phil. 4:15, the subject of the verse is actually the mission to Greece, during which Paul received support only from the Philip-

pians. In Philippi, for example, one would hardly have spoken of the mission in Corinth as the beginning of the proclamation of salvation.

188. The explanation offered by Dibelius in the second edition of his commentary breaks down in that there is simply no meaning when one has Paul saying "when I made a beginning among you" (p. 74) and has this immediately connected with his departure from Macedonia (= Philippi). (I have used the second edition of the commentary as well as the third, because it presents an independent contribution and, in this case, has illustrative value.)

Friedrich ("An die Philipper," ad loc.) interprets v. 15 as follows: "When the gospel was proclaimed among them, they had the privilege of participating with the apostle in the matter of giving and receiving." This is not the way the text reads. The text says that the Philippians were the only ones to support Paul during the mission to Greece, which followed on the departure from Macedonia. After many years, Paul views this mission in retrospect as the beginning of the gospel. It is, of course, also implied that the Philippians supported Paul during his stay in Philippi.

R. Jewett, A *Chronology of Paul's Life*, writes concerning the understanding of Phil. 4:15 presented here: "Lüdemann . . . overinterprets what is surely a reference to the start of the Macedonian ministry in Phil. 4:15" (p. 82). For support of this judgment, Jewett merely cites Friedrich's interpretation, which was just refuted.

189. E. Lohmeyer, *Die Briefe an die Philipper, an die Kolosser und an Philemon*, 184–85; J. Gnilka, *Der Philipperbrief*, 177. Suhl (*Paulus*, 92 n. 3) seems to follow the same view. The following statement by Lohmeyer is, at least, capable of creating misunderstanding: "If one takes the words as they stand, then the very beginning of the Pauline mission is said to be the proclamation of the gospel in Philippi" (p. 184). Paul, however, does not speak explicitly of the proclamation in Philippi. A similar problem underlies Gnilka's statement "For the apostle, the activity in Macedonia . . . forms the actual beginning of his proclamation" (p. 177). Gnilka has only spoken of Macedonia instead of Philippi. Both Gnilka and Lohmeyer understand *archē* in a punctual manner and do not note that the clause "when I left Macedonia" indicates that Paul had left Macedonia to travel toward Achaia (Suhl, *Paulus*, 103–4, correctly points this out in his discussion of Lohmeyer and Gnilka). Thus they do not see that Paul uses *archē* for the period in which he, setting out from Macedonia, pursued his mission to (the whole of) Greece.

Various answers are given to the question of whether "Macedonia" in Phil. 4:15 means "Philippi" (see the example above). Since Paul uses "Macedonia" for "Philippi" in 2 Cor. 11:9 (see pp. 103–4), the departure from Philippi could be intended in Phil. 4:15. There is, however, no absolute proof for this interpretation of 4:15. Thus, in the text above I have preferred to speak generally of Paul's departure from Macedonia. In terms of our inquiry, not much depends on the resolution of this problem.

136

190. This view was presented by J. C. K. von Hofmann, *Der Brief Pauli an die Philipper*: "The apostle differentiates an initial period of the gospel, when it went out into the world, from the present, when it was being proclaimed from Jerusalem to Rome. He thus is thinking of the founding proclamation in the regions that were decisive for the further, general expansion" (p. 159).

191. See H. Conzelmann, "'Was von Anfang war,'" in *Neutestamentliche Studien für Rudolf Bultmann*.

192. Of course, thesis (a) contains an element of truth insofar as the initial period of Paul's mission was also the beginning of the proclamation of the gospel in Philippi.

193. This is correctly stated by G. Delling, "Archō," *TDNT* 1:478–489, esp. 482. See, further, Ramsey, "Place of Galatians," 175ff.; and M. J. Suggs, "Concerning the Date of Paul's Macedonian Ministry." Ramsey and Suggs, however, inappropriately confound the interpretation of Phil. 1:5 and 4:15. The former passage may not be employed with certainty to argue for an early European mission by Paul, for *prōtē hēmera* refers to the first day in which the congregation took part in the gospel. Similar retrospects on the foundation of congregations are found in the proems at 1 Thess. 1:5 and 1 Cor. 1:6. They are an established part (along with the eschatological reference) of the thanksgiving. On this, see E. Synofzik, *Die Gerichts- und Vergeltungsaussagen bei Paulus*, 16–19.

An accurate translation of Phil. 4:15 is offered by *The New English Bible*, 2d ed. (Oxford: At the University Press, 1970): "As you know yourselves, Philippians, *in the early days of my mission, when I set out from Macedonia*, you alone of all our congregations were my partners in payments and receipts."

194. One more word may be added regarding the peculiar understanding of *archē* in Phil. 4:15 by Otto Glombitza. Glombitza would like to understand *en archē tou euaggeliou* as "at the beginning of the gospel" because he thinks that this expression was occasioned by polemics: "The gospel in its real form [began] in Macedonia first with his proclamation" ("Der Dank des Apostels," *NT* 7 [1964/65]: 138 n. 4). It may be said against this view that there is no trace of polemics in Phil. 4:15ff. Further, Paul founded the Philippian congregation.

195. On Suhl's denial of this route, see above, n. 185. Suhl further thinks that "Paul arrived in Corinth fairly destitute. It follows then that the money that he received at his departure from Macedonia would have been sufficient for a direct trip to Rome but quickly expired when he encountered external difficulties and took up a route that differed from the one originally planned" (*Paulus*, 111). "Since Corinth substituted for the destination Rome, which could not be reached at the time, it is probable that Paul stayed there a little longer" (ibid., 114). Such assertions, in my opinion, are without foundation. The opinion expressed by Suhl in this context, that Georg Heinrici ("Die Christengemeinde in Korinth und die religiösen Genossenschaften der Grie-

chen," *ZWTh* 19 [1876]: 465–526) "convincingly proved that the Christian congregation in Corinth . . . organized itself similar to the numerous Hellenistic associations of the time" (Suhl, *Paulus*, 115), overlooks a century of research and is certainly incorrect in this unqualified form. On this problem, see the fine work by A. J. Malherbe, *Social Aspects of Early Christianity*, 87–91 and throughout, where the most important literature on this subject has been evaluated.

196. An exact determination of how much time had passed between the founding visit in Thessalonica and the composition of 1 Thess. is hardly possible on the basis of 1 Thess. In any event, Hurd, *Origin*, 26, shows that (despite 1 Thess. 2:17–18) there is no absolute proof for the assumption that only a short period of time had passed.

197. The question, left open up to now, whether the Galatian congregations were located in the north or the south of the province seems to require, on the basis of the letters, an answer in favor of the territorial hypothesis, for Paul would hardly have addressed the residents of the southern part of the province as "foolish Celts." See Conzelmann and Lindemann, *Arbeitsbuch*, 194 (see pp. 192ff. for the various arguments for the territorial and provincial hypotheses). A different opinion on this point is expressed by F. F. Bruce, "Galatian Problems. 2. North or South Galatia?" 263–64; Gunther, *Paul*, 61. Noteworthy arguments for the "South Galatian theory" are presented by C. Clemen, *Paulus*, 1:25ff. I readily admit that a degree of uncertainty finally remains.

3

INTEGRATION OF THE
TRADITIONS OF ACTS INTO
THE FRAMEWORK ATTAINED SOLELY
ON THE BASIS OF PAUL'S LETTERS

3.1 CIRCUMSCRIPTION OF THE TASK

It is appropriate first to say a word delimiting what can and cannot be considered in the following step of the investigation. This is *not* a study of the value of the traditions[1] of Acts that would attempt to write a history of the traditions passed on to Luke. As desirable as such an investigation with all its known difficulties would be, it would involve an analysis of the whole of Acts. This step in our investigation is undertaken exclusively in the light of the chronology obtained on the basis of the letters. All the periods that go unmentioned in Paul's own letters, the "first missionary journey,"[2] the journey to Rome, the trial before Festus, and so on, do not fall within the scope of this investigation, even though an analysis of them would be desirable.

The following episodes in Acts, which fall within the period covered by the chronology developed on the basis of the letters, will also be left to one side.

(1) The (thrice-reported) story of Paul's conversion (Acts 9:1–19; 22:3–21; 26:9–18). This story is of no importance for the chronology, though it is important for the question indicated above about the age of the traditions contained in Acts. This problem cannot be thematically treated here.[3]

(2) The story about Paul's flight from Damascus will not be discussed here again, for the chronological information obtainable from this story, the year 41 C.E. as the *terminus ante quem* for Paul's first visit to Jerusalem, was already determined above (p. 31 n. 10) and will be assumed in the following.

(3) There will not be an analysis of Acts' reports about Paul's stays in Philippi (16:11ff.), Thessalonica (17:1ff.), and Ephesus (19:1ff.), because the references of the letters to the events, persons, and places in

139

these cities are very indeterminate. Thus, a direct comparison of these reports with Paul's letters leads to no conclusions.

Though analyses of these passages in Acts might be valuable for a "history of apostolic tradition" (and, after that, for Pauline chronology), it would be rash at the present to fill out the picture of Paul's stays in Philippi, Thessalonica, and Ephesus with the local traditions contained in Acts.

The limits and the aim of the following investigation are thus narrowly defined. We want to ask whether Paul's journeys before and after the Jerusalem Conference, which were identified on the basis of the letters, are reflected in the traditions of Acts. According to what was said in section 1.4.2.1, old traditions should be found most readily in the summarizing reports of the journeys.

Further, a decision must be made about the standard point of reference of the conventional chronology of Paul, the reference to Gallio. Does the above reconstruction render every sort of connection between Gallio and Paul impossible? In the event of a negative answer to this question, can the Gallio-inscription help us find an absolute datum, which we have not had up to now? Since Acts 18 contains another important piece of chronological data alongside the reference to Gallio, namely, the reference to the edict concerning the Jews by Emperor Claudius, it will be best to undertake an analysis of the entire report about Paul's stay in Corinth. Not only does the reference to the edict concerning the Jews provide another possible absolute datum, but chap. 18 as a whole contains other individual traditions that may be compared with the relatively plentiful information provided by the Corinthian correspondence. The analysis of Acts 18:1ff. will thus attempt to answer two questions: (a) Can absolute dates be determined for Pauline chronology? (b) Does the chapter contain (local) traditions that are verified by the letters?

Third and finally, a special problem is raised by Acts' information regarding the lengths of Paul's stays in the various localities. Since the chronology developed above provided a relatively set period for Paul's founding visit in Thessalonica (and in Corinth) as well as for the stay in Ephesus and the third visit to Corinth, it should be asked whether Acts' information about the lengths of the stays in these localities is compatible with this chronology.

We shall address these three problems in the order in which they were just listed, beginning with the summarizing report about Paul's travels in Acts 18:18–23.

3.2 THE TRANSITION IN ACTS FROM THE SECOND TO THE THIRD MISSIONARY JOURNEY AS THE TRANSITION IN THE CHRONOLOGY OF PAUL FROM THE FOUNDING VISIT TO THE VISIT FOR THE COLLECTION: ACTS 18:18–23

3.2.1 On the Interpretation of Acts 18:18–23 in Previous Research. The Problem

The conventional chronology finds the division of the second missionary journey from the third marked by Acts 18:22 and 18:23. After spending a few days in Corinth, Paul departs from here in v. 18 in order to travel to Syria. He leaves his travel companions Aquila and Priscilla in Ephesus, though he himself spends a few days there for discussion with the Jews in the synagogue. He soon departs from Ephesus for Palestine, even though the Jews ask him to stay longer. He travels by sea to Caesarea, goes up (to Jerusalem), greets the church, and then goes to Antioch. From there he travels on through the region of Galatia and Phrygia, where he strengthens the disciples. In Acts 19:1 he is back in Ephesus again.

In the exegesis of this text, which was just paraphrased, research has always taken a historicizing approach.[4] Even the two major introductions by Kümmel and Vielhauer make no exception to this rule.[5] They assume as self-evident that, after the conference, Paul undertook two trips to Greece starting out from Palestine and that he undertook one trip from there to Palestine before the journey to deliver the collection. They do not deal with the problem of whether a trip to Jerusalem was involved in the journey described in our text and of whether such a trip to Palestine should be viewed as historically possible. In the light of their silence about a possible trip to Jerusalem, one should actually conclude that they assume this trip to be a self-evident fact, since such a trip is reported by Luke and since these investigators allow Luke to prescribe for them the organizational idea of a "second and third missionary journey" in Pauline chronology (in contradiction to the letters).[6]

Investigators who at least mention the problem of the trip to Jerusalem intimated in Acts 18:22 maintain the historicity of the journey to Caesarea and either doubt that a trip to Jerusalem is presupposed in the report[7] or explain the hint about a trip to Jerusalem on the basis of Luke's theological penchant. "According to Luke's conviction Paul was on excellent terms with the congregation of Jerusalem; he has indeed just undertaken a missionary journey in the company of Silas, an *anēr hēgoumenos*, a leading man of this congregation. Hence from the viewpoint of Acts a Pauline visit to Jerusalem is quite reasonable" (Haenchen, 548).[8] As to why Caesarea (instead of Antioch) is the port of arrival, Haenchen explains that Paul was driven there by unfavorable winds. "In reality Paul will have wanted to go to Antioch in order, after his great missionary success, to bind relations with this congregation still closer" (ibid.). According to this view, Luke found the unusual indication of place, Caesarea, in the tradition and explained it by relating it to a Pauline trip to Jerusalem.

Haenchen's hypothesis is a good example of the tendency in research that this investigation intends to examine critically. This sort of research has gone only halfway in its criticism of Acts' chronological information in the light of Paul's letters. It does go so far as to exclude a Pauline visit to Jerusalem between the trip for the Jerusalem Conference and the trip to deliver the collection. It nevertheless maintains that a visit to Antioch during this time is plausible, even though this trip is reflected in the letters no more than the visit to Jerusalem just mentioned. We shall remain with this thesis for a moment longer and examine how it has been developed further in the most recent work on Pauline chronology, the work of A. Suhl.

Suhl accepts Haenchen's explanation that Paul's visit to Antioch served to reestablish relationships that had broken down at the time of the incident in Antioch. He goes beyond Haenchen insofar as he attempts to state more fully why the trip to Antioch is not documented in the primary source, Paul's letters. "That there were weighty reasons for Paul to undertake this journey can at most be a supplementary argument for the historical reconstruction. Much more important is whether not only the secondary source but also the primary source make it necessary to consider the journey to Antioch historical. There are indeed a few reasons to this effect."[9]

Suhl lists three main arguments:

(1) The explanation for the creation of a party of Cephas in Corinth during Paul's absence is supposedly that "Paul's visit to Antioch brought news of the existence of this congregation to the East, and this gave rise to these influences" (p. 133).

(2) The later opponents in Galatia supposedly heard about the Gala-

tian congregations and about Paul's plans to gather a collection there through Paul's report in Antioch. Therefore, they went to Galatia (ibid.).

(3) "The most important indication of the visit to Antioch is the reappearance of Titus after the end of the founding visit in Corinth" (p. 134). According to Suhl, Titus did not accompany Paul after the Jerusalem Conference on the missionary journey to Europe but rather stayed in Antioch (after the incident in Antioch). Titus does not appear alongside Paul, Silvanus, and Timothy either as a co-founder of the Corinthian congregation or as a co-author of 1 Thessalonians. After Paul's visit of reconciliation in Antioch, "Titus evidently departed from Antioch with Paul in order to carry out the collection" (p. 134).[10]

Apart from the fact that all Suhl's claims are hypotheses of the second order, none of them attains even a degree of probability.

As regards (1), it is much more conceivable that in the event that Cephas was not himself in Corinth, Paul had spoken of Cephas during his founding visit (cf. the tradition about Cephas in 1 Cor. 15:5) and that, from this, veneration of Cephas arose in Corinth and found expression in the formula *egō de Kēpha* (1 Cor. 1:12). Further, Paul's arguments in 1 Corinthians are not aimed merely against the party of Cephas. They are directed against parties of all sorts, even against the party of Paul.

As regards (2), the opponents in Galatia, in any event, are connected with the group at the conference that demanded that Gentile Christians be circumcised. This was already evident from the fact that they were well informed about the agreements and emphasized to the Galatians that Paul's apostleship was either not recognized or else not dealt with in Jerusalem. They did not need to hear from Paul that Paul was gathering a collection in Galatia. They will have gathered information themselves about the transgressions of the law in the Pauline congregations. From this information they knew about what was taking place there.

As regards (3), it is improbable that Titus agreed to a separation from Paul and remained in a congregation that was ready for compromises and that—according to Suhl—Paul had left after the incident in Antioch. Titus was the one against whom the Judaistic demand for circumcision of Gentile Christians was raised in Jerusalem and whom Paul held to be a living symbol for Gentile Christianity free of the law. Further, would this Titus, who according to Suhl acquiesced to the Judaists in Antioch, be able to overcome the Judaists in Corinth and swing the congregation back to Paul's side? Does not his successful mission in Corinth presuppose that he was acquainted with the congregation there and was familiar with the Corinthian situation?

Suhl's hypotheses, which build on Ernst Haenchen's hypothesis of the historicity of an intermediary visit to Antioch and speculatively develop it further, disclose clearly the impasse to which historicizing exegesis of Acts 18:18–23 leads. This impasse makes it advisable to abandon this approach quickly and to test on this passage the literary and redaction-historical method that has been so successful in research into Acts. This is all the more advisable since the chronology that was developed above solely on the basis of the letters excludes not only the historicity of a trip to Jerusalem between the conference and the delivery of the collection but also the historicity of a trip to Antioch during this same period.

3.2.2 Separation of Redaction and Tradition in Acts 18:18–23

Research is virtually unanimous in deriving our passage from a document that lay before Luke and that he redactionally expanded in a few places. We shall proceed on the basis of this same assumption. Our concern will be with separating out the Lukan elements in order to recover from the present text the source available to Luke.

Verse 18a reports Paul's departure for Syria. Following Haenchen's assumption that Antioch was the actual goal of the journey, we should then have a source that indicated in preview the final intended destination of the journey. Since, however, Syria is mentioned in connection with a trip to Jerusalem also in Acts 20:3 and 21:3, Haenchen's assumption is impermissible. The statement can be understood as the source's preview of a trip to Jerusalem.

The statement that Paul took Priscilla and Aquila with him from Corinth to Ephesus (*v. 18b*) is, in view of the construction of the sentence, open to the suspicion of being a redactional addition: *kai syn autō Priskilla kai Akylas, keiramenos en Kegchreais tēn kephalēn· eichen gar euchēn.* "What do Aquila's hair and the fact that he had it . . . cut have to do with anything? These matters are not really connected with the context but are rather totally separate."[11] Even if *keiramenos,* contra Wellhausen and despite the stylistic difficulty, should be taken in reference to Paul and not to Aquila,[12] the question is still similarly pressing whether "and with him Priscilla and Aquila" is

144

an addition. It is not clear whether one may attribute to Luke such a stylistically weak move as the insertion of *kai syn autō Priskilla kai Akylas* after *Syrian* in the text *exeplei eis tēn Syrian keiramenos en Kegchreais tēn kephalēn' eichen gar euchēn*. One cannot convincingly deny the redactional character of such a move by referring to v. 19 and stating "that the source already reported of a joint journey" (Conzelmann, ad loc.). Luke needs the couple for the episode involving Apollos (v. 26). On the other hand, the brevity of the note in v. 19 about Paul's leaving the two behind makes it possible that the report of the joint journey of Paul and the couple from Corinth to Ephesus is also traditional. And why should not the entire passage "at Cenchreae he cut his hair, for he had a vow" derive from Luke's redaction? "A (Nazirite) vow counted as a meritorious work. It could be discharged only at the temple" (Conzelmann, ad loc.). If it can be proven that Luke is following or abbreviating a source in Acts 18:18ff. that spoke of a trip to Jerusalem (see below), then the report that Paul cut his hair because of a vow would make good (Lukan) sense. It presents Paul as a loyal adherent of the Jewish law (cf. 21:23–24) on his way to Jerusalem (i.e., to the temple). In deference to this concern, Luke would then be responsible for the stylistically awkward expansion of his source, which recounted Paul's trip to Ephesus with Priscilla and Aquila, through the statement "he cut his hair. . . ."

In any event, it is clear that the report of the move of the married couple from Corinth to Ephesus is historical (see 1 Cor. 16:19 and below, pp. 173–75).

Verses 19b–21a (Paul's preaching in the synagogue and the Jews' request for Paul to stay) are clearly redactional. This is clear from the content and for formal (literary-critical) reasons. The statement "He left them there [in Ephesus]; but he himself went into the synagogue" (v. 19) creates the impression that the synagogue is not situated in Ephesus.[13] That this impression was not created intentionally is revealed by the description of Paul's departure from Ephesus in v. 21b and by the anticipation of Paul's return to Ephesus "if God wills" in v. 21a (the return is presented in 19:1ff.). After the "if God wills," the travel report begins again with Paul's departure from Ephesus. This literary-critical separation of vv. 19b–21a from the succinct travel report[14] can be bolstered by observations on the content. The content, too, derives from the redactor Luke. Verse 19b contains the well-known Lukan schema of beginning with the Jews: Paul preaches first

145

in the synagogue. Verse 21 looks forward to Paul's possible return. When this event is depicted in 19:1, however, the text speaks only of Paul's "arrival," as if this were his first visit there. Thus the prospect of a return in v. 21 cannot have been in the source.[15] The underlying reason for composing Acts 18:19b–21a can be determined in light of the following passage (vv. 24ff.), which reveals that there were Christians in Ephesus prior to Paul's arrival. In this scene Luke wants to have Paul "appear as the first Christian preacher in the city" (Conzelmann, ad loc.).[16]

In sum, Acts 18:19b–21a has thus been shown to be a Lukan composition.[17]

The very brevity of the report on the journey following the departure from Ephesus (18:22–23) poses several riddles for exegetes: "'From Ephesus, to Caesarea, up to greet the brethren, down to Antioch, then back through Galatia and Phrygia.' With plans made at a moment's notice and reported in telegraphic style, no American could have done it better."[18]

Before we evaluate the epitomic style so brilliantly described by Wellhausen, we must examine (a) whether this passage contains a visit to Jerusalem and (b) whether this visit derives from Lukan redaction.

As regards (a), the expression "he went up" intimates that Paul went from Caesarea up to the higher-situated Jerusalem. If one were to understand Paul's ascent as expressing his intention to greet the church in Caesarea, one would be faced with the difficulty posed by the use of the verb *katabainein* (v. 22), which predominantly indicates movement from Jerusalem (or Palestine) to another locality (in this case, Antioch).[19]

As regards (b), the absence of an explicit reference to Jerusalem as the destination of the journey is a clear point against the thesis that the allusion to a journey to Jerusalem is Lukan. Haenchen's attempted explanation, "As an author Luke is thrifty; he wastes no space" (p. 548), shows he is in a quandary. In the other passage where it is *certain* that Luke has composed a report about a trip to Jerusalem (11:27ff.), Luke writes at greater length. One cannot—as do Haenchen and Suhl—on the one hand say that Luke is a thrifty author and then on the other hand charge this allusion with theological importance and see here (Luke's) illustration of the good relations between Paul and the primitive congregation. To be sure, it would not have been contrary to Luke's interests for Paul to visit and greet the brethren in Jerusalem during the time described in Acts 18:22. If, however, this trip to Jerusalem, to which—as noted above—there is only allusion, did derive from Lukan redaction, then certainly Luke would have emphasized it more strongly. The terseness, that is, the epitomic style[20] characteristic of the entire report of the journey from Corinth, especially as regards the trip to Jerusalem,[21] supports the assumption that the tradition Luke possessed for this report was a list of stations supplemented through other bits of information, some of which were omitted by Luke. The list probably contained the following stations: Corinth, Ephesus, Caesarea, Jerusalem, Antioch, Galatia, Phrygia. Phrygia will have been followed by Ephesus as the next station (Acts 19:1b).

Having now recovered the above list of stations as the tradition behind Acts 18:18ff., we may turn to evaluating the list in terms of the history of traditions. Here we shall want to develop further Wellhausen's brilliant observations, noted above.

3.2.3 Considerations on the History of the Traditions in the List of Stations in Acts 18:18ff.

It is well known that Paul's letters witness to three journeys by Paul to Jerusalem (the first journey in order to get to know Cephas, the second for the conference, and the third to deliver the collection). Acts, in contrast, reports five trips to the Holy City (9:26ff.; 11:27ff.; 15:1ff.; 18:22; 21:15). Since hypotheses such as the suggestion that Paul suppressed information about a trip to Jerusalem[22] can be left to one side,[23] one can only conclude that two of the trips reported in Acts should be ascribed to Lukan redaction. Strecker has demonstrated that Paul's second trip to Jerusalem in Acts (11:27ff.) is a Lukan construction (see above, pp. 13–14). The question remains which of the three following journeys should be attributed to Luke.

3.2.3.1 THE TRIP TO JERUSALEM IN ACTS 18:22 AS A DOUBLET OF ACTS 21:15?

In 1907, J. Wellhausen had already surpassed the historicizing explanations of Acts 18:22 mentioned above. His thesis was that the trip to Jerusalem in Acts 18:22 should be viewed as a doublet of Paul's last visit to Jerusalem in Acts 21:15.[24] Wellhausen referred to the doubling of the second trip in Acts 11:27ff. and 15:1ff. as an analogy for the doubling of the third trip to Jerusalem.

Suhl objects to this view: "This, however, is not convincing. Acts 11:27ff. mentions no more than a trip from Antioch to Jerusalem. This information does not contradict the more precise description of the route in Acts 15:3ff. The journey in Acts 20:3ff., in contrast, follows a completely different route from that described in Acts 18:18ff."[25] Contra Suhl's last statement, the following parallels between the two passages should be noted:

18:18: Paul boards a ship in Corinth for Syria.

~20:3: Paul's plan to sail to Syria is hindered.

18:21: Departure from Ephesus.

~21:1: Departure from Miletus: On the assumption that this passage is a doublet, this information may indeed be evaluated as a parallel. Luke knows that Paul cannot show his face in Ephesus and thus substitutes Miletus for Ephesus since it was situated nearby.

18:22: Paul in Caesarea.

~21:8: Paul in Caesarea: The choice of different havens for the arrival (18:22: Caesarea; 21:3: Tyre) may be explained as an artificial literary maneuver in order to avoid repetition.

18:22: Paul in Jerusalem.

~21:17: Paul in Jerusalem.

Thus, contra Suhl's critique, reasons can be found in the text for Wellhausen's thesis that Paul's fourth trip to Jerusalem in Acts is an abbreviated version of the fifth and final trip. Wellhausen's reference to the parallel doubling of the second trip to Jerusalem is insightful, for there both reports (11:27ff. and 15:1ff.) not only cover the same distance (Antioch—Jerusalem) but also have the same personages (Paul and Barnabas). In the fourth and fifth trips, Paul is the only main personage, and in each case the same distance, Corinth—Jerusalem, is covered.

Though Wellhausen's thesis is still impressive today, it can no longer be maintained, for it failed to give due consideration to two observations:

(1) Acts 18:18ff. is epitomic in character, whereas Acts 20:3ff. is loaded with details. Wellhausen assumes that Acts 18:18ff. is a shortened, abbreviated form of Acts 20:3ff. Counterquestion: Why should Luke present, precisely at this point in Acts, an epitome of a journey later described more extensively? This would make sense only if Luke had a particular purpose for the journey or if the trip to Jerusalem could be explained as playing an integral part in the structure of Luke's composition. If this had been the case, Luke would have made this

function more evident. Thus it seems more likely that Luke here short-ened or abbreviated a tradition because he did not know what to do with it at this point. He nevertheless presented it here, for it provided the transition to the stay in Ephesus depicted in chap. 19.[26]

(2) The epitomic travel report carries on in a similarly abbreviated way even after the station "Jerusalem." Since the localities listed after the station "Jerusalem" evidently belong to the same tradition as the stations listed before the Holy City, one may, contra Wellhausen, rule out the possibility that Acts 18:22 is a doublet of Paul's last trip to Jerusalem. The trip to Jerusalem mentioned in Acts 18:22 is rather part of an independent tradition, abbreviated in Acts, which reported a trip by Paul from Greece to Jerusalem *and back.* Is it possible to rediscover the original place of this tradition, which probably lay before Luke in a written form as a travel report and which told of a trip by Paul from Greece to Jerusalem and back?

3.2.3.2 THE ORIGINAL LOCATION OF THE VISIT TO JERUSALEM IN ACTS 18:22

The analysis should proceed from the observation that of all five[27] of Paul's trips to Jerusalem reported by Acts, the fourth (Acts 18:22) strikes one as the most inornate. For this reason, it is most likely that this report derives from old tradition.

The following will present the thesis that Acts 11:27ff; 15:1ff.; and 18:22 are a tripling[28] of Paul's second visit to Jerusalem and that Acts 18:22 represents its original historical location—after the journey from Greece to Palestine. This thesis will first be argued on the basis of Acts itself and then be verified through a comparison with the chronology presented above.

3.2.3.2.1 *Acts 11:27ff.; 15:1ff.; 18:22 as a Tripling of Paul's Second Visit to Jerusalem*

It was shown above (pp. 13–14) that in Acts 11:27ff. Luke constructed a trip by Paul to Jerusalem. This was evident from observations on the language (Lukan language) and on the content. Luke's intention was to establish the continuity of salvation history by having the An-tiochene congregation act in support of Jerusalem.[29] The following will similarly present observations on (a) the language and (b) the content that support the thesis that the trip in Acts 15:1ff. is a Lukan construction.

(a) The following observations on the language and expressions in

Acts 15:1ff. support the conclusion that Luke is the originator of this passage. Luke's favorite expressions are strewn throughout the report of the journey in Acts 15:1–4: *katelthein*,[30] *adelphos*,[31] *ethos*[32] (v. 1); *ouk oligos*,[33] *zētēma*[34] (v. 2); *dierchesthai*,[35] *chara*,[36] *ekklēsia*[37] (v. 3). The following phrases also do not come into consideration as being part of any trip that lay before Luke in the tradition, for they are found in the immediate context of 15:1–4 and are therefore suspected of having been transported from there into the report about the journey:

Verse 1: "Unless you are circumcised according to the custom of Moses" corresponds to 15:5.

Verse 2: "There arose dissension and debate" corresponds to 15:7.

Verse 4: "They declared all that God had done with them" picks up on 14:27 and reappears in a similar form in 15:12.

Verse 4: "By the church and the apostles and the elders" corresponds to 15:22.

While this thus demonstrates that the redactor Luke has firmly imprinted the mark of his hand on 15:1–4, it is nevertheless clear that in this passage (as similarly in 11:27ff. [see Strecker's demonstration]) Luke did not freely compose without any point of contact in the tradition. Just as in 11:27ff., where the reference to the persons Barnabas and Paul as well as the mention of the collection derives from old traditions relating to Paul's visit to Jerusalem, so too in our passage there is old tradition: Paul and Barnabas, the ones whom 15:1ff. presents as undertaking the journey to Jerusalem, went to Jerusalem according to Paul's own statement in Galatians 2.

Luke probably adopted the reason and occasion for Paul and Barnabas's trip from traditions about the conference that were available to him. He then worked this information into the report of the journey. This information probably only partially corresponds with historical truth, even though the demand for circumcision of the Gentile Christian Titus was actually raised at the conference. The direct occasion for the conference was probably the conflicts that arose in the mixed congregations and that had to do with the table fellowship of Gentile and Jewish Christians (on Acts 15 as the Antiochene version of the conference, see above, p. 74).

Comparison of the *journey* reported in Acts 15:1ff. with Paul's statement in Galatians thus reveals that there is actually only one real point of agreement, namely, that Paul and Barnabas traveled together to Jerusalem. The following will point out several major differences that

150

further confirm that the journey in Acts 15:1ff. is not historical. (1) Acts is silent about the fact that Paul went to Jerusalem because of a revelation and that this journey was undertaken so that Paul might present to the Jerusalem apostles the gospel he preached among the Gentiles. (2) The person who is important for Paul, the Gentile Christian Titus, is not even mentioned in Acts. (3) According to Acts 15:1ff., Barnabas and Paul were sent from Antioch to Jerusalem; contrary to what is often falsely assumed, Galatians does not state that Paul traveled to Jerusalem from Antioch.[38] These differences already reveal that the report of the journey in 15:1ff. has left out certain information because of a particular slant. Thus in (1) and (3) it is implied that Paul's major mission had not yet been undertaken, and in (2) the intention is to remove all dangerous conflicts from every connection with the conference. These observations may serve as the transition to the demonstration of the material reasons—in terms of content and redaction history—that led Luke to locate the report of the meeting in Jerusalem at this point.

If it can be convincingly proven that the location of Paul's third visit to Jerusalem and the conference at this place is redactionally conditioned, then there will be, in addition to the above demonstration of characteristically Lukan language, a second and even weightier argument against the historicity of Paul's third trip to Jerusalem in Acts.

(b) The so-called second visit to Jerusalem by Paul with Barnabas had the function of "confirming also through the action of the Antiochene congregation the continuity of salvation history that had been established through the connection with Jerusalem."[39] Something similar applies—*mutatis mutandis*—to the third visit to Jerusalem for the conference at this point.

The conference, which occurs before Paul's actual mission, is the pivotal point where the transition from the Jerusalem *and* the Antiochene mission to the worldwide Pauline mission takes place. It is at the conference that Paul's mission receives its internal legitimation by the Jerusalem apostles.[40] From the time of the conference onward, there is also no more room for Paul as an Antiochene missionary. Thus the conference also effects the transition from the Antiochene mission to the Pauline mission, while previously Luke had meshed the two by constructing an exemplary journey (Acts 13–14). After this point, not only do James and Peter no longer have a place in Acts, but the same applies to the representative of the Antiochene congregation, Barnabas, for dogmatic reasons prevent him from being mentioned again in Acts 18:22. Otherwise, this historical—because we can verify it through Paul's own witness—information would have meant limiting the importance of the universal Pauline mission that extended materially into Luke's own time.[41]

To be sure, Luke possesses correct bits of information about the conference, and on the basis of these sources he draws a conclusion about how the conference was occasioned. Since, however, the author of Acts develops proper chronology from proper dogmatics, the location of the Jerusalem Conference *before* Paul's worldwide mission must be viewed as a Lukan construction.[42]

If this assumption, which remains to be verified in the following on the basis of the above chronology, is correct, there is an explanation for why one could get the impression from Acts 18:21bff. that "the particulars are understandable only to the one who made the epitome [namely, Luke] but no longer to his reader. This impression is strengthened when one also considers 19:1" (Conzelmann, ad loc.). The epitomic character finds its explanation in light of the early placement of the conference and the Lukan construction of the so-called third trip to Jerusalem by Paul.

3.2.3.2.2 The Verification of Acts 18:22 as Paul's Second Trip to Jerusalem on the Basis of the Chronology Developed Solely from the Letters

Once the references to places conditioned through Lukan redaction are removed, the stations in Paul's mission which are mentioned before Acts 18:22 are paralleled exactly by the places where, according to the above chronology based solely on the letters, Paul stayed between the first and second visits to Jerusalem. This will be elucidated in the following.

After the conference in Acts 15, Paul travels to Antioch, Syria, Cilicia, Derbe, Lystra, Phrygia, and the region of Galatia. Then comes the mission in Philippi, Thessalonica, Athens, and Corinth. Paul next travels from Corinth to Ephesus, Caesarea, and Jerusalem.

A large portion of the places of travel and stay just listed agree even in their order with the chronology reconstructed above for the time between the first and second visits to Jerusalem. This applies to the stations Syria, Cilicia, and Philippi to Corinth[43] (see above, p. 108).

The following stations mentioned in Acts cannot be verified by the above chronology for the time between Paul's first and second visits to Jerusalem:[44]

Acts 15:30–39: Paul and Barnabas in Antioch. The dispute about John Mark.

Acts 16:1–5: Paul in Derbe and Lystra. The circumcision of Timothy.

Acts 16:6–8: The journey through Phrygia, the region of Galatia, Mysia, and Bithynia.

All these passages are suspected of deriving from Lukan redaction.

Acts 15:30–39: In Acts the dispute between Paul and Barnabas forms the transition to Paul's independent mission to the Gentiles —after the material presupposition for this mission was established by the conference.

The conflict probably reflects the historical separation of Paul from the Antiochene congregation. It cannot be demonstrated, however, that the conflict was related to the incident in Antioch (Gal. 2:11ff.). On the one hand, Acts 15:30ff. has transformed a material conflict, the nature of which is no longer recognizable for us, into a personal conflict. On the other hand, the opponent in the incident at Antioch is not Barnabas but rather Cephas and, above all, the people from James.

What has already been said has revealed one redactional motive for Paul's separation from Barnabas after the conference. Two observations demonstrate the secondary character of 15:30ff. (in contrast to the following section).

(1) In 15:40–41, Paul selects as his companion Silas, who, however, was already sent off to Jerusalem in 15:33.[45] From this it should be concluded that a new source begins in vv. 40ff. (Conzelmann [ad loc.] comes, questioning, to the same result).

(2) 15:40–41 reports that Paul traveled through Syria and Cilicia. This report evidently presupposes that Paul departed from Palestine and not from Antioch, which is located in Syria, and where, according to Acts 15:30ff., the conflict between Barnabas and Paul occurred.

Acts 16:1–5: Derbe, Lystra, and the circumcision of Timothy. The report about Paul's stay in Derbe says nothing about Paul preaching there. It depicts only the delivery of the decisions made at the conference (16:4), Paul's circumcision of Timothy, and Paul's decision to have Timothy accompany him (16:3). Apart from the unhistorical character of Paul's circumcision of Timothy (see Conzelmann, ad loc.), 16:1–5 also does not enter into question as being part of a source, for the episode about Paul's stay in Derbe and Lystra is a Lukan doubling of the stay reported in Acts 14:6ff. Luke reports again after the conference about Paul's journey to these localities, for he wants to report about Timothy as Paul's companion only after Paul's independent mission has begun. If he had reported about Timothy's connection with Paul during the "first missionary journey," the misunderstanding could have arisen that Timothy had also joined up with Barnabas. Further, this episode serves to illustrate the continuity of the church, for the congregations founded before the conference had to be informed of the decisions of the Jerusalem Conference (the Apostolic Decree), insofar as they were not informed of these decisions by letter.[46]

Acts 16:6–8: Phrygia, the region of Galatia, Mysia, Bithynia. The description of the journey through Phrygia and the region of Galatia is peculiar. It strikes one as "a purposefully nonmissionary journey" (Conzelmann, ad loc.). The statement "They were hindered from speaking the word in Asia" (v. 6) reflects—in a historically correct way—the difficulties that Paul encountered in Asia and that are possibly documented in 1 Cor. 15:32 and 2 Cor. 1:8. At the present place in Acts, this peculiar nonmissionary journey through Phrygia and the region of Galatia, the hindrance of the pronouncement of the word in Asia, and the unsuccessful attempt to missionize Mysia and Bithynia form a conscious contrast (notice also, in connection with this, v. 9) to the following European mission. Luke's redactional hand is also evident when one compares v. 6 with Acts 18:23, where Luke reports a trip by Paul through the region of Galatia and Phrygia with similar words and in inverse order.

We thus conclude that Acts 16:6–8 is a Lukan composition based on individual traditions that can no longer be clearly distinguished (on 18:23, however, see more on pp. 155–56).

In summary, of the stations reported in Acts between the "conference" and the trip to Jerusalem in Acts 18:22, all those that do not agree with the stations recovered from Paul's letters for the period between the first and second visits to Jerusalem should be attributed largely to Lukan redaction. This shows that the tradition reworked in Acts 16–18 has major agreements with the stations that were reconstructed solely on the basis of the letters for the time between Paul's first and second visits to Jerusalem.

Are the agreements of the stations after Acts 18:22 with the above chronology after the conference equally strong? In the case of an affirmative answer to this question, there would be a further reason for the view that Acts 18:22 reflects Paul's actual second visit to Jerusalem.

After the visit to Jerusalem in Acts 18:22, Paul stays in the following places: Antioch, the region of Galatia, Phrygia, Ephesus (19:1), Macedonia (20:2), Greece (20:3 = Corinth).

We are unable to verify the localities mentioned after this (Philippi [20:3], Troas [20:6], etc.), for Romans was written during the stay in Corinth mentioned in 20:3. Thus the chronological information that can be recovered from the letters breaks off at this point.

When we compare the route of the journey in Acts with the above chronology, there is amazing agreement. According to Paul's own statements, Paul undertook a trip to organize the collection after the conference. The first station we reconstructed above was Galatia (i.e., Paul's second visit there, the purpose being to institute and organize the collection).

While on the basis of the letters alone we were unable to make an *assured* decision between the South Galatian hypothesis and the North Galatian hypothesis, the existence of Pauline congregations in the region Galatia (North Galatian hypothesis) nevertheless appeared to be more probable, because Paul would hardly have addressed the residents of Pisidia and Lycaonia as "Galatians" (Gal. 3:1). If it may thus be assumed that Paul's Galatian congregations should be located in the north of the province, then Paul can have traveled to this location only by the overland route via the Cilician pass. This, however, presupposes—even in light of Paul's relationship to the congregation in Antioch—that Paul at least passed through Antioch. These considerations yield the identity of the first two stations after the conference, according to both Paul's own statements and Acts: Antioch, the region of Galatia.

In retrospect on what has been said about 18:23 (the journey through the region of Galatia), it should be recalled that according to the above chronology Paul's stay in Galatia after the conference is the apostle's second visit to this congregation. Now, 16:6 already mentions that Paul visited the Galatian region. Is it possible that the founding visit is glimmering through here? Does Luke's source contain more information about this mission? Is Luke suppressing traditions because they reported little that was edifying with respect to the apostle to the Gentiles and his sickness? What we in fact know from the letters is that the founding of the Galatian congregations resulted from Paul's sickness.

There is agreement also as regards the next stations. At the time of the composition of 1 Corinthians, Paul is in Ephesus, and he came to Ephesus from Galatia. Since the normal route from Galatia to Ephesus passes through Phrygia,[47] Acts and Paul agree regarding the third and fourth stations, Phrygia and Ephesus. The next stations in Acts' source, Macedonia and Corinth (compare also Acts 19:21 with 1 Cor. 16:5), correspond with the above chronology, the only exception being that the intervening visit (i.e., the second visit) to Corinth is not mentioned. In the event that this visit was recorded in the source, Luke would certainly have left it out, for there could hardly have been anything edifying in this report—probably even in the source.[48]

3.2.4 Summarizing Considerations

The first step in comparing the results of the chronology developed solely on the basis of the letters with Acts revealed that after the redactionally conditioned chronological arrangement of the second half of Luke's two-volume work was retrogressively removed, there was a surprising confirmation of the chronology of Paul reconstructed above. Admittedly, the agreement extended to a large degree only to the stations and their order. This makes it likely that Luke used a list of stations embellished with various episodes and that this source derived from a companion of Paul. This list of stations, which dealt briefly with Paul's journeys from the first visit to Jerusalem until the third stay in Corinth, was supplemented by Luke with additional routes. Luke also filled out the report with local traditions, whereby he partially included individual episodes that were preserved with the list of stations.

The above observations, which were obtained primarily by comparing Acts with the chronology presented above, thus constructively lead one step beyond H. Conzelmann's position, which was developed in discussion with M. Dibelius's classical thesis of an itinerary. We believe that we have recognized a tradition or source of a continuous nature that runs through and undergirds Acts 16–20. On the other hand, the reserve expressed above with regard to M. Dibelius's thesis of an itinerary and its modification by P. Vielhauer remains in force, for they consider the itinerary equal in importance to Paul's letters, and they maintain, for example, that the itinerary stands behind Acts 13–14. It should be emphasized that we, on the contrary, could never have been able to recover the above source without recourse to Paul's letters.

We remarked above that Luke filled out the list of stations available to him with local traditions, whereby he partially included individual episodes from the source. When Acts 18:1–17 is analyzed in the following, with the elements of the Lukan redaction being taken into consideration and a comparison being made with Paul's letters, will there be a similarly surprising confirmation of the results of the above chronology? Does Acts 18:1–17 even still provide us with an absolute datum for the chronology?

3.3 ON THE QUESTION OF THE INDIVIDUAL TRADITIONS CONTAINED IN ACTS 18:1–17

3.3.1 The Structure and Train of Thought

The text may be divided into three units. After the transition in v. 1, which contains characteristically Lukan vocabulary (*meta tauta*: eight times in the New Testament, seven of which occur in Luke's two volumes: Luke 5:27; 10:1; 12:4; 17:8; Acts 7:7; 13:20; 15:16; Mark 16:17 [secondary ending of Mark]), the text is best divided in the following manner.

(I) Verses 2–3: Paul meets Aquila and Priscilla in Corinth. They had lately (*prosphatōs*) come from Italy, for Claudius had expelled all the Jews from Rome. Paul resides with them. He also works with the couple, since they practiced the same trade, tentmaking.

Verse 4, the report that Paul preached in the synagogue every sabbath and thereby persuaded Jews and Greeks, should be attributed to the Lukan mode of connecting episodes. It does not necessarily belong to unit I. Verse 4 is more readily understandable as the transition to the next unit.

(II) Verses 5–8 report Paul's intensified missionary activity after the arrival of Silas and Timothy (v. 5: "Paul was occupied with preaching").[49] Verse 4 reported preaching every sabbath as a *less intense* level of missionary activity (only once a week) and is the internal presupposition of this *intensified* missionary activity.

Verses 5–6 are, so to speak, the detailed explication of the persuasion (*peithein*) of the Jews mentioned in the first part of the transition in v. 4. As this fails, Paul turns to the Gentiles with a symbolic action against the Jews (v. 6: "Your blood be upon your heads!"). This is the explication of the second part of the transition in v. 4, the persuasion of the Greeks.

Verse 7: Paul goes to the house of Titius, a worshiper of God. The

157

success of his proclamation has increased since he turned away from the Jews. The conversion of Crispus, the ruler of the synagogue, brings about a wave of conversions (v. 8).

Paul's vision of Christ (or, more precisely, Paul's audition of Christ) in the following verses (vv. 9–10) (a) explains the length of Paul's stay in Corinth (v. 11: eighteen months), (b) illustrates the importance of the Corinthian congregation in Luke's time (cf. *1 Clem.*), and, above all, (c) serves as a *transition* to the following episode about Gallio, for these verses announce in advance that no harm will come to Paul.

(III) Verses 12–17: "Paul before Gallio" deals with, as vv. 6–7 have already done, Paul's conflict with the Jews and thereby takes up a thoroughly Lukan theme.

Verse 12 is set apart almost abruptly from the preceding: "But when Gallio was proconsul of Achaia. . . ." One almost gets the impression that Luke had not previously reported anything about Paul's stay in Corinth.

It should be noticed that Paul does not have to speak a single word for the Jews' accusation to be undermined. Before Paul is able to say a word, Gallio rejects the Jews' accusation in a manner that, in Luke's opinion, is exemplary for a government official involved in a controversy between the church and Judaism: Gallio presides over cases of wrongdoing only, not over the disputes about Jewish law (v. 15).

After Gallio has driven the Jews from the tribunal, the people seize Sosthenes, the ruler of the synagogue (who evidently was not driven away?), and beat him. The righteous wrath of the people over the Jews' attempted illegal action is expressed by beating their representative. The slug returns to the sluggers. That this internal connection between "the Jews' accusation" and "the beating of the Jews" was intended by Luke is shown by the following sentence: "But Gallio paid no attention to this" (v. 17). The beating is part of the scene before Gallio.

3.3.2 Questions on the History of Traditions in Acts 18:1–17

We noted above that Luke usually groups together into *one* passage whatever local traditions were available to him about a given locality. If he mentions the same locality again, he presents no more than a summarizing report. Thus the account of the second (historically, the third) visit to Corinth contains only the statement that Paul stayed there three months (on this, see p. 178) and the similarly Lukan report of the Jews' plot against Paul that made it necessary for him to travel on to Macedonia (20:3). This finding raises the question of the interrelationship of the traditions that have been worked into Acts 18:1–17. Do they all derive from Paul's founding visit in Corinth? Or did Luke, in accordance with the redactional tendency just mentioned, rework the traditions available to him on Paul's three visits into *one* report?[50]

We shall methodically approach this question by first determining whether the units isolated above could derive from several mutually exclusive times of Paul's stays in Corinth. As we investigate each unit, we shall ask which elements Luke found in the tradition. In the event that such elements can be isolated, only these elements will enable final judgment as to whether Acts 18:1–17 contains traditions about several of Paul's stays in Corinth.

The following observation seems to enable us to assume that our text reflects at least two of Paul's visits to Corinth. There is no internal connection between units I and II and unit III. Both (a) literary and (b) material reasons stand in support of this observation. The literary reasons are as follows.

(1) The chronological reference to eighteen months (v. 11) apparently delimits the period described in vv. 2–8 (10).[51]

(2) The phrase "But when Gallio was proconsul" is—as stated above—an abrupt opening. It is as if nothing has previously been reported of Paul's stay in Corinth.

(3) Unit III is completely understandable in itself.

A weighty *material* reason for the assumption that units I, II, and III reflect several of Paul's visits to Corinth is that in v. 8 the ruler of the synagogue is Crispus (unit II), whereas in v. 17 Sosthenes is given this title (unit III). The conclusion that arises from this observation is that we are confronted here with a change in the office of the ruler of the synagogue that cannot be accommodated into any one of Paul's stays in Corinth. Against this conclusion it may not be said that there were several rulers of the synagogue[52] or that another person was elected to be ruler of the synagogue because Crispus had become a Christian.[53] This latter argument historicizes in a way that is inappropriate to the text.

Above it was seen that units I, II, and III, even in their redactional form, reflect various stays in Corinth. We now ask about the traditional elements that have been worked into unit III and that seem to offer further confirmation of the above result.

The name of the ruler of the synagogue, Sosthenes, probably derives from old tradition. Why should Luke have invented this name? We know nothing else of a Sosthenes who was the ruler of the synagogue in Corinth. The assumption that he became a Christian and appears as a co-author of 1 Corinthians is unprovable. It is most probable that Luke knew a tradition that associated a ruler of the synagogue named Sosthenes with one of Paul's stays in Corinth (on the relationship of this Sosthenes to the person of Gallio in this tradition, see immediately below).

As regards the historicity of a trial of Paul before Gallio, we should remember what was said above (p. 18) about Luke's apologetical tendency: Gallio reacts in a manner that Luke considers exemplary for a representative of the state who is involved in a controversy between Jews and Christians. This insight prohibits us from viewing such[54] a trial of Paul as historical. A further argument against such a supposition, which is based solely on Acts, arises from the literary character of unit III.

Verses 12ff. are not a report of a trial; they are an intentional presentation of a nontrial and an explication of the reasons such a trial may not even take place. A strict reading reveals that there is absolutely no reported conversation between Paul and Gallio. Conversation occurs only between the Jews and Gallio.

Thus, redaction-historical and literary reasons stand against the generally held opinion that there was a trial of Paul before Gallio in Corinth that resulted from a conspiracy of the Jews.

It is in general certain that Luke does not simply create episodes but rather formulates on the basis of tradition and develops and interprets this tradition in accord with his theology. For this reason, denial of the historicity of a trial before Gallio does not automatically mean denial of every sort of relationship between the apostle to the Gentiles and the proconsul. It is most likely that Luke had a tradition in which one of Paul's visits to Corinth was connected with the person of Gallio and that Luke then developed this tradition—in accord with his theology—into the episode of a nontrial of Paul before Gallio. Luke possibly received from the same tradition the person of Sosthenes, who gets beaten by the Corinthians after the nontrial. This is likely in light of the observation that the figure of Sosthenes, seen in terms of literary criticism, does not fit very well into the Lukan scene of the Jews' accusation and Gallio's response. The scene seems to have reached its conclusion when the Jews are driven away from the tribunal (v. 16). The following report about the beating of Sosthenes in v. 17 comes a little too late and stands in tension with v. 16; it presupposes that the ruler of the synagogue evidently was not driven away—otherwise the people would not have been able to beat him before the tribunal.

For this reason, it is most probable that Luke found the persons of Gallio and Sosthenes together in the same tradition about one of Paul's visits to Corinth. It is likely that Luke developed this tradition into a "nontrial," where the Jews spoke against Paul before Gallio, and that he exemplified the punishment of the Jews by having the ruler of the synagogue, Sosthenes, beaten.

We have now shown that unit III (Acts 18:12ff.) is a disparate entity when compared with units I and II, and we have isolated the traditional elements contained in this unit. We shall now examine whether units I and II are similarly disparate.

The internal structure of the passage (see section 3.3.1) revealed that units I and II are clearly distinguishable units that Luke has linked together through the transitional v. 4. Whether units I and II can be understood independently of one another depends on the exegesis of v. 7: "And he left there and went to the house of a man named Titius Justus, a worshiper of God." If this indicates a change of residence, as Haenchen (ad loc.) thinks (see also Codex Bezae [D]), we could conclude experimentally that there was a tradition about one of Paul's stays in Corinth according to which Paul resided in the house of Titius Justus. Unit I would then, in contrast, preserve a tradition about Paul residing in Priscilla and Aquila's house. If v. 7 indicates merely a change in the location of Paul's teaching,[55] the preceding hypothesis would not be convincing. The change in the place of instruction (in the house of Titius Justus instead of in the synagogue) would have resulted from the Jews' hostile attitude (notice, however, that the house mentioned lies in the vicinity of the synagogue).

The decision will have to be made on the basis of whether units I and II, after removal of the Lukan elements, present an internally consistent layer of tradition that is understandable in itself. This is actually the case if one understands v. 7 to indicate a change in the place of instruction. If we remove Paul's proclamation every sabbath in the synagogue (v. 4, which derives from Luke's mode of connecting episodes), the symbolic turn away from the Jews (v. 6), and the change in the place of instruction (v. 7, which again derives from Luke's mode of ordering episodes), there remains a core of tradition that is understandable in itself: Paul's work and residence with Priscilla and Aquila, the arrival of Timothy and Silas from Macedonia, Paul's preaching in the

161

house of Titius Justus, and the conversion of Crispus, the ruler of the synagogue.

With regard to the question of the traditional character of the connection between Claudius's edict concerning the Jews and the presence of Priscilla and Aquila, the same applies as applied to Paul's trial before Gallio: After the removal of the Lukan elements, the core of this report probably derives from old tradition. In the following comparison of the traditions recovered from Acts 18 with letters, we shall have to check whether one of Paul's stays in Corinth can be brought into a chronological relationship with the edict of Claudius.

3.3.3 Comparison of the Traditions Recovered from Acts 18:1–17 with the Chronology Obtained Solely on the Basis of the Letters

We are now in the position to venture an answer to the two questions to which our analysis of Acts 18:1–17 has been leading: (1) Can we obtain absolute dates for Paul's chronology from the traditions that are reflected in Acts 18? (2) Are the traditions reworked in Acts 18 confirmed by the foregoing chronology? We shall begin with the first question.

3.3.3.1 ON THE DATA IN ACTS 18 RELEVANT TO ABSOLUTE CHRONOLOGY

The two world-historical data contained in the traditions of Acts 18 and verifiable through secular historical sources are the references to (a) the expulsion of the Jews from Rome and (b) the proconsulate of Gallio in Achaia. These data of Acts 18:1–17 are found respectively in units where the traditional element reflects different visits by Paul to Corinth, which were separated from each other by a considerable length of time (enough time for a new ruler of the synagogue to take office). Literary criticism and observation of Luke's redactional tendency in using local traditions similarly led us to the conclusion that the traditions in Acts 18 reflect various visits. Our task in this section is first to employ the extant secular historical sources to determine the exact chronological dates of Gallio's proconsulate and of Claudius's edict concerning the Jews. If we find that these two events were separated by a considerable period of time, this finding would confirm our assumption above that Acts 18 has reworked traditions from various visits by

Paul. On the other hand, this finding would also provide some support for the reliability of the two data relevant to the absolute chronology.

After these two chronological questions have been dealt with, it must be asked whether the above chronology, which was obtained solely on the basis of the letters, stands in harmony with these absolute dates.

3.3.3.1.1 The Gallio-Inscription

In his book on Paul,[56] A. Deissmann made available to the general public four fragments of the Gallio-inscription, which was discovered in Delphi. The four fragments preserve parts of a letter by the emperor Claudius. Since reference to the twenty-sixth imperatorial acclamation is clearly legible in the inscription, and since this date may be determined on the basis of the extant sources, the letter can be dated between 25 January and 1 August of the year 52 C.E.

According to Plassart's analysis, the edition of five further fragments,[57] three of which were known to Deissmann,[58] leads to the conclusion that the letter was directed not to the city of Delphi, as Deissmann[59] still assumed, but to a proconsul of the province Achaia. The letter pertains to the city of Delphi and mentions Gallio.[60] Since the reference to Gallio is in the nominative, Gallio cannot have been the letter's recipient. He nevertheless could have been the recipient's proconsular predecessor. This is clear because Claudius's letter evidently presents the imperial decision about a controversy in Delphi, of which the emperor had been informed by a letter from Gallio. This leads to the following conclusion regarding Gallio's year of service. Since the letter was composed between January and August 52 C.E., the recipient was in office *at the latest* by the year 52 (did the term of office begin on 1 May in Achaia?). The other possibility, that Claudius's letter reached Gallio's successor during the last part of his term and that he had been proconsul since 1 May 51, is unlikely, because the imperial letter is written in response to Gallio's inquiry ("Claudius refers to a correspondence of Gallio when he prescribes the measures that should be taken"[61]) and because it would have been extremely unusual if Claudius had allowed such a relatively long period of time to pass between Gallio's report and his decision.

Result: The edition of the five further fragments of the Gallio-inscription has shown that the recipient of the imperial letter was probably Gallio's *successor*. Nothing changes, however, as regards the usual dating[62] of Gallio's term of office. It should be reckoned as falling chronologically in the years 51/52 C.E.

3.3.3.1.2 Claudius's Edict Concerning the Jews[63]

It was already noted above (p. 2) that the conventional chronology relies on Orosius's report for the date of the Jews' expulsion from Rome. Orosius reports that it occurred in the ninth year of Claudius, that is, 49 C.E. (Claudius reigned from 41 to 54). The passage reads: "Anno eiusdem nono expulsos per Claudium Urbe Iudaeos Iosephus refert. Sed me magis Suetonius movet, qui ait hoc modo: Claudius Iudaeos impulsore Chresto adsidue tumultuantes Roma expulit" ("Josephus reports that the Jews were expelled from the city by Claudius in his ninth year. I, however, am more convinced by Suetonius, who asserts as follows: Claudius expelled the Jews from Rome who were exceedingly riotous because of the instigator Chrestus" [*Historiae adversum paganos* 7.6.15, tr.]).[64]

The well-known passage from Suetonius,[65] *Caes. Claudius* 25, is accurately cited by Orosius. The origin of the first part of the passage in Orosius, together with the indication of the year, is still today a moot point. If one follows Harnack in viewing Julius Africanus as perhaps responsible for the tradition (see above, p. 6)—for nothing of the sort is found in the works of Josephus, which have been preserved in their complete form[66]—then the problem is simply shoved from one place to another, and nothing much has been gained as regards the question of the reliability of the indication of the year.

In view of the secondary character of Orosius's historical work, both in general and in the dubious indication of the source in this special case, one should, for reasons of method, in any event *not* proceed on the basis of the date of the Jews' expulsion that he has preserved.

In the following analysis of the texts that are relevant to Claudius's edict against the Jews, we should first make a remark about the passage from Suetonius mentioned above. Attention to the wording of the text reveals that the statement should be understood in an exclusive sense, indicating that (only) those Jews were expelled who were directly connected with the disturbances involving Chrestus: "Iudaeos impulsore Chresto assidue tumultuantes Roma expulit" (*Caes. Claudius* 25).

Dio Cassius 60.6.6 also reports on an edict by Claudius concerning the Jews (though this report pertains to the year 41 C.E.):[67] "As for the Jews, who had again increased so greatly that by reason of their multitude it would have been hard without raising a tumult to bar them from the city, he did not drive them out, but ordered them, while continuing their traditional mode of life, not to hold meetings" (trans. E. Cary).

What is the relationship between the traditions of Suetonius and those of Dio? Both report measures taken by Claudius against the Jews living in Rome. Dio, however, explicitly expresses doubt about what Suetonius assumes, namely, that the Jews were expelled "without raising a tumult." This remarkable situation cannot be fortuitous and demands an explanation in terms of the history of traditions, especially since both measures again have it in common that they stand in the context of dealing with a concrete incident that endangered the political peace in Rome. This context of Dio's statement is clear from the sentence that directly follows: "He also disbanded the clubs, which had been reintroduced by Gaius." The edict concerning the Jews, alongside the disbandment of the clubs just mentioned, is related to the suppression of the institution of associations and should be understood, in Dio's opinion, as a retraction of the right of association granted the Jews.[68] This act was intended to establish control over the political intrigues that accompanied the change of power in Rome after Gaius was murdered. Roman officials considered the associations, especially in Rome, to be revolutionary nuclei that should be disbanded as soon "as tendencies are uncovered that endanger the state."[69]

The *political* context of Suetonius's report of Claudius's measure is self-evident. Disturbances among the Jews living in Rome which were related to a messianic figure—whether Christian or Jewish made no difference to the Romans—gave rise to the suspicion of intentional revolutionary intrigues and demanded governmental involvement.

This demonstration that both texts report *political* measures against Roman Jewry permits us to suggest that both traditions derive from the same incident. The following observations on the history of traditions supply further confirmation of this hypothesis.

Dio, of course, was not an eyewitness; he reworks sources.[70] When he states that an expulsion of the Jews from Rome would have been impossible for the first year of Claudius's reign (41 C.E.)[71] and then immediately thereafter reports an ersatz measure pertaining to the Jews (precisely because expulsion was impossible!), it sounds as if he is correcting[72] a tradition that actually asserted the historicity of such a (impossible) measure during the first year of Claudius's reign. As the object of correction, Suetonius's report comes into consideration. It is possible that Dio understood Suetonius's report in an inclusive sense.

In view of the literary relationship of Dio and Suetonius in other matters,[73] it is more probable, however, that both authors drew upon a common source. Dio seems to have had access to other sources, which enabled him to add that the imperial edict occurred in the first year of Claudius's reign and which allowed him to correct the misunderstanding that could arise from his other source.[74]

The source that Dio corrected and that Suetonius copied nevertheless probably contains an element of truth insofar as an imperial edict concerning the Jews also brought about the expulsion of some Jews, especially since disbandment of a *collegium* in Rome usually resulted in expulsions.[75] Further, the source seems to have accurately preserved the occasion of the edict, disturbances involving Chrestus (see below).[76] Accordingly, the solid historical kernel of the reports about Claudius's edict concerning the Jews in the year 41 C.E.[77] is the following. The emperor expelled the people who were directly involved in the disturbances involving Chrestus in a Roman Jewish synagogue. Fearing political implications, he denied the other members of the synagogue the right to meet together and thus retracted the right of association. Dio seems to have generalized unhistorically when he spoke of *the* Jews in his account.

Unfortunately these considerations can only be said to be probable, for we know only partially what events Dio reported for the year 49 and thus are unable to verify the above conclusions. Though Dio's eighty-volume work on Roman history extends into the year 229, it ceases to be an original work with the report on the year 46 (apart from small sections on the years 217–219, books 79–80). Further, the report covering the year 49 (among other years) has been preserved only in Byzantine extracts. These extracts say nothing about an edict concerning the Jews in the year 49, but this does not necessarily mean that the original did not mention an edict.

On the other hand, another argument against the historicity of an edict concerning the Jews in the year 49 is that the silence of Tacitus (whose report on the first six years of Claudius has been lost) would otherwise be hardly understandable.

We concluded above, primarily on the basis of the history of traditions, that the reports of Dio and Suetonius derive from the same strand of tradition. We still need to evaluate critically the arguments of investigators who assume that Claudius enacted two different measures concerning the Jews in Rome. If their arguments can be defused, this would be a further plus for the thesis presented above.

The impossibility of an expulsion of the Jews from Rome in the year

41 is evident to some investigators[78] from Claudius's friendly politics with regard to the Jews at the beginning of his reign. This friendliness is documented in the emperor's letters to the city of Alexandria and the "rest of the world" (*allē oikoumenē*) that are preserved in Josephus,[79] *Ant.* 19.280ff., 286ff.[80] Here the privileges and rights of the Jews that were revoked under Gaius are reinstated (even though one probably cannot conclude on the basis of this passage that Alexandrian Jewry received the full rights of citizenship[81]).

This attitude is supposedly understandable in view of the close relations between the emperor and the grandson of Herod the Great, Agrippa, who was living in Rome and who had been living there with his mother Berenice even under Tiberius's government, though at the end of Tiberius's reign he had fallen from grace and had been imprisoned for a few months (Josephus, *Ant.* 18.188ff.). Later, under Caligula, with whom he had formed a close relationship in the time of Tiberius (Josephus, *Ant.* 18.166–67, 187–88), he was released and became king over a part of the kingdom of his grandfather Herod (Josephus, *Ant.* 18.237). Agrippa was evidently of substantial help to Claudius during the confusion that followed the murder of Gaius, and he apparently advised Claudius to accept the throne when Claudius was still undecided (Josephus, *Ant.* 19.236ff.). Thus it was no surprise when Claudius expressed his gratitude after he had taken office and added Judaea and other areas to Agrippa's kingdom, thereby making it even larger than the kingdom of Agrippa's grandfather Herod the Great (Josephus, *Ant.* 19.274–75; *Bell.* 2.215). The text documenting the gift, originally written on a bronze tablet, was placed with due ceremony in the Capitoline temple (Josephus, *Bell.* 2.216). Agrippa received the insignia of a consul and expressed his gratitude in a speech delivered before the senate in Greek (Dio Cassius 60.8.2–3).

These close relations to the Jewish crown and Claudius's measures reestablishing the Jews' privileges in Alexandria and the "rest of the world" are cited by the investigators who maintain that these facts cannot be harmonized with the assumption that the Jews were expelled from Rome during the same period. In view of the good relationship between Claudius and Agrippa, such an edict is considered a historical impossibility, especially since Agrippa's own influence was probably indirectly responsible for reinstatement of the privileges lost under Gaius. The following passage from the letter to the "rest of the world" seems to demonstrate this latter statement: "Kings Agrippa and Herod, my dearest friends, having petitioned me to permit the same privileges to be maintained for the Jews throughout the empire under the Romans as those in Alexandria enjoy . . ." (*Ant.* 19.288).

This argument, which is convincing at first, seems to be invalidated by a letter of Claudius to the city of Alexandria that was discovered on a piece of papyrus in the year 1921.[82] The letter responds to a petition delivered by a delegation from the city. Its date can be determined with all desired certainty from the date on which the governor, Aemilius Rectus, made its contents known to Egypt: 10 November 41.[83] This means that the letter was written not long after the letters preserved by Josephus mentioned above, which reinstated the Jews' privileges in the empire.

In this letter Claudius admonishes the Alexandrians not to desecrate the rites of the Jews in prayer to their God, but he also warns the Jews:

> . . . And on the other hand I explicitly order the Jews not to agitate for more privileges than they formerly possessed, and not in the future to send out a separate embassy as if they lived in a separate city, . . . and not to bring in or admit Jews who come down the river from Syria or Egypt, a proceeding which will compel me to conceive serious suspicions; otherwise I will by all means take vengeance on them as fomenters of what is a general plague infecting the whole world.[84]

Research has analyzed this letter primarily to determine whether it witnesses to the expansion of Christianity all the way to Alexandria by the year 41 C.E. This question, which I think should be answered in the affirmative even though the majority of investigators have answered it in the negative, does not call for further treatment here.[85]

More important for us is that the letter indicates that Claudius's attitude toward the Jews—even at the beginning of his term—was hardly characterized by sympathy; it was politically motivated. To conclude from Agrippa's good relations with Claudius that Claudius was benevolent toward the Jews, as those investigators mentioned above do, is misleading (and besides, it psychologizes in an impermissible manner). All three of the reported actions mentioned above—the reinstatement of the privileges of Alexandrian Jewry (and of Jews in the "rest of the world"), the threat of severe punishment of the Alexandrian Jews (in the same year!), and finally the measures taken against the Jews in Rome that are visible behind the reports of Dio and Suetonius—reflect the same basic political stance.[86] Exercise of religion is generally allowed; political implications are suppressed through appropriate means, including expulsion.[87] Even the reinstatement of the Jews' privileges in Alexandria may be explained on the basis of the political consideration that, in view of the peculiar nature of the Jewish people, the danger of a political uprising would have been greater if these privileges had not been guaranteed. Such a situation is illustrated well by the Jewish reaction to Gaius's attempt to erect his statue in the temple at Jerusalem.[88]

The result of these considerations is that reference to the friendly nature of Claudius's politics concerning the Jews at the beginning of his reign cannot be used as an argument against the historicity of the expulsion of Jews from Rome at approximately the same time. Thus, the decisive reason for assuming that there were two edicts concerning the Jews in Rome during Claudius's reign does not hold water. This is all the more the case since it was shown above on the basis of the history of traditions that the texts employed for the hypothesis of two edicts against the Jews derive from the same tradition and that Dio's dating (in contrast to Orosius's dating) of the edict reflected in this tradition should be trusted until the contrary is proven.[89]

Reference to the absence of Chrestus in Dio's report signifies nothing, for—as was already stated above (p. 189 n. 76)—Dio was generally silent about Christianity. In recent times it has been claimed repeatedly that Chrestus was a Jewish disturber and that the presence of this name in Suetonius's report does not reflect Christianity's penetration into Roman Jewry.[90] This view, however, is extremely improbable, especially since "Chrestus" was used for "Christ" in popular language,[91] since Tacitus knows the designation *Chrestianoi* (*Annals* 15.44.2),[92] and since the name *Chrestiani* was still used as a designation for Christians in the second century.[93] Suetonius's mistake is that he considers the cultic hero to be an earthly person who was present in Rome.[94] Moreover, a word of warning should be said against placing too much weight on the importance of this question for the chronology. Even if Chrestus was the name of a Jewish disturber in Rome, and Claudius's edict was intended to suppress an uprising (or something similar) that involved this Chrestus, Christians were nevertheless in danger of being expelled from Rome, for they were considered Jews by the Roman officials.

The final bastion of the thesis that the edict concerning the Jews (or one such edict) should be dated in the year 49 is the witness of Acts 18:2, insofar as one combines this with the reference to Gallio. Lake, for example, writes the following about Claudius's measure that affected the Jews (he evidently considers Suetonius and Dio Cassius to be dependent on the same tradition): "It must be admitted that if there were no reason to the contrary it would probably be put down to A.D. 41. Acts, however, distinctly says that Aquila and Priscilla had 'recently' (*prosphatōs*) arrived from Italy, and 41 is far too early to be a conceivable date for Paul in Corinth."[95]

Momigliano's thesis that the Jews were expelled from Rome in the year 49 seems to be based primarily on Acts: "We cannot dismiss . . . the evidence of two such independent authorities as Suetonius and the Acts, though we may dismiss Orosius."[96]

Authors such as Leon, who speak of only one edict concerning the Jews, namely, the one in the year 41, nevertheless attempt to fit this date into the chronology of Paul that is based on the reference to Gallio. They try to avoid contradicting Acts by assuming that the couple acquainted with Paul took several years for their trip from Rome to Corinth: "It need not, however, be assumed that this couple went to Corinth immediately after leaving Rome. They may well have spent several years elsewhere in the interim, so that the first year of Claudius, 41, is not necessarily excluded."[97]

The historicizing use of Acts evident in all three of the above quotations is impermissible in our investigation for the reasons of method stated above. Thus the date implied by Acts for the edict against the Jews, shortly before the year 50, cannot be used as an argument against the year 41. Moreover, apart from this renewed methodological objection, it should be emphasized that Luke—contrary to what is silently assumed in the above opinion—*does not date* the expulsion of the Jews or Gallio's period of office,[98] and he is probably not even aware of the chronological relationship between the two. The argument from Acts 18 against dating Claudius's edict concerning the Jews in 41 arises only because we are fortunately able to determine Gallio's period of office. On the basis of this external information, one *extracts* the conclusion that the expulsion of the Jews occurred at approximately this time. This conclusion, which rests on a number of assumptions, should never be viewed as an "independent witness" for the year 49 C.E. as the date of the edict concerning the Jews. For reasons of method, one should proceed rather in the inverse manner and throw light from the truly independent traditions onto Acts' report.

Our analysis of the extant sources for the edict concerning the Jews has yielded a great degree of probability for the following result: The edict of Claudius concerning the Jews that is reflected in Acts 18:2 was issued in the year 41.[99] The effect of the edict was that those who participated directly in the controversy involving Chrestus had to leave the city of Rome. The Jewish Christians Priscilla and Aquila were subject to expulsion and arrived in Corinth shortly after 41.

The chronological determination of the two pieces of world-historical data in Acts 18 as belonging, respectively, in the years 41 and 51/52 has confirmed the above analysis of Acts 18 from the perspective of the history of traditions and literary criticism. This analysis revealed that Acts 18 reflects more than one stay in Corinth, especially since each datum appears in a different unit (I and III) and since these units were already relegated, experimentally, to two chronologically separated visits. Our confirmation gives the two absolute dates a certain amount of credibility, even though this is not yet a decisive degree of credibility. The actual decision as to whether the two datable events recorded in Luke's tradition can and may be used for Pauline chronology must be made in the following, where we shall ask whether these events fit into the framework obtained solely on the basis of the letters.

3.3.3.1.3 Paul's Stays in Corinth in the Years 41/42 and 51/52 as Part of a Chronology of Paul?

The *terminus post quem* for Paul's conversion is the death of Jesus and the appearances of the resurrected one shortly thereafter. Between these events and Paul's meeting with the heavenly Lord, some time will have passed, for (a) Paul's activity as a persecutor, however this should be construed, already presupposes the existence of a Christian congregation in Damascus and (b) in 1 Cor. 15:3ff. Paul describes Jesus' appearance to him as the last in the list of appearances and evidently assumes that some period of time separated the appearance to him from the appearances to Cephas, James, the five hundred brethren, and all the apostles. In the following we shall reckon the span of time from the death of Jesus to Paul's conversion as three years.[100] We are nevertheless conscious of the arbitrary nature of such a procedure. The exact chronological date of the death of Jesus cannot be determined with absolute certainty. Those years in which the fourteenth or fifteenth of Nisan fell on a Friday come into consideration, that is, 27, 30, and 33. One should not proceed exclusively from the arithmetic mean, 30,[101] but should also take the year 27 into consideration, for G. Hölscher has presented arguments for this date that as yet have not been thoroughly refuted.[102] The date of Paul's conversion would accordingly be the year 30 or 33.

One other uncertainty of Pauline chronology is evident when we take into account the above finding that Paul does not provide any information about the lengths of his stay in Arabia, of his journey to

Syria and Cilicia, and of his stay in Jerusalem for the Jerusalem Conference. As a working hypothesis, we shall reckon a total of two years for these periods, and we shall add in one further year for the time between the second visit to Jerusalem and the second stay in Galatia.

As regards the question of the periods covered by Paul's references "after three/fourteen years" (Gal. 1:18; 2:1), it should be remembered that the ancient mode of counting reckoned the first and last years as full years. This means that the following formulas apply to the references just mentioned:[103]

$$\text{"after three years"} = x + 1 + y$$
$$\text{"after fourteen years"} = x + 12 + y$$

For this reason, we shall calculate with the arithmetic means of two years and thirteen years.

These considerations yield the following table:

Conversion	30 (33)
Arabia	31 (34)
First visit to Jerusalem	33 (36)
Syria and Cilicia	34 (37)
Second visit to Jerusalem	47 (50)
Galatia	48 (51) in the summer
1 Corinthians (Ephesus)	49 (52)
Intervening visit to Corinth	49 (52)
Third stay in Corinth	51/52 (54/55)

While one will want to remain conscious of the various underlying assumptions of the above table, there is an amazing correspondence of the absolute dates of Acts with the chronology developed solely on the basis of the letters:

(a) Even when one takes into account the chronological uncertainties, it is possible that the founding visit to Corinth occurred shortly after 41.

(b) A visit by Paul to Corinth circa 51/52, which is implied by the reference to Gallio, fits in well with the above table and would correspond to the intervening visit or to the last stay.

In sum, these considerations impart a high degree of probability to the absolute chronological data isolated in Acts 18. The verification of these two data through the chronology developed solely on the basis of the letters permits us to accept them into this chronology.[104]

Though one will have to refrain from calculating a semi-exact date for Paul's conversion (the above table should not be construed as such, but rather as an *aid* to test the absolute dates in Acts 18), the two absolute dates recovered above do enable progress[105] insofar as they allow us to determine the time of Paul's mission in Greece and the chronological span separating 1 Thessalonians, which was composed during the founding visit in Corinth, and 1 Corinthians, which was written in Ephesus. If Paul was in Corinth, at the latest, shortly after the year 41, then he will have begun his actual missionary work in Philippi and Thessalonica at the end of the 30s. The chronological span between 1 Thessalonians and 1 Corinthians would then be circa eight to eleven years (that between the founding visit in Thessalonica and the composition of 1 Corinthians would be circa ten to thirteen years).

3.3.3.2 THE INDIVIDUAL TRADITIONS IN ACTS 18:1–17 AND THEIR INTEGRATION INTO THE ABOVE CHRONOLOGY

In the following we shall examine those traditional elements in Acts 18 that are also reflected in Paul's letters. We shall set to one side, because of the lack of parallels, the traditional fragments in unit III (Gallio and Sosthenes) and also Paul's preaching in the house of Titius Justus[106] in unit I. The following traditions remain: (1) Paul's work and residence with Priscilla and Aquila, (2) the arrival of Timothy and Silas in Corinth from Macedonia, and (3) the conversion of Crispus, the ruler of the synagogue. We shall investigate these traditions in the order just listed.

3.3.3.2.1 *Priscilla and Aquila*[107]

This couple is mentioned in Paul's letters at 1 Cor. 16:19 and Rom. 16:3. In 1 Corinthians they send greetings to the Corinthians. This permits the thesis that they were personally acquainted with the Corinthians. Since they are with Paul in Ephesus, it is most probable that they made Paul's acquaintance during his founding visit in Corinth. The phrase "together with the church in their house," which follows the reference to Priscilla and Aquila in 1 Cor. 16:19, enables us to catch a glimpse of the economic status of this couple. Regardless of whether the phrase "together with the church in their house" should be understood as referring to a congregation that met in their house or—more probably—to their household as a congregation (Rom. 16:5 should certainly be understood in this sense), it is clear that the couple is affluent. Thus probability is established not only for the tradition that Paul met Priscilla and Aquila in Corinth but also for the information preserved in Acts 18 that Paul worked for them in Corinth. That Paul performed manual labor in Corinth is firmly attested by his own words (1 Cor. 4:12 and elsewhere). The affluence of the couple allowed them to employ others, among whom Paul should be counted, especially in view of the fact that Priscilla and Aquila could recognize a (Jewish) Christian comrade in him. This simultaneously implies that they were Christians even before they came to Corinth.[108] The additional report of Acts that they were tentmakers cannot be verified by the letters. Nevertheless, this information is not contrary to what can be concluded from the above, namely, that they practiced the same trade as Paul.[109]

What has been said up to now has not proven that Aquila and Priscilla had anything to do with Claudius's edict concerning the Jews, as is indicated in Acts. They could have already been in Corinth for a considerable period of time, and Luke's reason for their coming to Corinth, the edict of Claudius, could derive from Luke's penchant for meshing salvation history with world history. Apart from the correspondence of the date of the edict concerning the Jews and the time of Paul's first mission in Greece, the following observations support the view that they had recently arrived from Rome.

Paul sends greetings to the couple in Rom. 16:3. Since the assumption that Romans 16 is actually a letter to Ephesus creates more new problems than solutions to old problems,[110] one should proceed from the view that chap. 16 originally belonged to the letter to the Romans and assume that the couple was in Rome at the time when Romans was composed.[111] A plausible explanation of their presence in Rome at this time is the assumption that after having been expelled in the year 41 they returned to Rome around the end of Claudius's reign. (In not following the usual dating of the edict to the year 49, our chronology has the advantage of not having to postulate an unreasonably short period between the couple's expulsion and their return.)

In Rom. 16:4, Paul gives the couple special praise for aiding him (literally, they "risked their necks" for his life). This passage permits the hypothesis that this deed occurred in connection with the dangers that Paul encountered in the vicinity of Ephesus (see 1 Cor. 15:32; 2 Cor. 1:8–9). This assistance and the reference to the couple in 1 Corinthians presuppose that they were in Ephesus until shortly before Paul's third visit to Corinth. Since Paul wrote Romans during this visit, the couple's emigration to Rome will have occurred not long before the composition of this letter. Their return to their old residence would have had eminent importance for Paul's missionary plans, as is evident from the location of the reference to the couple in the list of greetings in Romans. Together with the other people mentioned in the greetings who were acquainted with Paul, they were evidently supposed to get things ready for Paul's arrival at the starting base for his future missionary activity in Spain, the congregation in Rome. Or else they were supposed to ensure that he received a warm reception there.[112]

In sum, our comparison of the traditions about Priscilla and Aquila preserved in Acts 18 and the references to the couple in Paul's letters showed that the traditions in Acts are largely confirmed by the letters. This finding also gave us the methodological right to combine the witness of the letters with the traditions about the couple in Acts 18. We obtained thereby a picture of the importance of Aquila and Priscilla in the Pauline mission that the letters alone would not have allowed.

3.3.3.2.2 Crispus

The conversion of Crispus (the ruler of the synagogue) is confirmed by Paul's own statements. In 1 Cor. 1:14, Paul even remarks that contrary to his custom of not baptizing, he baptized Crispus and Gaius (who is not mentioned in Acts). In view of the context of this statement in 1 Corinthians, this baptism can have occurred only during the founding visit. While the tradition in Acts 18 does not explicitly say that Paul baptized Crispus, it nevertheless also reports that Crispus's conversion and baptism (v. 8!) occurred during the founding visit. This point of agreement speaks in favor of the antiquity (and reliability) of the tradition about Crispus in Acts 18.

3.3.3.2.3 The Arrival of Silas and Timothy from Macedonia

It is certain that Timothy and Silas were in Corinth during the founding visit there. This is clear from the description of the initial proclamation in 2 Cor. 1:19, "the Son of God, Jesus Christ, whom we preached among you, Silvanus and Timothy and I," and further from the opening of 1 Thessalonians, which was composed in Corinth (1 Thess. 1:1). That Timothy and Paul did not arrive in Corinth at the same time is evident from 1 Thess. 3:6, where it is presupposed that Paul was already present in Corinth when Timothy arrived from Thessalonica. Thus, not only could the order of events in the first part of Acts 18 be correct (first Paul worked with Priscilla and Aquila, *then* Timothy arrived), but the chapter also correctly reports that Timothy and Silas were present during the founding visit. Further, the statement that Timothy came to Corinth from Macedonia does not contradict 1 Thess. 3:6, which says that Timothy came from Thessalonica to Paul (in Corinth; Thessalonica was the capital of the Roman province Macedonia).

Now it was seen above, on the basis of the letters alone, that Paul received money from the Philippians also while he was in Corinth for the founding visit (see above, pp. 103ff.). Hence, there is a certain degree of probability that Timothy was part of a delegation that brought the gift to Paul in Corinth. Paul's statement that he had sent Timothy to Thessalonica from Athens (1 Thess. 3:1–2) does not contradict this view. Timothy could have also planned to make an excursion to Philippi during his visit to Thessalonica. The report in Lukan language in Acts 18:5 that Paul "was occupied with preaching" after the arrival of Timothy and Silas from Macedonia could be a redacted form of a tradition on the arrival of Timothy and Silas that spoke of a monetary gift from the Philippian congregation.

The information of Acts and the letters about "Timothy and Silas in Corinth" thus proves to be practically identical. For the sake of completeness, we should mention one exception here. Paul's letters do not confirm that Silas came to Corinth from Macedonia. If one does not want to assume that Silas—without being mentioned, of course—was part of the same delegation from Philippi as Timothy was, one may simply leave the question open. This changes nothing regarding the surprising confirmation of even this third tradition by Paul's letters. This agreement in the main points permits us in this case, too, to attribute to the tradition a value almost equal to that of the primary source and to combine the two carefully. The result yields nothing new beyond the fact, also attainable from the letters, that Paul received money from Philippi while he was in Corinth. The circumstances and purpose of this monetary gift from Philippi, however, receive new illumination through the combination of the letters and Acts on this point: Timothy apparently played an active role in gathering this gift, and the purpose of this gift was evidently to relieve Paul from the necessity of daily work so that he might devote himself to the proclamation of the gospel—here the statement formulated in Lukan

176

vocabulary, "Paul was occupied with preaching," may have preserved a kernel of truth.

The statements above about Timothy's arrival in Corinth do not place us at odds with the tension noted in the introduction between the presentations of Timothy's journey in 1 Thessalonians 3 and Acts, which was used above as an argument against combining information in Acts with information in Paul's letters. The introduction was concerned with the question of combining *Lukan* information and the *Lukan* framework with the letters of Paul. Here the question is that of the relationship of Paul's letters to the specific *traditions* available to Luke.

In summary of this section, we may venture to state the thesis that the individual *traditions* reworked by Luke possess a high degree of historical reliability once they have been integrated into the chronological framework obtained solely on the basis of the letters. When they are combined with the information from the letters, they yield a more precise picture of Paul's activity than would be possible on the basis of the letters alone, and they attain to a historical value almost equal to that of the primary source.

3.4 ACTS' EXPLICIT CHRONOLOGICAL REFERENCES PERTAINING TO PAUL'S STAY IN THESSALONICA, CORINTH, AND EPHESUS

The above chronology has enabled us to locate chronologically a few of Paul's stays with a relatively large degree of probability. Thus, in the following we shall compare the chronological references in Acts with the dates suggested by our chronology.

3.4.1 Thessalonica

Acts delimits the length of the founding visit in Thessalonica as three to four weeks, for according to Acts 17:2 Paul went to the synagogue on three sabbaths.

This chronological information cannot even raise a claim to possible historicity, because 1 Thessalonians presupposes a much longer stay: (a) Paul worked in order not to be a burden to anyone, and (b) he received support from Philippi several times (Phil. 4:16: "once and again"). Particularly this latter fact shows that the visit lasted much longer than three to four weeks.[113]

3.4.2 Corinth

According to Acts 18:11, the founding visit to Corinth spanned one and a half years. The evidence we have to check this information is not as clear as the evidence we had for the founding visit in Thessalonica. Paul met Aquila and Priscilla in Corinth shortly after the year 41. On the other hand, he traveled to the Jerusalem Conference first circa 49 (46). Assuming it to be correct that Paul's first visit to Corinth lasted one and a half years, we are confronted with difficulties in accommodating the intervening period into Paul's chronology. This is all the more a problem since we do not know at which point within the eighteen months Paul met the couple. If we suppose, in contrast, that Aquila and Priscilla had already been in Corinth for a while before Paul arrived, then it might be possible to bring the eighteen months into harmony with the date of the conference, 47/50 C.E. This assumption, however, overlooks that the date given for the conference derives from an auxiliary construction, which leaves open the possibility that the date could be up to three years earlier and that this date means nothing when isolated from the overall construction. The absolute date for the edict concerning the Jews is, in contrast, certain (41 C.E.). One will thus have to be content with being unable to verify the length of Paul's founding visit to Corinth by the letters.

The situation is better in the case of checking the report that the last stay in Corinth lasted three months (Acts 20:3). This number derives from the principle of round numbers and is redactional, as will be proven in the next section.

3.4.3 Ephesus

Acts 19:8 describes Paul's stay in Ephesus as entailing three months of proclamation to the Jews. Verse 10 then mentions two years of teaching in the hall of Tyrannus. Finally, Acts 20:31 speaks of three years. These references immediately create the impression of schematism (three months of proclamation to the Jews, two years of teaching in the hall of Tyrannus) and thus do not evoke credence. Further, the "three years" stands in tension with the other two references, for it does not presuppose a period of proclamation to the Jews. Finally, Acts' chronological data on Paul's stay in Ephesus are, in general, not confirmed by the above chronology. According to this chronology, Paul stayed in Ephesus around eighteen to twenty-two months (see the table on pp. 108–9). The question arises whether it is possible to separate tradition and redaction in Luke's references here. This actually seems to be possible. We may begin with the observation that "three" is a favorite Lukan number. See Acts 7:20; 9:9; 10:19 vl.; 11:11; 17:2; 20:3; 25:1; 28:7, 11, 12, 17. Then it should be noted that the above proclamation to the Jews derives from Luke's schema for connecting episodes. Luke had access to a local tradition which connected Paul's teaching in Ephesus with the hall of Tyrannus and which indicated that Paul taught for two years. Since Luke had to create a proclamation by Paul to the Jews in Ephesus too (because this was dogmatically correct), and since he had the chronological specification of "two years" for Paul's teaching in the hall of Tyrannus, he felt it necessary to indicate the length of the period of the proclamation to the Jews. He adopted his usual chronological specification, "three months" (see, similarly, Acts 7:20; 20:3; 28:11), and takes these months into account when he speaks of "three years" in Acts 20:32 (a year that has begun is counted as a full year).[114] What has been said leads to the conclusion that the "three months" and the "three years" are redactional specifications of the stay in Ephesus (further, three is a "round" number), while the reference to two years for Paul's teaching in the hall of Tyrannus reflects old, reliable tradition. The chronology constructed solely on the basis of the letters leads to the same conclusion, for it has Paul staying in Ephesus for almost two years.

This surprising agreement between the above chronology and the tradition in Acts may be considered further confirmation of the above reconstruction. It also demonstrates again, and clearly, that Acts contains old traditions, though these of course can be recovered only after a comparison with the chronology constructed solely on the basis of the letters.

Thus, something similar should be said regarding the explicit chronological references in Acts as was said regarding the individual traditions, the data on world history, and the list of stations. When these references have been purified of Lukan redaction, they often contain old and valuable traditional material.

NOTES

1. Certainly false is, for example, the view that all the information about Paul that is not in the letters is a Lukan "creation." M. S. Enslin (see also above, p. 126 n. 109) apparently holds this view. Enslin assumes that Luke knew Paul's letters and believes, for instance, that Luke concluded on the ba-

sis of Gal. 1:21 that Paul was born in Tarsus. Why should Luke not have decided for Antioch? (See M. S. Enslin, "Luke, the Literary Physician," in *Studies in New Testament and Early Christian Literature*, 141.) Moreover, such expressions as "create" are not helpful for the investigation of Acts, for they distract from the concern of the narrator and direct it toward the modern question "historical or unhistorical (i.e., false)." Hasty historicizing attempts replace the task of style criticism outlined by Dibelius (see above, p. 43 n. 102). This statement is directed against Enslin, ibid., and also against A. Suhl, *Paulus und seine Briefe*, who proceeds on the basis of the methodologically inadequate assumption "that Luke hardly created freely all the details he reports" (p. 13). The expressions "create/creation" are found throughout Suhl's book, e.g., pp. 128, 136 n. 30, 283ff., 313 n. 66, and frequently elsewhere.

2. It is impossible to follow R. Jewett, *A Chronology of Paul's Life*, 11, in seeing in Acts 13–14 "part of the pre-Lukan material originating in Antioch, designed to emphasize the independent role of the Antioch congregation" and then concluding that there is a polemic here against Jerusalem because Peter is absent in Acts 13–14 (p. 12). There is no way to go back to the old style of literary criticism, even if one were to try on the basis of Jewett's statement "The best surmise is that the material in Acts 13–14 was formed from the Antioch recollection of the reports rendered by Barnabas and Paul at the conclusion of the journey" (ibid.). In contrast to Jewett's procedure, questions should be raised about the traditional elements underlying the Lukan composition in Acts 13–14. Contained in these traditional elements, though this cannot be further explicated here, are reflections of joint missionary activity (within the framework of the Antiochene mission) of Barnabas and Paul (see esp. Acts 14:14). The historicity of this activity can almost be proven on the basis of the letters (Gal. 2:1, 13; 1 Cor. 9:6). The sphere of this mission should be located in South Galatia (Antioch, Iconium, Lystra). Compare 2 Tim. 3:11 with Acts 13:50; 14:5, 19. This activity will have occurred directly before the beginning of Paul's worldwide mission and will have followed on the period mentioned in Gal. 1:21. I do not believe that probability for the historicity of a mission by Paul to Cyprus can be established. See, correctly, G. Schille, *Anfänge der Kirche*, 53–57. (Schille, pp. 58–59, also makes it clear that 2 Tim. 3:11 cannot have known the Lukan report; contra W. Meeks, "Jews and Christians in Antioch in the First Four Centuries," in *SBL 1976 Seminar Papers*, 58 n. 64.) The mission in South Galatia will be taken into consideration in the final survey.

3. This has been investigated by G. Lohfink, *Paulus vor Damaskus*; C. Burchard, *Der dreizehnte Zeuge*; K. Löning, *Die Saulustradition in der Apostelgeschichte*; and Volker Stolle, *Der Zeuge als Angeklagter*, BWANT 102 (Stuttgart: Kohlhammer, 1973). A critical survey of the literature is pre-

sented by C. Burchard, "Paulus in der Apostelgeschichte." I have not seen K. Obermeier, "Die Gestalt des Paulus in der lukanischen Verkündigung: Das Paulusbild der Apostelgeschichte" (Catholic theological diss., Bonn, 1975).

4. On the history of the exegesis of this journey, see J. Dupont, "Les problèmes du livre des actes entre 1940 et 1950," in *Études sur les Actes des Apôtres*, 51ff.; J. C. Hurd, *The Origin of 1 Corinthians*, 33f. n. 2.

5. W. G. Kümmel, *Introduction to the New Testament*, 252–55; P. Vielhauer, *Geschichte der urchristlichen Literatur*, 70–81. See now H.-M. Schenke and K. M. Fischer, *Einleitung in die Schriften des Neuen Testaments*, vol. 1 of 2 vols.: *Die Briefe des Paulus und Schriften des Paulinismus*, 45, who designate the visit in Antioch as "an attempt at rapprochement."

6. Even according to Luke's intention, however, the separation of a second missionary journey from a third is inappropriate. See above, pp. 36–37 n. 48.

7. E. Trocmé, *Le "Livre des Actes" et l'Histoire*: "Besides, Acts 18:22 perhaps does not even report of a visit by Paul to Jerusalem" (p. 93 n. 1).

8. See Suhl, *Paulus*, 130: The visit especially "fits well into the picture that Acts paints of Paul's relationship to Jerusalem and thus may be easily explained as a Lukan construction."

9. Ibid., 132. In the following, the page numbers of quotations from this book will be set in parentheses.

10. Wolf-Henning Ollrog, *Paulus und seine Mitarbeiter: Untersuchungen zu Theorie und Praxis der paulinischen Mission*, WMANT 50 (Neukirchen-Vluyn: Neukirchener Verlag, 1979), 36, agrees with this view.

11. J. Wellhausen, "Noten zur Apostelgeschichte," 14.

12. H. Conzelmann, *Die Apostelgeschichte*, ad loc.: "This demonstrates his [Paul's] faithful fulfillment of Jewish prescriptions, cf. 21:23f."

13. Wellhausen correctly asks, "Further, what is this supposed to mean: Paul left Priscilla and Aquila in Ephesus but went himself into the synagogue . . . ? The synagogue is situated in Ephesus too! More than one hand was at work on this cockeyed contrast. Such foolishness tends to arise through redaction" ("Noten," 14).

14. Notice how the "Western" text smooths this over: The tension between v. 19a and v. 19b is removed by reporting first in v. 21 that Paul left Aquila and Priscilla in Ephesus.

15. Nothing more is said of Priscilla and Aquila in 19:1ff. If at least part of 19:1ff. stood in the source, then this is a further reason for assuming that Luke also introduced the couple in 18:18 as well as in 18:26.

16. It is surprising how often the secondary literature holds this Lukan fiction to be historical. Even A. von Harnack, *The Mission and Expansion of Christianity in the First Three Centuries*, 2:222, accepted it. Similarly, Helmut Koester, in James M. Robinson and Helmut Koester, *Trajectories through Early Christianity* (Philadelphia: Fortress Press, 1971), 144. See,

against this view, C. Andresen, *Geschichte des Christentums*, vol. 1: *Von den Anfängen bis zur Hochscholastik*, 3. That there was a pre-Pauline Christianity in Ephesus is clear from Acts 18:27.

17. See also Ollrog, *Paulus*, 32–33.

18. Wellhausen, "Noten," 14.

19. While Caesarea also belongs to Palestine, "the verb *katabainō* would not be used of going from Caesarea, a seaport, to Antioch, an inland town" (F. F. Bruce, *The Acts of the Apostles*, 350).

20. The cluster of participles in Acts 18:22 is Lukan narrative style. See Bl.-Debr., 14th ed., sec. 421, p. 350.

21. See M. Dibelius, "The Acts of the Apostles in the Setting of the History of Early Christian Literature," in *Studies in the Acts of the Apostles*, 197, on the indication of the station "Jerusalem" as a part of the tradition.

22. This is evidently the implication of the article by C. H. Talbert, "Again: Paul's Visits to Jerusalem": "The visit of Gal. II 1ff equals that of Acts XI 27–30, XII 25. The visit of Acts XV belongs to the indirect occasion of the epistle and is echoed in the Syncretists' charges and the Pauline responses that make up our epistle to the Galatians" (p. 40). Talbert's analysis actually leads to an equation of primary and secondary sources that is methodologically unjustifiable. Unfortunately, Talbert does not deal with the article by G. Strecker, "Die sogenannte zweite Jerusalemreise des Paulus (Act 11,27–30)."

23. See also above, p. 37 n. 51.

24. Wellhausen, "Noten," 15, and his "Kritische Analyse der Apostelgeschichte," 37–38. Wellhausen's thesis was accepted by A. Loisy, *Les Actes des Apôtres*, 708–9. See also O. Kuss, *Paulus*, 66–67.

25. Suhl, *Paulus*, 131.

26. One cannot object to this by saying that Luke could have presented the information from Acts 19 about Paul's stay in Ephesus already in Acts 18:19ff. If he had done this, he would not have been able to claim as clearly as in the present form of Acts that Paul was the first to proclaim the Christian message in Ephesus.

27. The oldest readings of Acts 12:25 report a (further) visit by Paul (with Barnabas) to Jerusalem. On this, see Hurd, *Origin*, 33ff.

I consider it certain that *Luke* had a journey from Jerusalem to Antioch in mind (see also Strecker, "Jerusalemreise," 76 n. 53). Another opinion is emphatically presented by P. Parker, "Three Variant Readings in Luke-Acts," 168ff.

28. The best-known triplet in Acts is the account of Paul's conversion. Luke will have had *one* report of this event. E. Haenchen (*The Acts of the Apostles*, 544–45 n. 6) lists the representatives of the thesis that Acts 18:22 actually reflects Paul's second visit to Jerusalem (Gal. 2). It is curious that the most important defender of this view escaped him: Ernst Barnikol, *Die drei Jerusalemreisen des Paulus*, FEUC 2 (Kiel: W. G. Mühlau, 1929). On pp.

47ff. Barnikol gives a comprehensive survey of the representatives of the view that Gal. 2:1 corresponds to Acts 18:22. Barnikol's noteworthy work is, however, still too dominated by the literary-critical phase of research into Acts.

H. L. Ramsey, "The Place of Galatians in the Career of Paul," 255–56, and Jewett, *Chronology*, throughout, also think that Acts 18:22 reflects the visit for the conference.

29. See Strecker, "Jerusalemreise," 76.

30. The verb is used sixteen times in the New Testament. Fifteen of these are in Luke's two volumes.

31. *Adelphos* in Acts is a *terminus technicus* for the Christian brother: 1:15, 16; 2:29, 37, and frequently elsewhere.

32. This word is used twelve times in the New Testament. Ten of these are in Luke's two volumes.

33. Otherwise only in Acts 12:18; 14:28; 17:4, 12; 19:23, 24; 27:20.

34. In the New Testament the substantive is found only in Acts: 15:2; 18:15; 23:29, 25:19; 26:3.

35. See Luke 19:1; Acts 12:10; 13:6; 14:24, and frequently elsewhere.

36. See Acts 8:8; 12:14; 13:52, and frequently in Luke.

37. Twenty-three times in Acts.

38. This view is shared by M. Hengel, "Die Ursprünge der christlichen Mission," 18 n. 17, who correctly emphasizes this against Haenchen's exegesis.

39. Strecker, "Jerusalemreise," 76.

40. On this, see also above, pp. 37–38 n. 56.

41. See Hengel, "Ursprünge," 25: Luke "has a clear intention, to which everything else is subordinated: the presentation of the ideal mission to the world, i.e., the mission of Paul. His composition is *a tendentious history of the Pauline mission 'with an extensive introduction.'* The reports about the Hellenists, for example, have to function, in their harmonized form, as a bridge between the apostolic foundation that Luke considered to be authoritative and the actual hero of the composition. While all the other co-actors leave the stage ahead of time, the hero dominates the center of the stage until the curtain falls."

42. G. Ogg, "A New Chronology of Saint Paul's Life," objects, "But had that been Luke's purpose, he would have set the Conference before ch. 13 and not at the end of the first of Paul's great missionary journeys" (p. 121). Against this: Paul's actual mission to the world begins first in Acts 15:40.

43. Whether Paul traveled from Corinth to Jerusalem *via Ephesus* cannot be determined on the basis of the letters. In light of the traditional character of Acts 18:19–20, however, this question can probably be answered in the affirmative. Nevertheless, Paul's own witness in 1 Cor. 16:9 supports the assumption that Paul was first active as a missionary in Ephesus during his second journey from Palestine to Greece: When Paul speaks of the door that had

opened for him in Ephesus, this evidently excludes the possibility that there had been an earlier mission in this locality.

44. The following stations, which cannot be verified through the letters of Paul, do not stand in need of further confirmation, for they are intermediary stations that must have been passed through in order to arrive at verifiable stations such as Philippi and Jerusalem: Troas, Samothrace (Acts 16:11), Caesarea (Acts 18:22).

45. Schenke and Fischer, *Einleitung*, 43, would like to differentiate Paul's companion Silas from the Silas mentioned in Acts 15:22, 27, 32–33.

46. It should be noticed that the decree is *not* passed on to the congregations that are founded after the conference. This is one more reason not to assume that the decree was current in Luke's congregation (see above, p. 122 n. 97).

47. See also the map of roads in M. Grant, *Ancient History Atlas*, 58.

48. In the margin at this point we should return to our hypothesis that the incident in Antioch was the occasion for the conference. Is not this hypothesis contradicted by the source just recovered, which knows of Paul staying in Antioch only *after* the conference? Since the source reports in an unswerving, summary way and skips over Paul's intermediary visit to Corinth, the possibility cannot be excluded, however, that a stay in Antioch before the conference has also been omitted in our passage. Result: The hypothesis stated above regarding the time of the incident in Antioch does not necessarily stand in contradiction to the list of stations we have reconstructed.

49. *Syneicheto tō logō* is specifically Lukan language. *Synechō*: Luke 4:38; 8:37, 45; 12:50; 19:43; 22:63; Acts 7:57; 28:8. *Logos* used absolutely as a *terminus technicus* for the Christian proclamation: Acts 4:4; 6:4; 8:4; 10:44, and frequently elsewhere.

50. See Hurd, *Origin*, 30–31.

51. On the basis of this, Schille, *Anfänge*, concluded that the episode involving Gallio is not historical. "The Jews' accusations against Paul arise too late, for Paul had already separated himself from the synagogue a year and a half ago" (p. 97). M. Goguel sees the same problem of the location of the chronological reference. He attempts to explain away the problem in the following manner: "The incident involving Gallio should be located not toward the end of Paul's stay in Corinth but rather toward the beginning of this stay, approximately at the time when Paul, after the arrival of Silas and Timothy from Macedonia, had been induced to separate himself from the synagogue" ("La vision de Paul à Corinthe et sa comparution devant Gallion," 331).

Both investigators—Goguel to a greater degree than Schille—inquire in a manner that is much too historicizing. Attention should be given to Schille's observation that the episode involving Gallio does not derive from the founding visit (p. 97). Unfortunately, owing to the historicizing nature of his inquiry, he does not allow this negative insight to raise the question of whether the episode involving Gallio could derive from another of Paul's stays in Corinth.

52. This view is presented by Bruce, *Acts*, 348. Jewish prescriptions, however, preclude this possibility. See Bill., 4:145ff. The plural in Acts 13:15 is not a counterargument and, further, is not the only example of Luke's ignorance of Jewish prescriptions.

53. This is evidently the opinion of W. Wiefel, "Die jüdische Gemeinschaft im antiken Rom und die Anfänge des römischen Christentums," 75 n. 77. Such a view would be possible only if Luke were an eyewitness or if he derived the basic material of the *entire* chapter from the diary of a companion of Paul. Since such assumptions must be ruled out for reasons that are known, one should remain with literary analysis. Jewett, *Chronology*, 82, has by no means convinced me that some synagogues had several rulers at the same time. His reference to S. Applebaum, "The Organization of the Jewish Communities in the Diaspora," in *The Jewish People in the First Century*, ed. S. Safrai and M. Stern, 1:464–503, esp. 492–93, proves nothing, for Applebaum generally confirms our assumption above and is not able to (and does not want to) offer a single clear witness for multiple rulers in the same synagogue at the same time. See also, J. B. Frey, *Corpus Inscriptionum Judaicarum*, vol. 1 of 2 vols. (1936; reprint, New York: KTAV Publishing House, 1975), xcviiff.; and S. Safrai, "The Synagogue," in *Jewish People*, ed. Safrai and Stern, 2:908–944, esp. 933–35.

54. One should differentiate the question about the historical possibility of a trial of Paul initiated by the Jews (this question should be answered in the affirmative) from the question about the historicity of a trial before Gallio as reported in Acts 18. This last question should be answered in the negative for the reasons mentioned above.

55. This is the view of Conzelmann, *Apostelgeschichte*, ad loc.; Burchard, *Zeuge*, 167 n. 21; Suhl, *Paulus*, 120; A. Malherbe, *Social Aspects of Early Christianity*, 74f. n. 30.

56. A. Deissmann, *Paul*, 261–86.

57. A. Plassart, "Lettre de l'empereur Claude au gouverneur d'Achaïe (en 52)," in *Les inscriptions du temple du IVe siècle*, École française d'Athènes, *Fouilles de Delphes*, vol. 3, pt. 4 (Paris: Éditions de Boccard, 1970), 26–32 (no. 286). See also idem, "L'inscription de Delphes mentionnant le proconsul Gallion"; J. H. Oliver, "The Epistle of Claudius Which Mentions the Proconsul Junius Gallio" (Oliver again suggests that the recipient of the letter was the city of Delphi [or the council of the amphictyony] and thinks that Gallio was the proconsul at the time of the composition of the letter; this changes nothing as concerns the dating of Gallio's period of office; see below, n. 62); B. Schwank, "Der sogenannte Brief an Gallio und die Datierung des 1 Thess"; K. Haacker: "Die Gallio-Episode und die paulinische Chronologie."

Schenke and Fischer, *Einleitung*, 50–51, present the Greek text and a German translation that reflects the improvement undertaken by Oliver, "Epistle." Accordingly, they view Gallio as the recipient of the letter. It is not necessary, however, to follow Plassart in attaching the *se* in line 17 to *entellomai*. *Se* could be the accusative object of some verb that has not been preserved. *[T]ois* in line 16 may belong with the verb *entellomai*. Oliver's reconstruction involves one verb following directly on another. Further, it seems to be thoroughly understandable that Gallio would still be called proconsul in a writing addressed to his successor (this comment is made in reference to Schenke and Fischer, *Einleitung*, 63 n. 7).

58. I cannot understand why Plassart seeks to create the impression that Deissmann refused to take note of the three fragments: "Après Deissmann (et malgré l'affirmation expresse de Bourguet . . .), H. Pomtow se refusa—à tort—à tenir compte de ces trois fragments dans son texte de la *Sylloge*" ("Inscription," 375). In the second German edition of his *Paul*, which Plassart overlooks, Deissmann expressly says that he decided not to present a facsimile of the three fragments in deference to a request by Bourguet (p. 269). Since several facsimiles of the three fragments had already been published, he presents a transcription of the text on p. 269 and writes, "It does not appear to me possible to restore the whole at present."

59. Deissmann, *Paul*, 273.

60. See Plassart, "Inscription," 376.

61. Ibid.

62. For the reasoning here, see also Haenchen, *Acts*, 66 n. 3: If one maintains that Gallio was the proconsul at the time of the composition of the letter, then internal reasons force one to assume that his period of office fell in the year 51/52. The assumption of a proconsulate in the year 52/53 would involve an inordinate overburdening of a short period of time: It is hardly possible to fit Gallio's inquiry and the imperial response into the time between May (Gallio's accession) and August (the twenty-seventh acclamation).

63. On this, see most recently S. Safrai, "The Problem of the Expulsion of the Jews from Rome in the Time of Claudius," in *Jewish People*, ed. Safrai and Stern, 1:180–83, and the literature cited there; see also M. Stern, ed. and trans., *Greek and Latin Authors on Jews and Judaism*, 2:113–17. On Claudius, see V. M. Scramuzza, *The Emperor Claudius*; A. Garzetti, *From Tiberius to the Antonines*, 106–45 (and the copious references to literature in the supplement); A. Momigliano, *Claudius*; W. den Boer, "Claudius," *RAC* 3: cols. 179–81. On "Claudius and Christianity," see F. F. Bruce, *New Testament History* (London: Nelson, 1969), 275–87.

64. Orosius perhaps gave preference to Suetonius's report owing to apologetical reasons. Orosius was trying to collect the references to Christ by secular writers. For him, Chrestus was obviously—and here he was historically correct—(Jesus) Christ. On the apologetics of Orosius, see B. Lacroix, *Orose et ses Idées*, 51–69. Orosius nevertheless adopts the indication of the year

from "Josephus," for this suits the annalistic style he employs before and after our passage. According to Orosius, Christians first appeared in Rome at the beginning of the reign of Claudius—as a result of the proclamation by Peter (7.6.1–2). Orosius was sure, on the basis of the report of Suetonius (and Acts 18:2), that Claudius's decree concerning the Jews was related to Christ's impact in Rome. For chronological reasons he could hardly follow a tradition that reported an act by Claudius against the Jews (Jewish Christians) in the first year of his reign. Further, Orosius presents a very favorable picture of the first years of this emperor.

65. A report on research into Suetonius is presented by Julius Penndorf, "Sueton, Florus, Fronto, Justin: Bericht über das Schrifttum der Jahre 1929—1937," *JKAW* 273 (1941): 45–114 (p. 45: survey of research into Suetonius before 1929; pp. 49–78: after 1929).

66. On the relationship of Orosius to Josephus, see Heinz Schreckenberg, *Die Flavius-Josephus-Traditionen in Antike und Mittelalter*, ALGHL 5 (Leiden: E. J. Brill, 1972), 95.

67. I do not understand why W. Wiefel flatly denies that such an edict was pronounced in the first year of Claudius's reign (41 c.e.) and why he does not say something about the fact that Dio Cassius usually reports in an annalistic manner ("Gemeinschaft," 78). It is certainly right to say, "In the imperial period each period begins and ends with a collection of material taken out of its chronological setting and designed to illustrate the character and government of the Emperor concerned" (F. Millar, *A Study of Cassius Dio*, 40). It should be emphasized, however, that the general description ends in 60.3.1 and that after this Cassius begins his report of events from the year 41 (this is also stated by Millar, ibid.). A different view is nevertheless taken by Emil Schürer, *A History of the Jewish People in the Time of Jesus Christ*, div. 2, vol. 2 (New York: Charles Scribner's Sons, 1896), 237 n. 68, who thinks, "with the words *lexō de kath' hekaston hōn epoiēse*, c. 3, Dio passes over not to a chronological narrative, but to a description of the good side of Claudius." The wording of the transitional phrase and the immediate context (3.2), however, render the opposite opinion probable. The actual reason for Schürer's view is his claim "It is not credible that an unfavorable edict against the Jews should be carried into effect in the early days of Claudius, who was just then issuing an edict for their toleration" (ibid.). Concerning this assumption, which I consider to be misleading, see the text above.

The conclusion that the deeds of the emperor that are reported in the immediate context of Claudius's edict against the Jews belong to the initial period of his reign also arises from the observation that these deeds reverse the decrees of his predecessor (cf. 6.3, 7, 8; 7.1; 8.1). Such actions usually occur at the beginning of a new government. This observation provides further support for the view that Cassius proceeded in a chronologically conscious manner when he connected the edict concerning the Jews with these deeds.

Scruples similar to those raised against Wiefel's article should also be raised against S. Benko, "The Edict of Claudius of A.D. 49 and the Instigator Chrestus." Contrary to Wiefel, "Gemeinschaft," Benko agrees with Schürer, *History*, div. 2, vol. 2 (1896), p. 238, in thinking that Suetonius and Cassius are speaking of the same edict by Claudius. For the same reason presented by Schürer and Wiefel (Claudius's friendly politics with regard to the Jews at the beginning of his reign), Benko does not follow Cassius's dating but rather dates the edict, with Orosius, in 49 C.E. (Wiefel, who assumes that there were two edicts, thinks, in contrast, that the edict depicted by Cassius represents a partial mitigation of the general expulsion of the Jews in 49 C.E. and derives from a later period.)

68. The historical kernel of this report will be that the right of association was withdrawn from one synagogue (see below). The numerous Jews in Rome (50,000) were not centrally organized as they were in Alexandria. Rather, the individual synagogal associations were independent groups with their own forms of organization. They should probably be understood, similar to other associations, as *collegia licita*. The retraction of the right of association from one synagogue would not consequently involve revocation of the right from other synagogues. The question touched on here is in need of further investigation. See the survey by H. J. Leon, "The Organization of the Roman Jewish Community," in *The Jews of Ancient Rome*, 167–94. As a supplement, see S. L. Guterman, "The Synagogues and the Collegia," in *Religious Toleration and Persecution in Ancient Rome*, 130–56. On Leon's book, see the review by Arnaldo Momigliano in *Gn.* 34 (1962): 178–82. See now Romano Penna, "Les Juifs à Rome au temps de l'apôtre Paul," *NTS* 28 (1982): 321–47.

69. See W. Liebenam, *Zur Geschichte und Organisation des römischen Vereinswesens*, 178.

70. On the sources that come into consideration, see E. Schwartz, "Cassius Dio Cocceianus," Pauly-W. vol. 3, 2d ed. (1899): cols. 1684–1722 (= *Griechische Geschichtsschreiber*, 394–450).

71. Compare the previous expulsion in Tiberius's reign in 19 C.E.: Josephus, *Ant.* 18.81ff. (literature is cited in the edition by L. H. Feldman, *Antiquities*, vol. 9, LCL 433, pp. 59ff.; and also in E. Mary Smallwood, *The Jews under Roman Rule: From Pompey to Diocletian*, SJLA 20 [Leiden: E. J. Brill, 1976], 201–10 [on the edict by Claudius, see pp. 210–19]). The expulsion during Tiberius's reign is also witnessed by Tacitus, *Annals* 2.85; Suetonius, *Caes. Tiberius* 36; Dio Cassius 57.18; and Philo, *Leg. Gaj.* 24. This expulsion, too, did not apply to all Jews: "To suppose that all the Jews were banished by Tiberius involves an assumption as to that emperor's methods wholly at variance with what we know of him" (M. Radin, *The Jews among the Greeks and Romans*, 308).

72. Contra Jewett, *Chronology*, 126 n. 116: "Some scholars have erroneously concluded that Suetonius' reference was to this edict in the year 41, but

Dio Cassius explicitly states that the Jews were not expelled at this early date."
Source criticism should be performed before reconstruction of the historical
events. Source criticism allows only the conclusion that there was *one* edict by
Claudius against the Jews in the city of Rome (for more on this, see below).

73. Cf. the position taken by E. Schwartz: "One must remain by the view
that congruencies between Dio and Suetonius . . . derive from earlier report-
ers" ("Cassius," col. 1714).

74. Dio's remark that the Jews could not have been expelled because of
their great number, however, probably derives from his own reflections. It
will hardly have been in his source.

75. Membership in a *collegium illicitum* could be reckoned as a *crimen
maiestatis*. See Liebenam, *Geschichte*, 39, 237.

76. Independent of the question whether Dio Cassius used Suetonius's report or is dependent together with Suetonius on a common source (which is
more probable), we have plenty of reason to assume that Dio neglected to take
over the name "Chrestus" from his source. He persistently ignores Christianity: "It is difficult to believe that his total silence about Christianity was not de-
liberate" (Millar, *Study*, 179).

77. Suhl, *Paulus*, 326, and R. O. Hoerber, "The Decree of Claudius in
Acts 18:2," *CTM* 31 (1960): 690–94, correctly maintain the view that the reports by Cassius and Suetonius reflect only *one* edict against the Jews by
Claudius. Suhl nevertheless thinks that the dating by Orosius should be
trusted, though the logic behind this judgment escapes me: "Dio Cassius reports [of Claudius's action against the Jews] in the context of the events from
the year 41, though he does not precisely date the edict" (*Paulus*, 326). Is not
the attribution of the edict to the first year of Claudius's reign precise enough?
Hoerber, "Decree," 692, writes in the same vein, "But since Dio's remark is
general, without citing any date, he may [*sic*] not have intended to define the
incident with the year 41 A.D."

78. See, e.g., Hoerber, "Decree," 691.

79. The question whether Josephus reliably reproduces documents of this
sort is usually answered in the affirmative by research. Nevertheless, see H. R.
Moehring, "The *Acta pro Joudaeis* in the *Antiquities* of Flavius Josephus: A
Study in Hellenistic and Modern Apologetic Historiography," in *Christianity, Judaism, and Other Greco-Roman Cults*, pt. 3: *Judaism before 70*, who
places emphasis on Josephus's apologetic interest in these documents.

80. See M. Stern, in *Jewish People*, ed. Safrai and Stern, 1:128–29; Momigliano, *Claudius*, 96ff.; Feldman, ed., Josephus's *Antiquities*, 9:344ff.

81. On this problem, see, along with the contributions mentioned in the
preceding note, M. Stern, *Greek and Latin Authors*, 1:399ff. (commentary
on Josephus, *Ap.* 2.38).

82. The text was first edited by H. I. Bell, *Jews and Christians in Egypt*. A
convenient English translation is found in C. K. Barrett, *The New Testament*

Background, 44ff. A survey of the secondary literature is provided by M. Stern (see above, n. 80), 129ff.; Leon, *Jews*, 22–23; Momigliano, *Claudius*, 98. Also important is Victor Tcherikover and Alexander Fuks, *Corpus Papyrorum Judaicorum*, vol. 2 of 3 (Cambridge: Harvard University Press, 1960), no. 153, pp. 36–55 (text, translation, and an up-to-date discussion of the document).

83. See Stern in *Jewish People*, ed. Safrai and Stern, 1:130.

84. Text and translation according to Arthur Serridge Hunt and Campbell Cowan Edgar, ed., *Select Papyri*, vol. 2 of 3: *Non-literary Papyri, Public Documents*, LCL 282, no. 212, p. 86.

85. This view was affirmed by, e.g., S. Reinach, "La première allusion au Christianisme dans l'histoire," *RHR* 90 (1924): 108–22; F. Cumont, "La lettre de Claude aux Alexandrins et les Actes des Apôtres," *RHR* 91 (1925): 3–6. Against this view: W. Seston, "L'Empereur Claude et les Chrétiens," *RHPhR* [11] (1931): 275–304; P. Labriolle, *La réaction païenne*, 20–24. See also Momigliano, *Claudius*, 99 n. 32; Scramuzza, *Emperor*, 285–86; and H. Gülzow, *Christentum und Sklaverei in den ersten drei Jahrhunderten*, 11 n. 1, whose work as a whole provides a good insight into the situation of Jews and Jewish Christians in Rome and into Claudius's policy on religion.

86. The remarks above make it clear that I cannot share the noteworthy suggestions by Leon, *Jews* (see his summary on p. 26), about Claudius's personal development in his relations with the Jews. Even without the influence of Agrippa, Claudius would probably have reinstated—for political reasons—the privileges of Alexandrian Jews that had been lost under Gaius. See A. Loisy, *Actes*, 688.

87. See Scramuzza, *Emperor*, 151: "The cardinal point of that policy was to grant hospitality to foreign religions, but to consider them a menace the moment they took advantage of that courtesy to disturb the public peace."

88. On this matter, see J. P. V. D. Balsdon, *The Emperor Gaius (Caligula)*, 135–40. On Caligula, see also Garzetti, *Tiberius*, 80–105 and the appendix.

89. As support for the historicity of an expulsion of the Jews in 49 C.E., Momigliano attempts to employ the Nazareth inscription, which probably derives from Claudius (44 C.E.) and which establishes death as the penalty for opening graves (on this inscription [text and English translation], see Bruce M. Metzger, "The Nazareth Inscription Once Again," in *Jesus und Paulus: Festschrift für Werner Georg Kümmel*, ed. E. E. Ellis and E. Grässer [Göttingen: Vandenhoeck & Ruprecht, 1975], 221–38 [further literature is cited there]). According to Momigliano, Christianity was drawn to Claudius's attention by disturbances in Galilee. He thinks that the edict in the year 49 was a second measure taken to suppress a movement "that threatened the spirit of Roman religion" (p. 37). The following points speak against this view: (1) Momigliano's assumption that the Nazareth inscription should be con-

nected "with the story which must have then been current about the resurrection of Christ . . . , namely that the disciples had broken into the tomb and carried off the body" (p. 36), Matt. 28:12–15, neglects to take into consideration that we know nothing about the age and dissemination of this tradition, which presupposes the set theological affirmation of the empty grave that is not yet reflected in Paul's letters. Momigliano does consider the anti-Christian character of that tradition. But why should Claudius have believed one Jewish group more than the other? (2) The two actions taken by Claudius in the years 44 and 49, in the event that the latter date is correct, would have been reactions to concrete problems. Thus, they could not be employed in a speculative manner to trace Claudius's personal development in his relations to Christians—totally apart from the fact that Claudius did not differentiate between Jews and Christians. On a similar thesis, namely, that Claudius's edict concerning the Jews in the year 49 was part of the anti-oriental politics that prevailed during the second part of his reign, see the critical remarks by K. Lake, "The Chronology of Acts," in *The Beginnings of Christianity*, 5:460.

90. Benko, "Edict"; M. Borg, "A New Context for Romans XIII," 212. Following R. Eisler, E. Bammel, "Judenverfolgung und Naherwartung: Zur Eschatologie des Ersten Thessalonicherbriefs," even knows who this Chrestus was: Simon Magus!

91. Friedrich Blass, "*CHRĒSTIANOI—CHRISTIANOI*," *Hermes* 30 (1895): 465–70.

92. On this passage, see H. Fuchs, "Tacitus über die Christen," *VigChr* 4 (1950): 65–93 (= *Tacitus*, ed. Victor Pöschl, WdF 97 [Darmstadt: Wissenschaftliche Buchgesellschaft, 1969], 558–90).

93. Adolf von Harnack, *Die Mission und Ausbreitung des Christentums in den ersten drei Jahrhunderten*, 4th rev. ed., 2 vols. (Leipzig: J. C. Hinrichs, 1924), 1:425 n. 3.

94. The same misunderstanding is present, e.g., in the source on the Hellenists that Luke employed in Acts 8, where Philip is supposed to have encountered the cultic god of the Simonians.

95. Lake, "Chronology," 459.

96. Momigliano, *Claudius*, 31. Acts seems to be Momigliano's most important witness, for Suetonius does not date the edict. An argument similar to Momigliano's is presented by Harnack, *Mission*, 1:5f. n. 3.

97. Leon, *Jews*, 25.

98. "Acts differs from history in that there is no chronology. The occasional references to contemporary history do not have a chronological purpose. . . . In the second part, the only indications of time are those that are related to the stories about Paul. They remain relative, because there is no synchronization with absolute dates from contemporary history" (P. Wendland, *Die hellenistisch-römische Kultur in ihren Beziehungen zu Judentum und Christentum*, 325 n. 5).

99. The same conclusion was recently reached by Penna, "Juifs," 331; Stern, *Greek and Latin Authors*, 2:116.

100. See, however, Harnack, *Mission*, 1:60f. n. 5, who, on the basis of the idea found in apocryphal writings that Jesus associated with his disciples for eighteen months after the resurrection, concluded that Paul's conversion occurred eighteen months after the death of Jesus. For criticism of this argument, see M. Hengel, "Christologie und neutestamentliche Chronologie," in *Neues Testament und Geschichte*, 45 n. 10.

101. Probably most investigators advocate 30 C.E. as the year of Jesus' death. See, recently, A. Strobel, *Ursprung und Geschichte des frühchristlichen Osterkalenders*, 109–21 (further literature is cited there).

102. G. Hölscher, *Die Hohenpriesterliste bei Josephus und die evangelische Chronologie*. See also F. Hahn, *Mission in the New Testament*, 88. In any event, one should not object to the year 27 as the date for the death of Jesus because Luke 3:1 states that John the Baptist made his public appearance in the fifteenth year of Tiberius's reign (27/28). J. Jeremias, *The Eucharistic Words of Jesus*, 12 n. 3, uses this argument to dismiss the possibility of the year 27. However, it applies fundamentally that Luke's chronological information must be confirmed from other sources, not vice versa. On Luke 3:1, see already above, p. 34 n. 28. Strobel, *Ursprung*, 84–92 (see the literature cited there), attempts to show that in Luke 3:1 "the expression 'in the fifteenth year of the reign' of Tiberius should be understood as a reference to the year A.D. 26/27" (p. 92).

103. C. W. Emmet, "The Case for the Tradition," in *The Beginnings of Christianity*, 1/1: 281. Jewett, *Chronology*, takes note of the ancient mode of enumerating years but nevertheless states: "The only safe assumption is that even if Paul did not designate full years, the partial system might have come very close to the full three and fourteen year spans. If a chronology does not proceed on this assumption, its starting point will appear arbitrary" (p. 54). Directly before this statement, Jewett raises the following objection to the proposal of reckoning a total of fifteen years: "How can such probabilities be useful in making decisions about specific events? History, after all, is the arena of the unique rather than the average." In response to this statement, one should ask how the historian should approach the unique object of investigation if not through judgments that rest on probability. Similarly incorrect: Ramsey, "Place of Galatians," 165–66.

104. It may be noted in passing that the chronology constructed here makes an early date for the change of governors, Felix/Festus (Acts 24:27), most probable, regardless of whether the "two years" in Acts 24:27 should be taken as a reference to the length of Paul's imprisonment (this view accords with the Lukan context; see Conzelmann, *Apostelgeschichte*, ad loc.) or to Felix's term of office (Haenchen, *Acts*, 661, 663, and Suhl, *Paulus*, 333–38, think this

was the view of the source employed in Acts 24:27). If the latter view is correct, then our alternative chronology based on the year 30 as the date of the death of Jesus accommodates this date well. If the former view is correct, then the chronology based on 27 c.e. as the date of the crucifixion of Jesus accommodates this date well. Absolute precision cannot be attained here. Jewett, *Chronology*, 1, 81, overlooks the fact that our enumerations of years are only part of an auxiliary construction, in which both 27 and 30 are calculated in as the date of Jesus' death.

105. The early dating of the Jerusalem Conference in the winter of 43/44, which has again become popular (Suhl, *Paulus*, 316–21; Vielhauer, *Geschichte*, 77–78; Schenke and Fischer, *Einleitung*, 55–56), is, according to the above reconstruction, improbable and rests on an unpersuasive interpretation of Mark 10:38–39 as a reflection of a double martyrdom. Against this dating, see correctly D. Georgi, *Die Geschichte der Kollekte des Paulus für Jerusalem*, 91–92. Further, one should ask with Georgi, ibid., whether Gal. 2:9 (combined with Acts 12:2) does not rather presuppose the death of James the son of Zebedee: (a) Gal. 2:9 mentions only his brother (although he himself might have had a leading position in the primitive congregation), and (b) in Gal. 2:9 Paul no longer explains, as he still did in Gal. 1:19, which James was involved. See also Schille, *Anfänge*, 147 n. 50.

106. In passing, we draw attention to the reading of Sinaiticus, E, and syr[p], which have *Titou* instead of *Titiou*. In the event that this reading is correct, we should be able to find this companion of Paul in Acts, who is not mentioned elsewhere in the book. This reading would explain why Titus was not one of the preachers of the gospel during the first visit (see 2 Cor. 1:18) but nevertheless had such great success with regard to the collection. As a Corinthian, he would have been well acquainted with the Corinthian situation. If the identification of Paul's companion Titus with Tit(i)us Justus is correct, then the mission in Greece before the conference would be certain, for Titus accompanied Paul to the conference. The statement in Acts that Tit(i)us was a "fearer of God" fits in with Paul's report that he took the uncircumcised Titus *Hellēn ōn* with him to the conference (Gal. 2:1, 3).

107. See also Ollrog, *Paulus*, 24–27.

108. Paul calls the household of Stephanas *aparchē tēs Achaias* (1 Cor. 16:15).

109. In passing, we mention that practice of a trade and the social contact involved therein will have provided an excellent basis for the mission. See Georg Heinrici, "Zur Geschichte der Anfänge paulinischer Gemeinden," *ZWTh* 20 (1877): 89–130.

110. This is also the view of Kümmel, *Introduction*, 316ff. See U. Wilckens, "Über Abfassungszweck und Aufbau des Römerbriefs," in *Rechtfertigung als Freiheit*, 124–25 (he notes, against Kümmel, that Paul personally

had known all those who are greeted). A different opinion is expressed by Walter Schmithals, *Der Römerbrief als historisches Problem*, StNT 9 (Gütersloh: Gerd Mohn, 1975), 128ff.

111. See H. Y. Gamble, *The Textual History of the Letter to the Romans*. On the Ephesus hypothesis, see 36ff.

112. For an analogy, attention should be drawn to the group of Christians from Syria who traveled to Rome ahead of the bishop Ignatius (Ignatius, *R.* 10:2).

113. A different view is presented by A. von Harnack, "Die Zeitangaben in der Apostelgeschichte des Lukas," 384 n. 1 (revised and expanded in his *New Testament Studies III: The Acts of the Apostles* [New York: G. P. Putnam's Sons, 1909], pp. 22–44). Harnack thinks that almost all the chronological references in Acts are historically correct. M. Hengel, *Acts and the History of Earliest Christianity*, 39, also thinks that Acts' references to the length of Paul's stays in the various centers of his mission are of great historical value. For the reasons stated above in the text, I cannot admit the correctness of such claims in this sort of generality. I also cannot follow the view that "the sequence of Paul's letters, the length of his stay in missionary centers and the chronology of his activity—all these and much else would be completely or largely unknown to us without Acts" (ibid.). On the order of the letters, see above, pp. 22ff.

114. Accurate observations on Luke's use of the number three are made by G. Delling, "Treis," *TDNT* 8: 216–225, esp. 219–20.

4

SUMMARY OF
CHAPTERS 1 TO 3

The introductory chapter presented a critical survey of research into
Pauline chronology. It was shown, first, that the conventional view,
contrary to appearance (i.e., despite partial rejection of Acts' information), is actually based on a harmonization of Acts and the letters. This
was apparent, above all, in the unquestioned theses (a) that Paul's independent mission occurred only *after* the Jerusalem Conference and
(b) that Paul was arraigned before Gallio and thus was in Corinth in
the year 51/52 C.E.

Various arguments against this method of directly employing Acts'
chronological information were then gathered together. First, the witness of Galatians was seen to exclude the thesis that Paul was a missionary of the Antiochene congregation. Second, it was shown that
Luke reports only episodically in Acts. Third, it was demonstrated that
the information in Luke's two volumes regarding world history often
stands in direct contradiction to secular historical sources.

The next stage in the investigation was able to demonstrate that the
absolute chronological data in Luke's two volumes are to a large extent
conditioned by redaction, as is also the notion that Paul's worldwide
mission occurred *after* the Jerusalem Conference. Luke's chronological data are involved with his interest in depicting Christianity as a cos-
mopolitan religion. They are supposed to interweave world history and
the history of salvation in such a way as to bring attention to the public
claim and the urbanity of Christianity within the Roman state. The
presentation of Paul's worldwide mission as occurring *after* the
conference is based on the idea that before this mission could actually
begin it had to be legitimized by the conference. This is the means by
which continuity is established between Luke's church, which is represented by Paul's mission, and the earliest church in Jerusalem. It was
determined here that for Luke correct chronology arises from proper
dogma.

With regard to the question of Pauline chronology, these observations could serve only as warnings against the old sort of harmoniza-

tion of Acts and the letters. At the same time, the usual employment of Paul's letters (particularly of Galatians 1–2) for chronological purposes was also in need of criticism. The chronological references of the letters are too quickly, and without regard for the occasion and genre of Paul's statements, transposed onto a historical drawing board. While it is correct to suppose that Paul was not silent about a visit to Jerusalem in Galatians 1–2, the other chronological references are unclear and disjointed. Thus it was noted with regard to the chronological location of the incident in Antioch, for example, that the (almost) unanimous attribution of this event to the time *after* the conference rests on the assumption that Paul is reporting as a historian.

The *conclusion* drawn in the introductory chapter was that there was a need to construct a chronology of Paul solely on the basis of the letters—with due consideration being given to what was said about "Paul as a historian." Only afterward should there be an attempt to integrate Acts' witness into this chronology, though the possibility that the traditions reworked by Luke derived from old material was to be left open, especially since at various points it had already become evident that Luke did not simply "create" episodes but rather reworked traditions.

The reconstruction of a chronology of Paul based solely on the letters began with an analysis of Gal. 1:6—2:14, the central pillar for every chronology of Paul. The Judaistic opponents who had found entry into Paul's Galatian congregations had forced him to give a summary of his relations with the Jerusalem apostles. Paul was probably under this constraint because the opponents claimed that he and his gospel were either inferior to the pillars and the gospel of circumcision or else dependent on them. They thought they had the right to supplement the Pauline proclamation with the demand for observance of the law. In the first step of the investigation (form criticism), we proceeded from H. D. Betz's thesis that Galatians belongs form-critically to the genre "apologetic letter," a form that has many parallels, particularly in the "apologetic speeches" of ancient rhetoric. We were able to show that Gal. 1:13—2:14 stands in close accord with the stylistic laws for one part of the apologetic letter, the *narratio*. It was prescribed that the *narratio* should employ extreme brevity, bypassing everything not directly related to the issue at stake. Paul noticeably follows this prescription in Gal. 1:13ff., for—far from giving a complete account of his life from the time of the conversion to the time of the Jerusalem Conference—he relates only matters pertaining directly to Jerusalem (the journeys *to* and *from* Jerusalem) and summarizes the rest of the time with references to numbers of years. But even these references serve in a broader way to emphasize his independence from those in Jerusalem and thus to controvert the opponents' claim. As regards the important chronological question of the time from which the explicit indications of years should be reckoned, we were able to determine that they have the same reference point as the particle *epeita* that is connected with them. This meant that the "three years" in Gal. 1:18 should be reckoned as starting with the return to Damascus, just as the "fourteen years" in Gal. 2:1 should be reckoned as starting with the (completion of the) journey to the province of Syria and Cilicia. While Gal. 1:20 rendered it clear that Paul worked as a missionary in this last area and that this period of activity belongs within the "fourteen years," we nevertheless had to reject the view that Paul's activity before the conference was confined to this area. Apart from the fact that such a thesis involves an *argumentum e silentio*, the following considerations on Gal. 2:7ff. produced indications against such a claim. It was possible to determine that vv. 7–8 preserved a personal tradition current in Paul's Greek-speaking congregations. This tradition dealt with Paul's first visit to Jerusalem and paralleled Paul's mission with Peter's mission. The fact that Paul quotes this tradition as something known to the Galatians (see the parenthesis, v. 8) provided an indication that the Galatian congregations existed before the conference. The address in Gal. 3:1 allowed it to be determined that these congregations were located in the region "Galatia" (in the north). The assumption that these congregations existed before the conference seemed to gain support from Paul's affirmation that he did not yield to the false brethren so "that the truth of the gospel might be preserved for you" (v. 5) as well as from the agreement quoted in v. 9, which presupposes the existence of an independent Pauline mission: "We should go to the Gentiles and they to the circumcised." This agreement entailed no additional stipulations for Paul's Gentile Christian congregations ("Those, I say, who were of repute *added nothing to me*"), though there probably were additional injunctions for the Antiochene congregation represented by Barnabas. Here a statement similar to the Apostolic Decree henceforth regulated the unity of the congregation and the table fellowship of Gentile and Jewish Christians.

This thesis was also rendered probable by the observation that the regulation in v. 9 contained a restrictive element, first made it possible to oblige a

Jewish Christian who belonged to a mixed congregation to observe the law, and ruled out any future establishment of mixed congregations. Hence the agreement at the conference pertaining to the separation of areas for the mission, or of groups for the mission, necessarily involved a special clause for the mixed congregations (which could no longer be established) unless a division was agreed on.

It could be determined that the agreement regulating the separation of the mission carried a Judaistic seal because the agreement was supposed to keep Jews who had adopted Christianity from acting against the law. Since the regulation in v. 9 also reads like a reaction to such cases and, above all, since the common life of Jewish and Gentile Christians in the same congregation provided many occasions for transgression of the law, the suggestion lay at hand that one motive behind the conference was Judaistic questioning of table fellowship between Jewish and Gentile Christians before the conference in mixed congregations. At this point, we seriously considered the possibility that the incident in Antioch was the direct occasion for the conference.

That Paul operated his own mission at the time of the conference also seemed to be indicated by the statement that Paul and Barnabas should henceforth remember the poor, which Paul strove to do (v. 10). The simplest explanation of this sentence was that Paul is speaking of a request made of the two representatives of the mission to the Gentiles for material support for the poor in Jerusalem and that Paul is able to say for his own part that he had immediately taken steps to fulfill this request.

In the event that this last conclusion was correct, a further argument arose *against* the thesis that the tradition contained in v. 9 ("We should go to the Gentiles and they to the circumcised") witnesses to a common mission by Paul and Barnabas directly before and after the conference, and *for* our proposal that the tradition in v. 9 presupposes an independent mission by Paul, even though Paul and Barnabas appear as a group that is contrasted with those in Jerusalem. In the agreement regarding the collection ("they would have us remember the poor"), Paul and Barnabas similarly appear as a group,[1] even though Paul organizes the collection in his own congregations (without any apparent involvement of Barnabas).

Thus the exegesis of Gal. 1:6—2:14 not only provided a relative chronological framework but also made it probable that Pauline congregations outside Syria and Cilicia (e.g., in Galatia) existed before the

198

conference. The exegesis simultaneously drew attention to a matter that was determinative for Paul's life and activity for some time after the conference, the gathering and organization of the collection.

In the following section, we employed the collection as an external criterion to determine the order of the letters. We then combined the results with the chronological and topographical data contained in the passages of the letters dealing with the collection (1 Cor. 16:1ff.; 2 Corinthians 8–9; Gal. 2:10; Rom. 15:26). The result was a chronology of Paul and his co-workers that spanned three to four years (see the table on pp. 108–9). A particularly important observation was that the collection was evidently not a subject of discussion during the founding visit. This striking finding was a first point of support for the thesis that the founding visit occurred at a time when the agreement about the collection did not yet exist, that is, before the conference. A second pointer in the same direction was that—as could be concluded on the basis of 1 Corinthians—a relatively long period had passed between the time of the composition of this letter and the founding visit. This period can hardly be accommodated into the usual chronology, which reckons about four years between the founding visit and 1 Corinthians. Finally, the two letters that had not been employed for reasons of method (because they do not refer to the collection), 1 Thessalonians and Philippians, rendered the thesis of a Pauline mission in Greece *before* the conference certain, for Phil. 4:15 ascribes the mission that started out from Macedonia to the initial period of the Pauline proclamation, and it is to this period that 1 Thessalonians, which was composed shortly after the founding of the Thessalonian congregation, witnesses.

The next stage in the investigation attempted to integrate the traditions in Acts into the chronology obtained solely on the basis of Paul's letters. This resulted in the conclusion that Paul's visit to Jerusalem reflected in Acts 18:22 was Paul's second trip to Jerusalem (for the conference), while 11:27ff. and 15:1ff. derive from Lukan redaction. This conclusion was confirmed not only by the observation that for dogmatic reasons Luke neither could nor wanted to report of a conference that legitimized Paul's worldwide mission after it had already begun but also by the observation that the stations mentioned before and after Acts 18:22 unexpectedly and strikingly agree with the stations determined on the basis of the letters for the period before and after the second visit to Jerusalem. For these reasons, the conclusion lay at hand that for this passsage Luke had access to a source that derived from a companion of Paul. The source was probably in the form of a list of stations supplemented with various episodes.

A detailed analysis of Acts 18:1–17 led to a similar surprise. In his report about Paul's stay in Corinth, Luke reworked traditions that derived from two different visits. This was clear not only from the content and formal structure of Acts 18:1–17 but also from the fact that Gallio's proconsulate should be dated to the year 51/52 while Claudius's edict concerning the Jews, which is reflected in v. 2, should be dated to the year 41. The year 41 as the date for a stay in Corinth fit in well with what had been said about the initial period of the Pauline proclamation. The period 51/52 also corresponded to Paul's second or third visit in the chronology developed solely on the basis of the letters. Our calculations involved dating Jesus' death to the year 27/30, assuming three years for the time between Jesus' death and Paul's conversion, presupposing a sum of two years for the stay in Arabia, the trip to Syria/Cilicia, and the second stay in Jerusalem, and figuring in another year for the time between the conference and Paul's stay in Galatia.

While the *traditions* of Acts thus furnished a surprising confirmation of the chronology developed solely on the basis of the letters, we consciously refrained from attempting to plot out Paul's activity in precise terms of days, months, and years. The sources themselves made such an attempt impossible. They allowed only calculations that took into account a factor of uncertainty of about three years (for a synopsis of the results, see the tables on pp. 108–9 and 172).

What has been said up to now has not brought us to the end of our new proposal for a chronology of Paul. It is possible to verify the main thesis above, namely, that Paul missionized Greece at an early stage, by studying the eschatological statements in 1 Thess. 4:13–18 and 1 Cor. 15:51–52. Examination of Paul's intentions in these passages to a certain extent leads to the third volume of our investigation, for which the present chronology is merely a preliminary study.

NOTE

1. James and Cephas also appear as a group, although we have no evidence that they undertook a mission together.

5

THE ESCHATOLOGICAL STATEMENTS
IN 1 THESS. 4:13–18 AND
1 COR. 15:51–52 AS CONFIRMATION OF
PAUL'S EARLY MACEDONIAN MISSION

5.1 FORMULATION OF THE QUESTION
AND THE METHOD

At the beginning of our investigation, we explained that it is appropriate to waive the employment of internal criteria such as "developments in Paul's theology" when one reconstructs the (relative) chronology of Paul's life and the order of his letters. Instead one should use external criteria. The chronology developed above began with the collection as an external criterion and employed, for reasons of method, first the letters of Paul without maintaining an eye on Acts. Thereby we reached a view of the time and place of Paul's missionary activity that stands in considerable tension with the view held by research up to this point. The presentation climaxed with the thesis that Paul's founding visit to Macedonia occurred at the end of the 30s and that 1 Thessalonians was composed at the beginning of the 40s.

The following is an attempt to anchor this thesis more firmly. The method will nevertheless be the same as the method that guided the chronological reconstruction above: We shall proceed solely on the basis of Paul's letters and shall base the investigation on an external point of reference.

What, apart from the collection, can serve as an external criterion?

We can start with the insight that the earliest beginnings of Christianity were characterized by an apocalyptic tenor and were dominated by an ardent expectation of the end.[1] Though the evaluation of Jesus' own imminent expectation may be controversial,[2] there is absolutely no doubt about the imminent expectation of the first generation. This is the case even though the thesis promoted by A. Schweitzer and his students, that the delay of the parousia[3] was the central crisis of primitive Christianity and the factor that sparked the Hellenization of Christianity, did not meet with general approval.[4]

The concepts "apocalyptic" and "imminent expectation" and the related notion of the proximity of the kingdom of God are not, however, explicit enough to serve us as an external criterion for an "early dating" of 1 Thessalonians. Previous discussion of apocalyptic or the imminent expectation as a part, or the decisive moment, of Paul's theology has already shown that both concepts need to be defined more precisely in the study of Pauline theology. This need is evident, for example, in the claim that Paul held on "firmly throughout his life to the imminent expectation that was already central for apocalyptic"[5] or in the thesis that Paul was an adherent of apocalyptic before his call.[6]

It should be clear that the need for differentiation in the use of the terms "apocalyptic" and "imminent expectation" in the study of Paul's theology is even greater when one uses these terms for determining Paul's chronology. This is all the more the case since apocalyptic elements, or statements about the arrival of the day of judgment, and so on, appear in every letter (with the exception of Philemon). These statements could prohibit the chronological differentiation of the letters on the basis of Paul's imminent expectation or apocalyptic. They could, above all, serve to counter the chronological placement of 1 Thessalonians ten years earlier than usual.

The question thus arises whether one may more closely delineate the concept of imminent expectation and define it temporally so that it may be employed for chronological purposes. More specifically, we are concerned with the question of (a) whether statements about the end as arriving at a specific time were made in early Christianity and, above all, (b) whether this phenomenon is found in Paul's writings.

Should these questions be answered in the affirmative, then we should obtain an external point of reference for determining the order and approximate date of texts and letters. Their stance on the temporally set arrival of the end would be the key for such determinations.

The imminent expectation of primitive Christianity can be delineated precisely enough to enable us to say that the Christians of the first generation after the death and resurrection of Jesus generally thought they would no longer have to die, for the arrival of the Son of Man, or the kingdom of God, was immediately at hand.[7]

Evidence of this belief is found in texts that refer to the eschaton as immediately at hand, such as the logion on the imminent expectation in Matt. 10:23: "When they persecute you in one town, flee to the next; for truly, I say to you, you will not have gone through all the towns of Israel, before the Son of man comes." One can no longer follow A. Schweitzer in the view that this verse is a saying of the historical Jesus that remained unfulfilled.[8] Such a thesis neglects the literary and compositorial character of the speech of instructions for the mission in Matthew. The verse nevertheless incontestably reflects the conviction, which was connected with an ardent expectation, of experiencing the day of the Son of man. The hope is that one will live up to and through this event. For our purposes, it matters little whether one employs literary criticism to separate Matt. 10:23b from 10:23a and to understand the second part of the verse as "comfort in the face of the difficult task [the mission]: just begin and do not avoid exertion"[9] or—better—whether one views the entire verse as a logion of apocalyptic comfort in the face of persecution.[10] In any event, the text should be analyzed not as a part of the question of the infallibility of Jesus[11] but rather from the perspective of its being an apocalyptic proclamation of a temporally determined end. The statement that the disciples must endure persecution for only a short time (or, less probably, that they will not complete the mission to Israel before the arrival of the Son of Man) clearly presupposes that none (or only a minority) of them will die. Otherwise it would not make sense for the disciples to be the addressees.

The case is similar, though the occurrence of more deaths should be assumed, in Mark 13:30: "Truly, I say to you, this generation will not pass away before all these things take place." Here the *terminus ante quem* of the arrival of the end is the passing of the first generation.[12] The first deaths may have caused the community to undertake this modification of the statement on the parousia. Although a number of Christians have not lived to experience the end, the first generation will nevertheless witness the coming of the Son of Man. This phenomenon of stating that (at least) some of the first generation will not have to die is most readily understandable if the original expectation was that the first generation in its entirety would experience the end of time.

This judgment on Mark 13:30 also applies to Mark 9:1, a text that reflects the death of Christians but nevertheless comforts other Christians of the first generation by maintaining that they will not have to die:[13] "Truly, I say to you, there are some standing here who will not taste death before they see that the kingdom of God has come with power."

Finally, the conviction of the earliest Christians that they would live until the parousia is also reflected in a passage which rejects the opinion that the beloved disciple would not die, John 21:23. It is well known that John 21 is an appendix to the Gospel of John.[14] In light of the death of the beloved disciple, John 21:23 corrects the tradition, indigenous to the Johannine circle, that the beloved disciple would never die.[15]

We have now surveyed the texts in the Gospels which chronologically qualify the imminent expectation by stating that the end would occur during the time of the first generation. If one considers that these texts are found in the Gospels, which were composed at a much later date and which neither could still share such a specified expectation nor maintain an interest for the tradition of such extreme eschatological statements, then the content of these texts gains in importance and the thesis propounded above seems plausible: The very beginnings of Christianity were characterized by the conviction that the first generation would not pass away before the parousia occurred.

We have thus found a viable chronological criterion for determining the date of texts and traditions from the early period of Christianity. A text which presupposes that Christians do not have to die before the arrival of the eschaton[16] probably arose during the period that followed directly on the death and resurrection of Jesus, that is, not long after 27/30 C.E. On the other hand, a text that limits the number of those who will not die or assumes that all will die should be considered as belonging chronologically to the end of the first generation (47–57) or to a later generation. Though chronologically exact datings cannot be expected when this criterion is employed, approximate datings can be.

If we test this criterion on the texts cited above, we find confirmation for the result of literary criticism that John 21 (here the opinion that the beloved disciple would survive is presented as an error) is later than, for example, Mark 9:1, a text which assumes that a few will survive. One should also note that, according to the above criterion, Mark 9:1 lies nearer to the death and resurrection of Jesus than does the Gospel of Mark. In itself, this is a trivial observation, for Mark 9:1 is a tradition used by Mark and is thus older than the Gospel. This self-evident observation does, however, verify the efficiency of the above criterion.

This criterion has thus shown itself to be a useful instrument for approximate reconstruction of the chronological order of texts and for the determination of their proximity to (or distance from) the death and resurrection of Jesus (27/30 C.E.).

Can it be employed in a productive way for work on the letters of Paul?

The answer to this question depends on whether there are texts in the Pauline writings that not only contain apocalyptic elements but also use these elements to specify chronologically the imminent expectation. This applies, surprisingly, only to two texts, 1 Thess. 4:13–18 and 1 Cor. 15:51–52, where mention is made of existing groups of people who will experience the parousia. All the other manifold passages in the letters of Paul do not chronologically delimit the end[17] and for this reason are useless for the chronological question.[18]

Our task will be to examine by means of an exegesis of the relevant texts whether and how Paul speaks of the death of Christians before the parousia. By determining whether death of Christians is presupposed not at all, as an exception, or as the rule, we shall be able to specify an approximate date for each statement and to verify this through the above chronology. The exegesis of 1 Thess. 4:13–18 will naturally form the focus of our investigation, for this passage, above all, must bear the brunt of support for the central thesis of the above chronology.

5.2 EXEGESIS OF 1 THESS. 4:13–18

Historical understanding always proceeds in a circle. The determination of the meaning of a statement in a letter presupposes conjectures about the situation of the addressees, just as these conjectures are dependent on how the statements in the letter are understood. When we start in the following with a critical discussion of a few possible theses on the situation in Thessalonica, we are not trying to break out of this circle (on the contrary, we are entering into it at one particular point), but rather are attempting to achieve some initial clarification in view of the massive literature on this passage. This approach will also allow the elimination of certain proposals from the outset.

5.2.1 The Situation of the Congregation: The Occasion for Grief

The introductory word *peri* (4:13; cf., previously, 4:9 and, afterward, 5:1) shows that Paul is dealing here with a written or oral question. The concern of the question is evident from the word that *peri* introduces: "Those who are asleep." Since Paul left the Thessalonian congregation, at least two Thessalonian Christians have died.[19] Their deaths caused the Thessalonians to ask Paul about them. What concrete occasion and background is presupposed by such a question?

In the following, we shall differentiate and critically examine four types of exegesis.

5.2.1.1 GNOSIS IN THESSALONICA

Following W. Lütgert, W. Schmithals developed the thesis[20] that 1 Thess. 4:13–18 was occasioned by gnostic denial of the resurrection. A new case for this thesis was recently (1973) presented by W. Harnisch.[21] These authors presume that Paul preached the doctrine of the resurrection in Thessalonica but that this Jewish doctrine had since assumed dubious status for the congregation. A similar situation is said to be witnessed in the Corinthian denial of the resurrection of the dead. For this reason, we can recognize "behind the denial of the resurrection in Thessalonica that Gnostic agitation which is known to us above all from 1 Cor. 15, but can be inferred with some probability also for Philippi and Galatia."[22]

To answer the question why Paul responds to such similar situations in such different ways, Schmithals explains that in 1 Corinthians 15 Paul

> must set himself against the current argument of the false teachers, while here in [1 Thess. 4:13–18] he is comforting troubled members of the community. There Paul mistakenly takes the denial of the resurrection as an expression of utter hopelessness; here [1 Thess. 4:13–18], as in 2 Cor. 5:1ff., he no longer makes this assumption, at any rate not *expressis verbis*. Thus at the time of 1 Thess. 4:13ff. he may have been somewhat better informed than at the time of 1 Cor. 15.[23]

This awkward claim that different answers were given to the same situation has properly been criticized by U. Luz.[24] It involves the assumption that Paul has misunderstood the situation, something that always mars the credibility of a thesis. It finally takes recourse in the view that Paul directed his comments, on the one hand, against the opponents in 1 Corinthians (whom, furthermore, he misunderstands) and, on the other hand, to members of the congregation who have been set in grief by the opponents (1 Thessalonians). W. Harnisch has attempted to improve on all this with the thesis that Paul is not comforting the congregation but is rather warning them. "That you may not grieve as others do who have no hope" (1 Thess. 4:13b)

> hardly reflects a view that the congregation has already adopted. It rather attempts to counter the consequences of a certain mode of thought press-

ing upon the Thessalonians that, *according to Paul's conviction*, must necessarily arise. The apostle *asserts* that the congregation will necessarily fall into "grief" bordering on hopelessness insofar as it gives into this mode of thought.[25]

Harnisch further thinks that it was not a question from the congregation that caused Paul to make these statements. "It is more probable that certain information from Thessalonica (brought by Timothy?) provoked the apostle to take his stand on the issue."[26]

This undoubtedly relieves *one* weak point in Schmithals's explanation, where the different addressees and the different functions of 1 Corinthians 15 and 1 Thess. 4:13–18 were delineated, while at the same time the same opponents were supposedly involved. Paul is seen rather to be arguing against gnostic thought in both passages.

Does Harnisch's interpretation of 1 Thess. 4:13–18 provide a comprehensive, satisfactory solution? The following points speak against his view of a gnostic background to 1 Thess. 4:13–18.[27]

1. Harnisch assumes that the same gnostic opposition is involved in 1 Corinthians 15 and 1 Thessalonians 4. Why are there such different responses to the same situation in these two chapters? First Corinthians vehemently emphasizes the future resurrection of Christians. If one denies this resurrection, then Christ has not been raised (15:16). In 1 Thess. 4:13–18 there is the argument that Christians who have died suffer no disadvantage when compared with the living, for the dead too will be caught up[28] to participate in everlasting fellowship with Christ. This means, however, that in contrast to 1 Corinthians 15, 1 Thess. 4:13–18 does not even make the resurrection of Christians a point of discussion. For this reason, Harnisch's assumption that the resurrection of Christians had become a controversial point in Thessalonica is absurd.[29]

2. The assumption that there was a gnostic threat in Thessalonica does not accord with the content of the rest of the letter. At no point is there even a trace of disappointment over the relationship between the congregation and the apostle. How could Paul have said that he had no need to write to them regarding brotherly love (4:9) if incidents had occurred in their congregation that were similar to the incidents in Corinth?

3. The assertion that there were gnostic opponents in Galatia, Philippi, and Corinth, which supports the thesis of gnosis in Thessalonica, has not been confirmed by research. In general, Harnisch presents a view of gnosis that sovereignly bypasses the last twenty years of

research into gnosis. His view is founded on the position of R. Bultmann, who understood the renowned Valentinian statement *physei sōzesthai*[30] as the cornerstone of gnostic soteriology.[31] This is evident in the following statement by Harnisch:

> The gnostic knows that he has been removed once and for all from the grasp of the powers of darkness. He is no longer exposed to the threat of self that arises from historical being, and he has returned to the place of his origin, to which applies "There is peace and security."[32]

Which gnostic is Harnisch speaking about? In any case, there are many witnesses from gnostic texts that show that the historical dialectic denied by Harnisch for gnostics was indeed a part of gnostic existence.[33] Harnisch's picture of gnosis is an *interpretatio christiana* interested only in hermeneutical results, though it does not reveal itself as such. It can claim to be only partially historically verifiable.[34]

4. The following objection, which surprisingly has not been raised against the thesis of gnostic opponents in Thessalonica, relates to the chronological impossibility of 1 Thessalonians being composed during the "third missionary journey,"[35] or *after* 1 Corinthians. Schmithals's construction stands and falls with this thesis, and Harnisch is also obliged to accept it, even though he does not address the chronological question. If 1 Thessalonians was composed during the founding visit in Corinth, then no possibility remains for Schmithals's view that the gnostic movement entered at about the same time into the Christian congregations founded by Paul, unless one assumes that Paul encountered gnostic teachers from the outside during his founding visit in Corinth. Schmithals himself does not maintain this last point, and it is a view that the Corinthian correspondence completely rules out. In my opinion, the possibility that 1 Thessalonians was composed after 1 Corinthians is also excluded.[36] I say this because of the Pauline witness in 1 Thessalonians. We shall examine the reasons Schmithals presents in support of his claim of the inverse chronological order, and afterward we shall present positive proof of the contrary in each case.

1. "The external situation during the composition of 1 Thess., as it is to be inferred from 1 Thess. 3:1ff., is in no case to be harmonized with the account in the book of Acts of the second journey."[37] In light of the secondary character of Acts, this argument must be discounted.

2. Paul's several intended visits to the congregation (1 Thess. 2:17ff.) and the final sending of Timothy indicate, according to Schmithals, that 1 Thessalonians cannot have been written during the founding

mission in Greece, for a journey to Thessalonica at this time would not have been impossible for Paul.[38] This argument does not take into account the formal character of the wish for a visit in Paul's letters. R. W. Funk has analyzed this form and has designated it a "travelogue."[39] In any case, these statements should not be used to conclude that Paul was having troubles with his congregations and was thus hindered from fulfilling his wish to make a visit.

3. "According to 1 Thess. 1:8–9, the word of the Lord has sounded forth from Thessalonica 'not only in Macedonia and Achaia, but everywhere your faith in God has become known.' However broadly one may interpret these words, either clause is so little conceivable at the beginning of Paul's first stay in Corinth that Paul's words are unexplainable."[40] On the contrary, one should expect that this passage intends, in a not minor way, to create a rhetorical effect. Something similar is found in 2 Cor. 9:1ff., where Paul writes that he has boasted to the Macedonians about the Corinthians' zeal in gathering the collection. In reality, the readiness of the Corinthians was quite a different matter. This is evident from the need to send Titus and to exhort them to complete the collection.

4. According to Schmithals, it is impossible that some of the Thessalonians had died within approximately four months after the founding visit, even "if the community should have consisted in the main of old people."[41] Now, it is certainly not impossible that some died during this period, especially since no more than two deaths need have occurred. Besides, there is no reason to limit the chronological span between the visit and the composition of the letter to four months.[42]

It is clear, then, that none of the reasons supplied by Schmithals for dating 1 Thessalonians after 1 Corinthians is convincing. The following points speak rather for the composition of 1 Thessalonians in Corinth and before 1 Corinthians.

1. The list of senders in 1 Thessalonians: Paul, Silvanus, Timothy. These three preached the gospel to the Corinthians during the founding visit (2 Cor. 1:19).

2. The proportion of Christians who will live until the parousia in 1 Thess. 4:13–18 has changed markedly in 1 Cor. 15:51–52. In 1 Thess. 4:13–18 survival until the parousia is the rule; in 1 Cor. 15:51–52, this is no longer the case (see below, pp. 240ff.). Thus 1 Thessalonians must have been written *before* 1 Corinthians.

In sum, the assumption of gnostic opponents in Thessalonica breaks down not only for internal reasons but also for chronological reasons.

5.2.1.2 THE RELATIVE ADVANTAGE OF THE LIVING
OVER THE DEAD

In order to determine the concern of the Thessalonians, another group of exegetes proceeds from v. 15b: "We who are alive . . . shall not precede those who have fallen asleep." According to this view, Paul had taught about the resurrection of Christians during his founding proclamation, but the Thessalonians were also informed about the apocalyptic schema possibly through Jewish circles (Acts 17:1ff.) and were told that the resurrection would occur only after the parousia. Since Paul did not present "an eschatological timetable in his proclamation of the resurrection and parousia,"[43] the Thessalonians expressed the fear, occasioned by the above apocalyptic schema, that any Christians who died would suffer disadvantage.

Occasionally this type of exegesis includes the view that the Thessalonians were acquainted with the apocalyptic doctrine of an intermediary messianic kingdom and that the congregation was afraid the dead would miss out on the blessedness of this intermediary kingdom. Accordingly, the relative disadvantage of the dead arising from the chronological order of parousia and resurrection would involve a much more important disadvantage.[44] Certain proof for the existence of the conception of an intermediary messianic kingdom is found, however, only after 70 C.E.[45] Thus this conception may not be drawn in here without further ado.

While this *variation* on the type of exegesis under consideration must thus be rejected,[46] other weighty objections apply to the type as a whole. One must admit that 1 Thess. 4:15b, with its stress on the equality of the living and the dead at the end of time, certainly is strongly reminiscent of Jewish apocalyptic texts that raise the question of the relationship of the living and dead in the final salvation. Compare, for example, 4 Ezra 5:41–42:

> "Yet behold, O Lord, thou dost have charge of those who are alive at the end, but what will those do who were before us, or we, or those who come after us?" He said to me, "I shall liken my judgment to a circle; just as for those who are last there is no slowness, so for those who are first there is no haste."[47]

Aside from the completely different situations of Pseudo-Ezra and the Thessalonian congregation,[48] the view of the Thessalonians, that the dead would be raised but that this would occur only *after* the parousia, would hardly have led to hopelessness or have caused Paul to depict their view as such.[49]

This type of exegesis must therefore also be rejected.

5.2.1.3 THE INABILITY OF THE THESSALONIANS AS THE CAUSE OF GRIEF

The type of exegesis described here characteristically assumes in various ways that the Thessalonians were unable to cope with death, even though Paul had already provided the means for this, namely, the doctrine of the resurrection of Christians.

According to R. Bultmann, for example, the doctrine of the resurrection that Paul propounded in his founding proclamation "died away without effect, so that he has to reassure that Church [the Thessalonians] of the resurrection (1 Thess. 4:13–18)."[50] Spörlein thinks that "this point of the apostolic proclamation [viz., the resurrection of the dead] . . . was unable to maintain its place in living faith owing to the strong influence of the nonbelieving environment and the seeming reality that contradicted every hope in the resurrection."[51] Finally, it has been suggested that the Thessalonians somehow misunderstood Paul and that Paul is correcting this misunderstanding in 1 Thess. 4:13–18.[52]

A more powerful proposal has been offered by U. Luz and P. Siber. According to them, when Paul was in Thessalonica he taught the Thessalonians to expect both the parousia and the resurrection (of Christians). The problem of the Thessalonians with respect to the death of a few members of the congregation arose not from a lack of theoretical knowledge but from the inability to apply the content of faith to their everyday lives. "If the Thessalonians had systematically considered the certainty that arises [sic] from the kerygma regarding the future resurrection of believers . . . , then they could have avoided falling into doubts when members of their congregation died."[53]

In criticism of this type of exegesis, we may say that Bultmann and Spörlein overlook the fact that 1 Thess. 4:13–18 is primarily concerned not with the resurrection of the dead as such[54] but rather with the specific problem of whether Christians who have fallen asleep before the parousia are at a disadvantage when compared with the living. Luz and Siber should be asked whether Paul could have left the congregation in Thessalonica without having correlated his ideas about the parousia and the notion of the resurrection if, as they assume, 1

Thessalonians was written twenty years after the death and resurrection of Jesus, that is, at a time when "both reckoning with one's own death and the hope of a resurrection of the dead was widespread in the churches."[55] Had Paul not already encountered similar problems in other congregations? Did he nevertheless refrain from connecting the two ideas? Does "the hopelessness of the Thessalonians have its material presupposition in the structure of Pauline proclamation and theology" (that does not systematically relate the future resurrection with the parousia in an apocalyptic manner)?[56]

Anyone who accepts the conventional dating of 1 Thessalonians can only ask these questions and *must* deny the propriety of the thesis to be presented in the following, namely, that Paul said nothing about the future resurrection of Christians during the founding proclamation.[57]

5.2.1.4 LACK OF INSTRUCTION ABOUT THE FUTURE RESURRECTION OF CHRISTIANS DURING THE FOUNDING VISIT AS THE CAUSE OF GRIEF

The proponents of this thesis[58] maintain that Paul did not deal thematically with the resurrection of the dead during his founding proclamation, owing to the expectation of an imminent parousia. Support for this view is found in the scattered references to the imminent end throughout the letter (1:9–10; 3:13; 5:23). Further, the introductory phrase "We would not have you ignorant" always introduces new information in Paul's writings. Thus this phrase indicates, in view of the subject it introduces (the *koimōmenoi*), that Paul had not previously dealt with the fate of Christians who died. Moreover, according to this view, Paul's maintenance of the old expectation of salvation, where the resurrection is spoken of as one event that will occur at the time of the parousia (i.e., the dead will arise in order to be caught up),[59] shows that Paul previously proclaimed this older form of expectation without connecting it with the notion of the resurrection of Christians.

This proposal is, in general and in my opinion, correct. The following analysis of the text will show whether more reasons can be brought forward in support of this view and whether this view may be stated more precisely. If this proves to be the case, then according to the external criterion developed above (see above, pp. 204–5), the date of the founding visit in Thessalonica would be very early.[60]

5.2.2 Analysis of 1 Thess. 4:13–18[61]

5.2.2.1 CONTEXT

In 1 Thess. 4:13–18 we find a distinct unit of thought within 1 Thessalonians. Verse 13 starts the new unit with a formula that Paul uses elsewhere to introduce new sections ("We would not have you ignorant"). The object of the following *peri, koimōmenōn*,[62] stands in reference to a question raised by the Thessalonians (probably orally) and indicates the subject of the following verses.

The *peri* at the beginning of our section is the second of three *peris* (4:9, 13; 5:1). Its relationship to the *peris* in 4:9 and 5:1 may be described as follows. In the other two cases instruction is expressly declared to be unnecessary. Thereby the importance of the instructions about Christians who have died is further enhanced.

This gives some indication of the way the unit is connected with the preceding text. Notice should also be taken of the parallelism between the final statement of 4:13–18, "Therefore comfort one another with these words," and the concluding statement of the following section, 5:1–11, which also begins with *peri*: "Therefore encourage one another and build one another up" (5:11).

Both 1 Thess. 4:13–18 and 5:1–11 are tailored to fit this congregation. There is a further parallelism between the two units insofar as they each refer to future fellowship with Christ as the salvation of living and dead Christians. See 5:10, where reference is made to the problem of living and dead Christians at the time of the parousia, which was dealt with in 4:13ff. The verbs *grēgorein* and *katheudein* in 5:10 are no longer used in a literal sense as in 5:6, 7.

5.2.2.2 STRUCTURE

I. *Introduction*: Indication of the theme and aim of Paul's discussion: In view of the death of a few Christians, Paul wants to avert heathen hopelessness on the part of the Thessalonians (v. 13).

II. *First response* to the problem posed by the theme: Recourse to the "faith" and application of it to the dead (v. 14).

III. *Second response* to the problem posed by the theme as a specification of the first response: A saying of the Lord (vv. 15–17).

III.1 Summary of the saying of the Lord (v. 15).

III.2 Quotation of the saying of the Lord (vv. 16–17).

IV. *The conclusion* of II and III stated as *paraklēsis*: Achievement of the aim indicated in I (v. 18).

5.2.2.3 EXEGESIS

5.2.2.3.1 Verses 13–14

Verse 13: "We would not have you ignorant." Paul often used this introductory formula to introduce something new or to present his congregations with previously unknown information.[63] Harnisch's thesis that this formula in Paul's writings indicates only "that Paul is placing special emphasis on the statement that follows"[64] is contradicted by the texts:

1. Harnisch himself admits that in Rom. 1:13 and 2 Cor. 1:8, where the formula is also used, the congregation is informed of something previously unknown.[65]

2. As regards Rom. 11:25, the explanation that Paul is only placing special emphasis on the following but is not telling the readers anything new is hardly satisfactory.[66] Insofar as the earlier message of the apostle to the Gentiles is known, it did not provide any basis for the conclusion or supposition that "all Israel will be saved" (see, to the contrary, Galatians and 1 Thess. 2:14ff.). Thus, the formula probably introduces something new here too.[67]

3. In 1 Cor. 10:1, Paul employs the formula again to introduce something new to the readers. Of course, what is new is not the biblical material, which is assumed to be known. "The new element which Paul has to offer is the interpretation introduced by *ou thelō hymas agnoein*, 'I would not have you ignorant.'"[68]

4. Similarly, 1 Cor. 12:1 makes sense only if the formula is employed here to introduce something *new*, though the aspect of emphasis is also involved. Paul is responding to the Corinthians' question about the gifts of the Spirit, and the ensuing discussion shows that Paul is correcting his congregation at several points. For this reason, even this last passage supports the thesis that in Paul's writings the formula always introduces something new.

The content of the instruction in 1 Thess. 4:13–18 concerns those Christians who have died in Thessalonica since Paul left that city. Their deaths have caused *lypē*, comparable only to the hopelessness of the heathens. Even the *elpis* of the living Christians has been drawn into danger through the death of a few Christians.[69] Since it is endangered, Paul has to present anew the reason for hope, with special attention being given to the deaths that have occurred.

Verse 14: "For since we believe that Jesus died and rose again, even so, through Jesus, God will bring with him those who have fallen asleep." How is the *elpis* defined? An indication that *elpis* is not understood primarily as hope in the resurrection arises from a comparison of our passsage with 1 Cor. 6:14. There it is stated, "And God raised the Lord and will also raise us up by his power." A corresponding final statement for 1 Thess. 4:14 would have been "Thus God will also raise those who have fallen asleep."[70] While 1 Cor. 6:14 explicates the resurrection of Christians according to the schema "as Christ—so the Christians," this schema has no importance in 1 Thess. 4:14. The statement about the resurrection of Christians is only indirectly important, for while their resurrection is the presupposition for being brought together with Christ, the emphasis is not placed on it. This will be explained in the following.

These preliminary remarks suffice as an *introduction to the problem*. A detailed exegesis of v. 14 must now be performed with the following questions in mind:

(a) The formula of faith in v. 14
(b) The question of the meaning and referent of *tous koimēthentas dia tou Iēsou*
(c) The problem of *axei syn autō*.

(a) It has long been recognized that Paul and other authors of the New Testament employ kerygmatic formulations in their letters. These formulas have been the subject of an intensified investigation in recent years, especially in German-speaking countries.[71] Despite differences with regard to the theological meaning, delineation, and classification of these formulas, New Testament exegesis has taken a great step forward in recognizing this phenomenon in almost all the letters of the New Testament, especially in the letters of Paul.

The last major work to have analyzed the type of formula found in 1 Thess. 4:14 derives from K. Wengst. In the first section of his book, Wengst deals with the type of formula that he calls the "raising formula" (*Auferweckungsformel*). The content of this type of formula is that God raised Jesus from the dead (catchword: *egeirein*). Wengst differentiates this raising formula from a resurrection formula (*Auferstehungsformel*), such as appears in 1 Thess. 4:14 and Rom. 14:9. The reason for this differentiation is that in these two passages Jesus is not the object of the resurrection but rather the subject. It is said that he *anestē* or *ezēsen* (Rom. 14:9).

Is this distinction between the raising formula and the resurrection formula legitimate? This question is particularly pressing because 1 Thess. 4:14 and Rom. 14:9 do not have the same wording.

On Rom. 14:9: Here the theme of dying and living is developed in the context, and the living and dying of Christians are described as occurring for Christ. It is therefore likely that Paul let the *ezēsen* slip into the formula from the context, thereby replacing an explicit statement concerning the resurrection.[72]

Does the recognition of the secondary character of *ezēsen* in Rom. 14:9 prove that Paul took over from tradition the *anestē* in the formula in 1 Thess. 4:14 and that *anestē* represents to a certain extent the archetype of the second part of the resurrection formula? Despite the singular character of *anestē* in Paul's writings, one will not be able to answer this question in the affirmative without further ado, as Wengst does, for no other "credo text" in the letters has the order *apethanen—anestē*.[73] For this reason it cannot be proven that the redactional *ezēsen* derives from *anestē*. In view of our observation that the context has affected the credo in Rom. 14:9, one should rather conclude that the *anestē* in 1 Thess. 4:14 arose from the context, that is, from v. 16, where it is said that "the dead . . . will rise (*anastēson-tai*)."[74] It should also be noted that an absolute *Iēsous* does not otherwise occur in the full *pistis*-formula[75] and that, in contrast to the other death-formulas, v. 14 does not explicate the meaning of Jesus' death. These observations lead to the conclusion that while v. 14 actually has the structure of a credo, the peculiar features just mentioned preclude it from being classified as a particular traditional type of formula. It should rather be viewed as an independent Pauline formulation.[76]

Further inquiry into the history of traditions of the individual elements in the formula combining the death and resurrection of Jesus in 1 Thess. 4:14 need not be undertaken here, for it would serve no purpose for our chronological question. For this reason, reference may simply be made to the secondary literature.[77]

(b) On the question of the meaning and referent of *tous koimēthentas dia tou Iēsou*: Since P. Hoffmann has recently undertaken a thorough investigation of the term *koimasthai* in the Pauline writings and their contemporary world, we can simply refer to this study and present its results summarily:

The characteristic of Paul's use of the word *koimasthai* may be said to be that he uses the verb in an unreflected, self-evident way. He shows no special interest for the word. Not a single text requires a specifically Christian meaning. A few passages speak against such an interpretation. The Christian reinterpretation of the verb, which understands death as "sleep until resurrection" and is witnessed for later times, neither determined nor influenced his usage.[78]

This view must, however, be defended against the thesis of J. Baumgarten, according to which *koimasthai* "in the Pauline stage of tradition inherently [includes] the expectation of resurrection."[79] Paul employs the verb nine times (1 Cor. 7:39; 11:30; 15:6, 18, 20, 51; 1 Thess. 4:13, 14, 15). Baumgarten arrives at his thesis because only "in 1 Cor. 7:39 and 11:30 . . . no direct connection with the hope of the resurrection"[80] is present. That is right. In terms of method, however, the question arises whether precisely in view of these two passages, which exclude a specifically Christian interpretation of *koimasthai* as "sleep until resurrection," all the other passages should be interpreted in this specifically Christian sense, even though not a single one of these passages demands a specifically Christian meaning.

Thus there is no compelling reason to revise Hoffmann's statements on *koimasthai* quoted above. By no means does the Pauline use of the verb inherently contain the hope for resurrection. The verb is rather employed as a neutral euphemism for "dying."[81]

(*Tous koimēthentas*) *dia tou Iēsou*: The question of what *dia tou Iēsou* modifies, and further whether *dia* should be translated in a causal or modal manner, is controversial. On the assumption that *dia* should be taken with *tous koimēthentas*, there are two possible interpretations:

(a) It has been proposed that v. 14 is speaking of the first Christian martyrs. In this case *dia* would have a causal[82] meaning. This thesis breaks down because neither the context of 4:13ff. nor the entire letter says anything about martyrs. In the passages in which Paul speaks of *thlipsis* (1:6; 3:3, 7), he is not speaking of death through persecution.[83]

(b) Another thesis is that *dia* should be understood in a modal sense, synonymous to *en*. The translation would be "those who have fallen asleep in Jesus" or "those who have fallen asleep" "in the case of whom there was a relationship to Jesus" (Dobschütz, 191). Sometimes a parallel is seen between *Iēsous apethanen* and *tous koimēthentas dia tou Iēsou*.[84]

The parallelism just mentioned reads a Pauline mode of thought

("as Christ—so the Christians") into our text where it is not (yet) present (see p. 215). Further, Paul knows how to differentiate between *dia*
and *en* (v. 16 speaks of the *nekroi en Christō*),[85] and "to fall asleep/die
through Jesus"[86] is meaningless if the thesis regarding martyrs is
incorrect.

Should *dia* even be taken with *tous koimēthentas*? The last argument for taking *dia* with *tous koimēthentas*, namely, that "*dia . . .*" is
usually placed after the word it modifies, may be countered with a stylistic argument. Paul placed *dia tou Iēsou* before its actual referent,
axei, for otherwise the two prepositional phrases *dia tou Iēsou* and *syn
autō* would have had to stand alongside one another.[87]

This sentence already anticipates a thesis concerning the referent of
dia tou Iēsou that must be further explicated in the framework of an
exegesis of v. 14. It also leads over to the next question, the meaning of
axei syn autō.

(c) *Axei syn autō*: With this phrase Paul refers to a future event, the
bringing together of the (dead) believers with Jesus.

Agein is "not a terminus technichus of eschatology,"[88] and attempts
to connect *agein* with traditions on the Passover or Exodus[89] fail.

The future *syn*-phrases in Paul (see Rom. 6:8; 8:32; 1 Thess. 4:17;
5:10) do not indicate a single act in the final drama but rather focus the
final drama, which is painted in bright colors in apocalyptic texts, on
the christologically founded meaning of salvation, the final state of
fellowship with Jesus.[90] While the *syn*-phrases in other Pauline texts,
such as Phil. 1:23, designate a fellowship with Christ that begins directly after death, the phrase in 4:14 is clearly involved with the idea of
the parousia, as is evident from the immediate (vv. 16ff.) and broader
context (1:9–10; 3:13).

After this clarification of the *individual terms*, we may now return to
the question of the meaning of *dia tou Iēsou*. Picking up on what was
said above as an introduction to the problem (p. 215), we may turn to
examine the flow of thought in v. 14 and the theological logic of Paul
that surfaces here. As was already clear from the analysis of the structure of the passage, v. 14 presents a first response to the problem that
had arisen in Thessalonica. Thus we may also keep in mind here the
question of whether the thesis we proposed above regarding the occasion of grief in Thessalonica can be verified.

The flow of thought in v. 14: On the basis of the kerygma of the
death and resurrection of Jesus that is acknowledged in Thessalonica,
Paul concludes that the Thessalonians who have died will participate

in future fellowship with Jesus: "For since we believe that Jesus died and rose again, even so, through Jesus, God will bring with him those who have fallen asleep."

The meaning of *dia tou Iēsou*, which was left unspecified above, should now be determined as serving to connect the first part of the sentence with the second. On the basis of what is said in the first part ("Jesus died and rose"), Paul uses the phrase to indicate the reason for *salvation*, the reason God will bring the dead together with Jesus. For the interpretation of *dia* this means that even though *dia* with the genitive should usually be understood in an instrumental sense, though not always,[91] a *causal* nuance[92] is also involved in our passage. This view is reinforced by the fact that even *ei* (in the first part of the sentence) can carry a causal meaning.[93]

The change of subjects in v. 14 (v. 14a: *Jesus* died and rose; v. 14b: *God* will bring the dead) has already been described as a stylistically awkward construction that is singular among Paul's credo formulations. It has occasioned various interpretations of v. 14. The stylistic awkwardness is further increased by the phrase *dia tou Iēsou*, which refers to *axei syn autō*. The construction is monstrous: God brings the dead through Jesus with Jesus. This disjointed mode of expression, however, intends to call forth an explanation.[94] It can be adequately explained only on the assumption that Paul is for the first time connecting the kerygma of the death and resurrection of Jesus with the death of a few Christians. When he does this, he maintains the old soteriological perspective that had been proclaimed in Thessalonica and that conceived of the (death and) resurrection of Jesus as the basis for his imminent arrival from heaven. That this was the old soteriological perspective is evident from the summary of the missionary proclamation in 1 Thess. 1:9–10[95] (cf. 3:13).[96] Apparently the death of Christians was not a topic of this initial proclamation because the parousia was thought to be immediately at hand. In the first theological reflection on the death of a few Christians, fellowship with the Lord at the parousia remains most important. Thus Paul does not say, "He will raise those who have fallen asleep (with him)," but rather keeps the focus on the statement concerning the parousia: "He will bring with him."[97] Observation of this maintenance of the old soteriological conception, even though it involved stylistic awkwardness, leads to the conclusion that Paul did not preach the resurrection of the dead (relating to Christians) during his first proclamation. A further argument for this conclusion may be drawn from the phrase in v. 13, "We would not have you ignorant," through which Paul always introduces something new.

Paul attempts to counter the grief of the Thessalonians that can lead only into the hopelessness of the heathen and thus to counter the endangerment of the *elpis* by referring to the credo in v. 14 (which is partially formulated in Pauline vocabulary). On the basis of this credo, Paul concludes that *those who have died* will participate in future fellowship with Christ. Thereby he proclaims something new.

Thus his initial proclamation in Thessalonica would not yet have had this content. Paul's theological logic is that *because* Jesus died and rose the dead will participate in the parousia. The *elpis* of the Thessalonians, which is focused on the parousia, need not collapse because of a few deaths.

The comments of the apostle in v. 14 were thus undoubtedly the result of considerable intellectual effort. Beyond establishing the causal relationship between the kerygma and the parousia and applying this to the dead Christians,[98] Paul's comments also provide a christological basis for understanding the fate of believers and already hint at the model "as Christ—so the Christians,"[99] which would be developed later.[100]

As is clear from the following verses, Paul actually imagines the "bringing" of the dead Christians in such a manner that they first rise and then are taken away with those still alive at the parousia. This means that Paul is introducing—for the dead Christians and as fulfillment of the condition for being taken away—the notion of resurrection for Christians, though the emphasis of Paul's statements in v. 14 and vv. 15ff. (see below) is on the (dead) Christians being "brought" or taken away. If our thesis that *anastēsontai* in v. 16 gave rise to the formulation *anestē* in the kerygma is correct, then Paul not only connected the idea of resurrection with the statement *axei syn autō* but also took a short step in the direction of the theological model "as Christ—so the Christians."[101]

Result of the exegesis of vv. 13–14: Alongside providing an insight into Paul's theological thought as it developed from the kerygma of death and resurrection, the exegesis of vv. 13–14 has supplied confirmation of the hypothesis that is important for our inquiry, namely, that Paul said nothing about the resurrection of Christians in his initial proclamation in Thessalonica.

We may now analyze vv. 15–17.

5.2.2.3.2 *Analysis of Verses 15–17: The* Logos Kyriou *and Its Interpretation by Paul*

For this (*touto gar*) we declare to you by the word of the Lord (*en logō kyriou*), that we who are alive, who are left until the coming of the Lord, shall not precede those who have fallen asleep. For the Lord himself will descend from heaven with a cry of command, with the archangel's call, and with the sound of the trumpet of God. And the dead in Christ will rise first; then we who are alive, who are left, shall be caught up together with them in the clouds to meet the Lord in the air; and so we shall always be with the Lord.

The particle *gar* shows that Paul understands these verses as further support for what he said in v. 14. *Touto* refers to v. 15b and marks the beginning of a new section in the course of the argument.

Questions arise concerning the meaning of *en logō kyriou*. Research has suggested the following possibilities:

(a) It is based on a saying of the earthly Jesus.
(b) It is based on a saying of the raised one that derives either from a prophetic pronouncement or from Paul, who received it directly from the Lord.

Further, the delimitation of the saying of the Lord is uncertain. While most interpreters find it in vv. 16–17 and understand v. 15 as a Pauline summary of the saying and application to the Thessalonian situation, some exegetes view v. 15b as the saying of the Lord and see an apocalyptic specification of it in vv. 16–17.

In the light of these divergent views of the text, it seems proper first to separate redaction and tradition in vv. 15–17, and to do this on the basis of (a) observations of internal tensions in the text and (b) word statistics.

5.2.2.3.2.1 *Separation of Redaction and Tradition*

5.2.2.3.2.1.1 *Internal Tensions in the Text*

The following observations reveal the disparity of v. 15 and vv. 16–17:

(a) Verse 15 is written in epistolary style, as is clear from the first-person plural. Verses 16–17 are dominated by the third person, which is altered to the first-person plural only in v. 17 where the application is drawn out.

(b) Verse 15 strikes one rather as a statement (of comfort) directed to a particular situation. Verses 16–17 offer a general description of the events at the end of time.

(c) As is clear from the statement that the living shall not precede the dead, v. 15 is speaking of a moment in time *after* the events pictured in v. 16 and corresponding to the stage of being taken away in v. 17. The statement (of comfort) in v. 15 evidently finds the meaning of vv. 16–17 concentrated in the statement about being taken away in v. 17. It simply cannot be a coincidence that this part of v. 17 is taken up in v. 15: *hoi zōntes hoi perileipomenoi.*

Thus observation of tensions in vv. 15–17 permits us to make the preliminary suggestion that v. 15 and vv. 16–17 do not belong to the same layer of tradition. Rather, v. 15 offers an exegesis of vv. 16–17.

5.2.2.3.2.1.2 Word Statistics

Verse 15: legein is thoroughly Pauline (cf. Rom. 15:8; Gal. 5:2, etc.).

En logō kyriou: logos kyriou is found elsewhere only in 1 Thess. 1:8, where, however, it designates "the gospel" in general. In our passsage it refers to a particular piece of apocalyptic information. *Kyrios* as a designation for the raised one is Pauline.

Hēmeis hoi zōntes: zaō is frequently witnessed in the Pauline writings (see the concordance). The first-person plural is certainly a Pauline formulation.

Perileipomenoi is found in Paul's writings only here and in v. 16.

Parousia (tou kyriou) is found in an apocalyptic sense elsewhere only in 1 Thess. 2:19; 3:13; 5:23; 1 Cor. 15:23 (*parousia tou Christou*).

Ou mē: This negative is also found in 1 Thess. 5:3; Rom. 4:8 (quotation); 1 Cor. 8:13; Gal. 4:30 (quotation); 5:16.

Phthasōmen: phthanein with the sense "precede" is found in Paul's writings only here. Elsewhere Paul uses the verb with the sense "come," "attain to": 1 Thess. 2:16; 2 Cor. 10:14; Rom. 9:31.

Tous koimēthentas: koimasthai is thoroughly Pauline. See 1 Cor. 7:39; 11:30; 15:6, 18, 20, 51; 1 Thess. 4:13, 14.

Verse 16: autos ho (kyrios). The phrase *autos ho* is used in Pauline writings in connection with God (1 Thess. 3:11; 5:23), with Christ (1 Cor. 15:28; 2 Cor. 8:19), with *pneuma* (Rom. 8:16, 26), with Satan (2 Cor. 11:14), and with the called (1 Cor. 1:24). See, further, *autos egō* in Rom. 7:25b, though the possibility that this verse is a gloss cannot be excluded.[102]

Ho kyrios as a designation for the coming one (*mare-kyrios*) corresponds with the usage both of the pre-Pauline Hellenistic church[103] and of Paul himself. Other than in our passsage, it is found five more times merely in 1 Thessalonians, and thus the phrase might be attributable to Pauline usage (cf. 2:19; 3:13; 4:17; without the article: 4:18; 5:2; all these passages, however, are formulaic).[104]

En keleusmati: keleusma is a *hapax legomenon* in the New Testament.

En phonē archaggelou: archaggelos is found once more the New Testament: Jude 9 (for Michael). The above usage is unique in the New Testament. *Phonē* is used elsewhere by Paul in a nonapocalyptic sense in 1 Cor. 14:7, 8, 10, 11; Gal. 4:20.

En salpiggi theou: salpigx in an apocalyptic context reappears in Paul only in 1 Cor. 15:52, and this passage probably stands in a genetic relationship with 1 Thess. 4:16 (see below; cf. further Rev. 1:10; 4:1; 8:2, 6, 13; 9:14, etc.).

Katabēsetai ap' ouranou: In apocalyptic usage the verb is a *hapax legomenon* in Paul's writing. Compare, otherwise, Rom. 10:7 (in a quotation, but also together with *ouranos*). Elsewhere in the New Testament, the verb is used in connection with the new Jerusalem (Rev. 3:12; 21:2, 10), with the *diabolos* (Rev. 12:12), with the angels (Rev. 10:1; 18:1; 20:1; Matt. 28:2), and with the Son of Man (John 3:13 and, picking up on this, 6:33, 38, 41, etc.).[105]

Hoi nekroi is totally Pauline (see the concordance). In 1 Thessalonians, however, Paul prefers *koimōmenoi/koimēthentes*. Elsewhere in 1 Thessalonians, *nekroi* appears only in the tradition in 1:9–10.

En Christō is clearly Pauline and, in the event that *hoi nekroi* should be part of the tradition despite its common use in Paul's letters, is certainly a redactional addition. This view finds further confirmation in that the expression *en Christō* was probably created by Paul.[106]

Anastēsontai is an unusual expression for Paul that, aside from the immediate context (v. 15), never reappears in the Pauline writings. Paul prefers the stem *egeir-*.

Prōton is thoroughly Pauline. See Rom. 1:8, 16, etc.

Verse 17: epeita probably derives from Paul (cf. 1 Cor. 12:28; 15:5, 6, 7; Gal. 1:18, 21; 2:1. This conclusion is likely also because the expression *prōton—epeita* appears in another Pauline apocalyptic text that is certainly marked by redaction, 1 Cor. 15:46 (cf. 15:23).

Hēmeis hoi zōntes hoi perileipomenoi must stand in a genetic relationship with v. 15 because the phrasing is identical (see the word statistics there).

Hama syn is also found in 1 Thess. 5:10. *Hama* by itself is found elsewhere in Philemon 22 and in the quotation in Rom. 3:12. Paul employs *syn* both for relationships between humans and for (future) fellowship with Christ.

Is it impossible, despite the presence of *hama syn* in a *Pauline* formulation in Thess. 5:10, to affirm that *hama syn* in this passage derives from Paul, because one should reckon with the possibility that a traditional *hama syn* in 1 Thess. 4:17 has affected the formulation in 1 Thess. 5:10?[107] This thesis does not give adequate attention to the following two points:

1. In each passage *hama* describes something different. In 4:17 it describes the joint withdrawal of the living and those who were previously dead. In 5:10 it describes fellowship with Christ. If one were to assume that the context affected the formulation, one would expect a more thoroughgoing parallelism in usage (as was the case with *anestē/ anastēsontai*).

2. *Hama syn* in 4:17 corresponds with the perspective expressed in v. 15, that the survivors will not have any advantage over the dead. For this reason, it should be understood as a Pauline clarification rather than as a part of the tradition that fit in remarkably well with Paul's intention. In other passages where Paul employs tradition, he similarly interprets the tradition in accord with his intention.

Conclusion regarding *hama syn*: It derives from Paul's redaction.

Harpagēsometha: Elsewhere Paul employs this verb only in 2 Cor. 12:2, 4, where it describes his ecstatic withdrawal into the third heaven or paradise. The use of the verb in connection with the events of the parousia is thus found only in this passage in Paul's writings. This may be taken as a sign of use of tradition.

En nephelais: Elsewhere Paul employs the word *nephelē* only in the midrash on the generation in the desert in 1 Cor. 10:1, 2.

Apantēsis is not employed elsewhere in the Pauline writings or in the New Testament.

Aēr is elsewhere used by Paul only in 1 Cor. 9:26 and 14:9, each time as part of a metaphor.

Kai houtōs pantote syn kyriō esometha: This sentence is marked thoroughly by Paul's hand. *Kai houtōs*: Compare Rom. 5:12; 1 Cor. 7:17, 36; 11:28, Gal. 6:2. *Pantote*: Thirty-nine times in the New Testament, nineteen times in Paul. *Syn kuriō einai*: 1 Thess. 5:10; 2 Cor. 4:4 (*syn Iēsou*), cf. Rom. 6:8: *syzēsomen autō* [*Christō*].

The word statistics have thus shown that non-Pauline expressions are found mainly in vv. 16–17.

To conclude the section "Separation of Redaction and Tradition" (5.2.2.3.2.1), it may be said that, owing to its epistolary style, its content, and its Pauline vocabulary, v. 15 should be viewed as an application of vv. 16–17 to the Thessalonian situation.

Parallels to this manner of presenting the meaning of a quotation before the quotation is actually made may be found in the Pauline writings in Rom. 14:10c (Paul's pointed application of vv. 11–12) and 1 Cor. 15:51 (Paul's summary of vv. 52–53.)

We must now turn to the following tasks: (a) analysis of vv. 16–17 in terms of form criticism and the history of traditions, which may be able to verify the above separation of redaction and tradition, (b) determination of the meaning of vv. 16–17 at the level of the tradition, and (c) determination of the meaning of vv. 16–17 at the level of redaction, including examination of whether this agrees with the intention of the Pauline application in v. 15.

5.2.2.3.2.2 Analysis of Verses 16–17 in Terms of Form Criticism and the History of Traditions

If we separate out the expressions that have been identified as Pauline additions on the basis of word statistics, and if we remove the first-person plural, which was occasioned by the epistolary setting, we have the following text:

Whether *ho kyrios* is part of the tradition could not be decided on the basis of word statistics. Since only form criticism and the history of traditions can enable a decision, we shall postpone the question and assume for the moment that *ho kyrios* is part of the tradition:

"The Lord will descend from heaven with a cry of command, with the archangel's call, and with the sound of the trumpet of God. And the dead will rise. Those who are left will be caught up into the clouds to meet the Lord in the air" (tr.).

If one uses the term "apocalyptic" to designate "first of all the literary genre of the Apocalypses, i.e. revelatory writings which disclose the secrets of the beyond and especially of the end of time, and then secondly, the realm of ideas from which this literature originates,"[108] then our tradition should be classified as an apocalyptic document or, in terms of form criticism, "a miniature apocalypse" (Vielhauer).

This classification is correct because (a) the motifs of the passage all derive from the world of apocalyptic imagery and (b) the basic structure of the passage is that of a revelatory writing that discloses a mystery pertaining to the end of time.

On (a): *katabainein* ("to descend") is used in connection with traditions on the Son of Man (see Matt. 24:30; Mark 14:62 par.; John 3:13 [see below, p. 227]) and generally in the context of the arrival of eschatological events.[109] A list of the signs of the end of time is part of apocalyptic style (Matt. 24:30–31; *Did.* 16:6), and the call of the archangel and the sound of the trumpet are accompaniments of the arrival of the end. The sound of the trumpet may serve as a prelude both to the resurrection of the dead and to judgment, as well as to the gathering of the congregation of the saved.[110] The resurrection of the dead is an apocalyptic idea. The same applies to the notion of the remnant, or those left behind, in connection with the final events and to "being caught up" (see *S. Bar.* 13:3; 76:2, etc.; *Ethiopic Enoch* 70–71; Rev. 11:12). The "cloud motif" also belongs to the same world of ideas (see Dan. 7:13 and, again, Rev. 11:12).[111]

On (b): Verses 16–17 disclose the mystery of the end of time in a compressed form. The verses end with the aerial meeting of the *kyrios* with those who are his own.

Owing to his lack of interest in pictorial presentations, Paul breaks off the tradition here and merely summarizes its content with the words "and so we shall always be with the Lord." We do not know for sure how the tradition continued. It may be assumed as probable, however, that the miniature apocalypse next presented the arrival of the *kyrios* and his own on the earth. The following considerations render this a likely assumption: (a) *Katabainein* shows that the *kyrios* "is actually coming down to earth to build up his kingdom here." (b) "The *apantēsis* . . . takes place in order to receive the Lord as he descends and to return to earth with him."[112]

There seems to be a serious objection to understanding vv. 16–17 as a unified tradition that may be classified in the history of forms as a miniature apocalypse. (It will be seen, however, that this objection only strengthens what has already been said.) If one considers the chronology of events in the tradition above, the statements that the dead will rise and that the living will be caught up into the air to meet the Lord pose problems for an understanding of vv. 16–17 as a *unified* tradition. According to this objection, the statements on the resurrection and the withdrawal flatly contradict each other, for it is assumed that those who have risen will *not* be carried off to the Lord (Paul's understanding is *different*).

If one looks more closely, one may see that when Paul's redaction has been removed the statements about the resurrection and the withdrawal are not intended to indicate that one of these events will chronologically follow the other. Rather, each event is separately connected with the arrival of the *kyrios*. For this reason, it does not seem to be impermissible to place, in an experimental way, the resurrection of the dead chronologically after the withdrawal of the living in the reconstructed tradition. This seems all the more permissible since the express chronological priority of the resurrection derives from Paul's redaction (*prōton—epeita*) and since the portrayal of the parousia in vv. 16–17, with the resurrection of the dead occurring before the arrival of the *kyrios* (on earth), does not correspond to the Jewish schema. While this hypothesis has not yet proven that vv. 16–17 derive from a more or less unified apocalypse that ended with the resurrection of the dead, it is nevertheless justified to ask whether any analogous apocalyptic models from the surrounding world of the New Testament may be cited as parallels to the miniature apocalypse that presumably stands behind vv. 16–17.

The report of the appearance of the Son of Man in 4 Ezra 13 is particularly similar to our passage (italics indicate noticeable agreements in expression with 1 Thess. 4:16–17): 13:3: "I looked, and behold, this wind made something like the figure of a man come up out of the heart of the sea. And I looked, and behold, that man flew with the *clouds* of heaven; . . . 4: and whenever his *voice* issued from his mouth, all who heard his *voice* melted. . . . 12: After this I saw the same man *come down* from the mountain. . . . 13: Then many people came to him. . . . [who are, according to the interpretation in v.] 48: those who are *left* of your people."
It is well known that 4 Ezra does not connect the messianic kingdom with the resurrection of the dead. According to Pseudo-Ezra "those who are left are more blessed than those who have died" (13:24). The resurrection of the dead will occur only after the messianic reign has drawn to an end, when "the earth shall give up those who are asleep in it, and the dust those who dwell silently in it; and the chambers shall give up the souls which have been committed to them. And the Most High shall be revealed upon the seat of judgment" (4 Ezra 7:32–33).
It was said above, however, that the separation of the intervening messianic kingdom from the future eon and the concurrent resurrection of the dead reflects a conception that can be documented only for the period after 70 C.E. In Judaism before 70 C.E., belief in the resurrection is closely connected with the coming time of salvation, which is identical with the messianic kingdom. "Thus the Old Testament passage Dan. 12:2—the only one other than Isa

26:19—already seeks to answer the question of whether the pious ones who do not live to experience the change of worlds at the initiation of the blessed era will miss out on salvation. The answer is supplied precisely by the belief in the resurrection."[113]

These remarks have rendered it clear that our miniature apocalypse with its connection of the coming of the *kyrios* with the resurrection of the dead reflects Jewish tradition. A question that is in need of further clarification pertains to the relationship of those who remain and who are withdrawn to those who are raised. Do Jewish apocalyptic texts deal with the relationship of these two groups, or must we revert to the thesis that the fragmentary nature of the apocalypse contained in vv. 16–17 makes its derivation from the history of traditions impossible?

Almost all apocalypses share the conviction that the end is at hand. Even "the first apocalyptist is convinced that he will experience the end of times; this conviction is maintained throughout the ages."[114] Since these same apocalyptists expected the resurrection of the dead to be part of the imminent era of salvation, one should expect to find somewhere reflections on the relationship of the survivors to those who are raised.

Syriac Apocalypse of Baruch 29–30 seems to be an example of such reflection. Chap. 29 reports of the hardship that will come on the earth in the final days. In 28:7 the question is raised "Is it in one place or in one of the parts of the earth that those things are [to] come to pass, or will the whole earth experience (them)?" The apocalyptist receives an answer in 29:1: ". . . 'Whatever will then befall (will befall) the whole earth; therefore all who live will experience (them). 2: For at that time I will protect only those who are found in those self-same days in this land. 3: And it shall come to pass when all is accomplished that was to come to pass in those parts, that the Messiah shall then begin to be revealed. [This is followed by a description of the paradisaic state such as:] 8: And it shall come to pass at that self-same time that the treasury of manna shall again descend from on high, and they will eat of it in those years, because these are they who have come to the consummation of time. 30:1: And it shall come to pass after these things, when the time of the advent of the Messiah is fulfilled, that He shall return in glory. Then all who have fallen asleep in hope of Him shall rise again. 2: . . . the treasuries will be opened . . . , and the first shall rejoice and the last shall not be grieved. 3: For they know that the time has come of which it is said, that it is the consummation of the times.'"

Chap. 49 seems to present chaps. 29–30 in a varied form and to have arisen from apologetical interests.[115] The apocalyptist inquires in 49:2, "In what shape will those live[116] who live in Thy day?" The answer reads in 50:2: "For the earth shall then assuredly restore the dead, [which it now receives, in order to preserve them]. It shall make no change in their form. . . . 3: For then it will be necessary to show to the living that the dead have come to life again. . . . 4: When they have severally recognized those whom they now know, then judgement shall grow strong. . . . 51:8: [The righteous] shall behold the world which is now invisible to them, and they shall behold the time which is now hidden from them. 9: And time shall no longer age them. 10: For in the heights of that world shall they dwell, and they shall be made like unto the angels, and be made equal to the stars, and they shall be changed into every form they desire. . . ."

Previous research has often understood the *Syriac Apocalypse of Baruch* 29–30 to contain the conception of an intervening messianic kingdom.[117] According to this view, 29:3ff. is describing the paradisaic joys of the Messiah's reign, which only those who are alive at the time will enjoy. *S. Bar.* 30:1 supposedly reports the Messiah's return to heaven. The righteous rise only after this event.

Do these statements really differentiate two periods, the time of the Messiah and the eternal time of salvation, which is introduced by the resurrection of the dead?

First, against such a view is the fact that the 'statement in *S. Bar.* 30:1—that the Messiah returns to heaven and then those who have fallen asleep in hope of him rise again—has been suspected of being a Christian interpolation.[118]

Second, the messianic era as it is portrayed in chaps. 73–74 (cf. 74:2) is already considered to be the end of time (29:8; 30:3).

Third, there is no mention of the rebellion of evil, which is usually depicted as occurring between the messianic kingdom and the eternal kingdom.

Fourth, from the perspective of the history of traditions, chaps. 49–50, which belong together with chap. 30, deal with the relationship of the survivors and the dead. If, as is usually assumed, both sections (30 and 49–50) refer to the eternal time of salvation that follows the intervening kingdom, then it is inexplicable how there can be a discussion of the relationship of survivors and raised ones in chap. 50, for according to the usual understanding of the intervening kingdom all die after its completion (cf. 4 Ezra 7:28ff.).[119] How can *Syriac Apocalypse of Baruch* 50 assume that some humans will experience the day other than if the *Syriac Apocalypse of Baruch* envisions only *one turning point* in history?[120]

It should be concluded from what has been said that the *Syriac Apocalypse of Baruch* does *not* contain the conception of an intervening messianic kingdom. There is rather a relationship between the survivors in chap. 49 and those in chap. 29. In each case the survivors are groups of humans who are still alive at the arrival of the end.

The *Syriac Apocalypse of Baruch* is thus one example of how apocalyptic circles in Judaism viewed the relationship between the survivors and the dead at the time of salvation. The righteous, both those still alive and those who have died, will participate in the time of salvation, which is inaugurated by the arrival of the Messiah. The dead are raised after the arrival of the Messiah. Both groups, survivors and resurrected ones, will be transformed after the judgment (50:8).

It has thus been shown that the basic structure of the tradition in 1 Thess. 4:16–17 is analogous to Jewish apocalypses that report of the appearance of the Son of Man / Messiah on earth, of the assemblage of the surviving chosen ones (the remnant), and of the resurrection of the righteous and unrighteous.

In view of this relationship of 1 Thess. 4:16–17 to Jewish apocalyptic models, a relationship that has been reconstructed via the history of traditions, it seems advisable to replace *kyrios* by "Son of Man" at the level of tradition, especially since the recovered text reveals no Christian elements.

Up to now, one special feature of the recovered text behind 1 Thess. 4:16–17 has not been discussed, namely, the aerial *apantēsis* of the living with the Son of Man. Some Jewish statements about the gathering of the chosen by the angel of the Son of Man (cf. Mark 13:27; *Eth. En.* 61:1, 5; in connection with a statement about withdrawal: Luke 17:34) approximate our tradition about the withdrawal of the living to meet the Son of Man. However, these statements do not contain parallels to the specific imagery connected with the word *apantēsis*. Peterson has convincingly shown that *apantēsis* "is to be understood as a tech. term for a civic custom of antiquity whereby a public welcome was accorded by a city to important visitors."[121] The use of this word in our context means that a custom deriving from political life has been transported into the apocalyptic sphere.[122] Apocalyptic Hellenistic Judaism can use this word in order (a) to illustrate graphically the meeting of the Son of Man with the survivors and (b) to highlight the grandeur of the Son of Man.

The description of the withdrawal in our text should be understood in view of this meaning of *apantēsis*. The notion of withdrawal does not compete or conflict with the notion of resurrection. Rather, withdrawal involves nothing more than a sudden change of location.[123] Those who survive to the end of time will be withdrawn for the reception of the Son of Man. At the gateways of the world they will ceremoniously receive the one who is portrayed as a person of high rank. They will then return with him to the world, where the resurrection of the dead will occur.

In sum, it is possible to recognize the outline of an apocalypse from a Jewish Hellenistic environment in the tradition behind 1 Thess. 4:16–

17.[124] If one attempts to characterize the content of this apocalypse, one may say that it is an oracle regarding the future that proclaims salvation for those who survive until the parousia and for the righteous who have died. On the basis of the text, it cannot be decided with certainty whether the apocalyptist numbered himself among the survivors. At best, one could reach this conclusion through the general consideration that every apocalyptist numbered himself among the last generation (however, see the qualification of this consideration above, p. 249 n. 48).

Though further elucidation of the meaning of our miniature apocalypse at the level of tradition may not be possible because of its fragmentary character, knowledge about the form of 1 Thess. 4:16–17 is not completely without importance for the question about the *logos kyriou* that was left open above.

5.2.2.3.2.3 Consequences of the Form-Critical Analysis for the Meaning of Logos Kyriou *in 1 Thess. 4:15*

Previous research has focused primarily on the question of whether 1 Thess. 4:15–17 presents us with a saying of the earthly Jesus or the raised Christ. There is no real parallel to 1 Thess. 4:15–17 in the Gospels.[125] To designate such a saying as an *agraphon*[126] is always a precarious undertaking. This is especially the case with this saying, since the relationship of the *kyrios* in the saying of the Lord to the *kyrios* who supposedly spoke the saying would have to be clarified. For these reasons, there seems to be a consensus that the *logos kyriou* should be understood as a saying of the raised Christ and that it was spoken by a prophet in the name of the *kyrios*.[127]

In the light of the form-critical analysis undertaken above, this view should be modified as follows: According to Paul's understanding, this is certainly a saying of the raised one, but the kernel of vv. 16–17 derives from a *Jewish* apocalypse, which was understood by Paul as a saying[128] of the Lord.

An analogy from the beginnings of Christianity for such a process of placing a sort of apocalypse onto the lips of the raised one is found in Mark 13, where a Jewish apocalypse clearly glimmers through as the kernel (13:7–8, 12, 14–22, 24–27) of the apocalyptic speech. "Important . . . [is] the fact that a Jewish apocalypse was taken over and used as a saying of Jesus, so that the Messiah (21f.) or the Son of Man (26f.) was simply identified with Jesus."[129]

In view of the Jewish origin of the kernel of 1 Thess. 4:16–17, it is not possible to evaluate, through the history of traditions, the unit that Paul calls a *logos kyriou* in order to illuminate a pre-Pauline congregation whose situation "was not very different from that in Thessalonica."[130]

Apart from the fact that a purely Jewish substratum in vv. 16–17 would—as has been said—exclude such a thesis, the two claims that would first allow this thesis are probably faulty:

(a) *Hama syn* belongs to the substratum. This was already shown to be improbable (above, p. 224).

(b) The substratum supposedly had the expression "the dead in the Lord" instead of "the dead in Christ."

On (b): As an analogy for the phrase "the dead in the Lord," which U. Luz reconstructs, Luz refers to Rev. 14:13, "the dead who die in the Lord," which according to the suggestion of T. Holtz[131] derives from set traditional material. This verse, however, is a witness not for the expression "the dead in the Lord" but only for the statement that *martyrs* "die in the Lord."[132] For this reason, it seems quite risky to substitute "the dead in the Lord" in 1 Thess. 4:16, especially since Luz does not share the thesis that those who have died in Thessalonica were martyrs.

This defense of our thesis in two particulars thus perhaps provides support for the purely Jewish character of 1 Thess. 4:16–17.

This brings us to the question of the meaning of vv. 16–17 at the level of Pauline redaction.

5.2.2.3.2.4 The Meaning of 1 Thess. 4:16–17 at the Level of the Pauline Redaction

The following is concerned with determining the meaning of the Pauline additions to the Jewish substratum. Closely related to this task is the need to determine Paul's understanding of the passage. This last need arises from the mere adoption of the Jewish substratum and its particular statements for the situation of the Thessalonian congregation.

The separation of redaction and tradition revealed the following Pauline additions: "(dead) in Christ," "first/then," "we who are alive," "together with them," "and so we shall always be with the Lord." Further, Paul changed the third person in the presentation of the substratum, insofar as it referred to the dead and the survivors, into the first person. Finally, Paul seems to have modified the traditional order, "parousia—resurrection," so that the resurrection has been inserted between the beginning of the parousia and its completion.[133] The Pauline redaction of the substratum and the interest expressed through the mere adoption of this substratum reveal two concerns:

(a) The concern with the problem, which has arisen through a few deaths, of the fate of the dead Christians.
(b) A concern to emphasize the expectation of the parousia.

On (b): Paul is able to employ the Jewish substratum because it speaks of the imminent final events. He radicalizes and actualizes the statement that a remnant will be caught up into the air to the Lord by impressing on it the imminent expectation he nurtured at the time of 1 Thessalonians: "We who are alive, who are left." The statement now reads as if no further deaths are "planned."

On (a): Paul is also partially able to adopt the Jewish substratum because it deals with the same type of people that had given rise to hopelessness in Thessalonica and because it contains the same answer to the problem of death that was known to him as a Jew, namely, belief in the resurrection.

At the level of the Pauline redaction, the "dead" in the tradition become "the dead in Christ." The meaning of the text is not presented adequately when one explains the addition "in Christ" as indicating merely that those who had died were Christians.[134] While it must be admitted that "in Christ" in Paul's later letters often means "Christian,"[135] it must be taken into account that at the time of 1 Thessalonians, as the introductory formula "We would not have you ignorant, brethren, concerning those who are asleep" shows, the problem of dead Christians had not yet been theologically mastered. While this thus raises the question of whether the addition "in Christ" after "the dead" carries more than technical meaning, two further redactional alterations undertaken by Paul indicate that Paul did actually have to draw on new theological models in the light of the experience of death. In order to examine these models, we need to broaden our perspective. The point of the argument is reached in v. 17, where the focus falls on the future, lasting fellowship with Christ (literally, fellowship with the *kyrios*) of the dead and the (until the parousia) living Christians. In order to guarantee the fellowship of the dead Christians too with the *kyrios*, Paul consciously inverts the order of events in the Jewish substratum. There the resurrection of the dead chronologically followed the withdrawal of the living. Paul differentiates these two events by having the resurrection occur *prōton* and by letting the withdrawal occur *epeita* (cf. 1 Cor. 15:46 for a similar rearrangement of the order arising out of the desire to make a particular point). Further, Paul has the resurrection occurring only in order to enable the raised ones to be taken up together with the survivors, among whom Paul numbers himself and all the living Thessalonian Christians. Thus the Pauline expression "together with"[136] serves to confirm the future fellowship with Christ of the dead (and living) members of the congregation by emphasizing the simultaneity[137] of the withdrawal of the living and the dead. The presupposition for such a simultaneous withdrawal, in Paul's logic, is, however, the resurrection of the dead Christians.

From what has been said, it is clear that the statement about the resurrection was formulated in accommodation to the statement about withdrawal. It was seen in (b) (above, p. 233) that Paul radicalizes and actualizes the imminent expectation of the Jewish substratum and does *not* think that there will be further deaths. The most probable conclusion to be drawn from these observations, other than that the resurrection of Christians is still considered to be the exception, is that Paul is introducing the notion of the resurrection of dead Christians to the Thessalonians for the first time in 1 Thess. 4:13ff. Its introduction into the argument through the reception and redaction of a Jewish substratum serves to verify that the dead too will participate in fellowship with Christ.

In terms of the problem left open above about the precise meaning of "in Christ" after "the dead," this means not only that "in Christ" has technical meaning but also that Paul uses the qualification of the dead as "in Christ" to indicate that death cannot hinder future fellowship with Christ.[138] This was evidently the fear that arose in Thessalonica after the first deaths occurred.

If we were to extend Paul's thought systematically on this point, we could say that participation in Christ, which cannot be disrupted by death, is the foundation for the future fellowship with Christ. The goal of the "in Christ" is the "with Christ," which in turn is founded in the "in Christ." Such theological thinking by Paul, which admittedly appears in a pure form only in the later letters, is already intimated in 1 Thessalonians, and thus one step has been made toward a christological understanding of Christian existence.

A similar observation was already made regarding v. 14, where Paul employed "through Jesus" to indicate expressly that the saving event of the death and resurrection of Jesus described in the credo was the *reason* that the dead too would participate in fellowship with Christ.

Another, farther-reaching step toward a christological understanding of human existence was seen in the way that the resurrection of the dead was described in a manner parallel to the description of the resurrection of Jesus ("the dead will rise"/"Jesus rose"). Here we already catch a glimpse of the theological model "as Christ—so the Christians."

Of course, these are only intimations. The basis of 1 Thess. 4:13ff. remains the model *"since* Christ died and rose, *therefore* the living and the dead will participate in the future fellowship with him."* This causal relationship between the saving event and future fellowship with Christ may be seen best in the phrase "through Jesus" and in the addition "in Christ": If we are in Christ through the death and resurrection of Jesus, therefore we, the dead and the living, because we are in Christ, will participate in the future fellowship with Christ. This theological model of "since—therefore," which was just explicated, does not yet actually involve the model "as (Christ)—so (the Christians)," because Paul envisions the death of Christians before the parousia as an exception at the time of 1 Thessalonians. The notion of the resurrection in 1 Thess. 4:13–18 has only an auxiliary function. To say this in a pointed manner, the notion of the resurrection is accommodated into the model "since—therefore" and carries no weight of its own.

Once more: The model "as Christ—so the Christians" is already implicitly present in 1 Thess. 4:13–18 and, as 1 Thess. 5:10 also shows, this kept the increasing delay of the parousia from being perceived as such.

Excursus: Transformation in 1 Thess. 4:16–17?

At this point it seems advisable to discuss briefly the often repeated thesis that the idea of a transformation underlies our passage and thus that Paul is not clearly saying anything different from what he says in 1 Cor. 15:51–52.

In light of what has been said about the auxiliary function of the notion of the resurrection in 1 Thess. 4:13–18, it may be said against this thesis that the idea of a transformation is foreign to our passage. The function of the resurrection of the dead is to place them on equal footing with the living in order that they might be withdrawn at the same time, that is, might participate in fellowship with Christ. It is probably assumed here that death, which is perceived as a disadvantage, is compensated for by the restitution of the same bodies the dead had before their separation.

Reference in the history of religions for an analogous realistic conception of the resurrection[139] may be made to the passage in the *Syriac Apocalypse of*

Baruch quoted above, *S. Bar.* 50:2. Here the dead are placed on equal footing with the living insofar as they recover the same bodies that they had before their deaths. Thus they can be recognized by the living. Paul, too, apparently "assumes that the ones who are raised will be individually recognizable—otherwise the *hama syn autois* in 4:17 would not be readily imaginable."[140] For this reason, the notion of a transformation should not be introduced into 1 Thess. 4:13–18,[141] especially since even in *Syriac Apocalypse of Baruch* 51 the transformation of the believers is presented only later and is not connected with the resurrection.[142]

5.2.2.3.2.5 The Pauline Meaning of Verse 15

Paul's statement in v. 15, just as in vv. 16–17, runs in two directions. (a) It takes a stance on the fate of the dead and (b) it takes a stance on the imminent expectation.

On (b): "We who are alive, we who are left" is also found in vv. 16–17 and has been taken over from there. "We who are alive" derives from the Pauline application of the tradition to the present situation. One should notice how the imminent expectation is radicalized. Paul equates the "remnant" in the tradition with the surviving majority in the redaction. Though it remains uncertain whether, at the level of tradition, the apocalyptist reckoned himself to be part of the remnant that would still be alive at the end of time, this is certainly the case for Paul. Even more, Paul has actually transcended the notion of the remnant insofar as he assumes in v. 15 that all Christians still alive will survive until the parousia.

The image of the descent of the *kyrios* from heaven and of the withdrawal of the Christians into the clouds is replaced in v. 15 by the *parousia tou kyriou*.[143] Despite the radicalization and actualization of the imminent expectation,[144] one may observe here a reduction[145] of apocalyptic by Paul, just as was the case at the end of v. 14 ("God will bring with him").

On (a): The other point of the statement in v. 15 relates to those who have died: The living will by no means precede them. The wording of this statement reminds one of the concerns expressed in the Jewish apocalypses for the fate of the dead (see above, pp. 210–11). With regard to the Thessalonian situation, this statement can be correctly understood only if the goal of Christian hope, fellowship with the *kyrios* at the end of time, is properly kept in mind. This goal is reflected at the end of v. 14 ("God will bring with him"), at the end of v. 17 ("We shall

236

always be with the Lord"), and in v. 15 through "until the coming of the Lord." Verse 15 should thus be paraphrased "The living will not precede the dead in the attainment of fellowship with Christ."[146] The dead will rather enter into participation in the same manner as the living.

Thus the two aims of the Pauline statements in v. 15 and vv. 16–17 prove to be identical in form and content. It should also be remarked on v. 15 that such an emphasized reassurance that the living will not precede the dead is understandable only when the question was "whether the dead are to be included at all."[147]

This problem could have arisen, however, only if Paul had not dealt with the fate of dead Christians, that is, the resurrection of Christians, during his initial proclamation.

We have now analyzed the Pauline meaning of v. 15 and vv. 16–17 and, insofar as it was important for our inquiry, have clarified the content of Paul's initial proclamation and of 1 Thessalonians with regard to the resurrection and to the death of Christians. We may now draw together the results of the entire section dealing with 1 Thess. 4:13–18.

5.2.3 Summary of the Results of the Exegesis of 1 Thess. 4:13–18

The death of some members of the congregation in Thessalonica had led others in the congregation into a grief that could be compared only with the hopelessness of the heathen. The death of a few fellow Christians had threatened the *elpis* of the congregation that, via the notion of the parousia, was directed toward future fellowship with Christ. The question that arose was "Will the dead miss out on future fellowship with Christ?" By referring to the "faith," the traditional credo of the death and resurrection of Christ, Paul finds assurance that even dead Christians will participate in the future fellowship (v. 14).

In the second part of the section, Paul provides further confirmation for this thesis, which was *new* to the Thessalonians. He does this by referring to a "saying of the Lord," which derives from a Jewish apocalypse and is accommodated to the situation through redactional additions. This saying elucidates Paul's own assumption, namely, that the dead Christians will rise. When the parousia arrives, the dead will be at absolutely no disadvantage in comparison with the living, for the dead will be raised at the beginning of the eschaton and will thereby be placed in the same situation as the living. After this, both groups will be withdrawn to participate in fellowship with Christ.

5.2.4 Implications for the Chronological Question

What has been said yields a confirmation of the thesis of Ernst Teichmann and others that was summarized with initial approval at the outset of the inquiry (section 5.2.1.4): Paul did not deal with the resurrection of Christians during his founding proclamation in Thessalonica.[148]

Our exegesis further revealed that Paul employs the old hope of fellowship with Christ conceived in terms of the parousia to deal with the problem of dead Christians even in 1 Thess. 4:13–18. In any event, Paul presents the death of Christians before the parousia as a rare exception to the rule.

When the external criterion described above (pp. 204–5) is applied, the implications for the chronology are evident. The founding proclamation in Thessalonica can have occurred, at the latest, at the end of the 30s. The composition of 1 Thessalonians must have taken place not much later, even though one catches a glimpse of factual considerations—as has been shown—in the statement about the resurrection of those who have died (of course, this is still viewed as an exception).

If we compare this result with the chronology we developed above solely on the basis of the letters, we see that the two agree that Paul operated a mission in Macedonia at the end of the 30s. The date determined above for the composition of 1 Thessalonians, circa the year 41, fits in well with the dating of the letter "not long after the end of the 30s," the dating we just determined. Ten to twelve years after the death and resurrection of Jesus, at the latest, Paul will have encountered deaths among the Christians in other localities too. This forced him to make some first steps toward an *explicit* theological response to the death of Christians.

The investigation of 1 Thess. 4:13–18 has thus provided confirmation of the main thesis of the chronology developed solely on the basis of the letters, the early missionary activity of Paul in Macedonia. For this reason, it seems worthwhile to investigate the second text in Paul's writings that provides an explicit chronological delimitation of the imminent expectation, 1 Cor. 15:51–52.

5.3 EXEGESIS OF 1 COR. 15:51–52

5.3.1 Procedure

The description of the task of our inquiry above indicated that it focuses primarily on chronology and intends to evaluate texts in Paul's writings on the basis of their stance on experiencing the parousia. Thus we do not need to present an extensive analysis of 1 Cor. 15:51–52, which would necessarily include an analysis of the whole of 1 Corinthians 15. We can also refrain from performing an extensive exegesis of 1 Cor. 15:51–52, because we do not have to recover from this passage the content of Paul's founding proclamation about "the last things." This can be determined from 1 Thess. 4:13–18, for 1 Thessalonians was composed in Corinth and the content of the founding proclamation in Corinth is probably reflected in the basic structure of the theology of 1 Thessalonians.

Finally, we can refrain from an extensive analysis of the context together with an intensive investigation of the situation in Corinth because 1 Cor. 15:51–52 has clearly been formulated in dependence on 1 Thess. 4:13–18[149] (see below). This thus gives us the right to interpret 1 Cor. 15:51–52 in close connection and comparison with 1 Thess. 4:13–18.

We shall ask (1) how the proportional relationship of living to dead in 1 Cor. 15:51–52 compares with the same in 1 Thess. 4:13–18 and (2) how the description of the resurrection in 1 Cor. 15:51–52 compares with the same in 1 Thess. 4:13–18. Before asking (4) how 1 Cor. 15:51–52 should be evaluated for Pauline chronology, it should be asked, at least in a general way, (3) how the theological rationale of the conception of the resurrection in 1 Cor. 15:51–52 compares with the same in 1 Thess. 4:13–18.

5.3.2 The Proportional Relationship of Living to Dead in 1 Cor. 15:51–52 in Comparison with 1 Thess. 4:13–18

5.3.2.1 1 COR. 15:51–52 AS THE CONTINUATION OF 1 THESS. 4:13–18

Our text reveals itself to be the continuation of 1 Thess. 4:13–18 through the following reminiscences of this text:

Verse 51 corresponds with 1 Thess. 4:15. There Paul speaks of a *logos kyriou*; here he speaks of a *mystērion*. There is probably no material difference between the terms, especially since the *logos kyriou* in 1 Thess. 4:15 proved to be a Jewish apocalypse, and *mystērion* is a *terminus technicus* for the content of such an apocalypse.[150]

The passages also resemble each other insofar as in part the same group of motifs appears in both: *koimasthai* (1 Thess. 4:13, 14, 15 / 1 Cor. 15:51), *nekroi* (1 Thess. 4:16 / 1 Cor. 15:52), *salpigx* (1 Thess. 4:16 / 1 Cor. 15:52).[151]

There is a further similarity in structure. After the reference to the *logos kyriou* or the *mystērion* and before the apocalyptic presentation (1 Thess. 4:16–17 / 1 Cor. 15:52), each passage has a sentential application of the following in the first-person plural. 1 Thess. 4:15b: "We who are alive . . . shall not precede those who have fallen asleep"; 1 Cor. 15:51b: "We shall not all sleep, but we shall all be changed."

The order of events at the parousia in 1 Cor. 15:52d-e also corresponds exactly with the order in 1 Thess. 4:15–16: First the dead, then the living.

This demonstration of similarities seems to render certain the view that the two passages stand in a genetic connection, and it gives us the right to interpret the passages in close relationship with one another. It should be mentioned, however, that it is impossible to reconstruct the clear outline of a substratum in 1 Cor. 15:51–52 (as in 1 Thess. 4:16–17). Only the rudiments of such a substratum appear ("in a moment, in the twinkling of an eye, at the last trumpet"). Nevertheless, *that* a substratum was used should not be disputed. The passage could even be based on the same substratum as 1 Thess. 4:16–17.[152]

5.3.2.2 SURVIVAL AS THE EXCEPTION

It could be determined for 1 Thess. 4:13–18 that the relationship of survivors to dead was such that the deaths of Christians were considered exceptions. The rule was survival until the parousia.

In 1 Cor. 15:51–52 precisely the inverse[153] appears to be the case. This is evident from Paul's formulation in v. 51b: "We shall not all sleep, but we shall all be changed."[154] The emphasis of this statement is clearly that *all*[155] will be transformed, the dead as well as the living. This statement assumes that a quantitative change has occurred in the proportions of the (still) living and the (in the meantime) dead in Paul's circles and thus also in Corinth. This change effected the shift in Paul's formulation. Now, "the present generation of Christians can retain only the certainty that not all of them will fall among the group of *nekroi*."[156] The wording of 1 Cor. 15:51b thus leads to the view that most will die before the parousia. Reference may also be made to other passages in 1 Corinthians which demonstrate that death has become something normal in the Corinthian congregation:

(a) 1 Cor. 11:30 mentions that many (*hikanoi*) have fallen asleep.

(b) The formula in 1 Cor. 6:14, "God raised the Lord and will also raise us," for which 1 Corinthians 15 provides a commentary (see Conzelmann, 111), assumes that death has become the normal case.[157]

(c) The statement that "some" of the five hundred brethren, to whom the Lord appeared, have died also assumes an advanced situation. Though the "relative clause . . . intends to allow verification of the assertion by inquiry of one of the survivors,"[158] it is all the more significant that Paul *acknowledges* that "some" of the witnesses have died (1 Cor. 15:6).

(d) Paul speaks in a self-evident manner of "those who have fallen asleep in Christ" (1 Cor. 15:18).[159]

Whether Paul himself still hoped to experience the parousia will be dealt with in the next section, which will ask how the description of the resurrection in 1 Cor. 15:51–52 compares with that of 1 Thess. 4:13–18.

5.3.3 The Description of the Resurrection in 1 Cor. 15:51–52 in Comparison with 1 Thess. 4:13–18

5.3.3.1 THE IMAGE OF TRANSFORMATION IN 1 COR. 15:51–52

As the heading for the following, 1 Cor. 15:51b states that all, dead as well as living Christians, will be transformed (at the parousia). This is further explicated in v. 52d-e: (After the parousia) "the dead will be raised imperishable, and we shall be changed."

There is a consensus in research that according to 1 Corinthians 15 all Christians will be given a resurrectional body after the parousia and that the transformation results in a *sōma pneumatikon*, which is contrasted with the earthly body, the *sōma psychikon*.[160]

The interpretation of the double "we" in 1 Cor. 15:51–52 is controversial. Is the "we" at the end of v. 52 identical with the "we" in v. 51b (*allagēsometha*)? An affirmative answer to this question would mean that the dead will be raised imperishable and the dead *and* the living Christians will be transformed together.[161] This proposal, however, is improbable for the following reasons. "We shall all be changed" stands as a heading for the following. Nothing speaks against the view that this statement about the transformation of the dead and the living at the parousia is specified, on the one hand, for the dead through the statement "they shall be raised imperishable" and, on the other hand, for the living through the repeated words of the heading "we shall be changed." The context reveals that being "imperishable" is identical with being transformed.[162] Compare v. 42, "What is sown is perishable, what is raised is imperishable," and v. 53, "This perishable nature must put on the imperishable."

If it thus seems probable that "we shall be changed" should be related to the group of the living at the parousia,[163] then it follows from this that at the time of the composition of 1 Corinthians, Paul thought he would experience the parousia.

5.3.3.2 COMPARISON OF THE DESCRIPTIONS OF THE RESURRECTION IN 1 COR. 15:51–52 AND 1 THESS. 4:13–18

We saw above that the description of the resurrection in 1 Thess. 4:13–18 can be called realistic and that the concept of a transformation should not be associated with this passage. The resurrection was mentioned in the context of the assertion that the living do not have any advantage over the dead, and its function was to place the dead on equal footing with the living so that they might be withdrawn together. An analogous depiction of the resurrection was found in the *Syriac Apocalypse of Baruch*, where the living recognize the raised dead. In 1 Corinthians, by contrast, the resurrection is depicted within a *dualistic* framework, where the present *sōma psychikon* is distinguished from the *sōma pneumatikon*, the product of the transformation.

Both conceptions of the resurrection, the realistic conception and the supernatural conception that involves the notion of a transformation, were known to Paul from Judaism. They are even found alongside one another in the *Syriac Apocalypse of Baruch* (50–51). Surely Paul did *not* use the notion of the resurrection that involved the transformation to explicate the Christ-event at the time of the composition of 1 Thessalonians because the resurrection of Christians could not yet have been a separate, developed theme in his theology.

This brings us to the question of the occasion and rationale of Paul's view of the resurrection in 1 Cor. 15:51–52.

5.3.4 On the Occasion and Rationale of Paul's View of the Resurrection in 1 Cor. 15:51–52

Teaching about the resurrection (of Christians) was a subordinate part of the founding proclamation in Corinth. Paul also passed on to the Corinthians the kerygma of the death and resurrection of Jesus. It is clear from 1 Cor. 15:12 that even those who denied the resurrection acknowledged this kerygma. It seems that the Corinthians also asked Paul a question about what body the dead would assume when they were raised (15:35). The answer to this involves a dualistic separation of the psychic body from the pneumatic body (vv. 36ff.). The rationale for this answer is christological:

Verse 45: "'The first man Adam became a living being'; the last Adam became a life-giving spirit." Verse 47: "The first man was from the earth, a man of dust; the second man is from heaven." Verse 48: Those who belong to them are as they are. Verse 49: The Christians, who have borne the image of the earthly man, will bear the image of the heavenly man, Christ. In the light of v. 48, one may add that they will become "heavenly beings" just like the "heavenly man."

Paul's argument in 1 Cor. 15:45ff. allows us to answer the question of the theological rationale of the statement on the resurrection in 1 Cor. 15:51–52. For the sake of clarity, we may broaden our perspective and trace the development of the rationale supplied for the resurrection (of Christians) from 1 Thess. 4:13ff. to 1 Corinthians.

In 1 Thessalonians, Paul argues for the certainty of future fellowship with Christ, which has been threatened by the first deaths, by referring to the kerygma and by introducing the notion of resurrection. *Because* Jesus died and rose, the dead are also assured of participation in future fellowship with Christ. They will rise precisely in order to be withdrawn with the survivors. When death had become the normal case at the time of the composition of 1 Corinthians, the notion of the resurrection that was introduced as an auxiliary thought in 1 Thessalonians gained increasing importance, for resurrection of Christians had become the norm. In Corinth this situation provoked the question about the manner of the resurrection and the nature of the resurrectional body. This question, in the end, forced Paul to make this issue a *subject* of discussion.[164]

In his response to this question, Paul consistently develops further the christological rationale for the resurrection of Christians that was intimated in 1 Thess. 4:13ff. The fundamental principle is now "as Christ—so the Christians." Christians will become *just as* the heavenly one is now (15:48). Each will obtain—either as one who has died or as a survivor—a pneumatic *sōma*, that is, each will be transformed. In other words, Paul answers the question concerning the resurrectional body also by referring to the kerygma.

The further problem of whether Paul maintained this conception of the resurrectional body in 2 Corinthians or Philippians may only be mentioned here. An exegesis of the relevant passages (2 Cor. 5:1ff.; Phil. 1:23) would, however, presumably reveal that Paul's concern was not with the images—that is, not with the image of the resurrection of Christians or with the image of the resurrectional body—but rather with the *syn Christō*, which already played a role in 1 Thess. 4:17.

This realization, which leads to the very heart of Pauline theology, should not, however, cause us to neglect the task of checking and investigating when and where Paul employs particular images. Such work is not only able to provide insights into Paul's correspondents, but is also able, as our study has attempted to demonstrate, to unlock doors in the study of the chronology of Paul's life and letters. This, in turn, may contribute to an enriched interpretation of the letters.

5.3.5 Implications for the Chronology

At the time of 1 Corinthians, the proportion of dead Christians outweighed the proportion of living Christians, even though Paul still numbered himself among those who would survive until the parousia. This state of affairs is best conceivable at the end of the first generation, that is, around the year 50. Since this date is approximated by the date determined for the composition of 1 Corinthians in the chronology developed above solely on the basis of the letters, the investigation of 1 Cor. 15:51–52 thus also provides support for our chronology. This support is even more substantial because the difference[165] in the descriptions of the resurrection (of Christians) and the shift in the proportion of living and dead in 1 Cor. 15:51–52 and 1 Thess. 4:13–18 also find a satisfactory explanation in the above chronology insofar as it places a span of eight to eleven years between the two letters.

NOTES

1. It was probably the work of R. Kabisch, *Die Eschatologie des Paulus in ihren Zusammenhängen mit dem Gesamtbegriff des Paulinismus*, that pro-

244

vided the decisive impetus for the recognition of the apocalyptic background of Pauline theology. Kabisch's interpretation was approved by A. Schweitzer, *Paul and his Interpreters*, 58–59, but met with extremely strong disapproval by William Wrede (*ThLZ* 19 [1894]: cols. 131–37). In particular, Wrede thought that Kabisch placed too much emphasis on the real and substantial aspect of Paul's ideas. In light of what Wrede himself says about the doctrine of redemption in his *Paul*, this criticism is unexpected. A short time later, Wrede softened his criticism: "In retrospect I wish that I had recognized more clearly that the strong emphasis upon eschatology in Paul's thought and upon his connection with Judaism was a corrective to the usual view and performed a useful service" (W. Wrede, "The Task and Methods of 'New Testament Theology,'" in *The Nature of New Testament Theology*, 191 n. 71). Since the first edition of Wrede's book on Paul appeared in 1904, his sharp rejection of Kabisch in 1894 and his adoption of the main lines of Kabisch's work in his book on Paul in 1904 do not directly contradict each other. During the intervening years Wrede evidently corrected his views on Pauline eschatology. Unfortunately we do not have a biography of Wrede. See, nevertheless, Georg Strecker, "William Wrede," *ZThK* 57 (1960): 67–91; Wolfgang Wiefel, "Zur Würdigung William Wredes," *ZRGG* 23 (1971): 60–83. See Hans Rollmann's forthcoming two-volume biography of Wrede to be published by Vandenhoeck & Ruprecht.

On Kabisch's book, see also L. Kessler, "Die Eschatologie des Paulus und die religiös-bildliche Erkenntnis," *ZSTh* 7 (1929/30): 573–97. On A. Schweitzer's opinion of Kabisch's work, see W. G. Kümmel, "Albert Schweitzer als Paulusforscher," in *Rechtfertigung*, 274, 280.

On Schweitzer's interpretation of Paul, see the important book by H. Groos, *Albert Schweitzer*, 313–72, the critical continuation by E. P. Sanders, *Paul and Palestinian Judaism*, 431–523, and Erich Grässer, *Albert Schweitzer als Theologe*, BHTh 60 (Tübingen: J. C. B. Mohr [Paul Siebeck], 1979), 155–205.

2. E. Linnemann, *Parables of Jesus*, 132 n. 26, presented the thesis that there "is not one saying of Jesus that speaks expressly of the nearness of the kingdom of God, the authenticity of which is not at least disputed." She defended this thesis again in her "Zeitansage und Zeitvorstellungen in der Verkündigung Jesu," in *Jesus Christus in Historie und Theologie*. Against this thesis, and correctly, see E. Grässer, *Die Naherwartung Jesu*, 78ff. On the various evaluations of the apocalyptic elements in the proclamation of Jesus, see further the relevant contributions in the Conzelmann Festschrift and, recently, the instructive introductory chapter in E. Grässer, *Das Problem der Parusieverzögerung in den synoptischen Evangelien und in der Apostelgeschichte*, ix–xxxii (on Linnemann, "Zeitansage," see the criticism by Grässer, *Problem*, xiv–xv).

3. The phenomenon of delay in the arrival of a proclaimed future event is

not peculiar to primitive Christianity. On Qumran, see Kurt Schubert in J. Maier and K. Schubert, *Die Qumran-Essener*, 88ff. Interesting parallels between primitive Christianity and other chiliastic movements are presented by J. G. Gager, *Kingdom and Community*, 20ff., where attention is given to the important book by Leon Festinger, Henry W. Riecken, and Stanley Schachter, *When Prophecy Fails* (Minneapolis: University of Minnesota Press, 1956). Just as in certain groups in primitive Christianity and at Qumran, delay in the arrival of the predicted future event did not create a major crisis in the group studied by Festinger et al. On the contrary, "When the central belief of the group [the destruction of the world on December 21] had been unequivocally disconfirmed, the members responded not by disbanding but by intensifying their previous low level of proselytizing" (Gager, *Kingdom*, 39).

4. See the survey in Grässer, *Naherwartung*, 28ff., 91ff.

5. P. Stuhlmacher, *Gerechtigkeit Gottes bei Paulus*, 203. For criticism of this thesis, see G. Klein, "Apokalyptische Naherwartung bei Paulus," in *Neues Testament und christliche Existenz*.

6. This is the thesis of E. Käsemann and U. Wilckens. For criticism, see J. Baumgarten, *Paulus und die Apokalyptik*, 227.

7. A somewhat different view is taken by P. Siber, *Mit Christus leben*, 21: "Whether the ardent imminent expectation in the earliest period totally excluded thoughts about deaths before the parousia is questionable." Siber does admit, however, that deaths remained the rare exception in the primitive Christian imminent expectation. Grässer seems to have more adequately depicted the situation. The earliest church "soon experienced deaths and was then faced with the task of accommodating these deaths into their expectation of the parousia" (*Problem*, 136). This statement implies that the most ancient church did not reckon with deaths. Grässer's statement "One should rather assume that the question of death before the parousia played a certain role in the primitive church; Paul may be cited as the oldest witness to this question" (ibid., 135) applies to a second stage in the early Christian expectation of the parousia that is inconceivable unless the original view was that no one would die.

8. A. Schweitzer, *The Kingdom of God and Primitive Christianity*, 115; idem, *The Quest of the Historical Jesus*, 360.

9. Grässer, *Problem*, 138. Similarly, F. Hahn, *Mission in the New Testament*, 41ff.

10. This is the view of Philipp Vielhauer, "Gottesreich und Menschensohn in der Verkündigung Jesu," in *Festschrift für Günther Dehn*, ed. W. Schneemelcher (Neukirchen-Vluyn: Neukirchener Verlag, 1957), 51–79 (= Philipp Vielhauer, *Aufsätze zum Neuen Testament*, ThB 31 [Munich: Chr. Kaiser Verlag, 1965], 64–65); cf. G. Strecker, *Der Weg der Gerechtigkeit*, 42 n. 2, 246.

11. Contra M. Künzi, *Das Naherwartungslogion Matthäus 10,23*, 182.

12. We do not need to consider here the apologetic attempts of Schniewind and others to translate "this generation" as "the Jewish people." On this translation, see the correct judgment of W. G. Kümmel, *Promise and Fulfillment*, 59–60.

13. Contra ibid., 25–28, Mark 9:1 does not derive from the historical Jesus. Our view is shared by J. Wellhausen, *Das Evangelium Marci*, 74; R. Bultmann, *The History of the Synoptic Tradition*, 121; G. Bornkamm, "Die Verzögerung der Parusie," in *In Memoriam Ernst Lohmeyer* (= *Geschichte und Glaube I, Gesammelte Aufsätze*,3:46–49); Grässer, *Problem*, 131ff.; idem, *Naherwartung*, 102ff. (on Kümmel's view of Jesus that allows him to derive Mark 9:1 from the historical Jesus). The question of the relationship of Mark 9:1 to Mark 13:30 in the history of traditions does not need to be dealt with here. On this, see the literature mentioned in Rudolf Bultmann, *Die Geschichte der synoptischen Tradition, Ergänzungsheft*, ed. G. Theissen and P. Vielhauer, 4th ed. (Göttingen: Vandenhoeck & Ruprecht, 1971), 47, 50. For the history of exegesis of Mark 9:1, see M. Künzi, *Das Naherwartungslogion Markus 9, 1 par* (on Mark 13:30 par., see pp. 213–24). Norman Perrin (*What Is Redaction Criticism?* [Philadelphia: Fortress Press, 1969], 48ff.), however, thinks that Mark 9:1 is redactional.

14. In spite of Günter Reim, "Johannes 21—Ein Anhang?" in *Studies in New Testament Language and Text: Essays in Honour of George D. Kilpatrick*, ed. J. K. Elliot, *NT.S* 44 (Leiden: E. J. Brill, 1976), 330–37.

15. See Grässer, *Problem*, 135. It could well be that, as R. Bultmann (*The Gospel of John* [Oxford: Basil Blackwell, 1971], 716) thinks, John 21:23 reflects the fact that "a disciple of the Lord attained a surprisingly old age, so that the idea arose that he would remain alive till the parousia." This notion is understandable, however, only if the conviction of primitive Christianity was that the first generation would experience the parousia.

16. "Before the arrival of the eschaton" should be understood in an apocalyptic sense (meaning the parousia) and is a necessary qualification of the sentence in the text above, for the idea of not having to die could also arise from present eschatology (see Menander in Justin, *Apol.* 26, and Irenacus, *Haer.* 1.23.5).

17. See the references in Klein, "Apokalyptische Naherwartung." A. Suhl, *Paulus und seine Briefe*, 192, incorrectly places Phil. 3:11, 20–21 alongside 1 Thess. 4:13–18 and 1 Cor. 15:51–52. In the passage in Philippians, Paul does *not* say he expects to experience the parousia.

18. This noteworthy observation is of great importance for the question of the value that Paul placed on temporal concepts. It reveals that Paul was evidently not concerned with such concepts. Such concepts are, nevertheless, important for our chronological inquiry.

19. The Thessalonians were concerned here about particular cases of death

(notice the article in *tōn koimōmenōn*) and not about dead people in general.

20. Wilhelm Lütgert, *Die Vollkommenen im Philipperbrief und die Enthusiasten in Thessalonich*, BFChTh 13.6 (Gütersloh: C. Bertelsmann, 1909); W. Schmithals, "The Historical Situation of the Thessalonian Epistles," in *Paul and the Gnostics*, 123–218.

21. W. Harnisch, *Eschatologische Existenz*.

22. Schmithals, "Situation," 164.

23. Ibid., 164 n. 146.

24. U. Luz, *Das Geschichtsverständnis des Paulus*, 320–21.

25. Harnisch, *Existenz*, 24.

26. Ibid., 25f. n. 36.

27. Since Harnisch bases most of the details of his exposition on Schmithals's theses regarding both 1 Thess. and the other letters of Paul, the following will also contain arguments against Schmithals's theses.

28. Harnisch, *Existenz*, 35 n. 33, argues against this in controversy with W. Marxsen's "Auslegung von 1 Thess 4, 13–18": "The accusation of importing foreign ideas may be raised against Marxsen himself when he maintains the 'imagery used' in v. 14b (*axei syn autō*) belongs 'to the complex withdrawal/parousia.'. . . Withdrawal is something that happens to the living and not to the dead." Harnisch does not notice that in 1 Thess. 4:13–18, to say it pointedly, the dead arise only in order to be withdrawn (v. 17). Thus the withdrawal actually affects only the living. Further, Harnisch's generalizing statement that there is only a withdrawal of the living stands in need of correction. See G. Strecker, "Entrückung," *RAC* 5: cols. 461–76.

29. See, correctly, Marxsen, "Auslegung," 31; Luz, *Geschichtsverständnis*, 321.

30. Clement of Alexandria, *Strom.* 2.10.2; 2.115.1–2; 4.89.4; 5.3.3; *Exc. Theod.* 56.3; Irenaeus, *Haer.* 1.6.2.

31. See R. Bultmann, *Theology of the New Testament*, 1:178.

32. Harnisch, *Existenz*, 80–81.

33. See L. Schottroff, "Animae naturaliter salvandae," in *Christentum und Gnosis*, 65–97. The texts mentioned by Schottroff should be supplemented with Hippolytus, *Ref.* 6.14.6 (*Megalē Apophasis*); Irenaeus, *Haer.* 1.23.2 (Simonian Helen). See G. Luedemann, *Untersuchungen zur simonianischen Gnosis*, 77.

34. On *physei sōzesthai* in gnosticism, see also E. H. Pagels, *The Johannine Gospel in Gnostic Exegesis*, 83, 90–91, 98ff.

35. While Harnisch writes (against O. Merk, *Handeln aus Glauben*, 54 n. 76), "Whoever in view of 1 Thess. 4:13ff. denies Schmithals's assumption of a gnostic front in Thessalonica . . . must *prove* this point contra Schmithals on the basis of the whole letter" (*Existenz*, 23 n. 23), he does not even raise the question of whether someone who accepts Schmithals's thesis of gnosis in

Thessalonica must necessarily demonstrate the possibility that 1 Thess. could have been written after 1 Cor. Schmithals at least attempted to do this.

36. Schmithals's hypothesis for the division of 1 Thess. may be left out of consideration here, for according to his opinion both 1 Thess. 2:13—4:2 (written in Athens after the intervening visit to Corinth) and 1 Thess. 1:1—2:12; 4:3—5:28 (written from Athens before the intervening visit) were composed after 1 Cor. See W. Schmithals, "Die Thessalonicherbriefe als Briefkompositionen," in *Zeit und Geschichte*. For criticism of Schmithals's division of the letter, see C. Demke, "Theologie und Literarkritik im 1. Thessalonicherbrief," in *Wort und Existenz*.

37. Schmithals, "Situation," 183.

38. Ibid.

39. See R. W. Funk, *Language, Hermeneutic, and Word of God*, 263ff.; idem, "The Apostolic *Parousia*: Form and Significance," in *Christian History and Interpretation*, 249–68.

40. Schmithals, "Situation," 184.

41. Ibid., 185.

42. See also the reasons that F. C. Baur (*Paul*, 2:88–89,) supplies for the view that a considerable period of time had elapsed between the visit and the composition of the letter. See, further, H. L. Ramsey, "The Place of Galatians in the Career of Paul," 187–88.

43. H.-A. Wilcke, *Das Problem eines messianischen Zwischenreichs bei Paulus*, 122.

44. This is the view of A. Schweitzer, *The Mysticism of Paul the Apostle*, 90ff., and the authors mentioned by Wilcke, *Problem*, 120–21.

45. Detailed proof of this statement is supplied by Wilcke, *Problem*.

46. Most recently upheld by G. Friedrich, "Der erste Brief an die Thessalonicher," ad loc.

47. See, further, the following texts that view the participation of the dead in final salvation as a problem: *Ps. Sol.* 18:7; 4 Ezra 7:26ff.; 11–13; *Syriac Apocalypse of Baruch* 29, 40, 73; *Apocalypse of Abraham*; *Ethiopic Enoch* 103.

48. Pseudo-Ezra is concerned about his predecessors and his descendants and thus does not expect his generation to experience the end. The Thessalonians are not concerned with their predecessors but only with Christians who have died. They are also not concerned about their descendants, for they themselves (in contrast to Pseudo-Ezra) expect to experience the end.

49. The same or similar arguments are brought against this type of exegesis also by Luz, *Geschichtsverständnis*, 318–19; Harnisch, *Existenz*, 20–21; E. Grässer, "Bibelarbeit über 1Thess. 4,13–18," in *Bibelarbeiten, gehalten auf der rheinischen Landessynode 1967 in Bad Godesberg*, 15–16; and B. Spörlein, *Die Leugnung der Auferstehung*, 124.

50. Bultmann, *Theology*, 1:77

51. Spörlein, *Leugnung*, 125.

52. V. Furnish, "Development in Paul's Thought," 294, says that a misunderstanding on the part of the Thessalonians is "possible" but prefers the following interpretation: "The point [whether everyone would experience the parousia] had not been covered by the apostle at all and thus was simply assumed by everyone concerned" (ibid.). When Furnish finds support for his thesis in "Paul's reference to their 'ignorance' (4:13)" (ibid.), he overlooks the fact that "ignorance" is part of an introductory formula that Paul employs when he presents *new* information. In our case, the new information is that the dead will participate in fellowship with the *kyrios*. The supposedly false view of the Thessalonians about their survival is actually bolstered by Paul in the following (see below, pp. 233–34).

53. Luz, *Geschichtsverständnis*, 321–22; similarly, Siber, *Christus*, 22.

54. This view is, nevertheless, widely held. See also Klaus Wegenast, *Das Verständnis der Tradition bei Paulus und in den Deuteropaulinen*, WMANT 8 (Neukirchen-Vluyn: Neukirchener Verlag, 1962), 108–9.

55. Luz, *Geschichtsverständnis*, 320.

56. Ibid., 322.

57. What do the words "the certainty that arises from the kerygma regarding the future resurrection of believers" (Luz, *Geschichtsverständnis*, 321–22) actually mean? In any event, some Corinthian Christians understood the kerygma to contain an exclusively present eschatology, a view that could perhaps find support in the early Paul (see J. Héring, "Saint Paul a-t-il enseigné deux résurrections?"; and J. C. Hurd, *The Origin of 1 Corinthians*, 284–87). These questions will be treated extensively in the third part of this trilogy.

58. E. Teichmann, *Die paulinischen Vorstellungen von Auferstehung und Gericht und ihre Beziehungen zur jüdischen Apokalyptik*; F. Guntermann, *Die Eschatologie des hl. Paulus*, 35ff.; M. Dibelius, *An die Thessalonicher I.II, An die Philipper*, 23–28; Hurd, *Origin*, 284; Marxsen, "Auslegung"; Klein, "Apokalyptische Naherwartung"; J. Becker, *Auferstehung der Toten im Urchristentum*.

59. "The image of the resurrection of the dead has slipped in between" (Marxsen, "Auslegung," 29). However, compare this statement with p. 259 n. 148, below.

60. It is strange that no representative of this type of exegesis (with the exception of Hurd, *Origin*) has ventured to date 1 Thess. much earlier than the date ascribed by the conventional chronology. Luz and Siber (similarly, Grässer, "Bibelarbeit," 16) use the twenty years that the conventional chronology sets between the death of Jesus and Paul's stay in Greece as an argument against the thesis that Paul did not speak about the resurrection of Christians while he was in Thessalonica. This argument implicitly rests on the underlying assumption of our work, namely, that if Paul did not deal with the resurrection of Christians during his founding proclamation, he must have been in Macedonia at a very early date.

61. I assume the literary integrity of 1 Thess. For recent studies of 1 Thess. 4:13–18, see Niels Hyldahl, "Auferstehung Christi—Auferstehung der Toten (1 Thess. 4,13–18)," in *The Pauline Literature and Theology*, ed. Sigfred Pedersen, Theologiske Studier 7 (Arhus: Forlaget Aros; Göttingen: Vandenhoeck & Ruprecht, 1980), 119–35; Hans-Heinrich Schade, *Apokalyptische Christologie bei Paulus*, GTA 18 (Göttingen: Vandenhoeck & Ruprecht, 1981), 157–62, 282–87 (polemicizing against my position though curiously adopting it—without telling the reader); Walter Radl, *Ankunft des Herrn* (Frankfurt: P. D. Lang, 1981), 113–56.

62. D. G. Bradley, "The *Topos* as a Form in the Pauline Paraenesis," would like to deny that the *peris* in 1 Thess. refer to current issues, for 4:9–12, 13–18, and 5:1–11 (perhaps also 4:3–8) supposedly correspond to the Hellenistic epistolary genre *topos*. Against this view, see H. Boers, "The Form Critical Study of Paul's Letters: I Thessalonians as a Case Study," 157.

63. In agreement with Klein, "Apokalyptische Naherwartung," 245 n. 22.

64. Harnisch, *Existenz*, 22.

65. Ibid., 22 n. 16.

66. Contra Luz, *Geschichtsverständnis*, 286 and n. 84.

67. Contra Siber, *Christus*, 15 n. 8, who thinks that the content of Rom. 11:25 could have already been known to the readers. Does not the designation for the content of Rom. 11:25, *mystērion* (cf. 1 Cor. 15:51), speak against such a thesis? On Rom. 11:25, see now my booklet *Paulus und das Judentum*, TEH 215 (Munich: Chr. Kaiser Verlag, 1983), 33–35.

68. H. Conzelmann, *1 Corinthians*, 165.

69. See also the other passages in 1 Thess. where *elpis* occurs: 1:3; 2:19; 5:8. All these are related to the expectation of the parousia.

70. The difference between 1 Thess. 4:14, on the one hand, and 1 Cor. 6:14; Rom. 6:8; 2 Cor. 4:14, on the other hand, is demonstrated superbly by Siber, *Christus*, 26 (but contra Siber, ibid., 1 Thess. 5:10 does not make a statement regarding the resurrection of Christ).

71. Reference may be made simply to Hans Conzelmann, "Was glaubte die frühe Christenheit?" (1955) in idem, *Theologie als Schriftauslegung*, BEvTh 65 (Munich: Chr. Kaiser Verlag, 1974), 106–19; W. Kramer, *Christ, Lord, Son of God*; K. Wengst, *Christologische Formeln und Lieder des Urchristentums*. For criticism (and a survey), see Martin Rese, "Formeln und Lieder im Neuen Testament: Einige notwendige Anmerkungen," VF 15.2 (1970): 75–95. See also Hans von Campenhausen, "Das Bekenntnis im Urchristentum," ZNW 63 (1972): 210–53; U. Luz, "Zum Aufbau von Röm. 1–8" (disputes Conzelmann's important thesis that Romans could be understood as a commentary to the formulas of faith).

72. This is the opinion of most investigators, e.g., Wengst, *Formeln*, 45–46; Luz, *Geschichtsverständnis*, 325f. n. 30.

73. See the presentation in Siber, *Christus*, 24–25. The order *apethanen—anestē* is nevertheless found in the pre-Markan summary of the

passion in Mark 8:31 (cf. 9:31; 10:32ff.). On this passage, see G. Strecker, "Die Leidens- und Auferstehungsvoraussagen im Markusevangelium." Further investigation is necessary before one could say whether this pre-Markan summary of the passion can be related in the history of traditions to 1 Thess. 4:14. Both passages are connected with the Son of Man (on 1 Thess. 4:14, see below, pp. 219ff.). On Mark 8:31, see also Paul Hoffmann, "Mk 8,31: Zur Herkunft und markinischen Rezeption einer alten Überlieferung," in *Orientierung an Jesus: Zur Theologie der Synoptiker. Für Josef Schmid*, ed. P. Hoffmann, N. Brox, and W. Pesch (Freiburg: Herder, 1973), 170–204, and the literature cited there. Hoffmann arrives at the conclusion that at the level of tradition in Mark 8:31 "the *statement about the resurrection* still stands in a close relationship with the exaltation of Jesus to be the Son of Man and with the expectation of his return as the Son of Man/judge" (p. 200). He considers 1 Thess. 1:10 and Rom. 1:3–4 to be the closest parallels to this tradition.

74. See Helmut Koester, "The Structure and Criteria of Early Christian Beliefs," in James M. Robinson and Helmut Koester, *Trajectories through Early Christianity* (Philadelphia: Fortress Press, 1971), 227 n. 49.

75. See Siber, *Christus*, 24.

76. See, similarly, Luz, *Geschichtsverständnis*, 308 n. 38; Harnisch, *Existenz*, 32–33.

77. Kramer, *Christ*, 32–33 (sec. 6a-b); P. Vielhauer, *Geschichte der urchristlichen Literatur*, 9ff.

78. P. Hoffmann, *Die Toten in Christus*, 206.

79. Baumgarten, *Paulus*, 115.

80. Ibid.

81. See also Conzelmann, *1 Corinthians*, 266 n. 30, and the literature cited there.

82. For this possibility, see Bauer, *Lexicon*, 180.

83. This is said in reference to J. Jeremias, *Unknown Sayings of Jesus*, 82; P. Nepper-Christensen, "Das verborgene Herrnwort," 138 n. 10.

84. Cf. J. Dupont, *SYN CHRISTŌI: L'union avec le Christ suivant Saint Paul*, 1:42 n. 2.

85. The statement by B. Rigaux "The equivalence of *dia* and *en* is not grammatical but rather conceptual" (*Saint Paul: Les épîtres aux Thessaloniciens*, 536, following Frame) shows that he is really at a loss for an explanation.

86. E. Schweizer, however, thinks, "Paul speaks of falling asleep 'through Christ' but of the eschatological coming 'with him'" ("Die 'Mystik' des Sterbens und Auferstehens mit Christus bei Paulus" [= *Beiträge zur Theologie des Neuen Testaments*, 184]). A similar view is presented by A. Feuillet, "Mort du Christ et mort du chrétien d'après les épîtres pauliniennes," 511, and by J. Plevnik, "The Parousia as Implication of Christ's Resurrection," in *Word and Spirit*, 210ff.

87. Luz, *Geschichtsverständnis*, 326 n. 32.

88. Siber, *Christus*, 30 n. 54.

89. A. Strobel, "In dieser Nacht (Luk 17,34)," 23: "Just as Moses once brought the people of God to God's revelation at Sinai, so Christ, at his parousia, will bring the assembly of the pious to God." Strobel repeats this thesis in the continuation of this article in "Der Berg der Offenbarung (Mt 28,16; Apg 1,12)," in *Verborum Veritas*, 142 n. 37 (for criticism of Strobel's thesis of the expectation of the parousia during the night of the Passover, see W. Huber, *Passa und Ostern*, 215ff.). It may be said against this view that in 1 Thess. 4:13ff. God brings the dead to Jesus. An understanding of 1 Thess. 4:13ff. similar to Strobel's view is also presented by Dupont, *Union*, 64ff.; Plevnik, "Parousia," 212ff.

90. Siber, *Christus*, 29–30.

91. See p. 252 n. 82.

92. See also Wilcke, *Problem*, 128.

93. For a causal understanding of *ei*, see Bauer, *Lexicon*, 219.

94. This should be done in a manner precisely opposite to the way that Robert C. Tannehill evaluates it: "This construction can only be explained by the fact that Paul began the sentence with the thought that what is true of Jesus, that he died and arose, also holds for the believers on the basis of Jesus' death and resurrection" (*Dying and Rising with Christ*, BZNW 32 [Berlin: A. Töpelmann, 1967], 132). A similar view—with reference to Tannehill—is taken by J. W. Drane, "Theological Diversity in the Letters of St. Paul," 21.

95. There is no need for us to demonstrate again that Paul is quoting tradition in 1 Thess. 1:9–10 (see G. Friedrich, "Ein Tauflied hellenistischer Judenchristen: 1. Thess. 1,9f.").

96. *Meta tōn hagiōn* refers, of course, to Jesus coming not with the dead Christians (thus Teichmann, *Vorstellungen*, 21–22; Rigaux, *Thessaloniciens*, ad loc.) but rather with the angels (see Martin Dibelius, *Die Geisterwelt im Glauben des Paulus* [Göttingen: Vandenhoeck & Ruprecht, 1909], 30–31). For the designation of angels as *hagioi*, see Zech. 14:5 (LXX); Job 15:15; Ps. 88 (89): 6, 8; *Eth. En.* 1:9 (quoted in Jude 14). See also Heinz-Wolfgang Kuhn, *Enderwartung und gegenwärtiges Heil*, StUNT 4 (Göttingen: Vandenhoeck & Ruprecht, 1966), 90ff. ("Exkurs IV: Der Ausdruck 'die Heiligen' in den Qumrantexten und im sonstigen Spätjudentum"). In the event that our text is related to Matt. 24:31 in the history of traditions, this would be a further witness for the traditions on the Son of Man in 1 Thess.

97. The same view is taken by Hoffmann, *Toten*, 217–18.

98. This is indicated by the *dia tou Iēsou* that interprets the preceding clause about the death and resurrection of Jesus as the salvational *reason* that the dead Christians will participate in fellowship with Jesus.

99. Whether Paul already possessed the model "as Christ—so the Christians" in baptismal traditions that paralleled the fate of Christians with that of

Christ depends on the decision whether baptism had already been interpreted before Paul (in the Hellenistic congregations) as the establishment of a common fate between Christ and the baptized and on the decision about the importance of baptism in Paul's theology. For reasons of method, the question that is touched on here will be excluded from the present inquiry. We should also keep the possibility open that Paul's understanding of baptism underwent a development (see Becker, *Auferstehung*, 49 n. 5).

100. Consider also the verb *anestē* that appears in the credo formula and that, according to the analysis above, was chosen by Paul in accommodation to the context, which deals with the resurrection of dead Christians (v. 16).

101. It should also be remarked that where the model "as Christ—so the Christians" appears in its pure form, in Romans 6, it is developed primarily on the basis of the kerygma. The notion of being buried with Christ by baptism in Rom. 6:4 could probably have arisen only as an interpretation of baptism in the light of the kerygmatic tradition "died—buried—raised" (1 Cor. 15:3–4). See Niklaus Gäumann, *Taufe und Ethik*, BEvTh 47 (Munich: Chr. Kaiser Verlag, 1967), 61ff.

102. See Rudolf Bultmann, "Glossen im Römerbrief," *ThLZ* 72 (1947): cols. 197–202 (= *Exegetica*, ed. E. Dinkler [Tübingen: J. C. B. Mohr (Paul Siebeck), 1967], 278–84). A different opinion is defended by Josef Kürzinger, "Der Schlüssel zum Verständnis von Röm 7," *BZ*, n.s. 7 (1963): 270–74.

103. See Kramer, *Christ*, 99–107 (sec. 23a-g).

104. See ibid., 173 (sec. 48a): "With only three exceptions it is the title *Lord* which is linked in the Pauline corpus with the parousia."

105. *Ap' ouranou* is probably a Pauline formulation for *apo tōn ouranōn*. Cf. *ap' ouranou* in Rom. 1:18; *ex ouranou* in 1 Cor. 15:47; 2 Cor. 5:2; Gal. 1:8. Paul evidently prefers the singular without the article. Cf. also 2 Cor. 12:2: *heōs tritou ouranou*; 1 Cor. 8:5: *en ouranō*. In contrast to these passages, the following passages have the plural: 2 Cor. 5:1; 1 Thess. 1:10; Phil. 3:20. All three passages are perhaps traditional. On 1 Thess. 1:10, see above, p. 253 n. 95. On Phil. 3:20, see Georg Strecker, "Redaktion und Tradition im Christushymnus Phil 2,6–11," *ZNW* 55 (1964): 75ff. On 2 Cor. 5:1, see Peter von der Osten-Sacken, *Römer 8 als Beispiel paulinischer Soteriologie*, FRLANT 112 (Göttingen: Vandenhoeck & Ruprecht, 1975), pp. 104ff.

Of course, proof that *ap' ouranou* is a redactional insertion for *apo tōn ouranōn* would not be of direct import for the interpretation and can be omitted in the following.

106. On "in Christ" in Paul, see Udo Schnelle, *Gerechtigkeit und Christusgegenwart*, GTA 24 (Göttingen: Vandenhoeck & Ruprecht, 1983), 106–22, 225–35, and the literature cited there.

107. This is the thesis of Luz, *Geschichtsverständnis*, 328 n. 48. Harnisch, *Existenz*, 43 n. 20, agrees.

108. P. Vielhauer, "Apocalypses and Related Subjects: Introduction. Apocalyptic in Early Christianity," in E. Hennecke, *New Testament Apocrypha*, 2:582.

109. See J. Schneider, "Bainō," *TDNT* 1:518–23.

110. See G. Friedrich, "Salpigx," *TDNT* 7:72–88; Bill. 1:459–60.

111. See A. Oepke, "Nephelē," *TDNT* 4:902–10.

112. K. Deissner, *Auferstehungshoffnung und Pneumagedanke bei Paulus*, 15–16. The same view is taken by Teichmann, *Vorstellungen*, 35–36, and Nepper-Christensen, "Herrnwort," 148–49.

113. Dibelius, *An die Thessalonicher*, 2d ed., p. 23 (3d ed., p. 27). On the close connection of the messianic era and the resurrection of the dead, see Bill. 3:827–28; 4:799ff.

114. Paul Volz, *Die Eschatologie der jüdischen Gemeinde im neutestamentlichen Zeitalter* (1934; reprint, Hildesheim: G. Olms, 1966), 136. See, however, the qualification of this statement above, p. 249 n. 48, and Bill. 4:988–89; L. Hartman, "The Function of Some So-Called Apocalyptic Timetables," esp. 1, 11–13.

115. One may note the following differences: 30:1–4 speaks of a resurrection of the righteous from the treasuries; chaps. 49–50, in contrast, speak of a general resurrection from the earth into the old corporality. Nevertheless, the godless are also in mind in 30:4 (i.e., their resurrection for judgment), and their punishment, which is reported in chap. 51, is already implied in chap. 30. "The author of 2 *Bar.* probably was hardly aware of a contradiction between 30:1–4 and chapters 49–51" (G. Stemberger, *Der Leib der Auferstehung*, 95). Even from the perspective of the history of traditions it probably is hardly justified to derive chap. 30 and chaps. 49ff. from different sources.

116. The question stands in considerable tension with the answer. The answer speaks about the corporality of the dead, while the question asks about the corporality of the survivors. This means that a new source probably begins after the question.

117. This view was most recently presented by P. Bogaert, ed., *Apocalypse de Baruch*, SC 144, 145, 2 vols. (Paris: Éditions du Cerf, 1969), 1:416ff.; H. C. Cavallin, *Life after Death*, 86–94.

118. See U. B. Müller, *Messias und Menschensohn in jüdischen Apokalypsen und in der Offenbarung des Johannes*, 142ff.; Wilcke, *Problem*, 43.

119. 4 Ezra 12:34 stands in tension with this (?).

120. Müller, *Messias*, is not clear at this point: "In S. *Bar.* 29f. we do not find an actual division of history into three parts: this age—intervening kingdom—new world" (p. 144). Shortly before this it is said, "In 30:1 the original text would have read something like the following: 'After this, when the time of the presence of the Messiah has drawn to an end, all those who have fallen asleep will rise'" (pp. 143–44). In order to avoid the division of history into three parts, which is properly rejected by Müller, one must remove 30:1 to-

tally, for this verse artificially separates two traditions that refer to the same period of salvation. Compare merely 29:8 (consummation of time) with 30:3 (consummation of the times). See also C. K. Barrett, *The New Testament Background*, 248.

121. E. Peterson, "Apantēsis," *TDNT* 1:380; idem, "Die Einholung des Kyrios."

122. Something similar is also the case with *politeuma*. It designates an entity that is political as well as religious and apocalyptic (cf. Phil. 3:20). See H. Strathmann, "Polis," *TDNT* 6:516–35. In general, the transformation of the hope for a *political basileia* into the hope for a transcendental (*religious and apocalyptic*) *basileia* is a well-known phenomenon for Judaism at the turn of the era.

123. On "withdrawal," see Strecker, "Entrückung" (see above, p. 248 n. 28); G. Lohfink, *Die Himmelfahrt Jesu*; G. Friedrich, "Die Auferstehung Jesu, eine Tat Gottes oder ein Interpretament der Jünger?" 170ff.; idem, "Luk 9,51 und die Entrückungschristologie des Lukas," in *Orientierung*, 48–77; Armin Schmitt, *Entrückung—Aufnahme—Himmelfahrt*, FzB 10, 2d ed. (Stuttgart: Verlag Katholisches Bibelwerk, 1976) (Old Testament and Near East; on this, see also Riekele Borger, "Die Beschwörungsserie *bīt mēseri* und die Himmelfahrt Henochs," *JNES* 33 [1974]: 183–96).

124. See already Dibelius, *An die Thessalonicher*, 2d ed., p. 22: "Perhaps we are dealing with part of an apocalypse (such as Mark 13 par.) that had been placed on the lips of Jesus and from which Paul quotes the expressions or clauses that are decisive for his question." Dibelius is even more definite in the 3d ed. (p. 25): "The best explanation is that 16f. are quoted (literally or with alterations) from an apocalypse that Paul introduces as a *logos kyriou* (perhaps because it, as Mark 13, had been placed on the lips of the Lord?)."

125. Luz, *Geschichtsverständnis*, 327, lists the following passages from the New Testament that have been cited as parallels up to now: Matt. 10:39; 16:25, 28; 20:1ff.; 24:31, 34; 25:6; 26:64; Luke 13:30; John 5:25; 6:39–40.

126. Jeremias, *Unknown Sayings*, 82.

127. Luz, *Geschichtsverständnis*, 327–28; Siber, *Christus*, 39ff.; Baumgarten, *Paulus*, 94, to mention just a few.

128. *Logos kyriou* does not necessarily designate a *single* saying. See G. Kittel, "Legō," *TDNT* 4:69–143, esp. 105. L. Hartman correctly emphasizes that *logos*, "like its Hebrew equivalent . . . may be used both of a complex of doctrine and of parts of such a complex" (*Prophecy Interpreted*, 182).

129. Bultmann, *History*, 122. The same phenomenon is present in 1 Thess. 4:15–16: The designation *logos kyriou* attributes the apocalypse to Jesus, and Jesus himself is the redeeming figure in the apocalypse. On the thesis that Mark 13 is based on a Jewish apocalypse, see also R. Pesch, *Naherwartungen*, 215ff. A different view is taken by F. Hahn, "Die Rede von der Parusie des Menschensohnes Markus 13," in *Jesus und der Menschensohn*,

240–66, esp. 257ff. Since the Gospel of Mark was composed shortly after 70, does not Hahn run into chronological difficulties when he considers the pre-Markan, Christian apocalyptic speech to have arisen "first in the era in which a renaissance of apocalyptic in certain traditions of early Christianity is elsewhere noticeable and demonstrable" (p. 259)? Hahn refers to 2 Thess. and Rev., which belong "similarly to the time after A.D. 70" (p. 258 n. 70).

130. Luz, *Geschichtsverständnis*, 329. A similar view was already expressed by H. Koester, "Die ausserkanonischen Herrenworte als Produkte der christlichen Gemeinde." When Koester says that the *logos kyriou* reflects the situation of the congregation during the transition from the first generation to the second (pp. 233–34), one must ask how Paul, in this case, could still assume that the majority would survive.

131. T. Holtz, *Die Christologie der Apokalypse des Johannes*, 11. Further, Holtz reckons with Pauline influence in Rev. 14:13.

132. For *en kyriō* as a fixed ecclesiastical expression, see 1 Thess. 3:8 and 5:12. It is possible that Paul would not have changed an *en kyriō* in the tradition.

133. This modification gave the statement about withdrawal a content that differs totally from its meaning in the tradition. In our passage, the withdrawal means the transition to the final state of salvation. Thereby, the meaning of the apocalypse is changed totally, especially since the descent to earth of the Son of Man and those who belong to him is left out. This example demonstrates how Paul radically reinterprets apocalyptic traditions in terms of the meaning that the Christ-event has given them for him. For a parallel to this sort of interpretation, reference may be made to his use of the Old Testament (see 1 Cor. 9:9). See Philipp Vielhauer, "Paulus und das Alte Testament," in *Studien zur Geschichte und Theologie der Reformation: Festschrift für Ernst Bizer*, ed. L. Abramowski and J. F. G. Goeters (Neukirchen-Vluyn: Neukirchener Verlag, 1969), 33–62.

134. See, e.g., Siber, *Christus*, 57 n. 162.

135. See H. Conzelmann, *An Outline of the Theology of the New Testament*, 209.

136. Deissner, *Auferstehungshoffnung*, 15, writes that *hama syn autois* emphasizes once more that "the *zōntes* do not have any advantage over the *koimēthentes*."

137. W. Baird, "Pauline Eschatology in Hermeneutical Perspective," 322, does not notice that the withdrawal involves both the living and the dead. He writes, "I Thessalonians lists the descent of the Lord, . . . the resurrection of the dead, and the catching up of those who are alive for meeting the Lord in the air" (ibid.). As was shown above, resurrection and withdrawal are not parallel events. Rather, the resurrection is an auxiliary idea and is accommodated within the notion of withdrawal. Luz, *Geschichtsverständnis*, 355, also incorrectly writes that in 1 Thess. 4:13ff. "the subject is the withdrawal of

those who are still alive at the parousia." No. Those who have been raised will also be caught up.

138. Paul does not say anything about the state of the dead. Although it would have been appropriately consistent at this point to say something about their present fellowship with Christ, Paul had not yet arrived at this form of hope at the time of 1 Thess. The reason he had not yet arrived at this form of hope is apparently that survival was the rule and that his hope was still exclusively focused on the notion of the parousia. Phil. 1 differs here.

139. Cf. 2 Macc. 7:11; 14:46; Pseudo-Phocylides 100–104 (?); *Sib.* 4:181; *Gn.r.* 14:5; *Lv.r.* 14:9 (on the last two passages, see Cavallin, *Life*, 171ff.).

140. Dibelius, *An die Thessalonicher*, 2d ed., p. 21 (3d ed., p. 24).

141. Contra Furnish, "Development," 297; W. Wiefel, "Die Hauptrichtung des Wandels im eschatologischen Denken des Paulus," 70. See, against this view, J. Jeremias, "'Flesh and Blood Cannot Inherit the Kingdom of God' (1 Cor. XV.50)" (= *Abba*, 298–307).

142. Certainly one is free to assume that "at the time of the composition of 1 Thess. Paul had already adopted the idea of a transformation" (Deissner, *Auferstehungshoffnung*, 49). The decisive question, however, is whether the statement about the resurrection in 4:16 implies and demands the presence of a notion of transformation. This question should be answered in the negative. It is a completely different question whether Paul assumes that there will be a pneumatic mode of existence, and thus a transformation, involved in future fellowship with Christ (this remark pertains to ibid., 53). One may answer this question in the affirmative without assuming that the idea of a transformation underlies 4:16 (see the order of events in the *Syriac Apocalypse of Baruch* 49ff.: realistic resurrection and, then, transformation).

The investigators who, in order to maintain a unified system for Paul, always explain the different answers on the basis of the different situations involved should be asked the following question: Owing to the *different* situation that arose as time went on and more deaths occurred, did not Paul *have to* change his conception or his language if he wanted to retain the same meaning? I can only briefly touch on this point here, and I should like to refer to the third part of this trilogy. Important in this regard are the programmatic remarks by J. M. Robinson, "World in Modern Theology and in New Testament Theology," in *Soli Deo Gloria*, 100ff.

143. "*Parousia* as a [*terminus technicus*] for the 'coming' of Christ in Messianic glory seems to have made its way into primitive Christianity with Paul" (A. Oepke, "Parousia," *TDNT* 5:858–871, esp. 865). In the secular realm, the word designates the arrival of distinguished persons such as caesars and kings (see K. Deissner, "Parusie," *RGG*, 2d ed., vol. 4: cols. 978–81). It is thus possible that Paul drew this concept, which he later abandoned, from a tradition similar to 1 Thess. 4:16–17 (cf. Matt. 24:3, 27, 37, 39). In this tradition, the arrival of the Son of Man would have been pictured similarly to the

arrival of an earthly king, whom the citizens of the earth (i.e., the chosen/the remnant) rush to meet (*eis apantēsin*). The translation of *parousia* as "return" certainly seems to be ineradicable!

144. In any event, it should not be denied that "we who are alive, who are left until the coming of the Lord" implies that Paul is hardly counting on more deaths (in agreement with Klein, "Apokalyptische Naherwartung," 247 n. 25; see also M. J. Harris, "2 Corinthians 5:1–10: Watershed in Paul's Eschatology?" 36–37).

145. Grässer, "Bibelarbeit," 19, accurately notes: "The content of the hope itself and the application of the hope thus stand in crass inconformity. The tradition is full of fantasy here. Paul himself is very reserved."

146. This statement provides one argument for the view that Paul did *not* think that the dead already participated in fellowship with Christ (see above, n. 138; Phil. 1:23 presents a different opinion).

147. L. E. Keck, "The First Letter of Paul to the Thessalonians," 871.

148. The reason for this was not that he did not believe in a general resurrection (he was, of course, a Pharisee, and he acknowledged the resurrection of Jesus), but rather that he believed that the end of time lay directly at hand. The statements above do not intend to deny that the doctrine of a general resurrection could have been part of Paul's initial proclamation in Thessalonica. One should, however, differentiate from this issue the question of how Paul presented the hope that was applicable to him and to the congregation. In 1 Thess. 4:13ff., it is not the case that the "general resurrection . . . [has] slipped in between" (Grässer, "Bibelarbeit," 16, mirroring Marxsen, "Auslegung," 29; see above, p. 250 n. 59). Rather, as a result of the incipient *delay of the parousia*, Paul introduces the auxiliary notion of the resurrection of the dead Christians (*hoi nekroi en Christō*) in order to maintain the old conception of withdrawal. The general resurrection of the dead and the judgment are not affected by this addition. This process would hardly be understandable twenty years after the death of Jesus, though not if this time were cut in half.

149. Becker, *Auferstehung*, deals with 1 Cor. 15:50ff., not without justification, under the title 1 Cor. "15:50–58 as a Reinterpretation of 1 Thess. 4" (p. 96).

150. On *mystērion* in apocalyptic, see G. Bornkamm, "Mystērion," *TDNT* 4:802–828, esp. 815–17.

151. A noteworthy parallel to both passages is found in *Did.* 16:6–7.

152. See E. Best, *A Commentary on the First and Second Epistles to the Thessalonians*, 193. Gebhard Löhr, "1 Thess 4 15–17: Das 'Herrenwort,'" *ZNW* 71 (1980): 269–73, ventures to reconstruct the precise wording of the common tradition.

153. In 1 Cor. 15:51 "a change in emphasis appears . . . in comparison with 1 Thess. 4.15; it is now the survivors who are treated as exceptional" (C. K. Barrett, "New Testament Eschatology," *SJTh* 6 [1953]: 143).

154. For the text, which is problematical in terms of textual criticism, I follow Nestle and Conzelmann, *1 Corinthians*, 290, contra Helmut Saake, "Die kodikologisch problematische Nachstellung der Negation," *ZNW* 63 (1972): 277–79.

155. For this reason, "the parallelism [is] established . . . by the placement of the words *pantes ou*, understandable only in the sense of *ou pantes*" (Bl.-Debr., 14th ed., sec. 433 n. 3, p. 361). See E. W. Burton, *Syntax of the Moods and Tenses in New Testament Greek*, 31; J. H. Moulton, *A Grammar of New Testament Greek*, vol. 3 of 4 vols.: N. Turner, *Syntax*, 287; C. F. D. Moule, *An Idiom Book of New Testament Greek*, 168. The translation "all of us will not sleep, but all will rather be transformed" (H. J. Holtzmann, *Lehrbuch der neutestamentlichen Theologie*, 2:216) is thus incorrect. See, however, the same view expressed by G. B. Winer, *A Treatise on the Grammar of New Testament Greek*, 695–96 (note the literature cited there); A. T. Robertson, *A Grammar of the Greek New Testament in the Light of Historical Research*, 753. See also the survey presented by Hurd, *Origin*, 230f. n. 1.

156. Klein, "Apokalyptische Naherwartung," 251. See Becker, *Auferstehung*, 98; Baird, "Eschatology," 315; Hurd, *Origin*, 232–33 (further literature is cited there).

157. J. Weiss, *Earliest Christianity*, 2:531 n. 13, differs here: The resurrection of the dead is a phrase that "has become such a fixed dogma with Paul that he occasionally uses it of Christians of whom he elsewhere takes it for granted that they will live to see the Parousia." Precisely at the time of 1 Cor. that appears no longer to have been the case.

158. J. Weiss, *Der erste Korintherbrief*, 350. See also Becker, *Auferstehung*, 45, 64. If the emphasis of the relative clause is not "on the fact that the majority are still alive, but on the fact that some have already died" (Conzelmann, *1 Corinthians*, 258), why does Paul say that *most* of them are still alive? Clearly, this statement intends to emphasize that the appearances are strongly witnessed (H. Lietzmann, *An die Korinther I.II*, 77). See also P. von der Osten-Sacken, "Die Apologie des paulinischen Apostolats in 1Kor 15,1–11," 259.

159. In the margin, it may be noted that the enigmatic vicarious baptism (1 Cor. 15:29) is probably conceivable only if occurrences of death in Corinth had advanced beyond the initial stage.

160. One should not follow Deissner in denying that the *sōma pneumatikon* is material in character, even if the emphasis is placed on the "qualitatively different principles of life in the *sōmata*" (*Auferstehungshoffnung*, 34). See H. Gunkel, *The Influence of the Holy Spirit*, 62–63, 124.

161. This is the view of Klein, "Apokalyptische Naherwartung," 253.

162. Luz, *Geschichtsverständnis*, 355 n. 136.

163. Admittedly, *certainty* in the resolution of this problem cannot be obtained. This is not very important for our inquiry. While our proposal must

wrestle with a double "we," because "we" does not indicate the same group of people each time, Klein's thesis must wrestle with the relationship of *aphthartoi* to *allagēsometha* in v. 52, for the statement that the dead will be raised imperishable already implicitly contains a transformation.

164. The Corinthians did not reject the resurrection of the dead as a whole. See Hurd, *Origin*, 197–98.

165. Baird, "Eschatology," raises the following objection to the thesis that approximately ten years had passed between 1 Thess. and 1 Cor.: "But if this is the case, how are we to explain the minimal change in Paul's eschatology in the ten-year interval between 1 Thessalonians and 1 Corinthians . . . ?" (p. 316). I hope that I have shown that a "maximal change" has occurred, and I suspect that Baird's judgment rests on an imprecise exegesis of 1 Thess. 4:13ff. (see above, pp. 257–58 n. 137).

6

CHRONOLOGICAL CHART

The results of this book may now be summarized in the following chronological chart. It should be emphasized that the numbers are part of an auxiliary construction drawn up in order to check Luke's information and that other uncertainties had to be taken into consideration. Further, for the reasons mentioned above, it is necessary to proceed on the basis of two possible dates for the death of Jesus.

27 (30) C.E.	Crucifixion of Jesus.
30 (33)	Paul's conversion in/near Damascus. Stay in Arabia. Return to Damascus.
33 (36)	Paul's first visit to Jerusalem.
34 (37)	Journey to Syria and Cilicia. Mission there and in South Galatia together with Barnabas and under the auspices of the Antiochene mission.
From ca. 36 (39)	Paul's independent mission in Europe: Philippi, Thessalonica.
41	*Edict of Claudius concerning the Jews.*
Ca. 41	Paul in Corinth: 1 Thessalonians.
Before or after the mission in Greece	Founding of the Galatian congregations owing to sickness. Incident in Antioch, which was perhaps the direct occasion for the
47 (50)	Second visit to Jerusalem: Jerusalem Conference. Following this, the journey to the Pauline congregations to organize the collection.
Summer 48 (51)	Paul in Galatia.

Fall 48 (51)—
Spring 50 (53)   Paul in Ephesus.

Fall 48 (51)   Sending of Timothy to Macedonia and Corinth; the previous letter to Corinth with instruction for the collection (or this latter through a messenger).

Winter 48/49 (51/52)   Timothy in Macedonia.

Spring 49 (52)   Letter of the Corinthians with question about the collection (or this by oral inquiry).

Ca. Easter 49 (52)   1 Corinthians.

Summer 49 (52)   After bad news from Corinth by Timothy, Paul's intervening visit to Corinth and precipitate return to Ephesus; letter of tears and the sending of Titus to Corinth.

Winter 49/50 (52/53)   Deadly danger for Paul (imprisonment in Ephesus?).

Spring 50 (53)   Journey of Paul with Timothy from Ephesus to Troas; further journey to Macedonia.

Summer 50 (53)   Arrival of Titus in Macedonia from Corinth; bad news from Galatia; composition of 2 Corinthians 1–9, 2 Corinthians 10–13 / Galatians; sending of Titus with 2 Corinthians to Corinth in order to organize the completion of the collection.

Winter 50/51 (53/54)   Paul in Macedonia; completion of the collection there.

51/52   *Gallio as proconsul of Achaia.*

Spring/Summer 51 (54) Journey of Paul with Macedonian attendants to Corinth; completion of the collection there.

Winter 51/52 (54/55)   Paul in Corinth: Romans.

Spring 52 (55)   Journey to Jerusalem in order to deliver the collection.

7

BIBLIOGRAPHY

7.1 SOURCES

The Apocrypha and Pseudepigrapha of the Old Testament. 2 vols. Trans. R. H. Charles. Oxford: At the Clarendon Press, 1913. See also *Apocalypse de Baruch.* 2 vols. Edited by P. Bogaert. SC 144, 145. 1969.

Aristotle. *Ethica Nicomachea.* Edited by J. Bywater. SCBO. 1894. See also *The Nicomachean Ethics.* Trans. H. Rackham. LCL. 1934.

Cicero. *Treatise on Rhetorical Invention (De inventione).* Trans. H. M. Hubbell. LCL. 1949.

————. *Treatise on Oration (De oratore).* 2 vols. Trans. E. W. Sutton and H. Rackham. LCL. 1942.

(Pseudo-) Cicero. *Treatise on Rhetoric (Rhetorica ad Herennium).* Trans. H. Caplan. LCL. 1954.

Clement of Alexandria (Clemens Alexandrinus). *Miscellanies (Stromata).* In *Fathers of the Second Century.* Edited by A. C. Coxe. ANF 2:299–568. (1979 reprint).

Dio Cassius. *Roman History (Historia Romana).* 9 vols. Trans. by E. Cary on the basis of the version by H. B. Foster (1905–6). Vol. 7: Books LVI–LX. LCL. 1924.

Diodorus of Sicily (Diodorus Siculus). *Library of History (Bibliotheca historica).* 12 vols. Vol. 9: Books XVIII–XIX.65. Trans. R. M. Geer. LCL. 1947.

Dionysius of Halicarnassus. *Opuscula.* Edited by H. Usener and L. Radermacher. Vol. 1. BSGRT. 1899.

Euripides. *Medea.* Trans. A. S. Way. LCL. 1912.

Fortunatianus. *Ars rhetorica.* In *Rhetores Latini minores,* ed. C. Halm, 79–134. Leipzig: Teubner, 1863.

Hippolytus. *The Refutation of All Heresies (Refutatio omnium haeresium).* In *Fathers of the Third Century.* Edited by A. C. Coxe. ANF 5:9–162. (1978 reprint).

Iamblichus. *De vita Pythagorica.* Edited by L. Deubner. BSGRT. 1937.

Irenaeus (of Lyon). *Against Heresies (Adversus haereses).* In *The Apostolic Fathers with Justin Martyr and Irenaeus.* Edited by A. C. Coxe. ANF 1:309–567. (1979 reprint).

Isocrates. *Orations (Orationes).* 3 vols. Trans. G. Norlin and L. R. V. Hook. LCL. 1928–45.

Josephus, Flavius. *Antiquities (Antiquitates)*. 6 vols. of 9. Trans. L. H. Feldman. Vol. 9: Books XVIII–XX. LCL. 1965.

————. *The Jewish War (De bello Judaico)*. 2 vols. of 10. Trans. H. St. J. Thackeray. Vol. 2: Books I–III. LCL. 1927.

Justin (Martyr). *The First Apology (Apologia)* and *Dialogue with Trypho, A Jew (Dialogus)*. In *The Apostolic Fathers with Justin Martyr and Irenaeus*. Edited by A. C. Coxe. ANF 1:159–87, 194–270. (1979 reprint).

Novum Testamentum Graece. Edited by K. Aland, M. Black, C. M. Martini, B. M. Metzger, and A. Wikgren. 26th ed. Stuttgart: Deutsche Bibelstiftung, 1979.

Origen. *Against Celsus (Contra Celsum)*. Trans., intro., and notes by H. Chadwick. Cambridge: At the University Press, 1965.

Orosius, Paulus. *Historiae adversum paganos*. Edited by C. Zangemeister. CSEL 5. 1882.

Ovid. *The Art of Love (Ars amatoria)*. Trans. J. H. Mozley. Rev. 2d ed. by G. P. Goold. LCL. 1979.

Philo of Alexandria. *Complete Works*. 12 vols. Trans. F. H. Colson, G. H. Whitaker, and R. Marcus. LCL. 1929–62.

Pindar. *Odes*. Trans. J. E. Sandys. LCL. 1911.

Plato. *Complete Works*. 12 vols. Trans. H. N. Fowler, W. R. M. Lamb, P. Shorey, and R. G. Bury. LCL. 1914–35.

Plutarch. *Moralia*. 16 vols. Trans. F. C. Babbitt. Vol. 1. LCL. 1927.

Quintilian. *The Institutes of Eloquence (Institutio oratoria)*. 4 vols. Trans. H. E. Butler. LCL. 1920–22. See also Quintilian, *Ausbildung des Redners (Institutio oratoria)*, 2 vols. Edited by H. Rahn. TzF 2, 3. 1972–75.

Septuaginta. 2 vols. Edited by A. Rahlfs. 8th ed. Stuttgart: Württembergische Bibelanstalt, 1965.

Suetonius. *Lives of the Caesars (De vita Caesarum)*. 2 vols. Trans. J. C. Rolfe. LCL. 1914.

Tacitus. *Annals (Annales)*. 3 vols. Trans. J. Jackson. LCL. 1931–37.

Theophrastus. *Characters (Characteres)*. Trans. J. M. Edmonds. LCL. 1929. See also Theophrast, *Charaktere*, 2 vols. Edited by P. Steinmetz. Das Wort der Antike 7. Munich: Hueber, 1960–62.

7.2 COMMENTARIES

Barrett, Charles Kingsley. *A Commentary on the Epistle to the Romans*. HNTC. 1958. [= BNTC, 1957]

————. *A Commentary on the First Epistle to the Corinthians*. HNTC. 1968. [= BNTC, 1971]

————. *A Commentary on the Second Epistle to the Corinthians*. HNTC. 1968. [= BNTC, 1973]

Best, Ernest. A *Commentary on the First and Second Epistles to the Thessalonians*. HNTC. 1972. [= BNTC, 1972]

Betz, Hans Dieter. *Galatians: A Commentary on Paul's Letter to the Churches in Galatia*. Hermeneia. 1979.

Bonnard, Pierre. *L'Épître de Saint Paul aux Galates*. CNT 9. 2d rev. ed. 1972.

Bousset, Wilhelm. "Der Brief an die Galater." In *Die Schriften des Neuen Testaments*, 3d rev. ed. 2d of 4 vols.: *Die paulinischen Briefe und die Pastoralbriefe*, ed. W. Bousset and W. Heitmüller, 31–74. Göttingen: Vandenhoeck & Ruprecht, 1917.

Bruce, Frederick Fyvie. *The Acts of the Apostles*. 2d ed. Grand Rapids: Wm. B. Eerdmans, 1973; London: Tyndale Press, 1951.

Bultmann, Rudolf. *The Gospel of John: A Commentary*. Trans. G. R. Beasley-Murray. Edited by R. W. N. Hoare and J. K. Riches. Philadelphia: Westminster Press; Oxford: Basil Blackwell, 1971.

Burton, Ernest de Witt. *A Critical and Exegetical Commentary on the Epistle to the Galatians*. ICC. 1921.

Conzelmann, Hans. *Die Apostelgeschichte*. HNT 7. 2d ed. 1972. (Trans. in preparation for Hermeneia.)

———. *1 Corinthians: A Commentary on the First Epistle to the Corinthians*. Trans. J. W. Leitch. Edited by G. MacRae. Hermeneia. 1975.

Dibelius, Martin. *An die Thessalonicher I.II, An die Philipper*. HNT 11. 2d ed., 1925. 3rd ed., 1937.

———. *James: A Commentary on the Epistle of James*. Rev. by H. Greeven. Trans. M. A. Williams. Edited by H. Koester. Hermeneia. 1976.

Dobschütz, Ernst von. *Die Thessalonicher-Briefe*. Edited by F. Hahn. Bibliography by O. Merk. KEK 10. 1974.

Friedrich, Gerhard. "Der Brief an die Philipper." In *Die kleineren Briefe des Apostels Paulus*, NTD 8, pp. 125–75. (1976).

———. "Der erste Briefe an die Thessalonicher." In *Die kleineren Briefe des Apostels Paulus*. NTD 8, pp. 203–41. (1976).

Gnilka, Joachim. *Der Philipperbrief*. HThK 10.3. 2d ed. 1976.

Haenchen, Ernst. *The Acts of the Apostles: A Commentary*. Trans. B. Noble, G. Shinn, H. Anderson, and R. M. Wilson. Philadelphia: Westminster Press; Oxford: Basil Blackwell, 1971.

Heinrici, Georg. *Der zweite Brief an die Korinther*. KEK 6. 3d ed., with Appendix: "Zum Hellenismus des Paulus." 1900.

Hofmann, Johann Christian Konrad von. *Der Brief Pauli an die Philipper*. Die hl. Schrift neuen Testaments 4.3. Nördlingen: C. Beck, 1871.

Keck, Leander E. "The First Letter of Paul to the Thessalonians." In *The Interpreter's One Volume Commentary on the Bible*, ed. C. M. Laymon, 865–74. Nashville: Abingdon Press, 1971.

Klostermann, Erich. *Das Lukasevangelium.* HNT 5. 3d ed. 1975.

Lietzmann, Hans. *An Die Korinther I.II.* Rev. and supp. by W. G. Kümmel. HNT 9. 5th ed. 1969.

————. *An die Galater.* HNT 10. 4th ed. 1971.

Lightfoot, Joseph Barber. *The Epistles of St. Paul.* Vol. 2, pt. 3: *St. Paul's Epistle to the Galatians.* 10th ed. New York and London: Macmillan, 1890.

Lipsius, Richard Adelbert. *Briefe an die Galater, Römer, Philipper.* HC 2.2. 1891.

Lohmeyer, Ernst. *Die Briefe an die Philipper, an die Kolosser und an Philemon.* KEK 9. 6th ed. 1964.

Loisy, Alfred. *Les Actes des Apôtres.* Paris: E. Nourry, 1920.

Masson, Charles. *Les deux épîtres de saint Paul aux Thessaloniciens.* CNT 11a. 1957.

Michel, Otto. *Der Brief an die Römer.* KEK 4. 4th ed. 1966.

Mussner, Franz. *Der Galaterbrief.* HThK 9. 1974.

Oepke, Albrecht. *Der Brief des Paulus an die Galater.* Rev. by J. Rhode. ThHK 9. 3d ed. 1973.

Orr, William F., and James Arthur Walther. *1 Corinthians.* AncB. 1976.

Rigaux, Béda. *Saint Paul: Les épîtres aux Thessaloniciens.* EtB. 1956.

Schlier, Heinrich. *Der Brief an die Galater.* KEK 7. 4th ed. 1965.

Schürmann, Heinz. *Das Lukasevangelium I: Kommentar zu Kap.1, 1–9, 50.* HThK 3.1. 1969.

Sieffert, Friedrich. *Der Brief und die Galater.* KEK 7. 4th ed. 1899.

Weiss, Johannes. *Der erste Korintherbrief.* KEK 5. 1910.

Wellhausen, Julius. *Das Evangelium Marci.* 2d ed. Berlin: G. Reimer, 1909.

Windisch, Hans. *Der zweite Korintherbrief.* Edited by G. Strecker. KEK 6. 1970.

7.3 SECONDARY LITERATURE

Altaner, Berthold, and Alfred Stuiber. *Patrology.* Trans. H. C. Graef. New York: Herder & Herder, 1960.

Andresen, Carl. *Geschichte des Christentums.* Vol. 1 of 2: *Von den Anfängen bis zur Hochscholastik.* ThW 6. Stuttgart: Kohlhammer, 1975.

Bacon, Benjamin W. "The Reading *hois oude* in Gal. 2:5." *JBL* 42 (1923): 69–80.

Baird, William. "Pauline Eschatology in Hermeneutical Perspective." *NTS* 17 (1970/71): 314–27.

Balsdon, John Percy Vyvian Dacre. *The Emperor Gaius (Caligula).* Oxford: Clarendon Press, 1934.

Bammel, Ernst. "Judenverfolgung und Naherwartung: Zur Eschatologie des Ersten Thessalonicherbriefs." *ZThK* 56 (1959): 294–315.

Barrett, Charles Kingsley. "New Testament Eschatology." *SJTh* 6 (1953): 136–55.

———. *The New Testament Background: Selected Documents.* New York: Harper & Row; London: SPCK, 1956.

———. "Titus." In *Neotestamentica et Semitica: Studies in Honour of Matthew Black*, ed. E. E. Ellis and M. Wilcox, 1–14. Edinburgh: T. & T. Clark, 1969.

Bauer, Walter. *Orthodoxy and Heresy in Earliest Christianity.* Edited by G. Strecker. Trans. from 2d Ger. ed. Eng. ed. R. A. Kraft and G. Krodel. Philadelphia: Fortress Press, 1971.

———. *A Greek-English Lexicon of the New Testament and Other Early Christian Literature.* Trans. W. Arndt and F. W. Gingrich. 2d ed. Rev. and aug. F. W. Gingrich and F. W. Danker. Chicago: University of Chicago Press, 1979.

Baumgarten, Jörg. *Paulus und die Apokalyptik.* WMANT 44. Neukirchen-Vluyn: Neukirchener Verlag, 1975.

Baur, Ferdinand Christian. *Paul: The Apostle of Jesus Christ.* 2 vols. Edited by E. Zeller. Trans. A. Menzies. 2d ed. London: Williams & Norgate, 1875.

Becker, Jürgen. *Auferstehung der Toten im Urchristentum.* SBS 82. Stuttgart: KBW Verlag, 1976.

Bell, Harold Idris. *Jews and Christians in Egypt.* London: B. Quaritch; Oxford: At the University Press, 1924.

Benko, Stephen. "The Edict of Claudius of A.D. 49 and the Instigator Chrestus." *ThZ* 25 (1969): 406–18.

Berger, Klaus. "Zu den sogenannten Sätzen heiligen Rechts." *NTS* 17 (1970/71): 10–40.

———. "Apostelbrief und apostolische Rede/Zum Formular frühchristlicher Briefe." *ZNW* 65 (1974): 190–231.

———. "Almosen für Israel: Zum historischen Kontext der paulinischen Kollekte." *NTS* 23 (1977): 180–204.

Betz, Hans Dieter. *Der Apostel Paulus und die sokratische Tradition.* BHTh 45. Tübingen: J. C. B. Mohr (Paul Siebeck), 1972.

———. "Spirit, Freedom, and Law." *SEA* 39 (1974): 145–60.

———. "The Literary Composition and Function of Paul's Letter to the Galatians." *NTS* 21 (1975): 353–79.

———. "In Defense of the Spirit: Paul's Letter to the Galatians as a Document of Early Christian Apologetics." In *Aspects of Religious Propaganda in Judaism and Early Christianity*, ed. E. Schüssler Fiorenza, 99–114. University of Notre Dame Center for the Study of Judaism and Christianity in Antiquity 2. Notre Dame and London: University of Notre Dame Press, 1976.

Billerbeck, Paul. *Kommentar zum Neuen Testament aus Talmud und Midrasch*. 6 vols. Munich: C. H. Beck, 1922–61.

Blass, Friedrich, and Albert Debrunner. *A Greek Grammar of the New Testament and Other Early Christian Literature*. Trans. and rev. by R. W. Funk. Chicago: University of Chicago Press, 1961.

Boers, Hendrikus. "The Form Critical Study of Paul's Letters: 1 Thessalonians as a Case Study." *NTS* 22 (1976): 140–58.

Borg, Marcus. "A New Context for Romans XIII." *NTS* 19 (1972/73): 205–18.

Bornkamm, Günther. "Die Verzögerung der Parusie." In *In Memoriam Ernst Lohmeyer*, ed. W. Schmauch, 116–26. Stuttgart: Evangelisches Verlagswerk, 1951 (= *Geschichte und Glaube I, Gesammelte Aufsätze*, 3: 46–55, BEvTh 48 [Munich: Chr. Kaiser Verlag, 1968]).

———. *Paul*. Trans. D. M. G. Stalker. New York: Harper & Row, 1971.

———. "The Letter to Romans as Paul's Last Will and Testament." In *The Romans Debate*, ed. K. P. Donfried, 17–31. Minneapolis: Augsburg Publishing House, 1977.

Borse, Udo. "Die geschichtliche und theologische Einordnung des Römerbriefes." *BZ*, n.s. 16 (1972): 70–83.

———. *Der Standort des Galaterbriefes*. BBB 41. Cologne: Peter Hanstein, 1972.

Bouttier, Michel. "Complexio Oppositorum." *NTS* 23 (1977): 1–19.

Bradley, David G. "The *Topos* as a Form in the Pauline Paraenesis." *JBL* 72 (1953): 238–46.

Brandenburger, Egon. "Die Auferstehung der Glaubenden als historisches und theologisches Problem." *WuD* 9 (1967): 16–33.

———. *Frieden im Neuen Testament*. Gütersloh: Gerd Mohn, 1973.

Braunert, Horst. "Der römische Provinzialzensus und der Schätzungsbericht des Lukas-Evangeliums." *Hist.* 6 (1957): 192–214.

Brown, Schuyler. *Apostasy and Perseverance in the Theology of Luke*. AnBib 36. Rome: Pontifical Biblical Institute, 1969.

Bruce, Frederick Fyvie. "Galatian Problems. 2. North or South Galatians?" *BJRL* 52 (1969/70): 243–66.

Buck, Charles H. "The Collection for the Saints." *HThR* 43 (1950): 1–29.

———, and Greer Taylor. *Saint Paul: A Study of the Development of His Thought*. New York: Charles Scribner's Sons, 1969.

Bultmann, Rudolf. *Theology of the New Testament*. 2 vols. Trans. K. Grobel. New York: Charles Scribner's Sons, 1951–55.

———. *The History of the Synoptic Tradition*. Trans. J. Marsh. 2d ed. New York: Harper & Row, 1968.

Burchard, Christoph. *Der dreizehnte Zeuge.* FRLANT 103. Göttingen: Vandenhoeck & Ruprecht, 1970.

———. "Paulus in der Apostelgeschichte." *ThLZ* 100 (1975): cols. 881–95.

Burkert, Walter. "*GOĒS:* Zum griechischen 'Schamanismus.'" *RMP*, n.s. 105 (1962): 36–55.

Burton, Ernest de Witt. *Syntax of the Moods and Tenses in New Testament Greek.* 3d ed. Chicago: University of Chicago Press, 1900.

Cadbury, Henry J. *The Making of Luke-Acts.* 1927. Reprint. London: SPCK, 1968.

Campbell, Thomas H., "Paul's 'Missionary Journeys' as Reflected in His Letters." *JBL* 74 (1955): 80–87.

Catchpole, David R. "Paul, James, and the Apostolic Decree." *NTS* 23 (1977): 428–44.

Cavallin, Hans Clemens Caesarius. *Life after Death: Paul's Argument for the Resurrection of the Dead in 1 Cor. 15.* CB.NT 7.1. Lund: C. W. K. Gleerup, 1974.

Clemen, Carl. *Paulus: Sein Leben und Wirken.* 2 vols. Giessen: A. Töpelmann, 1904.

Conzelmann, Hans. *The Theology of St. Luke.* Trans. G. Buswell. 1960. Reprint. Philadelphia: Fortress Press, 1982.

———. *An Outline of the Theology of the New Testament.* Trans. J. Bowden. New York: Harper & Row, 1969.

———. *A History of Primitive Christianity.* Trans. J. E. Steely. Nashville: Abingdon Press, 1973.

———. "Die Rechtfertigungslehre des Paulus: Theologie oder Anthropologie?" *EvTh* 28 (1968): 389–404 (= *Theologie als Schriftauslegung,* 191–206, BEvTh 65 [Munich: Chr. Kaiser Verlag, 1974]).

———. "'Was von Anfang war.'" In *Neutestamentliche Studien für Rudolf Bultmann,* ed. W. Eltester, 194–201. BZNW 21. Berlin: A. Töpelmann, 1954 (= *Theologie als Schriftauslegung,* 207–214, BEvTh 65 [Munich: Chr. Kaiser Verlag, 1974]).

———, and Andreas Lindemann. *Arbeitsbuch zum Neuen Testament.* UTB 52. 3d ed. Tübingen: J. C. B. Mohr (Paul Siebeck), 1977.

Cousin, Jean. *Études sur Quintilien.* Vol. 1 of 2 vols.: *Contribution à la recherche des sources de l'institution oratoire.* Paris: Boivin, 1935 (2 vols. reprinted in 1: Amsterdam: P. Schippers, 1967).

Cullmann, Oscar. *Peter: Disciple, Apostle, Martyr: A Historical and Theological Study.* Trans. F. V. Filson. 2d rev. ed. Philadelphia: Westminster Press, 1962.

Dahl, Nils Alstrup. "The Purpose of Luke-Acts." In *Jesus in the Memory of the Early Church,* 87–98. Minneapolis: Augsburg Publishing House, 1976.

———. "Paul and Possessions." In *Studies in Paul: Theology for the Early Christian Mission*, 22–39. Minneapolis: Augsburg Publishing House, 1977.

Davies, John Gordon. "The Genesis of Belief in an Imminent Parousia." *JThS*, n.s. 14 (1963): 104–7.

Davies, William David. *Christian Origins and Judaism*. Philadelphia: Westminster Press, 1962.

———. *The Setting of the Sermon on the Mount*. 2d ed. Cambridge: At the University Press, 1966.

———. *The Gospel and the Land*. Berkeley, Los Angeles, and London: University of California Press, 1974.

———. *Paul and Rabbinic Judaism: Some Rabbinic Elements in Pauline Theology*. 4th ed. Philadelphia : Fortress Press, 1980.

Deissmann, Gustav Adolf. *Light from the Ancient East: The New Testament Illustrated by Recently Discovered Texts of the Graeco-Roman World*. Trans. L. R. M. Strachan. London: Hodder & Stoughton, 1911.

———. *Paul: A Study in Social and Religious History*. Trans. W. E. Wilson. 2d rev. ed. New York: Doran, 1926.

———. *Bible Studies*. Trans. A. Grieve. 2d ed. 1923. Reprint. Edinburgh. T. & T. Clark, 1979.

Deissner, Kurt. *Auferstehungshoffnung und Pneumagedanke bei Paulus*. Leipzig: A. Deichert, 1912.

Demke, Christoph. "Theologie und Literarkritik im 1. Thessalonicherbrief." In *Wort und Existenz: Festschrift für Ernst Fuchs*, ed. G. Ebeling, E. Jüngel, and G. Schunack, 103–24. Tübingen: J. C. B. Mohr (Paul Siebeck), 1973.

Dexinger, Ferdinand. "Ein 'Messianisches Szenarium' als Gemeingut des Judentums in nachherodianischer Zeit?" *Kairos* 17 (1975): 249–78.

Dibelius, Martin. "Zur Formgeschichte des Neuen Testaments (ausserhalb der Evangelien)." *ThR*, n.s. 3 (1931): 207–42.

———. *Paul*. Ed. and completed by W. G. Kümmel. Trans. F. Clarke Philadelphia: Westminster Press, 1953.

———. "The Acts of the Apostles as an Historical Source." In *Studies in the Acts of the Apostles*, ed. H. Greeven, trans. M. Ling, 102–8. New York: Charles Scribner's Sons; London: SCM Press, 1956.

———. "The Acts of the Apostles in the Setting of the History of Early Christian Literature." In *Studies in the Acts of the Apostles*, ed. H. Greeven, trans. M. Ling, 192–206. New York: Charles Scribner's Sons; London: SCM Press, 1956.

———. "The First Christian Historian." In *Studies in the Acts of the Apostles*, ed. H. Greeven, trans. M. Ling, 123–37. New York: Charles Scribner's Sons; London: SCM Press, 1956.

———. "The Speeches in Acts and Ancient Historiography." In *Studies in the Acts of the Apostles*, ed. H. Greeven, trans. M. Ling, 138–85. New York: Charles Scribner's Sons; London: SCM Press, 1956.

———. "Style Criticism of the Book of Acts." In *Studies in the Acts of the Apostles*, ed. H. Greeven, trans. M. Ling, 1–25. New York: Charles Scribner's Sons; London: SCM Press, 1956.

———. *From Tradition to Gospel*. Trans. B. L. Woolf. 2d rev. ed. New York: Charles Scribner's Sons, 1965.

Dinkler, Erich. "Der Brief an die Galater: Zum Kommentar von Heinrich Schlier." VF 7 (1953/55): 175–83 (= *Signum Crucis: Aufsätze zum Neuen Testament und zur christlichen Archäologie*, 270–82 [Tübingen: J. C. B. Mohr (Paul Siebeck), 1967]).

Dix, Gregory. *Jew and Greek: A Study in the Primitive Church*. 2d ed. Westminster: Dacre Press, 1955.

Dockx, Stanislas J. "Chronologie paulinienne de l'année de la grande collecte." RB 81 (1974): 183–95 (= *Chronologies néotestamentaires et Vie de l'Église primitive*, 107–18 [Paris: Dulcot, 1976]).

Doty, William G. *Letters in Primitive Christianity*. Guides to Biblical Scholarship, New Testament Series. Philadelphia: Fortress Press, 1973.

Drane, John W. "Theological Diversity in the Letters of Saint Paul." *TynB* 27 (1976): 3–26.

Dupont, Jacques. *SYN CHRISTŌI: L'union avec le Christ suivant Saint Paul*. Paris: Éditions de L'Abbaye de Saint-Andre, 1952.

———. "Pierre et Paul à Antioche et à Jérusalem." RSR 45 (1957): 42–60, 225–39 (= *Études sur les actes des Apôtres*, 185–215, LeDiv 45 [Paris: Éditions du Cerf, 1967]).

———. "Les problèmes du livre des actes entre 1940 et 1950." In *Études sur les actes des Apôtres*, 11–124. LeDiv 45. Paris: Éditions du Cerf, 1967.

Eichholz, Georg. *Die Theologie des Paulus im Umriss*. Neukirchen-Vluyn: Neukirchener Verlag, 1972.

Ellis, E. Earle. *Paul and His Recent Interpreters*. 2d ed. Grand Rapids: Wm. B. Eerdmans, 1967.

Eltester, Walter. "Israel im lukanischen Werk und die Nazarethperikope." In *Jesus in Nazareth*, ed. E. Grässer, A. Strobel, R. C. Tannehill, and W. Eltester, 76–147. BZNW 40. New York and Berlin: Walter de Gruyter, 1976.

Emmet, Cyril William. "The Case for the Tradition." In *The Beginnings of Christianity*, ed. F. J. F. Jackson and K. Lake, pt. 1, vol. 1, pp. 265–97. 5 vols. London: Macmillan & Co., 1920–33.

Enslin, Morton S. "Once Again, Luke and Paul." ZNW 61 (1970): 253–71.

———. "Luke, the Literary Physician." In *Studies in New Testament and*

BIBLIOGRAPHY

Early Christian Literature: Essays in Honor of Allen P. Wikgren, ed. D. E. Aune, 135–43. *NT.S* 33. Leiden: E. J. Brill, 1972.

Faw, Chalmer E. "Death and Resurrection in Paul's Letters." *JBR* 27 (1959): 291–98.

———. "The Anomaly of Galatians." *BR* 4 (1960): 25–38.

Feuillet, André. "Mort du Christ et mort du chrétien d'après les épîtres pauliniennes." *RB* 66 (1959): 481–513.

Filson, Floyd Vivian. "The Journey Motif in Luke-Acts." In *Apostolic History and the Gospel: Historical Essays Presented to F. F. Bruce on His 60th Birthday*, ed. W. W. Gasque and R. P. Martin, 68–77. Grand Rapids: Wm. B. Eerdmans; Exeter: Paternoster Press, 1970.

Finegan, Jack. *Handbook of Biblical Chronology*. Princeton: Princeton University Press, 1964.

Friedländer, Paul. *Darstellungen aus der Sittengeschichte Roms in der Zeit von Augustus bis zum Ausgang der Antonine*. Vol. 1 of 4 vols. 10th ed. Leipzig: Hirzel, 1922.

Friedrich, Gerhard. "Ein Tauflied hellenistischer Judenchristen: 1. Thess. 1,9f." *ThZ* 21 (1965): 502–16.

———. "Die Auferstehung Jesu, eine Tat Gottes oder ein Interpretament der Jünger?" *KuD* 17 (1971): 153–87.

———. "Luk 9,51 und die Entrückungschristologie des Lukas." In *Orientierung an Jesus: Zur Theologie der Synoptiker. Für Josef Schmid zum 80. Geburtstag*, ed. P. Hoffmann, N. Brox, and W. Pesch, 48–77. Freiburg: Herder, 1973.

Funk, Robert W. "The Enigma of the Famine Visit." *JBL* 75 (1956): 130–36.

———. *Language, Hermeneutic, and Word of God: The Problem of Language in the New Testament and Contemporary Theology*. New York and London: Harper & Row, 1966.

———. "The Apostolic *Parousia*: Form and Significance." In *Christian History and Interpretation: Studies Presented to John Knox*, ed. W. R. Farmer, C. F. D. Moule, and R. R. Niebuhr, 249–68. Cambridge: At the University Press, 1967.

Furnish, Victor Paul. *Theology and Ethics in Paul*. Nashville: Abingdon Press, 1968.

———. "Development in Paul's Thought." *JAAR* 38 (1970): 289–303.

Gager, John G. *Kingdom and Community: The Social World of Early Christianity*. Englewood Cliffs, N.J.: Prentice-Hall, 1975.

Gamble, Harry Y. *The Textual History of the Letter to the Romans: A Study in Textual and Literary Criticism*. StD 42. Grand Rapids: Wm. B. Eerdmans, 1977.

Garzetti, Albino. *From Tiberius to the Antonines*. Trans. J. R. Foster. London: Methuen & Co., 1974.

273

Gauger, Jörg-Dieter. *Beiträge zur jüdischen Apologetik: Untersuchungen zur Authentizität von Urkunden bei Flavius Josephus und im 1. Makkabäerbuch.* BBB 49. Cologne: P. Hanstein, 1977.

Gayer, Roland. *Die Stellung des Sklaven in den paulinischen Gemeinden und bei Paulus: Zugleich eine sozialgeschichtlich vergleichender Beitrag zur Wertung des Sklaven in der Antike.* EHS.T 78. Bern: H. Lang, 1976.

Georgi, Dieter. *Die Geschichte der Kollekte des Paulus für Jerusalem.* ThF 38. Hamburg: H. Reich, 1965.

Goguel, Maurice. "La vision de Paul à Corinthe et sa comparution devant Gallion." *RHPhR* 12 (1932): 321–33.

———. "L'apôtre Pierre, a-t-il joué un rôle personnel dans les crises de Grèce et de Galatie?" *RHPhR* 14 (1934): 461–500.

Grabner-Haider, Anton. *Paraklese und Eschatologie bei Paulus.* NTA, n.s. 4. Münster: Aschendorff, 1968.

Grant, Michael. *Ancient History Atlas: 1700 B.C. to A.D. 565.* 2d rev. ed. London: Weidenfeld & Nicolson, 1974.

Grässer, Erich. "Die Apostelgeschichte in der Forschung der Gegenwart." *ThR*, n.s. 26 (1960): 93–167.

———. "Bibelarbeit über 1 Thess. 4,13–18." In *Bibelarbeiten, gehalten auf der rheinischen Landessynode 1967 in Bad Godesberg,* 10–20. Düsseldorf, 1967.

———. *Die Naherwartung Jesu.* SBS 61. Stuttgart: KBW Verlag, 1973.

———. "Acta-Forschung seit 1960." *ThR*, n.s. 41 (1976): 141–94, 259–90; 42 (1977): 1–68.

———. *Das Problem der Parusieverzögerung in den synoptischen Evangelien und in der Apostelgeschichte.* BZNW 22. 3d ed. New York and Berlin: Walter de Gruyter, 1978.

Greeven, Heinrich. "Kirche und Parusie Christi." *KuD* 10 (1964): 113–35.

Groos, Helmut. *Albert Schweitzer: Grösse und Grenzen.* Munich: E. Reinhardt, 1974.

Gülzow, Henneke. *Christentum und Sklaverei in den ersten drei Jahrhunderten.* Bonn: R. Habelt Verlag, 1969.

Gunkel, Hermann. *The Influence of the Holy Spirit: The Popular View of the Apostolic Age and the Teaching of the Apostles. A Biblical-Theological Study.* Trans. R. A. Harrisville and P. A. Quanbeck. Philadelphia: Fortress Press, 1979.

Guntermann, Friedrich. *Die Eschatologie des hl. Paulus.* NTA 13.4,5. Münster: Aschendorff, 1932.

Gunther, John J. *Paul: Messenger and Exile. A Study in the Chronology of His Life and Letters.* Valley Forge, Pa.: Judson Press, 1972.

Guterman, Simeon L. *Religious Toleration and Persecution in Ancient Rome.* London: Aiglon Press, 1951.

Güttgemanns, Erhardt. *Der leidende Apostel und sein Herr: Studien zur paulinischen Christologie.* FRLANT 90. Göttingen: Vandenhoeck & Ruprecht, 1966.

Haacker, Klaus. "Die Gallio-Episode und die paulinische Chronologie." *BZ,* n.s. 16 (1972): 252–55.

Haenchen, Ernst. "Petrus-Probleme." *NTS* 7 (1960/61): 187–97 (= *Gott und Mensch: Gesammelte Aufsätze,* vol. 1 of 2 vols., 55–67 [Tübingen: J. C. B. Mohr (Paul Siebeck), 1965]).

Hahn, Ferdinand. *Mission in the New Testament.* Trans. F. Clarke. SBT 47. London: SCM Press, 1965.

———. *The Titles of Jesus in Their History in Early Christianity.* Trans. H. Knight and D. Ogg. Cleveland: World Publishing, Meridian Books, 1969.

———. "Methodenprobleme einer Christologie des Neuen Testaments." *VF* 15.2 (1970): 3–41.

———. "Der Apostolat im Urchristentum." *KuD* 20 (1974): 54–77.

———. "Die Rede von der Parusie des Menschensohnes Markus 13." In *Jesus und der Menschensohn: Für Anton Vögtle,* ed. R. Pesch, R. Schnackenburg, and O. Kaiser, 240–66. Freiburg: Herder, 1975.

———. "Das Gesetzesverständnis im Römer- und Galaterbrief." *ZNW* 67 (1976): 29–63.

Hainz, Josef. *Ekklesia.* BU 9. Regensburg: F. Pustet, 1972.

Hare, Douglas R. A. *The Theme of Jewish Persecution of Christians in the Gospel According to St. Matthew.* SNTSMS 6. Cambridge: At the University Press, 1967.

Harnack, Adolf von. *New Testament Studies I: Luke the Physician, the Author of the Third Gospel and the Acts of the Apostles.* Trans. J. R. Wilkinson. Edited by W. D. Morrison. CTL 19. New York: G. P. Putnam's Sons, 1907.

———. "Die Zeitangaben in der Apostelgeschichte des Lukas." In *SPAW.PH* (1907): 376–99.

———. *The Mission and Expansion of Christianity in the First Three Centuries.* 2 vols. Trans. J. Moffatt. 2d rev. ed. New York: G. P. Putnam's Sons; London: Williams & Norgate, 1908.

———. *New Testament Studies II: The Date of the Acts and the Synoptic Gospels.* Trans. J. R. Wilkinson. CTL 33. New York: G. P. Putnam's Sons, 1911.

———. "Chronologische Berechnung des 'Tags von Damaskus.'" *SPAW.PH* (1912): 673–82.

Harnisch, Wolfgang. *Eschatologische Existenz: Ein exegetischer Beitrag zum Sachanliegen von 1. Thessalonicher 4,13–5,11.* FRLANT 110. Göttingen: Vandenhoeck & Ruprecht, 1973.

Harris, M. J. "2 Corinthians 5:1–10: Watershed in Paul's Eschatology?" *TynB* 22 (1971): 32–57.

Hartman, Lars. *Prophecy Interpreted: The Formation of Some Jewish Apoca-*

lyptic Texts and of Eschatological Discourse in Mark 13. CB.NT 1. Lund: C. W. K. Gleerup, 1966.

———. "The Function of Some So-called Apocalyptic Timetables." *NTS* 22 (1976): 1–14.

Hartmann, Paul. "Das Verhältnis des Galaterbriefs zum zweiten Korintherbrief." *ZWTh* 42 (1899): 187–94.

Hengel, Martin. "Die Ursprünge der christlichen Mission." *NTS* 18 (1971/72): 15–38.

———. "Christologie und neutestamentliche Chronologie." In *Neues Testament und Geschichte: Historisches Geschehen und Deutung im Neuen Testament. Oscar Cullmann zum 70. Geburtstag,* ed. H. Baltensweiler and B. Reicke, 43–67. Zurich: Theologischer Verlag, 1972.

———. "Zwischen Jesus und Paulus: Die 'Hellenisten,' die 'Sieben' und Stephanus (Apg. 6,1–5; 7,54–8,3)." *ZThK* 72 (1975): 151–206.

———. *Acts and the History of Earliest Christianity.* Trans. J. Bowden. Philadelphia: Fortress Press; London: SCM Press, 1979.

Héring, Jean. "Saint Paul a-t-il enseigné deux résurrections?" *RHPhR* 12 (1932): 300–320.

Hirsch, Emanuel. "Petrus und Paulus: Ein Gespräch mit Hans Lietzmann." *ZNW* 29 (1930): 63–76.

Hoehner, Harold W. "Why Did Pilate Hand Jesus over to Antipas?" In *The Trial of Jesus: Cambridge Studies in Honour of C. F. D. Moule,* ed. E. Bammel, 84–90. SBT 2d series, 13. 2d ed. London: SCM Press, 1970.

Hoerber, Robert O. "The Decree of Claudius in Acts 18:2." *CTM* 31 (1960): 690–94.

Hoffmann, Paul. *Die Toten in Christus.* NTA, n.s. 2. Münster: Aschendorff, 1966.

Hölscher, Gustav. *Die Hohenpriesterliste bei Josephus und die evangelische Chronologie.* SHAW.PH (1939/40), 3d treatise. Heidelberg: Carl Winters Universitätsbuchhandlung, 1940.

Holtz, Traugott. *Die Christologie der Apokalypse des Johannes.* TU 85. 2d ed. Berlin: Akademie Verlag, 1971.

———. "Die Bedeutung des Apostelkonzils für Paulus." *NT* 16 (1974): 110–48.

Holtzmann, Heinrich Julius. *Lehrbuch der neutestamentlichen Theologie.* 2 vols. Edited by A. Jülicher and W. Bauer. 2d ed. Tübingen: J. C. B. Mohr (Paul Siebeck), 1911.

Huber, Wolfgang. *Passa und Ostern: Untersuchungen zur Osterfeier der alten Kirche.* BZNW 35. Berlin: A. Töpelmann, 1969.

Hübner, Hans. *Das Gesetz bei Paulus: Ein Beitrag zum Werden der paulinischen Theologie.* FRLANT 119. Göttingen: Vandenhoeck & Ruprecht, 1978.

Hunzinger, Claus-Hunno. "Die Hoffnung angesichts des Todes im Wandel der paulinischen Aussagen." In *Leben angesichts des Todes: Beiträge zum theologischen Problem des Todes. Helmut Thielicke zum 60. Geburtstag,* ed. B. Lohse and H. P. Schmidt, 69–88. Tübingen: J. C. B. Mohr (Paul Siebeck), 1968.

Hurd, John C. *The Origin of 1 Corinthians.* New York: Seabury Press; London: SPCK, 1965.

———. "Pauline Chronology and Pauline Theology." In *Christian History and Interpretation: Studies Presented to John Knox,* ed. W. R. Farmer, C. F. D. Moule, and R. Niebuhr, 225–48. Cambridge: At the University Press, 1967.

———. "The Sequence of Paul's Letters." *CJTh* 14 (1968): 189–200.

Hyldahl, Niels. "Die Frage nach der literarischen Einheit des Zweiten Korintherbriefes." *ZNW* 64 (1973): 289–306.

Jeremias, Joachim. *The Eucharistic Words of Jesus.* Trans. N. Perrin. 1955. Reprint. Philadelphia: Fortress Press, 1977.

———. *Unknown Sayings of Jesus.* Trans. R. H. Fuller. 2d ed. London: SPCK, 1964.

———. "Chiasmus in den Paulusbriefen." *ZNW* 49 (1958): 145–56 (= *Abba: Studien zur neutestamentlichen Theologie und Zeitgeschichte,* 276–90 [Göttingen: Vandenhoeck & Ruprecht, 1966]).

———. "'Flesh and Blood Cannot Inherit the Kingdom of God' (1 Cor. XV.50)." *NTS* 2 (1955/56): 151–59 (= *Abba: Studien zur neutestamentlichen Theologie und Zeitgeschichte,* 298–307 [Göttingen: Vandenhoeck & Ruprecht, 1966]).

———. "Sabbathjahr und neutestamentliche Chronologie." *ZNW* 27 (1928): 98–103 (= *Abba: Studien zur neutestamentlichen Theologie und Zeitgeschichte,* 233–38 [Göttingen: Vandenhoeck & Ruprecht, 1966]).

———. "Untersuchungen zum Quellenproblem der Apostelgeschichte." *ZNW* 36 (1937): 205–21 (= *Abba: Studien zur neutestamentlichen Theologie und Zeitgeschichte,* 238–55 [Göttingen: Vandenhoeck & Ruprecht, 1966]).

———. *Jerusalem in the Time of Jesus: An Investigation into Economic and Social Conditions during the New Testament Period.* Trans. F. H. Cave and C. H. Cave. Philadelphia: Fortress Press, 1969.

———. *Der Schlüssel zur Theologie des Apostels Paulus.* CwH 115. Stuttgart: Calwer Verlag, 1971.

Jervell, Jacob. "The Law in Luke-Acts." *HThR* 64 (1971): 21–36 (= *Luke and the People of God,* 133–51 [Minneapolis: Augsburg Publishing House, 1972]).

Jewett, Robert. *Paul's Anthropological Terms: A Study of Their Use in Conflict Settings.* AGJU 10. Leiden: E. J. Brill, 1971.

———. *A Chronology of Paul's Life.* Philadelphia: Fortress Press, 1979.

Kabisch, Richard. *Die Eschatologie des Paulus in ihren Zusammenhängen mit dem Gesamtbegriff des Paulinismus.* Göttingen: Vandenhoeck & Ruprecht, 1893.

Käsemann, Ernst. "Die Johannesjünger in Ephesus." In *Exegetische Versuche und Besinnungen*. 6th ed. Vol. 1 of 2 vols., 158–68. Göttingen: Vandenhoeck & Ruprecht, 1964 (= *ZThK* 49 [1952]: 144–54).

———. "Sentences of Holy Law in the New Testament." In *New Testament Questions of Today*, trans. W. J. Montague, 66–81. Philadelphia: Fortress Press, 1969.

Kasting, Heinrich. *Die Anfänge der urchristlichen Mission*. BEvTh 55. Munich: Chr. Kaiser Verlag, 1969.

Keck, Leander E. "The Poor among the Saints in the New Testament." ZNW 56 (1965): 100–129.

Kennedy, George. *The Art of Rhetoric in the Roman World 300 B.C.—A.D. 300*. History of Rhetoric, vol. 2 of 2 vols. Princeton: Princeton University Press, 1972.

Kertelge, Karl. "Das Apostelamt des Paulus, sein Ursprung und seine Bedeutung." *BZ*, n.s. 14 (1970): 161–81.

———. "Apokalypsis Jesou Christou (Gal 1,12)." In *Neues Testament und Kirche: Für Rudolf Schnackenburg zum 60. Geburtstag*, ed. J. Gnilka, 266–81. Freiburg: Herder, 1974.

Klausner, Joseph. *Jesus of Nazareth: His Life, Times and Teachings*. Trans. H. Danby. New York: Macmillan Co., 1925.

Klein, Günter. "Galater 2,6–9 und die Geschichte der Jerusalemer Urgemeinde." *ZThK* 57 (1960): 275–95 (= *Rekonstruktion und Interpretation*, 90–118, 118–28, BEvTh 50 [Munich: Chr. Kaiser Verlag, 1969]).

———. "Die Verleugnung des Petrus." *ZThK* 58 (1961): 285–348 (= *Rekonstruktion und Interpretation*, 49–90, 90–98, BEvTh 50 [Munich: Chr. Kaiser Verlag, 1969]).

———. "Apokalyptische Naherwartung bei Paulus." In *Neues Testament und christliche Existenz: Festschrift für Herbert Braun zum 70. Geburtstag*, ed. H. D. Betz and L. Schottroff, 241–62. Tübingen: J. C. B. Mohr (Paul Siebeck), 1973.

Klein, Hans. "Die lukanisch-johanneische Passionstradition." ZNW 67 (1976): 155–86.

Knox, John. "'Fourteen Years Later': A Note on the Pauline Chronology." *JR* 16 (1936): 341–49.

———. "The Pauline Chronology." *JBL* 58 (1939): 15–29.

———. *Marcion and the New Testament: An Essay in the Early History of the Church*. Chicago: University of Chicago Press, 1942.

———. *Chapters in a Life of Paul*. Nashville: Abingdon Press, 1950; London: A. & C. Black, 1954.

Koester, Helmut. "Die ausserkanonischen Herrenworte als Produkte der christlichen Gemeinde." ZNW 48 (1957): 220–37.

Kraeling, Carl H. "The Jewish Community at Antioch." *JBL* 51 (1932): 130–60.

Kramer, Werner. *Christ, Lord, Son of God.* Trans. B. Hardy. SBT 50. London: SCM Press, 1966.

Kümmel, Werner Georg. *Promise and Fulfillment.* Trans. by D. M. Barton. London: SCM Press, 1957.

————. *Introduction to the New Testament.* Trans. H. C. Kee. Rev. ed. Nashville: Abingdon Press; London: SCM Press, 1975.

————. "Albert Schweitzer als Paulusforscher." In *Rechtfertigung: Festschrift für Ernst Käsemann zum 70. Geburtstag,* ed. J. Friedrich, W. Pöhlmann, and P. Stuhlmacher, 269–89. Tübingen: J. C. B. Mohr (Paul Siebeck); Göttingen: Vandenhoeck & Ruprecht, 1976.

Künzi, Martin. *Das Naherwartungslogion Matthäus 10,23: Geschichte seiner Auslegung.* BGBE 9. Tübingen: J. C. B. Mohr (Paul Siebeck), 1970.

————. *Das Naherwartungslogion Markus 9,1 par.* BGBE 21. Tübingen: J. C. B. Mohr (Paul Siebeck), 1977.

Kuss, Otto. *Paulus: Die Rolle des Apostels in der theologischen Entwicklung der Urkirche.* Regensburg: F. Pustet, 1971.

Labriolle, Pierre Champagne de. *La réaction païenne: Étude sur la polémique antichrétienne du Ier au VIe siècle.* 3d ed. Paris: L'Artisan du Livre, 1934.

Lacroix, Benoit. *Orose et ses Idées.* Montreal and Paris: Institut d'études mediévales, 1965.

Lake, Kirsopp. "The Date of Q." *Exp.,* 7th ser., 7 (1909): 494–507.

————. "The Chronology of Acts." In *The Beginnings of Christianity,* ed. F. J. F. Jackson and K. Lake, pt. 1, vol. 5, 445–74. 5 vols. London: Macmillan & Co., 1920–33.

Laub, Franz. *Eschatologische Verkündigung und Lebensgestaltung nach Paulus: Eine Untersuchung zum Wirken des Apostels beim Aufbau der Gemeinde in Thessalonike.* BU 10. Regensburg: F. Pustet, 1973.

Lausberg, Heinrich. *Handbuch der literarischen Rhetorik.* 2d ed. 2 vols. Munich: Huebner, 1973.

Leon, Harry J. *The Jews of Ancient Rome.* Philadelphia: Jewish Publication Society of America, 1960.

Liebenam, Wilhelm. *Zur Geschichte und Organisation des römischen Vereinswesens.* 1890. Reprint. Aalen: Scientia Verlag, 1964.

Lindemann, Andreas. *Paulus im ältesten Christentum: Das Bild des Apostels und die Rezeption der paulinischen Theologie in der fruhchristlichen Literatur bis Marcion.* BHTh 58. Tübingen: J. C. B. Mohr (Paul Siebeck), 1979.

Linnemann, Eta. *Parables of Jesus.* Trans. G. J. Sturdy. London: SPCK, 1966.

————. *Studien zur Passionsgeschichte.* FRLANT 102. Göttingen: Vandenhoeck & Ruprecht, 1970.

─────. "Zeitansage und Zeitvorstellungen in der Verkündigung Jesu." In *Jesus Christus in Historie und Theologie: Neutestamentliche Festschrift für Hans Conzelmann zum 60. Geburtstag*, ed. G. Strecker, 237–63. Tübingen: J. C. B. Mohr (Paul Siebeck), 1975.

Lohfink, Gerhard. *Paulus vor Damaskus: Arbeitsweisen der neueren Bibelwissenschaft dargestellt an den Texten Apg. 9,1–19; 22,3–21; 26,9–18.* SBS 4. 3d ed. Stuttgart: Verlag Katholisches Bibelwerk, 1967.

─────. *Die Himmelfahrt Jesu: Untersuchungen zu den Himmelfahrts- und Erhöhungstexten bei Lukas.* StANT 26. Munich: Kösel Verlag, 1971.

Lohse, Bernhard. *Das Passafest der Quartadezimaner.* BFChTh, 2d ser. 54. Gütersloh: C. Bertelsmann, 1953.

Lohse, Eduard. "Lukas als Theologe der Heilsgeschichte." *EvTh* 14 (1954): 256–75 (= *Die Einheit des Neuen Testaments*, 145–64 [Göttingen: Vandenhoeck & Ruprecht, 1973]; and *Das Lukas-Evangelium: Die redaktions- und kompositionsgeschichtliche Forschung*, ed. G. Braumann, 64–90, WdF 280 [Darmstadt: Wissenschaftliche Buchgesellschaft, 1974]).

Löning, Karl. *Die Saulustradition in der Apostelgeschichte.* NTA, n.s. 9. Münster: Aschendorff, 1973.

Löwe, Hartmut. "Christus und die Christen." Theological dissertation. Heidelberg, 1965.

Luedemann, Gerd. *Untersuchungen zur simonianischen Gnosis.* GTA 1. Göttingen: Vandenhoeck & Ruprecht, 1975.

Lührmann, Dieter. "Wo man nicht mehr Sklave oder Freier ist." *WuD*, n.s. 13 (1975): 53–83.

Luz, Ulrich. *Das Geschichtsverständnis des Paulus.* BEvTh 49. Munich: Chr. Kaiser Verlag, 1968.

─────. "Zum Aufbau von Röm. 1—8." *ThZ* 25 (1969): 161–81.

Magie, David. *Roman Rule in Asia Minor to the End of the Third Century after Christ.* Vol. 2 of 2 vols.: *Notes.* Princeton: Princeton University Press, 1950.

Maier, Johann, and Kurt Schubert. *Die Qumran-Essener: Text der Schriftrollen und Lebensbild der Gemeinde.* UTB 224. Munich: E. Reinhardt, 1973.

Malherbe, Abraham J. *Social Aspects of Early Christianity.* Baton Rouge and London: Louisiana State University, 1977. 2d ed. enl. Philadelphia: Fortress Press, 1983.

Martin, Josef. *Antike Rhetorik: Technik und Methode.* HAW 2.3. Munich: C. H. Beck, 1974.

Marxsen, Willi. "Auslegung von 1 Thess 4,13–18." *ZThK* 66 (1969): 22–37.

McGiffert, Arthur Cushman. *A History of Christianity in the Apostolic Age.* 2d ed. New York: Charles Scribner's Sons, 1914.

Meeks, Wayne A. "Jews and Christians in Antioch in the First Four Centuries of the Common Era." In *SBL 1976 Seminar Papers*, ed. G. MacRae, 33–65. Missoula, Mont.: Scholars Press, 1976.

Merk, Otto. *Handeln aus Glauben: Die Motivierungen der paulinischen Ethik.* MThSt 5. Marburg: N. G. Elwert, 1968.

———. "Der Beginn der Paränese im Galaterbrief." ZNW 60 (1969): 83–104.

Merrill, Elmer Truesdell. "The Expulsion of Jews from Rome under Tiberius." CP 14 (1919): 365–72.

Meyer, Eduard. *Ursprung und Anfänge des Christentums.* 3 vols. 4/5th ed. Stuttgart: J. G. Cotta, 1921–23.

Millar, Fergus. *A Study of Cassius Dio.* Oxford: At the Clarendon Press, 1964.

Minear, Paul S. "The Jerusalem Fund and Pauline Chronology." AThR 25 (1943): 389–96.

Moehring, Horst R. "The Census in Luke as an Apologetic Device." In *Studies in New Testament and Early Christian Literature: Essays in Honor of Allen P. Wikgren,* ed. D. E. Aune, pp. 144–60. NT.S 33. Leiden: E. J. Brill, 1972.

———. "The *Acta pro Joudaeis* in the *Antiquities* of Flavius Josephus: A Study in Hellenistic and Modern Apologetic Historiography." In *Christianity, Judaism, and Other Greco-Roman Cults: Studies for Morton Smith at 60,* pt. 3: *Judaism before 70,* ed. J. Neusner, 124–58. SJLA 12.3. Leiden: E. J. Brill, 1975.

Momigliano, Arnaldo. *Claudius: The Emperor and His Achievement.* Trans. W. D. Hogarth. 2d ed. Cambridge: Heffer, 1961; New York: Barnes & Noble, 1962.

Moule, C. F. D. *An Idiom Book of New Testament Greek.* 2d ed. Cambridge: At the University Press, 1971.

Moulton, James Hope. *A Grammar of New Testament Greek.* Vol. 3 of 4 vols: *Syntax,* by N. Turner. Edinburgh: T. & T. Clark, 1963.

Moulton, William F., and Alfred S. Geden. *A Concordance to the Greek Testament.* Rev. by H. K. Moulton. 4th ed. Edinburgh: T. & T. Clark, 1963.

Müller, Ulrich B. *Messias und Menschensohn in jüdischen Apokalypsen und in der Offenbarung des Johannes.* StNT 6. Gütersloh: Gerd Mohn, 1972.

———. *Prophetie und Predigt im Neuen Testament: Formgeschichtliche Untersuchungen zur urchristlichen Prophetie.* StNT 10. Gütersloh: Gerd Mohn, 1975.

Munck, Johannes. *Paul and the Salvation of Mankind.* Trans. F. Clarke. Richmond: John Knox Press; London: SCM Press, 1959.

Mussner, Franz. "*Kathexēs* im Lukasprolog." In *Jesus und Paulus: Festschrift für Werner Georg Kümmel,* ed. E. E. Ellis and E. Grässer, 253–55. Göttingen: Vandenhoeck & Ruprecht, 1975.

Nembach, Ulrich. *Predigt des Evangeliums: Luther als Prediger, Pädagoge und Rhetor.* Neukirchen-Vluyn: Neukirchener Verlag, 1972.

Nepper-Christensen, Poul. "Das verborgene Herrnwort." StTh 19 (1965): 136–54.

Neugebauer, Fritz. In Christus: Eine Untersuchung zum paulinischen Glaubensverständnis. Göttingen: Vandenhoeck & Ruprecht, 1961.

Norden, Eduard. Die antike Kunstprosa vom VI. Jahrhundert v. Chr. bis in die Zeit der Renaissance. 2 vols. 1909–15. Reprint. Darmstadt: Wissenschaftliche Buchgesellschaft, 1974.

Ogg, George. "A New Chronology of Saint Paul's Life." ET 64 (1952/53): 120–23.

———. The Chronology of the Life of Paul. London: Epworth Press, 1968 (= The Odyssey of Paul [Old Tappan, N.J.: Revell, 1968]).

Oliver, James H. "The Epistle of Claudius Which Mentions the Proconsul Junius Gallio." Hesp. 40 (1971): 239–40.

Osten-Sacken, Peter von der. "Die Apologie des paulinischen Apostolats in 1Kor 15,1–11." ZNW 64 (1973): 245–62.

Otto, August. Die Sprichwörter und sprichwörtlichen Redensarten bei den Römern. 1890. Reprint. Hildesheim: G. Olms, 1962.

Overbeck, Franz. "Über die Anfänge der patristischen Literatur." HZ 48 (1882): 417–72. (Reprinted as Über die Anfänge der Patristischen Literatur, Libelli 15 [Darmstadt: Wissenschaftliche Buchgesellschaft, 1954, 1966]).

Pagels, Elaine. The Johannine Gospel in Gnostic Exegesis: Heracleon's Commentary on John. SBLMS 17. Nashville: Abingdon Press, 1973.

Parker, Pierson. "Three Variant Readings in Luke-Acts." JBL 83 (1964): 165–70.

Perrin, Norman. The New Testament: An Introduction. Proclamation, Paranesis, Myth, and History. New York: Harcourt Brace Jovanovich, 1974.

Pesch, Rudolf. Naherwartungen: Tradition und Redaktion in Mk 13 KBANT. Düsseldorf: Patmos-Verlag, 1968.

Peterson, Erik. "Die Einholung des Kyrios." ZSTh 7 (1930): 682–702.

Pincherle, Alberto. "Paul à Ephèse." In Congrès d'histoire du Christianisme: Jubilé A. Loisy, vol. 2 of 2 vols., pp. 51–69. Paris: Les Éditions Rieder; Amsterdam: Van Holkema & Warendorf, 1928.

Plassart, André. "L'inscription de Delphes mentionnant le proconsul Gallion." REG 80 (1967): 372–78.

Plevnik, Joseph. "The Parousia as Implication of Christ's Resurrection." In Word and Spirit: Essays in Honour of David Michael Stanley, S.J., on His 60th Birthday, 199–277. Willowdale: Regis College Press, 1975.

Plooij, Daniel. De Chronologie van het Leven van Paulus. Leiden: E. J. Brill, 1918.

Plümacher, Eckhard. Lukas als hellenistischer Schriftsteller. StUNT 9 Göttingen: Vandenhoeck & Ruprecht, 1972.

Radin, Max. *The Jews among the Greeks and Romans*. Philadelphia: Jewish Publication Society of America, 1915.

Ramsay, William M. *Pauline and Other Studies in Early Christian History*. London: Hodder & Stoughton, 1906.

Ramsey, Howard Lyn. "The Place of Galatians in the Career of Paul." Ph.D. diss., Columbia University, 1960; Ann Arbor: University Microfilms, 1961.

Rehkopf, Friedrich. *Die lukanische Sonderquelle: Ihr Umfang und Sprachgebrauch*. WUNT 5. Tübingen: J. C. B. Mohr (Paul Siebeck), 1959.

Riddle, Donald Wayne. *Paul: Man of Conflict. A Modern Biographical Sketch*. Nashville: Abingdon Press, 1940.

Robbins, Vernon K. "The We-Passages in Acts and Ancient Sea-Voyages." *BR* 20 (1975): 5–18.

Robertson, Archibald Thomas. *A Grammar of the Greek New Testament in the Light of Historical Research*. 3d ed. New York: Hodder & Stoughton, 1919.

Robinson, James M. "World in Modern Theology and in New Testament Theology." In *Soli Deo Gloria: New Testament Studies in Honor of William Childs Robinson*, ed. J. M. Richards, 88–110. Richmond: John Knox Press, 1968.

Robinson, William C. *Der Weg des Herrn: Studien zur Geschichte und Eschatologie im Lukas-Evangelium*. Trans. G. Strecker and G. Strecker. Response by H. Conzelmann. ThF 36. Hamburg: H. Reich, 1964.

————. "The Theological Context for Interpreting Luke's Travel Narrative." *JBL* 79 (1960): 20–31.

Roller, Otto. *Das Formular der paulinischen Briefe: Ein Beitrag zur Lehre vom antiken Briefe*. BWANT 58. Stuttgart: Kohlhammer, 1933.

Russell, David Syme. *The Method and Message of Jewish Apocalyptic: 200 B.C.—A.D. 100*. Philadelphia: Westminster Press; London: SCM Press, 1964.

Safrai, Samuel, and Menahem Stern, eds. *The Jewish People in the First Century: Historical Geography, Political History, Social, Cultural, and Religious Life and Institutions*. CRI 1. 2 vols. Philadelphia: Fortress Press; Assen: Van Gorcum & Co., 1974–76.

Sanders, Ed Parish. *Paul and Palestinian Judaism: A Comparison of Patterns of Religion*. Philadelphia: Fortress Press; London: SCM Press, 1977.

Sanders, Jack T. "Paul's 'Autobiographical' Statements in Galatians 1–2." *JBL* 85 (1966): 335–43.

Schenke, Hans-Martin. "Das Weiterwirken des Paulus und die Pflege seines Erbes durch die Paulus-Schule." *NTS* 21 (1975): 505–18.

————, and Karl Martin Fischer. *Einleitung in die Schriften des Neuen Testaments*. Vol. 1 of 2 vols.: *Die Briefe des Paulus und Schriften des Paulinismus*. Gütersloh: Gerd Mohn, 1978.

Schille, Gottfried. "Die Fragwürdigkeit eines Itinerars der Paulusreisen." *ThLZ* 84 (1959): cols. 165–74.

———. *Anfänge der Kirche: Erwägungen zur apostolischen Frühgeschichte.* BEvTh 43. Munich: Chr. Kaiser Verlag, 1966.

Schlier, Heinrich. *Der Apostel und seine Gemeinde: Auslegung des ersten Briefs an die Thessalonicher.* 2d ed. Freiburg: Herder, 1973.

Schmithals, Walter. *Paul and James.* Naperville, Ill.: Alec R. Allenson, 1965.

———. "Die Thessalonicherbriefe als Briefkompositionen." In *Zeit und Geschichte: Danksgabe an Rudolf Bultmann zum 80. Geburtstag,* ed. E. Dinkler, 295–315. Tübingen: J. C. B. Mohr (Paul Siebeck), 1964.

———. Review of *Die Geschichte der Kollekte des Paulus für Jerusalem,* by D. Georgi. *ThLZ* 92 (1967): cols. 668–72.

———. "The Heretics in Galatia." In *Paul and the Gnostics,* trans. J. E. Steely, 13–64. Nashville: Abingdon Press, 1972.

———. "The Historical Situation of the Thessalonian Epistles." In *Paul and the Gnostics,* trans. J. E. Steely, 123–218. Nashville: Abingdon Press, 1972.

Schnackenburg, Rudolf. *Baptism in the Thought of St. Paul: A Study in Pauline Theology.* Trans. G. R. Beasley-Murray. New York: Herder & Herder, 1964.

Schottroff, Luise. "Animae naturaliter salvandae." In *Christentum und Gnosis: Zum Problem der himmlischen Herkunft des Gnostikers,* ed. W. Eltester, 65–97. BZNW 37. Berlin: A Töpelmann, 1969.

Schrage, Wolfgang. "Zur Frontstellung der paulinischen Ehebewertung in 1Kor 7,1–7." ZNW 67 (1976): 214–34.

Schubert, Paul. "Form and Function of the Pauline Letters." *JR* 19 (1939): 365–77.

———. *Form and Function of the Pauline Thanksgivings.* BZNW 20. Berlin: A. Töpelmann, 1939.

Schürer, Emil. *The History of the Jewish People in the Age of Jesus Christ (175 B.C.—A.D. 135).* 2 vols. to date. Trans. A. Burkill. Rev. and ed. G. Vermes and F. Millar with P. Vermes and M. Black. Edinburgh: T. & T. Clark, 1973–79.

Schwank, Benedikt. "Der sogenannte Brief an Gallio und die Datierung des 1 Thess." *BZ,* n.s. 15 (1971): 265–66.

Schwartz, Eduard. *Charakterköpfe aus der antiken Literatur.* 2d ser. 3d ed. Leipzig: B. G. Teubner, 1919.

———. *Griechische Geschichtsschreiber.* Leipzig: Koehler & Amelang, 1957.

Schweitzer, Albert. *The Mysticism of Paul the Apostle.* Trans. W. Montgomery. New York: Macmillan Co., 1931.

———. *Paul and His Interpreters: A Critical History.* Trans. W. Montgomery. New York: Macmillan Co., 1951.

————. *The Kingdom of God and Primitive Christianity.* Ed. with introd. by U. Neuenschwander. Trans. L. A. Garrard. New York: Seabury Press, 1968.

————. *The Quest of the Historical Jesus.* Trans. W. Montgomery. New York: Macmillan Co., 1979.

Schweizer, Eduard. "Die 'Mystik' des Sterbens und Auferstehens mit Christus bei Paulus." *EvTh* 26 (1966): 239–57 (= *Beiträge zur Theologie des Neuen Testaments: Neutestamentliche Aufsätze,* 183–203 [Zurich: Zwingli-Verlag, 1970]).

Schwyzer, Eduard. *Griechische Grammatik.* Vol. 2 of 3 vols.: *Syntax und syntaktische Stilistik,* ed. A. Debrunner. HAW 2.1.2. 2d ed. Munich: C. H. Beck, 1959.

Scramuzza, Vincent Mary. *The Emperor Claudius.* HHS 44. Cambridge: Harvard University Press; London: H. Milford, 1940.

Seeberg, Alfred. *Der Katechismus der Urchristenheit.* Leipzig: A. Deichert, 1903 (= TB 26 [Munich: Chr. Kaiser Verlag, 1966]).

Selby, Donald Joseph. *Toward the Understanding of St. Paul.* Englewood Cliffs, N.J.: Prentice-Hall, 1962.

Sellin, Gerhard. "Komposition, Quellen und Funktion des lukanischen Reiseberichtes (Lk. IX 51—XIX 28)." *NT* 20 (1978): 100–135.

Siber, Peter. *Mit Christus leben: Eine Studie zur paulinischen Auferstehungshoffnung.* AThANT 61. Zurich: Theologischer Verlag, 1971.

Siegert, Folker. "Gottesfürchtige und Sympathisanten." *JSJ* 4 (1973): 109–64.

Spörlein, Bernhard. *Die Leugnung der Auferstehung: Eine historisch-kritische Untersuchung zu 1 Kor. 15.* BU 7. Regensburg: F. Pustet, 1971.

Stauffer, Ethelbert. *New Testament Theology.* Trans. J. Marsh. New York: Macmillan Co., 1956.

Stemberger, Günter. *Der Leib der Auferstehung: Studien zur Anthropologie und Eschatologie des palästinischen Judentums im neutestamentlichen Zeitalter.* AnBib 56. Rome: Pontifical Biblical Institute, 1972.

Stern, Menachem, ed. and trans. *Greek and Latin Authors on Jews and Judaism.* 2 vols. to date. Jerusalem: Israel Academy of Sciences and Humanities, 1974– .

Strecker, Georg. "Die sogenannte zweite Jerusalemreise des Paulus (Act 11,27–30)." *ZNW* 53 (1962): 67–77.

————. "Die Leidens- und Auferstehungsvoraussagen im Markusevangelium." *ZThK* 64 (1967): 16–39.

————. *Der Weg der Gerechtigkeit: Untersuchung zur Theologie des Matthäus.* FRLANT 82. 3d ed. Göttingen: Vandenhoeck & Ruprecht, 1971.

————. *Handlungsorientierter Glaube: Vorstudien zu einer Ethik des Neuen Testaments.* Stuttgart: Kreuz Verlag, 1972.

————. "Das Evangelium Jesu Christi." In *Jesus Christus in Historie und Theologie: Festschrift für Hans Conzelmann zum 60. Geburtstag,* ed. G. Strecker, 503–48. Tübingen: J. C. B. Mohr (Paul Siebeck), 1975.

————. "Befreiung und Rechtfertigung." In *Rechtfertigung: Festschrift für Ernst Käsemann zum 70. Geburtstag,* ed. J. Friedrich, W. Pöhlmann, and P. Stuhlmacher, 479–508. Göttingen: Vandenhoeck & Ruprecht; Tübingen: J. C. B. Mohr (Paul Siebeck), 1976.

Strobel, August. "In dieser Nacht (Luk 17,34)." *ZThK* 58 (1961): 16–29.

————. "Der Berg der Offenbarung (Mt 28,16; Apg 1,12)." In *Verborum Veritas: Festschrift für Gustav Stählin zum 70. Geburtstag,* ed. O. Böcher and K. Haacker, pp. 133–46. Wuppertal: Theologischer Verlag Brockhaus, 1970.

————. "Das Aposteldekret in Galatien: Zur Situation von Gal i und ii." *NTS* 20 (1974): 177–90.

————. *Ursprung und Geschichte des frühchristlichen Osterkalenders.* TU 121. Berlin: Akademie Verlag, 1977.

Stuhlmacher, Peter. *Gerechtigkeit Gottes bei Paulus.* FRLANT 87. 2d ed. Göttingen: Vandenhoeck & Ruprecht, 1966.

————. *Das paulinische Evangelium I: Vorgeschichte.* FRLANT 95. Göttingen: Vandenhoeck & Ruprecht, 1968.

Suggs, M. Jack. "Concerning the Date of Paul's Macedonian Ministry." *NT* 4 (1960): 60–68.

Suhl, Alfred. *Paulus und seine Briefe: Ein Beitrag zur paulinischen Chronologie.* StNT 11. Gütersloh: Gerd Mohn, 1975.

Surkau, Hans-Werner. *Martyrien in jüdischer und frühchristlicher Zeit.* FRLANT 54. Göttingen: Vandenhoeck & Ruprecht, 1938.

Synofzik, Ernst. *Die Gerichts- und Vergeltungsaussagen bei Paulus: Eine traditionsgeschichtliche Untersuchung.* GTA 8. Göttingen: Vandenhoeck & Ruprecht, 1977.

Tachau, Peter. *"Einst" und "Jetzt" im Neuen Testament: Beobachtungen zu einem urchristlichen Predigtschema in der neutestamentlichen Briefliteratur und zu seiner Vorgeschichte.* FRLANT 105. Göttingen: Vandenhoeck & Ruprecht, 1972.

Talbert, Charles H. "Again: Paul's Visits to Jerusalem." *NT* 9 (1967): 26–40.

Taylor, Vincent. *The Passion Narrative of St. Luke: A Critical and Historical Investigation.* Edited by O. E. Evans. SNTSMS 19. Cambridge: At the University Press, 1972.

Tcherikover, Victor. *Hellenistic Civilization and the Jews.* Trans. S. Applebaum. Philadelphia: Jewish Publication Society of America, 1959.

Teichmann, Ernst. *Die paulinischen Vorstellungen von Auferstehung und Gericht und ihre Beziehungen zur jüdischen Apokalyptik.* Tübingen: J. C. B. Mohr (Paul Siebeck), 1896.

Trocmé, Etienne. *Le "Livre des Actes" et l'Histoire.* EHPhR 45. Paris: Presses Universitaires, 1957.

Venetz, Hermann-Josef. *Der Glaube weiss um die Zeit: Zum paulinischen Verständnis der "Letzten Dinge."* BiBe 11. Fribourg: Verlag Schweizerisches Katholisches Bibelwerk, 1975.

Vielhauer, Philipp.. "Apocalypses and Related Subjects: Introduction. Apocalyptic in Early Christianity." In E. Hennecke, *New Testament Apocrypha*, ed. W. Schneemelcher. 2 vols. English trans. ed. R. M. Wilson, vol. 2, pp. 581–642. Philadelphia: Westminster Press, 1963–65.

———. Review of *Die Apostelgeschichte*, by H. Conzelmann. GGA 221 (1969): 1–19.

———. *Geschichte der urchristlichen Literatur: Einleitung in das Neue Testament, die Apokryphen und die Apostolischen Väter.* New York and Berlin: Walter de Gruyter, 1975.

———. "Paulus und die Kephaspartei in Korinth." NTS 21 (1975): 341–52.

———. "Gesetzesdienst und Stoicheiadienst im Galaterbrief." In *Rechtfertigung: Festschrift für Ernst Käsemann zum 70. Geburtstag*, ed. J. Friedrich, W. Pöhlmann, and P. Stuhlmacher, 543–55. Tübingen: J. C. B. Mohr (Paul Siebeck); Göttingen: Vandenhoeck & Ruprecht, 1976.

———. "On the 'Paulinism' of Acts." In *Studies in Luke-Acts: Essays Presented in Honor of Paul Schubert*, ed. L. E. Keck and J. L. Martyn, pp. 33–50. 1966. Reprint. Philadelphia: Fortress Press, 1980.

Vögtle, Anton. *Die Tugend- und Lasterkataloge im Neuen Testament exegetisch, religions- und formgeschichtlich untersucht.* NTA 16.4,5. Münster: Aschendorff, 1936.

Weiss, Johannes. *Earliest Christianity: A History of the Period A.D. 30–150.* 2 vols. Trans. F. C. Grant. 1937. Reprint. Gloucester: Peter Smith, 1970.

Weizsäcker, Carl. *The Apostolic Age of the Christian Church.* 2d rev. ed. 2 vols. New York: G. P. Putnam's Sons; London: Williams & Norgate, 1894–99.

Wellhausen, Julius. "Noten zur Apostelgeschichte." In NGG (1907): 1–21.

———. *Einleitung in die drei ersten Evangelien.* 2d ed. Berlin: G. Reimer, 1911.

———. "Kritische Analyse der Apostelgeschichte." In AGG, n.s. 15.2 (1914).

Wendland, Paul. *Die hellenistisch-römische Kultur in ihren Beziehungen zu Judentum und Christentum: Die urchristlichen Literaturformen.* 2d and 3d ed. HNT 1.2–3. Tübingen: J. C. B. Mohr (Paul Siebeck), 1912.

Wengst, Klaus. *Christologische Formeln und Lieder des Urchristentums.* StNT 7. 2d ed. Gütersloh: Gerd Mohn, 1974.

Wettstein, Johann Jakob. *HĒ KAINĒ DIATHĒKĒ: Novum Testamentum Graecum.* 2 vols. 1751–52. Reprint. Graz: Akademische Druck- und Verlagsanstalt, 1962.

Wiefel, Wolfgang. "Die jüdische Gemeinschaft im antiken Rom und die Anfänge des römischen Christentums." *Jud.* 26 (1970): 65–88.

———. "Die Hauptrichtung des Wandels im eschatologischen Denken des Paulus." *ThZ* 30 (1974): 65–81.

Wilcke, Hans-Alwin. *Das Problem eines messianischen Zwischenreichs bei Paulus.* AThANT 51. Stuttgart: Zwingli-Verlag, 1967.

Wilckens, Ulrich. "Der Ursprung der Überlieferung der Erscheinungen des Auferstandenen." In *Dogma und Denkstrukturen: Edmund Schlink in Verehrung und Dankbarkeit,* ed. W. Joest and W. Pannenberg, 56–95. Göttingen: Vandenhoeck & Ruprecht, 1963.

———. "Interpreting Luke-Acts in a Period of Existentialist Theology." In *Studies in Luke-Acts: Essays Presented in Honor of Paul Schubert,* ed. L. E. Keck and J. L. Martyn, 60–83. 1966. Reprint. Philadelphia: Fortress Press, 1980.

———. "Über Abfassungszweck und Aufbau des Römerbriefs." In *Recht-fertigung als Freiheit: Paulusstudien,* 110–70. Neukirchen-Vluyn: Neu-kirchener Verlag, 1974.

———. "Was heisst bei Paulus: 'Aus Werken des Gesetzes wird kein Mensch gerecht?'" EKK.V 1, 51–77. Zurich: Benziger Verlag, 1969 (= *Recht-fertigung als Freiheit: Paulusstudien,* 77–109 [Neukirchen-Vluyn: Neu-kirchener Verlag, 1974]).

Wilson, Robert McLachlan. "Gnostics—in Galatia?" In *StEv* 4 (= TU 102), 358–67.

Wilson, Stephen G. *The Gentiles and the Gentile Mission in Luke-Acts.* SNTSMS 23. Cambridge: At the University Press, 1973.

Winer, Georg Benedikt. *A Treatise on the Grammar of New Testament Greek.* Trans. W. F. Moulton. 9th expanded ed. Edinburgh: T. & T. Clark, 1882.

Winter, Paul. *On the Trial of Jesus.* Ed. T. A. Burkill and G. Vermes. SJ 1. 2d ed. Berlin: Walter de Gruyter, 1974.

Wrede, William. *Das literarische Rätsel des Hebräerbriefs.* FRLANT 8. Göttingen: Vandenhoeck & Ruprecht, 1906.

———. *Paul.* Trans. E. Lummis. London: P. Green, 1907.

———. "The Task and Methods of 'New Testament Theology.'" In *The Na-ture of New Testament Theology,* trans. and ed. R. Morgan, 68–116. SBT, 2d ser. 25. London: SCM Press, 1973.

POSTSCRIPT

The present volume is a translation of *Paulus, der Heidenapostel*, vol. 1: *Studien zur Chronologie*, FRLANT 123 (Göttingen: Vandenhoeck & Ruprecht, 1980), which was accepted in 1977 as a Habilitationsschrift in New Testament by the theological faculty of the University of Göttingen.[1] The translation was made by my student and friend F. Stanley Jones; the bibliographical work is by Ann E. Millin. I am grateful to both of them. For the English translation, I have dropped those parts of some footnotes that seemed to be unnecessary for the chronological argument. At the same time, I have done my best to add references to works that have been published since 1980. There have also been minor adjustments in the text. The present English translation can therefore be regarded as a second edition of my study of the chronology of Paul. The publication of the English version also affords me the opportunity to discuss briefly the responses to my work and thereby bring it more up-to-date.

Thus far I have seen the following reviews or articles that deal with my book: Jean-Noël Aletti, S.J., *RSR* 68 (1980): 570–72; H. Giesen, *Ordenskorrespondenz* (1981): 351–52; Joachim Gnilka, *BZ*, n.s. 25 (1981): 148–50; Andreas Lindemann, *ZKG* 92 (1981): 344–49; A. J. M. Wedderburn, *ET* 92 (1981): 103–8, and *SJTh* 20 (1981): 87–91; William R. Farmer, *JBL* 101 (1982): 296–97; Hans Hübner, *ThLZ* 107 (1982): cols. 741–44; Romano Penna, *Cristianesimo nella storia* 3 (1982): 218–21; Etienne Trocmé, *RHPhR* 62 (1982): 201–2; David Stanley, S.J., *CBQ* 44 (1982): 150–51; Edvin Larsson, *SEA* 48 (1983):176–79; Jerome Murphy-O'Connor, "Pauline Missions before the Jerusalem Conference," *RB* 89 (1982): 71–91; and Martin Rese, "Zur Geschichte des frühen Christentums—Ein kritischer Bericht über drei neue Bücher," *ThZ* 38 (1982): 98–110.

All in all, the reaction has been positive. The principle that the letters should be given priority also in the construction of a chronology of Paul has been generally agreed to, though the application of this principle has been disputed. Consequently, the book's way of dealing with Acts has sometimes been harshly criticized (Murphy-O'Connor, Trocmé, Wedderburn). It seems to me, however, that such criticism arises from inability to distinguish between primary and secondary sources[2] and failure to see that it was not until a chronology based solely on the letters was established that we used the material in Acts. The latter point is still in need of emphasis because, according to one reviewer (Andreas Lindemann), Acts has only slight historical value. Such an assumption is contradicted by the many agreements between Paul's letters and Acts (see pp. 139–94), unless one follows Lindemann in the improbable thesis that Luke knew and used Paul's letters.

In this respect, let me emphasize that Martin Hengel, in a polemical footnote to his brilliant article "'Christos' in Paul" (in his book *Between Jesus and Paul: Studies in the Earliest History of Christianity* [Philadelphia: Fortress Press; London: SCM Press, 1983], 186 n. 73), ascribes to me a view that I do not hold, namely, that I "accuse [*sic*] Luke of having written a kind of novel about Paul." I am convinced, as is Hengel, of the historical value of the material in Acts but I differ from him concerning the method for recovering that valuable material.[3]

The section of the book on the collection as an external criterion for the establishment of a chronology has been generally applauded. Even more important is that most reviewers who address the issue of the date of the edict of Claudius against the Jews adopt the dating in 41 C.E. rather than 49 C.E. (Lindemann, Murphy-O'Connor, Penna). Only Hübner disagrees with 41 C.E. as the date of the expulsion. In so doing, he refers to a private communication from D. Kienast (I remain unconvinced as long as Hübner does not give the details of this communication) and to E. Mary Smallwood, *The Jews under Roman Rule: From Pompey to Diocletian*, SJLA 20 (Leiden: E. J. Brill, 1976), 210ff., a book that, according to Hübner, I failed to use. Hübner is in error here, for I refer to Smallwood on p. 187 n. 70 of the original German edition (p. 188 n. 71 of the present edition). It is therefore to be hoped that the dating of Claudius's edict against the Jews to the year 41 C.E. will soon become part of common knowledge in New Testament scholarship.

The chronological reversal of the incident at Antioch and the Jerusalem Conference has been, in general, rejected by the reviewers and other critics (see esp. Dieter Zeller, "Theologie der Mission bei Paulus," in *Mission im Neuen Testament*, ed. K. Kertelge, QD 93 [Freiburg: Herder, 1982], 164–89, 175 n. 41. Incidentally, Zeller's footnote about the book reflects a lack of knowledge of its contents).

The reasons that have been given against the chronological reversal are insufficient. To mention only one: Hans Hübner insists that *hote de* in Gal. 2:11 has the same function as *epeita*. He notices that this *hote de* has a parallel in Gal. 1:15, where it is supposed to indicate chronological sequence. Hübner is mistaken again. The *hote de* of Gal. 1:15 emphasizes the *contrast* between Paul's Jewish zeal and his call to be an apostle and is not primarily a sequential adverb. In connection with the critics' objections to my treatment of Gal. 2:11ff., I hope that scholarship will not consider the proposed chronology to have been refuted if the incident at Antioch should be shown to belong actually to the period after the conference. Although I have not seen convincing reasons in favor of such a view, let me hasten to add that the chronological place of Gal. 2:11ff. is of little importance for the date of Paul's mission in Greece.

The chronological placement of Paul's mission in Greece *would*, however, be settled and the major thesis of the book refuted once and for all *if* Lindemann were right in his statement about Galatians 1, namely, that Paul would have mentioned an early Macedonian mission there if he had gone to Greece prior to the Jerusalem Conference (see also the similar but more cautious remarks by Gnilka and Penna). Had Paul mentioned such a mission in Galatians 1, there would be no doubt about the mission in Greece. Since that is not the case, the question arises as to how much weight an *argument from silence* should receive, for it is just such an argument that Lindemann and others invoke against my thesis. Should we not first look at the evidence of the other letters before deciding on the basis of Gal. 1:21 where Paul could and could not have been prior to the conference? I do not think that reference to Gal. 1:21 is a decisive objection to an early Macedonian mission, though I, too, certainly would have liked to have seen a mission in Greece mentioned in Galatians 1, for in that case, the present book would have been superfluous. (On the question of Gal. 1:21, see pp. 59–61 of the present volume.)

I am glad to report that the major thesis of the book, that is, a Pauline mission in Greece before the conference, has been confirmed by Murphy-O'Connor. His many brilliant insights make it easy for me to overlook the tone of some of his remarks against my book (see merely p. 73: Luedemann's "childlike faith in the objectivity of the sources used in the composition of *Acts*"; p. 81 n. 14: Luedemann's "hypothesis that the conflict at Antioch must have taken place before the Conference is rooted in a radical misunderstanding of the nature of the

Conference"; p. 89 n. 28: Luedemann's "obsession with the year A.D. 41 has led him to abandon any reasonable methodology"). While regretting the tone of his remarks, I would like to point out that Murphy-O'Connor has further established Paul's use of a rhetorical genre in Galatians 1–2 and has added strong arguments in favor of the book's claim that Gal. 2:7 goes back to Paul's first visit with Peter in Jerusalem (see Murphy-O'Connor, pp. 75ff.). Despite the remarks cited above, there is general agreement between the two of us, except as regards the date of Paul's Macedonian ministry. Following Jewett's hypothesis that the Aretas-datum (37–39 C.E.) is a rock on which a chronology can be based (see above p. 31 n. 10), Murphy-O'Connor dates the Macedonian mission in the late forties. Though endorsing 41 C.E. as the date of the edict of Claudius (see p. 170), Murphy-O'Connor questions "the relation between the edict and the advent of Aquila and Priscilla" (p. 89). Indeed, according to Murphy-O'Connor the arrival of Aquila and Priscilla in Corinth and the edict originally had nothing to do with each other. The connection of the two actually derives from Luke, who, in this instance, has interwoven world history and salvation history (see, similarly, Lindemann). I see no reason to reject Acts 18:2 as historically worthless if the chronology based solely on the letters leads me to an approximately similar datum, especially since the reference to Gallio (whose historical usefulness not even Murphy-O'Connor questions) is also a reliable piece of information. This latter point, too, follows from the chronology based solely on the letters. (I do not understand why Rese, p. 108, indirectly reproaches me for using the Gallio-inscription.)

In most cases, the final chapter of the book and its bearing on the chronology has been understood. Rese is an exception. He does not think that the different proportion of Christians dead or alive at the parousia can tell us anything about chronology ("Developments and changes in thought may simply not be computed chronologically," p. 109; see also the similar concern of Gnilka). Unlike most of the others, Rese has misunderstood what I meant when writing that around 50 C.E. "the proportion of dead Christians outweighed the proportion of living Christians" (p. 244). He claims, strangely, that I do not connect such a statement with those who, like Paul, became Christians soon after Jesus' death and resurrection (p. 109). Let me emphasize that I did make this connection, because only then, that is, only if you remain within the *first generation*, is the criterion of chapter 5 of this volume of use.

To sum up: The German original of the present English edition has received considerable attention thus far. Its main thesis has been rejected in the reviews by Hübner, Lindemann, Trocmé, and Wedderburn. Reviewers such as Aletti, Gnilka, Farmer, Penna, and Stanley have expressed approval, ranging from enthusiastic endorsement (Stanley) to cautious acceptance (Gnilka). Others, such as Rese or Murphy-O'Connor, have remained undecided (Rese) or, while approving of parts of the book, have developed their own solution (Murphy-O'Connor).

The main lines of the present chronology have been agreed to by Hans-Heinrich Schade, *Apokalyptische Christologie bei Paulus: Studien zum Zusammenhang von Christologie und Eschatologie in den Paulusbriefen*, GTA 18 (Göttingen: Vandenhoeck & Ruprecht, 1981), 173–75, 290–92 (who had access to the book in manuscript in 1977), and by Udo Schnelle, "Der erste Thessalonicherbrief und die Entstehung der paulinischen Anthropologie," *NTS* 31 (1985).

Further, the results of the present chronology have been adopted in the following textbooks: Kurt Rudolph, *Die Gnosis*, 2d ed. (Göttingen: Vandenhoeck & Ruprecht, 1980), 322, 406 (Eng. trans. and ed. R. Mc. Wilson, *Gnosis: The Nature and History of Gnosticism* [San Francisco: Harper & Row; Edinburgh: T. & T. Clark, 1983]); and Carl Andresen, "Die Anfänge christlicher Lehrentwicklung," in *Handbuch der Dogmen- und Theologiegeschichte*, vol. 1: *Die Lehrentwicklung im Rahmen der Katholizität* (Göttingen: Vandenhoeck & Ruprecht, 1982), 4.

I am grateful to all who, whether negatively or positively, have responded to the challenge of my studies in chronology. Most of all, however, I am grateful to John Knox, who was kind enough to write the Foreword to the present volume.[4] Without his insights, the present book would have never seen the light of day.

Gerd Luedemann
Georg-August-Universität
Fachbereich Theologie
Abteilung für frühchristliche Studien

NOTES

1. This volume is the first of my projected trilogy, *Paulus, der Heidenapostel*. The second part has recently been published: *Antipaulinismus im frühen Christentum*, FRLANT 130 (Göttingen: Vandenhoeck & Ruprecht, 1983).

2. See also Edvin Larsson, "Die paulinischen Schriften als Quellen zur

Geschichte des Urchristentums," *StTh* 37 (1983): 33–53, esp. 40–45, who thinks that combination of Acts and the letters cannot be avoided.

3. Since Hengel here and elsewhere in his book (see pp. 167 n. 12, 190 n. 1) simply attacks my study (supposedly) *ex cathedra* and fails to present a single counterargument, I see no reason to reply further to his statements.

4. See also Knox's recent article "Chapters in a Life of Paul—A Response to Robert Jewett and Gerd Luedemann," in *Colloquy on New Testament Studies: A Time for Reappraisal and Fresh Approaches*, ed. B. Corley (Macon, Ga.: Mercer University Press, 1983), 339ff. This volume also contains a summary presentation of my proposal for Pauline chronology (pp. 289ff.).

INDEX OF AUTHORS

INDEX OF PASSAGES

303

c) Jewish Writings

d) Church Fathers

E) Greek and Latin Writers

Undergraduate Lending Library